Designing Interfaces

Designing Interfaces

Second Edition

Jenifer Tidwell

O'REILLY®

Beijing · Cambridge · Farnham · Köln · Sebastopol · Tokyo

Designing Interfaces, Second Edition

by Jenifer Tidwell

Copyright © 2011 Jenifer Tidwell. All rights reserved.
Printed in Canada.

Published by O'Reilly Media, Inc., 1005 Gravenstein Highway North, Sebastopol, CA 95472.

O'Reilly books may be purchased for educational, business, or sales promotional use. Online editions are also available for most titles (*http://my.safaribooksonline.com*). For more information, contact our corporate/institutional sales department: 800-998-9938 or *corporate@oreilly.com*.

Editor: Mary Treseler	**Indexer:** Lucie Haskins
Production Editor: Rachel Monaghan	**Cover Designer:** Karen Montgomery
Copyeditor: Audrey Doyle	**Interior Designer:** Ron Bilodeau
Proofreader: Emily Quill	**Illustrator:** Robert Romano

Printing History:

November 2005: First Edition.

December 2010: Second Edition.

Revision History:

2010-12-06	First release
2011-07-08	Second release
2012-02-24	Third release
2013-03-15	Fourth release

Nutshell Handbook, the Nutshell Handbook logo, and the O'Reilly logo are registered trademarks of O'Reilly Media, Inc. *Designing Interfaces*, the image of a Mandarin duck, and related trade dress are trademarks of O'Reilly Media, Inc.

Many of the designations used by manufacturers and sellers to distinguish their products are claimed as trademarks. Where those designations appear in this book, and O'Reilly Media, Inc. was aware of a trademark claim, the designations have been printed in caps or initial caps.

While every precaution has been taken in the preparation of this book, the publisher and author assume no responsibility for errors or omissions, or for damages resulting from the use of the information contained herein.

ISBN: 978-1-449-37970-4

[TI]

Contents

Introduction to the Second Edition

In the five years since the first edition of *Designing Interfaces* was published, many things have changed.

Most user interface designers—who might now play the roles of user experience (UX) designers, or interaction designers, or information architects, or any of several other titles—now do their work on the Web. Countless websites, web services, web-delivered software, blogs, and online stores need good design, and it's becoming easier and easier to deliver these finished products in ridiculously short turnaround times. Many of these are highly interactive, but even traditional websites—static and straightforward in the past—now contain components that are dynamic and interactive, such as video players and social network content. There's a lot of designing going on!

Compared to a few years ago, not as much of that designing is being done for desktop applications. Of course, all of us technology users depend upon the complex software installed on our laptops and desktops. Our email clients, browsers, document editors, domain-specific software, and operating systems are still important parts of our online lives. But many aspects of their interface designs have stabilized. As a result, since the early 2000s, the audience for design books has shifted away from desktop design toward web-based design.

Here's another change: mobile design, which was still immature in 2005, has flourished. With iPhones and other complex mobile devices now spreading everywhere, putting the whole Web in our pockets, many designers have been forced to face the special problems inherent to mobile design. How should mobile concerns change interface design, especially for websites? That's a question we're still collectively trying to answer, but the design community has learned some approaches and techniques that work.

Also, designers cannot ignore the influence of online social networks. When I'm in the early phase of a design project, I need to think about its connections to blogs, Twitter, Facebook, comment areas, forums, and all the other ways that people talk to one another online. I would be remiss not to do so. Users spend a lot of their online time "doing" social interaction, and sophisticated users expect social-network support as a matter of course. It's unusual now to find any website that doesn't somehow connect to or from a social service (and usually several).

But wait, there's more! Since this book was first published, the UX design world has discovered the value of patterns, and other UX-related pattern collections have appeared on the scene. Many of them are quite good. Some took patterns originally set forth here and elaborated upon them, changed them, renamed them according to emergent conventions, or presented new information about them. Others created new patterns in areas that this book didn't cover well—especially social, mobile, gestural, search, and RIA-style interfaces. (I list the best of these other pattern collections in the preface, in the References section, and in the patterns themselves.)

So is the material written in 2005 still relevant?

To a large extent, yes. The human mind hasn't changed—visual hierarchies still work, progressive disclosure still works, and moving things still attract the attention of our reptilian brains. Good patterns based on fundamental design principles are just as valid now as they were 5, 10, or 20 years ago. But other patterns weren't as well grounded or have fallen out of favor. This second edition gave me the privilege of hindsight: I was granted the time to figure out how well these patterns have endured, and then report on them. And, indeed, a few have been removed from this book.

But most of them remain, because they still work. They've been updated with fresh examples, and in some cases with fresh research into their effectiveness. In addition, I've written (or borrowed) new patterns to reflect the changes of the last five years. The next section describes these changes in some detail.

Changes in the Second Edition

Here's what you're getting in this book:

A chapter about social media

> Chapter 9, *Using Social Media*, lays out some tactics and patterns for integrating social media into a site or application. The chapter does not cover all aspects of social interfaces; it's meant to be complementary to existing works on the subject, especially *Designing Social Interfaces* (O'Reilly, *http://oreilly.com/catalog/9780596154936/*).

A chapter about mobile design

> Chapter 10, *Going Mobile*, contains some patterns that are specific to mobile devices. In particular, the patterns are aimed at the platforms most designers are likely to target: touch-screen devices with full connectivity, such as iPhones. Both apps and websites are covered. Again, this is not intended to cover all aspects of mobile design—simply the patterns and ideas that can help you create a graceful mobile interface even if you're not a mobile UI specialist.

The existence of this chapter brings up an interesting point. A "good" pattern should be invariant across different platforms, perhaps including mobile ones. However, mobile design introduces so many new constraints on screen size, interactive gestures, social expectations, and latency that some patterns simply don't work well for it. Conversely, most of the patterns written specifically for mobile contexts don't work well (or aren't particularly salient design solutions) for larger screens; those patterns have a home in Chapter 10.

Reorganized chapters and rewritten introductions

Because there were so many old and new patterns about how to present lists of items, I chose to "refactor" three chapters to account for that. Chapter 5 is now simply about lists. It pulled patterns from the first edition's Chapter 2 (Two-Panel Selector, One-Window Drilldown) and Chapter 7 (Row Striping and Cascading Lists). I also added several new ones, such as List Inlay and Alphabetic Scroller.

Furthermore, the introductions to the chapters on information architecture (Chapter 2), navigation (Chapter 3), and page layout (Chapter 4) have been rewritten to reflect recent design thinking and a new emphasis on web-based or web-like designs.

New patterns that capture popular new interactions

Some techniques have really caught on in the last five years, and the ones that seem to be "pattern-like"—they are abstractable and cross-genre, they're common enough to be easy to find, and they can noticeably improve the user experience—are represented here. Examples include Fat Menus, Sitemap Footer, Hover Tools, Password Strength Meter, Data Spotlight, and Radial Table.

New patterns that aren't really "new," but that were not included in the first edition

These ideas have been kicking around for a while, but either I didn't recognize them as being important back in 2005, or they weren't especially salient back then. They are now. This list of patterns includes Dashboard, News Stream, Carousel, Grid of Equals, Microbreaks, Picture Manager, and Feature, Search, and Browse.

Renamed patterns, and patterns whose scope has changed

For instance, Card Stack was renamed to Module Tabs, and Closable Panels to Collapsible Panels; I made these changes to conform to current terminology and other pattern libraries. Similarly, Accordion was factored out from Collapsible Panels and made into its own pattern, since other designers, design writers, and pattern collections have converged on the term "accordion" for this particular technique. Meanwhile, One-Window Drilldown and Two-Panel Selector—both from the original book's chapter on information architecture—have been narrowed down to deal specifically with lists of items.

New examples, new research, and new connections to other pattern libraries

Almost every pattern has at least one new pictorial example, and many of them have an "In other libraries" section that directs the reader to the same pattern (or patterns that closely resemble it) in other collections. These might provide you with new insights or examples. Also, some patterns in this book have been slightly rewritten to account for new thinking or research on the issue. Row Striping is one of these; some experiments were run to find out the value of the technique, and the pattern refers you to those results.

Some individual patterns have been removed

Many of these have passed into the realm of "blindingly obvious to everyone," and while they're still useful as design tools, their value as part of this book is diminished. This list includes Extras on Demand, Intriguing Branches, Global Navigation, and Illustrated Choices. Others are no longer used much in contemporary designs, such as Color-Coded Sections.

The "Builders and Editors" chapter is gone

Designers still work on these types of applications, of course, but I honestly couldn't find much to change in that set of patterns in terms of new work and updated examples. I also discovered in a survey that readers found this to be one of the least valuable chapters. Because I wanted to keep the book size down to something reasonable, I chose to remove that chapter to make room for the new material.

Finally, I want to talk briefly about what you won't find in this new edition. The following areas are so well covered by other published (or forthcoming) pattern collections that I saw little need to put them into this edition:

- Search
- General social interfaces
- Gestural interfaces
- More depth in mobile design
- Types of animated transitions
- Help techniques

I hope that in the next few years, we'll see new sets of patterns for other areas of design: online games, geographic systems, online communities, and more. I see a rich and rewarding area of inquiry here, and that's terrific. I encourage other design thinkers to jump in and write other patterns—or challenge us pattern writers to make the existing collections better!

Preface

Once upon a time, interface designers worked with a woefully small toolbox.

We had a handful of simple controls: text fields, buttons, menus, tiny icons, and modal dialogs. We carefully put them together according to the Windows Style Guide or the Macintosh Human Interface Guidelines, and we hoped that users would understand the resulting interface—and too often, they didn't. We designed for small screens, few colors, slow CPUs, and slow networks (if the user was connected at all). We made them gray.

Things have changed. If you design interfaces today, you work with a much bigger palette of components and ideas. You have a choice of many more user interface toolkits than before, such as the Java toolkits, HTML/CSS, JavaScript, Flash, and numerous open source options. Apple's and Microsoft's native UI toolkits are richer and nicer-looking than they used to be. Display technology is better. Web applications often look as professionally designed as the websites they're embedded in, and some of those web sensibilities have migrated back into desktop applications in the form of blue underlined links, Back/Next buttons, beautiful fonts and background images, and non-gray color schemes.

But it's still not easy to design *good* interfaces. Let's say you're not a trained or self-taught interface designer. If you just use the UI toolkits the way they should be used, and if you follow the various style guides or imitate existing applications, you can probably create a mediocre but passable interface.

Alas, that may not be enough anymore. Users' expectations are higher than they used to be—if your interface isn't easy to use "out of the box," users will not think well of it. Even if the interface obeys all the standards, you may have misunderstood users' preferred workflow, used the wrong vocabulary, or made it too hard to figure out what the software even does. Impatient users often won't give you the benefit of the doubt. Worse, if you've built an unusable website or web application, frustrated users can give up and switch to your competitor with just the click of a button. So the cost of building a mediocre interface is higher than it used to be, too.

Devices like phones, TVs, and car dashboards once were the exclusive domain of industrial designers. But now those devices have become smart. Increasingly powerful computers drive them, and software-based features and applications are multiplying in response to market demands. They're here to stay, whether or not they are easy to use. At this rate, good interface and interaction design may be the only hope for our collective sanity in 10 years.

Small Interface Pieces, Loosely Joined

As an interface designer trying to make sense of all the technology changes in the last few years, I see two big effects on the craft of interface design. One is the proliferation of *interface idioms*: recognizable types or styles of interfaces, each with its own vocabulary of objects, actions, and visuals. You probably recognize all the ones shown in Figure P-1, and more are being invented all the time.

Figure P-1. *A sampler of interface idioms*

The second effect is a loosening of the rules for putting together interfaces from these idioms. It no longer surprises anyone to see several of these idioms mixed up in one interface, for instance, or to see parts of some controls mixed up with parts of other controls. Online help pages, which long have been formatted in hypertext anyway, might now include interactive applets, animations, or links to a web-based bulletin board. Interfaces themselves might have help texts on them, interleaved with forms or editors; this situation used to be rare. Combo boxes' drop-down menus might have funky layouts, like color grids or sliders, instead of the standard column of text items. You might see web applications that look like document-centered paint programs, but have no menu bars, and save the finished work only to a database somewhere.

The freeform-ness of web pages seems to have taught users to relax their expectations with respect to graphics and interactivity. It's OK now to break the old Windows style-guide strictures, as long as users can figure out what you're doing.

And that's the hard part. Some applications, devices, and web applications are easy to use. Many aren't. Following style guides never guaranteed usability anyhow, but now designers have even more choices than before (which, paradoxically, can make design a *lot* harder). What characterizes interfaces that are easy to use?

One could say, "The applications that are easy to use are designed to be intuitive." Well, yes. That's almost a tautology.

Except that the word "intuitive" is a little bit deceptive. Jef Raskin once pointed out that when we say "intuitive" in the context of software, we really mean "familiar." Computer mice aren't intuitive to someone who's never seen one (though a growling grizzly bear would be). There's nothing innate or instinctive in the human brain to account for it. But once you've taken ten seconds to learn to use a mouse, it's familiar, and you'll never forget it. Same for blue underlined text, play/pause buttons, and so on.

Rephrased: "The applications that are easy to use are designed to be *familiar*."

Now we're getting somewhere. "Familiar" doesn't necessarily mean that everything about a given application is identical to some genre-defining product (e.g., Word, Photoshop, Mac OS, or a Walkman). People are smarter than that. As long as the parts are recognizable enough and the relationships among the parts are clear, then people can apply their previous knowledge to a novel interface and figure it out.

That's where patterns come in. This book catalogs many of those familiar parts, in ways you can reuse in many different contexts. Patterns capture a common structure—often a very local one, such as a list layout—without being too concrete on the details, which gives you the flexibility to be creative.

If you know what users expect of your application, and if you choose carefully from your toolbox of idioms and frameworks (large-scale), individual elements (small-scale), and patterns (covering the range), then you can put together something that "feels familiar" while remaining original.

And that gets you the best of both worlds.

About Patterns in General

In essence, patterns are structural and behavioral features that improve the "habitability" of something—a user interface, a website, an object-oriented program, or a building. They make things easier to understand or more beautiful; they make tools more useful and usable.

As such, patterns can be a description of best practices within a given design domain. They capture common solutions to design tensions (usually called "forces" in pattern literature) and thus, by definition, are not novel. They aren't off-the-shelf components; each implementation of a pattern differs a little from every other. They aren't simple rules or heuristics either. And they won't walk you through an entire set of design decisions—if you're looking for a complete step-by-step description of how to design an interface, a pattern catalog isn't the place to find it!

Patterns are:

Concrete, not general

> All designers depend upon good design principles, like "Prevent errors," "Create a strong visual hierarchy," and "Don't make the user think." It's rather hard, however, to design an actual working interface starting from fundamental principles! Patterns are concrete enough to help fill the space between high-level general principles and the low-level "grammar" of user interface design (widgets, text, graphic elements, alignment grids, and so on).

Valid across different platforms and systems

> Patterns may be more concrete than principles or heuristics, but they do define abstractions—the best patterns aren't specific to a single platform or idiom. Some even work in both print and interactive systems. Ideally, each pattern captures some minor truth about how people work best with a created artifact, and it remains true even while the underlying technologies and media change.

Products, not processes

> Unlike heuristics or user-centered design techniques, which usually advise on how to go about *finding* a solution to an engineering or design problem, patterns *are* possible solutions.

Suggestions, not requirements

> You should almost always follow good design principles and heuristics, of course. And organizations need designers to follow style guides so that their products stay self-consistent. But patterns are intended to be only suggestions; you can follow them or reject them, depending on your design context and user needs.

Relationships among elements, not single elements

A text field is not a pattern. The spatial relationships between a text field and a piece of help text near it, however, might be a pattern. Likewise, changes in a set of elements over time—as a user interacts with the software—may constitute a pattern, though some patterns capture only static relationships.

Customized to each design context

When a pattern is instantiated in a design, the designer should adjust the pattern as needed to fit the situation. You could use some of the pattern examples verbatim, but as long as you understand why the pattern works, why not be creative? Fit the pattern to your particular users and requirements.

Some very complete sets of patterns make up a "pattern language." These patterns resemble visual languages in that they cover the entire vocabulary of elements used in a design (though pattern languages are more abstract and behavioral; visual languages talk about shapes, icons, colors, fonts, etc.). The set in this book isn't nearly as complete, and it contains techniques that don't qualify as traditional patterns. But at least it's concise enough to be manageable and useful.

Other Pattern Collections

The text that started it all dealt with physical buildings, not software. Christopher Alexander's *A Pattern Language* and its companion book *The Timeless Way of Building* established the concept of patterns and described a 250-pattern multilayered pattern language. It is often considered the gold standard for a pattern language because of its completeness, its rich interconnectedness, and its grounding in the human response to our built world.

In the mid-1990s, the publication of *Design Patterns* by Erich Gamma, Richard Helm, Ralph Johnson, and John Vlissides profoundly changed the practice of commercial software architecture. This book is a collection of patterns describing object-oriented "micro-architectures." If you have a background in software engineering, this is the book that probably introduced you to the idea of patterns. Many other authors have written books about software patterns since this book. Software patterns such as these do make software more habitable—for those who write the software, not those who use it!

The first substantial set of user-interface patterns was "Common Ground," the predecessor to the book you're reading now. Many other collections and languages followed, notably Martijn van Welie's *Interaction Design Patterns;* van Duyne, Landay, and Hong's *The Design of Sites*; the Little Springs mobile patterns, now known as Design4Mobile; the Yahoo! Design Pattern Library, which morphed into *Designing Web Interfaces;* and the rest of the O'Reilly design pattern library, including *Designing Social Interfaces, Designing Gestural Interfaces,* and the first edition of this book.

About the Patterns in This Book

So there's nothing really new in here. If you've done any web or UI design, or even thought much about it, you should say, "Oh, right, I know what that is" to most of these patterns. But a few of them might be new to you, and some of the familiar ones may not be part of your usual design repertoire.

These patterns work for both desktop applications and highly interactive websites. Many patterns also apply to mobile devices or TV-based interfaces (like digital recorders).

Though this book won't exhaustively describe all the interface idioms mentioned earlier, these idioms help to organize the book. Some chapters focus on the more common idioms: forms, information graphics, mobile interfaces, and interactions with social networks. Other chapters address subjects that are useful across many idioms, such as organization, navigation, actions, and visual style. (The book does not address idioms such as online games or communities, simply due to lack of space.)

This book is intended to be read by people who have some knowledge of such interface design concepts and terminology as dialog boxes, selection, combo boxes, navigation bars, and whitespace. It does not identify many widely accepted techniques, such as copy-and-paste, since you already know what they are. But, at the risk of belaboring the obvious, this book describes some common techniques to encourage their use in other contexts or to discuss them alongside alternative solutions.

This book does *not* present a complete process for constructing an interface design. When doing design, a sound process is critical. You need to have certain elements in a design process:

- Field research, to find out what the intended users are like and what they already do

- Goal and task analysis, to describe and clarify what users will do with what you're building

- Design models, such as personas (models of users), scenarios (models of common tasks and situations), and prototypes (models of the interface itself)

- Empirical testing of the design at various points during development, like usability testing and *in situ* observations of the design used by real users

- Enough time to iterate over several versions of the design, because you won't get it right the first time

These topics transcend the scope of this book, but there are plenty of other excellent resources and workshops out there that cover them in depth.

But there's a deeper reason why this book won't give you a recipe for designing an interface. Good design can't be reduced to a recipe. It's a creative process, and one that changes under you as you work—in any given project, for instance, you won't understand some design issues until you've designed your way into a dead end. I've personally done that many times.

And design isn't linear. Most chapters in this book are arranged more or less by scale, and therefore by their approximate order in the design progression: large decisions about content and scope are made first, followed by navigation, page design, and eventually the details of interactions with forms and toolbars and such. But you'll often find yourself moving back and forth through this progression. Maybe you'll know very early in a project how a certain screen should look, and that's a "fixed point;" you may have to work backward from there to figure out the right navigational structure. (It's not ideal, but things like this do happen in real life.)

Here are some ways you can use these patterns:

Learning

> If you don't have much design experience, a set of patterns can serve as a learning tool. You may want to read over it to get ideas, or refer back to specific patterns as the need arises. Just as expanding your vocabulary helps you express ideas in language, expanding your interface design "vocabulary" helps you create more expressive designs.

Examples

> Each pattern in this book has at least one example. Some have many; they might be useful to you as a sourcebook. You may find wisdom in the examples that is missing in the text of the pattern. If you're a designer who knows the patterns already, the examples may be the most useful aspect of the book for you.

Terminology

> If you talk to users, engineers, or managers about interface design, or if you write specifications, then you could use the pattern names as a way of communicating and discussing ideas. This is another well-known benefit of pattern languages. (The terms "singleton" and "factory," for instance, were originally pattern names, but they're now in common use among software engineers.)

Comparison of design alternatives

> If you initially decided to use Module Tabs to organize material on a page and it's not working quite as well as you hoped, you might use these patterns to come up with alternatives, such as Titled Sections or an Accordion. Other sets of "either/or" patterns are presented in this book, often with reasons to choose one pattern or another. Skilled designers know that presenting alternative designs to clients frequently leads to a better choice in the end.

Inspiration

> Each pattern description tries to capture the reasons why the pattern works to make an interface easier or more fun. If you get it, but want to do something a little different from the examples, you can be creative with your "eyes open." You could also use the book to jumpstart your creative process by flipping through it for ideas.

One more word of caution: a catalog of patterns is not a checklist. You cannot measure the quality of a thing by counting the patterns in it. Each design project has a unique context, and even if you need to solve a common design problem (such as how to fit too much content onto a page), a given pattern might be a poor solution within that context. No reference can substitute for good design judgment. Nor can it substitute for a good design process, which helps you find and recover from design mistakes.

Ultimately, you should be able to leave a reference like this behind. As you become an experienced designer, you will internalize these ideas to the point that you don't even notice you're using them anymore; the patterns become second nature and a permanent part of your toolbox.

Audience

If you design user interfaces in any capacity, you might find this book useful. It's intended for people who work on:

- Desktop applications
- Websites
- Web applications or "rich internet applications" (RIAs)
- Software for mobile devices or other consumer electronics
- Turnkey systems like kiosks
- Operating systems

Of course, profound differences exist among these different design platforms. However, I believe they have more in common than we generally think. You'll see examples from many different platforms in these patterns, and that's deliberate—they often use the same patterns to achieve the same ends.

From what readers said about the previous edition, this book has been more valuable to less experienced designers than to those who have been designing sites or interfaces for a while—they know this material already. However, even if you're just starting out with design, you should already know the basic "grammar" of UI design, such as available toolkits and control sets, concepts like drag-and-drop and focus, and the importance of usability testing and user feedback. If you don't, some excellent books listed in the References section can get you started with the essentials.

Specifically, this book targets the following audiences:

- Software developers who need to design the UIs that they build.
- Web page designers who are now asked to design web apps or sites with more interactivity.
- New interface designers and usability specialists.
- More experienced designers who want to see how other designs solve certain problems; the examples can serve as a sourcebook for ideas.
- Professionals in adjacent fields, such as technical writing, product design, and information architecture.

- Managers who want to understand what's involved in good interface design.

- Open source developers and enthusiasts. This isn't quite "open source design," but the idea is to open up interface design best practices for everyone's benefit.

How This Book Is Organized

The patterns in this book are grouped into thematic chapters, and each chapter has an introduction that briefly covers the concepts those patterns are built upon. I want to emphasize *briefly*. Some of these concepts could have entire books written about them. But the introductions will give you some context; if you already know this stuff, they'll be review material, and if not, they'll tell you what topics you might want to learn more about. The first set of chapters is applicable to almost any interface you might design, whether it's a desktop application, web application, website, hardware device, or whatever you can think of:

- Chapter 1, *What Users Do,* talks about common behavior and usage patterns supported by good interfaces.

- Chapter 2, *Organizing the Content,* discusses information architecture as it applies to highly interactive interfaces. It deals with different organizational patterns, recognizable interface types, and "guilds" of patterns (groups of smaller-scale patterns that work well together to support a certain type of interface).

- Chapter 3, *Getting Around,* discusses navigation. It describes patterns for moving around an interface—between pages, among windows, and within large virtual spaces.

- Chapter 4, *Organizing the Page,* describes patterns for the layout and placement of page elements. It talks about how to communicate meaning simply by putting things in the right places.

- Chapter 5, *Lists,* enumerates a set of patterns for displaying lists of items, along with criteria for choosing among them.

- Chapter 6, *Doing Things,* talks about how to present actions and commands; use these patterns to handle the "verbs" of an interface.

Next comes a set of chapters that deal with specific idioms. It's fine to read them all, but real-life projects probably won't use all of them. Chapters 7 and 8 are the most broadly applicable, since most modern interfaces use trees, tables, or forms in some fashion.

- Chapter 7, *Showing Complex Data,* contains patterns for trees, tables, charts, and information graphics in general. It discusses the cognitive aspects of data presentation and how to use them to communicate knowledge and meaning.

- Chapter 8, *Getting Input from Users,* deals with forms and controls. Along with the patterns, this chapter has a table that maps data types to various controls that can represent them.

- Chapter 9, *Using Social Media,* discusses the ways that one might integrate contemporary social media into a website or application design. Although designers don't always make these choices for a site, they sometimes do, and social media may influence your design in any case.

- Chapter 10, *Going Mobile,* presents techniques and concepts that designers ought to know in order to help their designs translate well to a mobile device. Patterns throughout the book may contain examples from mobile devices, but the patterns in this chapter are mobile-specific.

Finally, the last chapter comes at the end of the design progression, but it too applies to almost anything you design.

- Chapter 11, *Making It Look Good,* deals with aesthetics and fit-and-finish. It uses graphic design principles and patterns to show how (and why) to polish the look-and-feel of an interface once its behavior is established.

I chose this book's examples based on many factors. The most important is how well an example demonstrates a given pattern or concept, of course, but other considerations include general design fitness, printability, variety—desktop applications, websites, devices, etc.—and how well known and accessible these applications might be to readers. As such, the examples are weighted heavily toward Microsoft and Apple software, certain big-name websites such as Google and Yahoo! properties, and easy-to-find consumer software and devices. This is not to say that they always are paragons of good design—they're not, and I do not mean to slight the excellent work done by countless designers on lesser-known applications. If you know of examples that might meet most of these criteria, please suggest them to me.

Comments and Questions

Please address comments and questions concerning this book to the publisher:

O'Reilly Media, Inc.
1005 Gravenstein Highway North
Sebastopol, CA 95472
(800) 998-9938 (in the United States or Canada)
(707) 829-0515 (international or local)
(707) 829-0104 (fax)

We have a web page for this book, where we list errata, examples, and any additional information. You can access this page at:

http://oreilly.com/catalog/9781449379704/

To comment or ask technical questions about this book, send email to:

bookquestions@oreilly.com

For more information about our books, conferences, Resource Centers, and the O'Reilly Network, see our website at:

http://www.oreilly.com

Safari® Books Online

Safari Books Online is an on-demand digital library that lets you easily search over 7,500 technology and creative reference books and videos to find the answers you need quickly.

With a subscription, you can read any page and watch any video from our library online. Read books on your cell phone and mobile devices. Access new titles before they are available for print, and get exclusive access to manuscripts in development and post feedback for the authors. Copy and paste code samples, organize your favorites, download chapters, bookmark key sections, create notes, print out pages, and benefit from tons of other time-saving features.

O'Reilly Media has uploaded this book to the Safari Books Online service. To have full digital access to this book and others on similar topics from O'Reilly and other publishers, sign up for free at *http://my.safaribooksonline.com*.

Acknowledgments

First of all, I am indebted to my editor, Mary Treseler, who got this project rolling at just the right time. You knew a second edition was needed, and with the patience of a saint, you made sure I followed through with it. Thanks also to the rest of the O'Reilly production team: Rachel Monaghan, Audrey Doyle, Robert Romano, Ron Bilodeau, and anyone else I may have inadvertently missed. You all rocked.

The technical reviewers for this edition gave me fantastic feedback. Barbara Ballard, Erin Malone, Dan Saffer—thanks to you all!

The ideas in this second edition have been cooking for a long time. Both direct and indirect conversations with other UI designers and pattern writers have helped shape my thinking: Bill Scott, Luke Wroblewski, Martijn van Welie, Erin Malone, Christian Crumlish, Dan Saffer, James Reffell, Scott Jenson, and my UX colleagues at Google. I learned a ridiculous amount from all of you. I'm also grateful to the people who gave me feedback at the various and sundry presentations I've done for conferences and mini-conferences over the last few years.

To all who bought or read the first edition: thanks to you too! Without you, there would have been no second edition.

Finally, I am enormously grateful to Rich, who supported me wholeheartedly throughout this second-edition project; and to Matthew, who right now is too young to understand how helpful his sweet hugs actually were. I love you both!

Chapter 1

What Users Do

This book is almost entirely about the look and behavior of applications, web apps, and interactive devices. But this first chapter is the exception to the rule. No screenshots here; no layouts, no navigation, no diagrams, no visuals at all.

Why not? After all, that's probably why you picked up the book in the first place.

It's because good interface design doesn't start with pictures. It starts with an understanding of people: what they're like, why they use a given piece of software, and how they might interact with it. The more you know about them, and the more you empathize with them, the more effectively you can design for them. Software, after all, is merely a means to an end for the people who use it. The better you satisfy those ends, the happier those users will be.

Each time someone uses an application, or any digital product, he carries on a conversation with the machine. It may be literal, as with a command line or phone menu, or tacit, like the "conversation" an artist has with her paints and canvas—the give and take between the craftsperson and the thing being built. With social software, it may even be a conversation by proxy. Whatever the case, the user interface mediates that conversation, helping users achieve whatever ends they had in mind.

As the user interface designer, then, you get to script that conversation, or at least define its terms. And if you're going to script a conversation, you should understand the human's side as well as possible. What are the user's motives and intentions? What "vocabulary" of words, icons, and gestures does the user expect to employ? How can the application set expectations appropriately for the user? How do the user and the machine finally end up communicating meaning to each other?

There's a maxim in the field of interface design: "Know thy users, for they are not you!"

So, this chapter will talk about people. It covers a few fundamental ideas briefly in this introduction, and then discusses some patterns that differ from those in the rest of the book. They describe human behaviors—as opposed to system behaviors—that the software you design may need to support. Software that supports these human behaviors better helps users achieve their goals.

A Means to an End

Everyone who uses a tool—software or otherwise—has a reason for using it. For instance:

- Finding some fact or object
- Learning something
- Performing a transaction
- Controlling or monitoring something
- Creating something
- Conversing with other people
- Being entertained

Well-known idioms, user behaviors, and design patterns can support each of these abstract goals. User experience designers have learned, for example, how to help people search through vast amounts of online information for specific facts. They've learned how to present tasks so that it's easy to walk through them. They're learning ways to support the building of documents, illustrations, and code.

The first step in designing an interface is to figure out what its users are really trying to accomplish. Filling out a form, for example, is almost never a goal in and of itself—people only do it because they're trying to buy something online, renew their driver's license, or install software. They're performing some kind of transaction.

Asking the right questions can help you connect user goals to the design process. Users and clients typically speak to you in terms of desired features and solutions, not of needs and problems. When a user or client tells you he wants a certain feature, ask why he wants it—determine his immediate goal. Then to the answer of this question, ask "why" again. And again. Keep asking until you move well beyond the boundaries of the immediate design problem.*

Why should you ask these questions if you have clear requirements? Because if you love designing things, it's easy to get caught up in an interesting interface design problem. Maybe you're good at building forms that ask for just the right information, with the right controls, all laid out nicely. But the real art of interface design lies in *solving the right problem.*

So, don't get too fond of designing that form. If there's any way to finish the transaction without making the user go through that form at all, get rid of it altogether. That gets the user closer to his goal, with less time and effort spent on his part (and maybe yours, too).

Let's use the "why" approach to dig a little deeper into some typical design scenarios.

---

* This is the same principle that underlies a well-known technique called *root-cause analysis*. But root-cause analysis is a tool for fixing organizational failures; here, we use its "five whys" (more or less) to understand everyday user behaviors and feature requests.

- Why does a mid-level manager use an email client? Yes, of course—"to read email." Why does she read and send email in the first place? To converse with other people. Of course, other means might achieve the same ends: the phone, a hallway conversation, a formal document. But apparently, email fills some needs that the other methods don't. What are they, and why are they important to her? Privacy? The ability to archive a conversation? Social convention? What else?

- A father goes to an online travel agent, types in the city where his family will be taking a summer vacation, and tries to find plane ticket prices on various dates. He's learning from what he finds, but his goal isn't just to browse and explore different options. Ask why. His goal is actually a transaction: to buy plane tickets. Again, he could have done that at many different websites, or over the phone with a live travel agent. How is this site better than those other options? Is it faster? Friendlier? More likely to find a better deal?

- A mobile phone user wants a way to search through his contacts list more quickly. You, as the designer, can come up with some clever ideas to save keystrokes while searching. But why does he want it? It turns out that he makes a lot of calls while driving, and he doesn't want to take his eyes off the road more than he has to—he wants to make calls while staying safe (to the extent that that's possible). The ideal case is that he doesn't have to look at the phone at all! A better solution is voice dialing: all he has to do is speak the name, and the phone makes the call for him.

- Sometimes goal analysis really isn't straightforward at all. A snowboarding site might provide information (for learning), an online store (for transactions), and a set of Flash movies (for entertainment). Let's say someone visits the site for a purchase, but she gets sidetracked into the information on snowboarding tricks—she has switched goals from accomplishing a transaction to browsing and learning. Maybe she'll go back to purchasing something, maybe not. And does the entertainment part of the site successfully entertain both the 12-year-old and the 35-year-old? Will the 35-year-old go elsewhere to buy his new board if he doesn't feel at home there, or does he not care?

It's deceptively easy to model users as a single faceless entity—"The User"—walking through a set of simple use cases, with one task-oriented goal in mind. But that won't necessarily reflect your users' reality.

To do design well, you need to take many "softer" factors into account: gut reactions, preferences, social context, beliefs, and values. All of these factors could affect the design of an application or site. Among these softer factors, you may find the critical feature or design factor that makes your application more appealing and successful.

So, be curious. Specialize in finding out what your users are really like, and what they really think and feel.

The Basics of User Research

Empirical discovery is the only really good way to obtain this information. To get a design started, you'll need to characterize the kinds of people who will be using your design (including the softer factors just mentioned), and the best way to do that is to go out and meet them.

Each user group is unique, of course. The target audience for, say, a new mobile phone app will differ dramatically from the target audience for a piece of scientific software. Even if the same person uses both, his expectations for each are different—a researcher using scientific software might tolerate a less-polished interface in exchange for high functionality, whereas that same person may stop using the mobile app if he finds its UI to be too hard to use after a few days.

Each user is unique, too. What one person finds difficult, the next one won't. The trick is to figure out what's *generally* true about your users, which means learning about enough individual users to separate the quirks from the common behavior patterns.

Specifically, you'll want to learn:

- Their goals in using the software or site
- The specific tasks they undertake in pursuit of those goals
- The language and words they use to describe what they're doing
- Their skill at using software similar to what you're designing
- Their attitudes toward the kind of thing you're designing, and how different designs might affect those attitudes

I can't tell you what your particular target audience is like. You need to find out what they might do with the software or site, and how it fits into the broader context of their lives. Difficult though it may be, try to describe your potential audience in terms of how and why they might use your software. You might get several distinct answers, representing distinct user groups; that's OK. You might be tempted to throw up your hands and say, "I don't know who the users are" or "Everyone is a potential user." But that doesn't help you focus your design at all—without a concrete and honest description of those people, your design will proceed with no grounding in reality.

Unfortunately, this user-discovery phase will consume serious time early in the design cycle. It's expensive. But it's worth it, because you stand a better chance at solving the right problem—you'll build the right thing in the first place.

Fortunately, lots of books, courses, and methodologies now exist to help you. Although this book does not address user research, here are some methods and topics to consider:

Direct observation

Interviews and onsite user visits put you directly into the user's world. You can ask users about what their goals are and what tasks they typically do. Usually done "on location," where users would actually use the software (e.g., in a workplace or at home), interviews can be structured—with a predefined set of questions—or unstructured, where you probe whatever subject comes up. Interviews give you a lot of flexibility; you can do many or a few, long or short, formal or informal, on the phone or in person. These are great opportunities to learn what you don't know. Ask why. Ask it again.

Case studies

Case studies give you deep, detailed views into a few representative users or groups of users. You can sometimes use them to explore "extreme" users that push the boundaries of what the software can do, especially when the goal is a redesign of existing software. You can also use them as longitudinal studies—exploring the context of use over months or even years. Finally, if you're designing custom software for a single user or site, you'll want to learn as much as possible about the actual context of use.

Surveys

Written surveys can collect information from many users. You can actually get statistically significant numbers of respondents with these. Since there's no direct human contact, you will miss a lot of extra information—whatever you don't ask about, you won't learn about—but you can get a very clear picture of certain aspects of your target audience. Careful survey design is essential. If you want reliable numbers instead of a qualitative "feel" for the target audience, you absolutely must write the questions correctly, pick the survey recipients correctly, and analyze the answers correctly—and that's a science.

Personas

Personas aren't a data-gathering method, but they do help you figure out what to do with your data once you've got it. This is a design technique that "models" the target audiences. For each major user group, you create a fictional person that captures the most important aspects of the users in that group: what tasks they're trying to accomplish, their ultimate goals, and their experience levels in the subject domain and with computers in general. Personas can help you stay focused. As your design proceeds, you can ask yourself questions such as "Would this fictional person really do X? What would she do instead?"

You might notice that some of these methods and topics, such as interviews and surveys, sound suspiciously like marketing activities. That's exactly what they are. Focus groups can be useful, too (though not so much as the others), and the concept of market segmentation resembles the definition of target audiences used here. In both cases, the whole point is to understand the audience as best you can.

The difference is that as a designer, you're trying to understand the people who *use* the software. A marketing professional tries to understand those who buy it.

It's not easy to understand the real issues that underlie users' interactions with a system. Users don't always have the language or introspective skill to explain what they really need to accomplish their goals, and it takes a lot of work on your part to ferret out useful design concepts from what they *can* tell you—self-reported observations are usually biased in subtle ways.

Some of these techniques are very formal, and some aren't. Formal and quantitative methods are valuable because they're good science. When applied correctly, they help you see the world as it actually is, not how you think it is. If you do user research haphazardly, without accounting for biases such as the self-selection of users, you may end up with data that doesn't reflect your actual target audience—and that can only hurt your design in the long run.

But even if you don't have time for formal methods, it's better to just meet a few users informally than to not do any discovery at all. Talking with users is good for the soul. If you're able to empathize with users and imagine those individuals actually using your design, you'll produce something much better.

Users' Motivation to Learn

Before you start the design process, consider your overall approach. Think about how you might design the interface's overall interaction style—its personality, if you will.

When you carry on a conversation with someone about a given subject, you adjust what you say according to your understanding of the other person. You might consider how much he cares about the subject, how much he already knows about it, how receptive he is to learning from you, and whether he's even interested in the conversation in the first place. If you get any of that wrong, bad things happen—he might feel patronized, uninterested, impatient, or utterly baffled.

This analogy leads to some obvious design advice. The subject-specific vocabulary you use in your interface, for instance, should match your users' level of knowledge; if some users won't know that vocabulary, give them a way to learn the unfamiliar terms. If they don't know computers very well, don't make them use sophisticated widgetry or uncommon interface-design conventions. If their level of interest might be low, respect that, and don't ask for too much effort for too little reward.

Some of these concerns permeate the whole interface design in subtle ways. For example, do your users expect a short, tightly focused exchange about something very specific, or do they prefer a conversation that's more of a free-ranging exploration? In other words, how much openness is there in the interface? Too little, and your users feel trapped and unsatisfied; too much, and they stand there paralyzed, not knowing what to do next, unprepared for that level of interaction.

Therefore, you need to choose how much freedom your users have to act arbitrarily. At one end of the scale might be a software installation wizard: the user is carried through it with no opportunity to use anything other than Next, Previous, or Cancel. It's tightly focused and specific, but quite efficient—and satisfying, to the extent that it works and is quick. At the other end might be an application such as Excel, an "open floorplan" interface that exposes a huge number of features in one place. At any given time, the user has about 872 things that he can do next, but that's considered good, because self-directed, skilled users can do a lot with that interface. Again, it's satisfying, but for entirely different reasons.

Here's an even more fundamental question: how much effort are your users willing to spend to learn your interface?

It's easy to overestimate. Maybe they'll use it every day on the job—clearly they'd be motivated to learn it well in that case, but that's rare. Maybe they'll use it sometimes, and learn it only well enough to get by (Satisficing). Maybe they'll only see it once, for 30 seconds. Be honest: can you expect most users to become intermediates or experts, or will most users remain perpetual beginners?

Software designed for intermediate-to-expert users includes:

- Photoshop
- Dreamweaver
- Excel
- Code development environments
- System-administration tools for web servers

In contrast, here are some things designed for occasional users:

- Kiosks in tourist centers or museums
- Windows or Mac OS controls for setting desktop backgrounds
- Purchase pages for online stores
- Installation wizards
- Automated teller machines

The differences between the two groups are dramatic. Assumptions about users' tool knowledge permeate these interfaces, showing up in their screen-space usage, labeling, and widget sophistication, and in the places where help is (or isn't) offered.

The applications in the first group have lots of complex functionality, but they don't generally walk the user through tasks step by step. They assume users already know what to do, and they optimize for efficient operation, not learnability; they tend to be document-centered or list-driven (with a few being command-line applications). They often have entire books and courses written about them. Their learning curves are steep.

The applications in the second group are the opposite: restrained in functionality but helpful about explaining it along the way. They present simplified interfaces, assuming no prior knowledge of document- or list-centered application styles (e.g., menu bars, multiple selection, etc.). Wizards frequently show up, removing attention-focusing responsibility from the user. The key is that users aren't motivated to work hard at learning these applications—it's usually just not worth it!

Now that you've seen the extremes, look at the applications in the middle of the continuum:

- Microsoft PowerPoint
- Email clients
- Facebook
- Blog-writing tools

The truth is that most applications fall into this middle ground. They need to serve people on both ends adequately—to help new users learn the tool (and satisfy their need for instant gratification), while enabling frequent-user intermediates to get things done smoothly. Their designers probably knew that people wouldn't take a three-day course to learn an email client. Yet the interfaces hold up under repeated usage. People quickly learn the basics, reach a proficiency level that satisfies them, and don't bother learning more until they are motivated to do so for specific purposes.

You may someday find yourself in tension between the two ends of this spectrum. Naturally you want people to be able to use your design "out of the box," but you might also want to support frequent or expert users as much as possible. Find a balance that works for your situation. Organizational patterns in Chapter 2, such as Multi-Level Help, can help you serve both constituencies.

The Patterns

Even though individuals are unique, people behave predictably. Designers have been doing site visits and user observations for years; cognitive scientists and other researchers have spent many hundreds of hours watching how people do things and how they think about what they do.

So, when you observe people using your software, or doing whatever activity you want to support with new software, you can expect them to do certain things. The behavioral patterns that follow are often seen in user observations. Odds are good that you'll see them too, especially if you look for them.

(A note for pattern enthusiasts: these patterns aren't like the others in this book. They describe human behaviors—not interface design elements—and they're not prescriptive, like the patterns in other chapters. Instead of being structured like the other patterns, these are presented as small essays.)

Again, an interface that supports these patterns well will help users achieve their goals far more effectively than interfaces that don't support them. And the patterns are not just about the interface, either. Sometimes the entire package—interface, underlying architecture, feature choice, documentation, everything—needs to be considered in light of these behaviors. But as the interface designer or interaction designer, you should think about these as much as anyone on your team. You might be in a better place than anyone to advocate for the users.

1. Safe Exploration
2. Instant Gratification
3. Satisficing
4. Changes in Midstream
5. Deferred Choices
6. Incremental Construction
7. Habituation
8. Microbreaks
9. Spatial Memory
10. Prospective Memory
11. Streamlined Repetition
12. Keyboard Only
13. Other People's Advice
14. Personal Recommendations

Safe Exploration

"Let me explore without getting lost or getting into trouble."

When someone feels like she can explore an interface and not suffer dire consequences, she's likely to learn more—and feel more positive about it—than someone who doesn't explore. Good software allows people to try something unfamiliar, back out, and try something else, all without stress.

Those "dire consequences" don't even have to be very bad. Mere annoyance can be enough to deter someone from trying things out voluntarily. Clicking away pop-up windows, re-entering data that was mistakenly erased, suddenly muting the volume on one's laptop when a website unexpectedly plays loud music—all can be discouraging. When you design almost any kind of software interface, make many avenues of exploration available for users to experiment with, without costing the user anything.

Here are some examples:

- A photographer tries out a few image filters in an image-processing application. He then decides he doesn't like the results, and clicks Undo a few times to get back to where he was. Then he tries another filter, and another, each time being able to back out of what he did. (The pattern named Multi-Level Undo, in Chapter 6, describes how this works.)

- A new visitor to a company's home page clicks various links just to see what's there, trusting that the Back button will always get her back to the main page. No extra windows or pop ups open, and the Back button keeps working predictably. You can imagine that if a web app does something different in response to the Back button— or if an application offers a button that seems like a Back button, but doesn't behave quite like it—confusion might ensue. The user can get disoriented while navigating, and may abandon the app altogether.

Instant Gratification

"I want to accomplish something now, not later."

People like to see immediate results from the actions they take—it's human nature. If someone starts using an application and gets a "success experience" within the first few seconds, that's gratifying! He'll be more likely to keep using it, even if it gets harder later. He will feel more confident in the application, and more confident in himself, than if it had taken a while to figure things out.

The need to support instant gratification has many design ramifications. For instance, if you can predict the first thing a new user is likely to do, you should design the UI to make that first thing stunningly easy. If the user's goal is to create something, for instance, then create a new canvas, put a call to action on it, and place a palette next to it. If the user's goal is to accomplish some task, point the way toward a typical starting point.

This also means you shouldn't hide introductory functionality behind anything that needs to be read or waited for, such as registrations, long sets of instructions, slow-to-load screens, advertisements, and so on. These are discouraging because they block users from finishing that first task quickly.

Satisficing

"This is good enough.
I don't want to spend more time learning to do it better."

When people look at a new interface, they don't read every piece of it methodically and then decide, "Hmmm, I think this button has the best chance of getting me what I want." Instead, a user will rapidly scan the interface, pick whatever he sees first that might get him what he wants, and try it—even if it might be wrong.

The term *satisficing* is a combination of *satisfying* and *sufficing*. It was coined in 1957 by the social scientist Herbert Simon, who used it to describe the behavior of people in all kinds of economic and social situations. People are willing to accept "good enough" instead of "best" if learning all the alternatives might cost time or effort.

Satisficing is actually a very rational behavior, once you appreciate the mental work necessary to "parse" a complicated interface. As Steve Krug points out in his book *Don't Make Me Think* (New Riders), people don't like to think any more than they have to—it's work! But if the interface presents an obvious option or two that the user sees immediately, he'll try it. Chances are good that it will be the right choice, and if not, there's little cost in backing out and trying something else (assuming that the interface supports Safe Exploration).

This means several things for designers:

- Use "calls to action" in the interface. Give directions on what to do first: type here, drag an image here, tap here to begin, and so forth.

- Make labels short, plainly worded, and quick to read. (This includes menu items, buttons, links, and anything else identified by text.) They'll be scanned and guessed about; write them so that a user's first guess about meaning is correct. If he guesses wrong several times, he'll be frustrated, and you'll both be off to a bad start.

- Use the layout of the interface to communicate meaning. Chapter 4 explains how to do so in detail. Users "parse" color and form on sight, and they follow these cues more efficiently than labels that must be read.

- Make it easy to move around the interface, especially for going back to where a wrong choice might have been made hastily. Provide "escape hatches" (see Chapter 3). On typical websites, using the Back button is easy, so designing easy forward/backward navigation is especially important for web apps, installed applications, and mobile devices.

- Keep in mind that a complicated interface imposes a large cognitive cost on new users. Visual complexity will often tempt nonexperts to satisfice: they look for the first thing that may work.

Satisficing is why many users end up with odd habits after they've been using a system for a while. Long ago, a user may have learned Path A to do something, and even though a later version of the system offers Path B as a better alternative (or maybe it was there all along), he sees no benefit in learning it—that takes effort, after all—and keeps using the less-efficient Path A. It's not necessarily an irrational choice. Breaking old habits and learning something new takes energy, and a small improvement may not be worth the cost to the user.

Changes in Midstream

"I changed my mind about what I was doing."

Occasionally, people change what they're doing while in the middle of doing it. Someone may walk into a room with the intent of finding a key she had left there, but while she's there, she finds a newspaper and starts reading it. Or she may visit Amazon.com to read product reviews, but ends up buying a book instead. Maybe she's just sidetracked; maybe the change is deliberate. Either way, the user's goal changes while she's using the interface you designed.

This means designers should provide opportunities for people to do that. Make choices available. Don't lock users into a choice-poor environment with no connections to other pages or functionality unless there's a good reason to do so. Those reasons do exist. See the patterns called Wizard (Chapter 2) and Modal Panel (Chapter 3) for examples.

You can also make it easy for someone to start a process, stop in the middle, and come back to it later to pick up where he left off—a property often called *reentrance*. For instance, a lawyer may start entering information into a form on an iPad. Then, when a client comes into the room, the lawyer turns off the device, with the intent of coming back to finish the form later. The entered information shouldn't be lost.

To support reentrance, you can make dialogs and web forms remember values typed previously, and they don't usually need to be modal; if they're not modal, they can be dragged aside on the screen for later use. Builder-style applications—text editors, code development environments, and paint programs—can let a user work on multiple projects at one time, thus letting her put any number of projects aside while she works on another one. See the Many Workspaces pattern in Chapter 2 for more information.

Deferred Choices

"I don't want to answer that now; just let me finish!"

This follows from people's desire for instant gratification. If you ask a task-focused user unnecessary questions in the process, he may prefer to skip the questions and come back to them later.

For example, some web-based bulletin boards have long and complicated procedures for registering users. Screen names, email addresses, privacy preferences, avatars, self-descriptions…the list goes on and on. "But I just wanted to post one little thing," says the user plaintively. Why not allow him to skip most of the questions, answer the bare minimum, and come back later (if ever) to fill in the rest? Otherwise, he might be there for half an hour answering essay questions and finding the perfect avatar image.

Another example is creating a new project in a website editor. There are some things you do have to decide up front, such as the name of the project, but other choices—where on the server are you going to put this when you're done? I don't know yet!—can easily be deferred.

Sometimes it's just a matter of not wanting to answer the questions. At other times, the user may not have enough information to answer yet. What if a music-writing software package asked you up front for the title, key, and tempo of a new song, before you've even started writing it? (See Apple's GarageBand for this bit of "good" design.)

The implications for interface design are simple to understand, though not always easy to implement:

- Don't accost the user with too many upfront choices in the first place.

- On the forms that he does have to use, clearly mark the required fields, and don't make too many of them required. Let him move on without answering the optional ones.

- Sometimes you can separate the few important questions or options from others that are less important. Present the short list; hide the long list.

- Use Good Defaults (Chapter 8) wherever possible, to give users some reasonable default answers to start with. But keep in mind that prefilled answers still require the user to look at them, just in case they need to be changed. They have a small cost, too.

- Make it possible for users to return to the deferred fields later, and make them accessible in obvious places. Some dialog boxes show the user a short statement, such as "You can always change this later by clicking the Edit Project button." Some websites store a user's half-finished form entries or other persistent data, such as shopping carts with unpurchased items.

- If registration is required at a website that provides useful services, users may be far more likely to register if they're first allowed to experience the website—drawn in and engaged—and then asked later about who they are. Some sites let you complete an entire purchase without registering, then ask you at the end if you want to create a no-hassle login with the personal information provided in the purchase step.

Incremental Construction

"Let me change this. That doesn't look right; let me change it again.
That's better."

When people create things, they don't usually do it all in a precise order. Even an expert doesn't start at the beginning, work through the creation process methodically, and come out with something perfect and finished at the end.

Quite the opposite. Instead, she starts with some small piece of it, works on it, steps back and looks at it, tests it (if it's code or some other "runnable" thing), fixes what's wrong, and starts to build other parts of it. Or maybe she starts over, if she really doesn't like it. The creative process goes in fits and starts. It moves backward as much as forward sometimes, and it's often incremental, done in a series of small changes instead of a few big ones. Sometimes it's top-down; sometimes it's bottom-up.

Builder-style interfaces need to support that style of work. Make it easy for users to build small pieces. Keep the interface responsive to quick changes and saves. Feedback is critical: constantly show the user what the whole thing looks and behaves like, while the user works. If the user builds code, simulations, or other executable things, make the "compile" part of the cycle as short as possible, so the operational feedback feels immediate—leave little or no delay between the user making changes and seeing the results.

When creative activities are well supported by good tools, they can induce a state of *flow* in the user. This is a state of full absorption in the activity, during which time distorts, other distractions fall away, and the person can remain engaged for hours—the enjoyment of the activity is its own reward. Artists, athletes, and programmers all know this state.

But bad tools will keep users distracted, guaranteed. If the user has to wait even half a minute to see the results of the incremental change she just made, her concentration is broken; flow is disrupted.

If you want to read more about flow, read the books by Mihaly Csikszentmihalyi, who studied it for years.

Habituation

"That gesture works everywhere else; why doesn't it work here, too?"

When one uses an interface repeatedly, some frequent physical actions become reflexive: pressing Ctrl-S to save a document, clicking the Back button to leave a web page, pressing Return to close a modal dialog box, using gestures to show and hide windows—even pressing a car's brake pedal. The user no longer needs to think consciously about these actions. They've become habitual.

This tendency helps people become expert users of a tool (and helps create a sense of flow, too). Habituation also measurably improves efficiency, as you can imagine. But it can also lay traps for the user. If a gesture becomes a habit, and the user tries to use it in a situation when it doesn't work—or, worse, does something destructive—the user is caught short. He suddenly has to think about the tool again (What did I just do? How do I do what I intended?), and he might have to undo any damage done by the gesture.

For instance, Ctrl-X→Ctrl-S is the "save this file" key sequence used by the Emacs text editor. Ctrl-A moves the text-entry cursor to the beginning of a line. These keystrokes become habitual for Emacs users. When a user presses Ctrl-A→Ctrl-X→Ctrl-S in Emacs, it performs a fairly innocuous pair of operations: move the cursor, save the file.

Now what happens when he types that same habituated sequence in Microsoft Word?

1. Ctrl-A: Select all

2. Ctrl-X: Cut the selection (the whole document, in this case)

3. Ctrl-S: Save the document (whoops)

This is why consistency across applications is important! (And also why a robust "undo" is useful.)

Just as important, though, is consistency within an application. Some applications are evil because they establish an expectation that some gesture will do Action X, except in one special mode where it suddenly does Action Y. Don't do that. It's a sure bet that users will make mistakes, and the more experienced they are—that is, the more habituated they are—the more likely they are to make that mistake.

Consider this carefully if you're developing gesture-based interfaces for mobile devices. Once someone learns how to use his device and gets used to it, he will depend on the standard gestures working consistently on all applications. Check that gestures in your design all do the expected things.

This is also why confirmation dialog boxes often don't work to protect a user against accidental changes. When modal dialog boxes pop up, the user can easily get rid of them just by clicking OK or pressing Return (if the OK button is the default button). If the dialogs pop up all the time when the user makes intended changes, such as deleting files, clicking OK becomes a habituated response. Then, when it actually matters, the dialog box doesn't have any effect, because it slips right under the user's consciousness.

(I've seen at least one application that sets up the confirmation dialog box's buttons randomly from one invocation to another. One actually has to *read* the buttons to figure out what to click! This isn't necessarily the best way to do a confirmation dialog box—in fact, it's better to not have them at all under most circumstances—but at least this design sidesteps habituation creatively.)

Microbreaks

"I'm waiting for the train. Let me do something useful for two minutes."

People often find themselves with a few minutes of down time. They might need a mental break while working; they might be in line at a store or sitting in a traffic jam. They might be bored or impatient. They want to do something constructive or entertaining to pass the time, knowing they won't have enough time to get deep into an online activity.

This pattern is especially applicable to mobile devices, because people can easily pull them out at times such as these.

Here are some typical activities during microbreaks:

- Checking email
- Reading a News Stream (in Chapter 2) such as Facebook or Twitter
- Visiting a news site to find out what's going on in the world
- Watching a short video
- Doing a quick web search
- Reading an online book
- Playing a short game

The key to supporting microbreaks is to make an activity easy and fast to reach—as easy as turning on the device and selecting an application (or website). Don't require complicated setup. Don't take forever to load. And if the user needs to sign in to a service, try to retain the previous authentication so that she doesn't have to sign in every time.

For News Stream services, load the freshest content as quickly as possible and show it in the first screen the user sees. Other activities, such as games, videos, or online books, should remember where the user left them last time and restore the app or site to its previous state, without asking (thus supporting reentrance).

If you're designing an email application, or anything else for which the user needs to do "housekeeping" to maintain order, give her a way to triage items efficiently. This means showing enough data per item so that she can identify, for instance, a message's contents and sender. You can also give her a chance to "star" or otherwise annotate items of interest, delete items easily, and write short responses and updates.

Long load times deserve another mention. Taking too long to load content is a sure way to make users give up on your app—especially during microbreaks! Make sure the page is engineered so that readable, useful content loads first, and with very little delay.

Spatial Memory

"I swear that button was here a minute ago. Where did it go?"

When people manipulate objects and documents, they often find them again later by remembering where they are, not what they're named.

Take the Windows, Mac, or Linux desktop. Many people use the desktop background as a place to put documents, frequently used applications, and other such things. It turns out that people tend to use spatial memory to find things on the desktop, and it's very effective. People devise their own groupings, for instance, or recall that "this document was at the top right over by such-and-such." (Naturally, there are real-world equivalents, too. Many people's desks are "organized chaos," an apparent mess in which the office owner can find anything instantly. But heaven forbid that someone should clean it up for him.)

Many applications put their dialog buttons—OK, Cancel, and so on—in predictable places, partly because spatial memory for them is so strong. In complex applications, people may also find things by remembering where they are relative to other things: tools on toolbars, objects in hierarchies, and so forth. Therefore, you should use patterns such as Responsive Disclosure (Chapter 4) carefully. Adding items to blank spaces in an interface doesn't cause problems, but rearranging existing controls can disrupt spatial memory and make things harder to find. It depends. Try it out on your users if you're not sure.

Along with habituation, which is closely related, spatial memory is another reason why consistency across and within a platform's applications is good. People may expect to find similar functionality in similar places. See the Sign-in Tools pattern (Chapter 3) for an example.

Spatial memory explains why it's good to provide user-arranged areas for storing documents and objects, such as the aforementioned desktop. Such things aren't always practical, especially with large numbers of objects, but it works quite well with small numbers. When people arrange things themselves, they're likely to remember where they put them. (Just don't rearrange it for them unless they ask!) The Movable Panels pattern in Chapter 4 describes one particular way to do this.

Also, this is why changing menus dynamically can sometimes backfire. People get used to seeing certain items on the tops and bottoms of menus. Rearranging or compacting menu items "helpfully" can work against habituation and lead to user errors. So can changing navigation menus on web pages. Try to keep menu items in the same place, and in the same order, on all subpages in a site.

Incidentally, the tops and bottoms of lists and menus are special locations, cognitively speaking. People notice and remember them more than items in the middle of a list. The first and last items are perhaps the worst ones to change out from under the user.

Prospective Memory

"I'm putting this here to remind myself to deal with it later."

Prospective memory is a well-known phenomenon in psychology that doesn't seem to have gained much traction yet in interface design. But I think it should.

We engage in prospective memory when we plan to do something in the future, and we arrange some way of reminding ourselves to do it. For example, if you need to bring a book to work the next day, you might put it on a table beside the front door the night before. If you need to respond to someone's email later (just not right now!), you might leave that email on your screen as a physical reminder. Or if you tend to miss meetings, you might arrange for Outlook or your mobile device to ring an alarm tone five minutes before each meeting.

Basically, this is something almost everyone does. It's a part of how we cope with our complicated, highly scheduled, multitasked lives: we use knowledge "in the world" to aid our own imperfect memories. We need to be able to do it well.

Some software does support prospective remembering. Outlook and most mobile platforms, as mentioned earlier, implement it directly and actively; they have calendars, and they sound alarms. But what else can you use for prospective memory?

- Notes to oneself, like virtual "sticky notes"
- Windows left on-screen
- Annotations put directly into documents (such as "Finish me!")
- Browser bookmarks, for websites to be viewed later
- Documents stored on the desktop, rather than in the usual places in the filesystem
- Email kept in an inbox (and maybe flagged) instead of filed away

People use all kinds of artifacts to support passive prospective remembering. But notice that almost none of the techniques in the preceding list were designed with that in mind! What they *were* designed for is flexibility—and a laissez-faire attitude toward how users organize their stuff. A good email client lets you create folders with any names you want, and it doesn't care what you do with messages in your inbox. Text editors don't care what you type, or what giant bold magenta text means to you; code editors don't care that you have a "Finish this" comment in a method header. Browsers don't care why you keep certain bookmarks around.

In many cases, that kind of hands-off flexibility is all you really need. Give people the tools to create their own reminder systems. Just don't try to design a system that's too smart for its own good. For instance, don't assume that just because a window's been idle for a while, that no one's using it and it should be closed. In general, don't "helpfully" clean up files or objects that the system may think are useless; someone may be leaving them around for a reason. Also, don't organize or sort things automatically unless the user asks the system to do so.

As a designer, is there anything positive you can do for prospective memory? If someone leaves a form half-finished and closes it temporarily, you could retain the data in it for the next time—it will help remind the user where she left off. (See the Deferred Choices pattern.) Similarly, many applications recall the last few objects or documents they edited. You could offer bookmark-like lists of "objects of interest"—both past and future—and make those lists easily available for reading and editing. You can implement Many Workspaces, which lets users leave unfinished pages open while they work on something else.

Here's a bigger challenge: if the user starts tasks and leaves them without finishing them, think about how to leave some artifacts around, other than open windows, that identify the unfinished tasks. Another idea: how might a user gather reminders from different sources (email, documents, calendars, etc.) into one place? Be creative!

Streamlined Repetition

"I have to repeat this how many times?"

In many kinds of applications, users sometimes find themselves having to perform the same operation over and over again. The easier it is for them, the better. If you can help reduce that operation down to one keystroke or click per repetition—or, better, just a few keystrokes or clicks for all repetitions—you will spare users much tedium.

Find and Replace dialog boxes, often found in text editors (Word, email composers, etc.), are one good adaptation to this behavior. In these dialog boxes, the user types the old phrase and the new phrase. Then it takes only one Replace button click per occurrence in the whole document. And that's only if the user wants to see or veto each replacement—if she's confident that she really should replace all occurrences, she can click the Replace All button; one gesture does the whole job.

Here's a more general example. Photoshop lets you record "actions" when you want to perform some arbitrary sequence of actions with a single click. If you want to resize, crop, brighten, and save 20 images, you can record those four steps as they're done to the first image, and then click that action's Play button for each of the remaining 19. See the Macros pattern in Chapter 6 for more information.

Scripting environments are even more general. Unix and its variants allow you to script anything you can type into a shell. You can recall and execute single commands, even long ones, with a Ctrl-P and Return. You can take any set of commands you issue to the command line, put them in a for loop, and execute them by pressing the Return key once.

Or you can put them in a shell script (or in a for loop in a shell script) and execute them as a single command. Scripting is very powerful, and when complex, it becomes full-fledged programming.

Other variants include copy-and-paste capability (preventing the need to retype the same thing in a million places), user-defined "shortcuts" to applications on operating-system desktops (preventing the need to find those applications' directories in the filesystem), browser bookmarks (so users don't have to type URLs), and even keyboard shortcuts.

Direct observation of users can help you figure out just what kinds of repetitive tasks you need to support. Users won't always tell you outright. They may not even be aware that they're doing repetitive things that could be streamlined with the right tools—they may have been doing it so long that they don't even notice anymore. By watching them work, you may see what they don't see.

In any case, the idea is to offer users ways to streamline the repetitive tasks that could otherwise be time-consuming, tedious, and error-prone.

Keyboard Only

"Please don't make me use the mouse."

Some people have real physical trouble using a mouse. Others prefer not to keep switching between the mouse and keyboard because that takes time and effort—they'd rather keep their hands on the keyboard at all times. Still others can't see the screen, and their assistive technologies often interact with the software using just the keyboard API.

For the sakes of these users, some applications are designed to be "driven" entirely via the keyboard. They're usually mouse-driven too, but there is no operation that must be done with *only* the mouse—keyboard-only users aren't shut out of any functionality.

Several standard techniques exist for keyboard-only usage:

- You can define keyboard shortcuts, accelerators, and mnemonics for operations reachable via application menu bars, such as Ctrl-S for Save. See your platform style guide for the standard ones.

- Selection from lists, even multiple selection, is usually possible using arrow keys in combination with modifiers (such as the Shift key), though this depends on which component set you use.

- The Tab key typically moves the keyboard focus—the control that gets keyboard entries at the moment—from one control to the next, and Shift-Tab moves backward. This is sometimes called *tab traversal*. Many users expect it to work on form-style interfaces.

- Most standard controls, even radio buttons and combo boxes, let users change their values from the keyboard by using arrow keys, the Return key, or the space bar.

- Dialog boxes and web pages often have a "default button"—a button representing an action that says "I'm done with this task now." On web pages, it's often Submit or Done; on dialog boxes, OK or Cancel. When users press the Return key on this page or dialog box, that's the operation that occurs. Then it moves the user to the next page or returns him to the previous window.

There are more techniques. Forms, control panels, and standard web pages are fairly easy to drive from the keyboard. Graphic editors, and anything else that's mostly spatial, are much harder, though not impossible.

Keyboard-only usage is particularly important for data-entry applications. In these, speed of data entry is critical, and users can't afford to move their hands off the keyboard to the mouse every time they want to move from one field to another or even one page to another. (In fact, many of these forms don't even require users to press the Tab key to traverse between controls; it's done automatically.)

Other People's Advice

"What did everyone else say about this?"

People are social. As strong as our opinions may sometimes be, we tend to be influenced by what our peers think.

Witness the spectacular growth of online "user comments": Amazon for books (and everything else), IMDb for movies, Flickr for photographs, and countless retailers who offer space for user-submitted product reviews. Auction sites such as eBay formalize user opinions into actual prices. Blogs offer unlimited soapbox space for people to opine about and discuss anything they want, from products to programming to politics.

The advice of peers, whether direct or indirect, influences people's choices when they decide any number of things. Finding things online, performing transactions (Should I buy this product?), playing games (What have other players done here?), and even building things—people can be more effective when aided by others. If not, they might at least be happier with the outcome.

Here's a subtler example. Programmers use the MATLAB application to do scientific and mathematical tasks. Every few months, the company that makes MATLAB holds a public programming contest; for a few days, every contestant writes the best MATLAB code he can to solve a difficult science problem. The fastest, most accurate code wins. The catch is that every player can see everyone else's code—and copying is encouraged! The "advice" in this case is indirect, taking the form of shared code, but it's quite influential. In the end, the winning program is never truly original, but it's undoubtedly better code than any solo effort would have been. (In many respects, this is a microcosm of open source software development, which is driven by a powerful set of social dynamics.)

Not all applications and software systems can accommodate a social component, and not all should try. But consider whether it might enhance the user experience to do so. And you could get more creative than just tacking a web-based bulletin board onto an ordinary site—how can you persuade users to take part constructively? How can you integrate it into the typical user's workflow?

If the task is creative, maybe you can encourage people to post their creations for the public to view. If the goal is to find some fact or object, perhaps you can make it easy for users to see what other people found in similar searches.

Of the patterns in this book, Multi-Level Help (Chapter 2) most directly addresses this idea; an online support community is a valuable part of a complete help system for some applications.

Personal Recommendations

"My friend told me to read this, so it must be pretty good."

This pattern operates on the same principle as the previous one—we are strongly influenced by our peers. So much so, in fact, that we are much more likely to view the articles and videos that someone refers us to than those we find in some other way. The personal touch makes a big difference when we decide what to read online.

Therefore, support person-to-person sharing of content. Let people send a URL (or the content itself) to friends and family, either via email or via a social network such as Facebook or Buzz.

This implies a host of mechanisms that need to be used or designed in. First, what exactly are users sharing? If the content doesn't already have a URL, see if one can be constructed for it. (The Deep-linked State pattern in Chapter 3 talks about this.) This URL should direct the recipient to a page with the same content that the sender was seeing, to avoid confusion.

Second, whom will they share it with? Let users connect to a social network, or give them a way to send email.

Third, what implications does this reference have? If a user sends email to a few "close ties," along with a personal message—one the user typed, not an automatic "personal message!—that can potentially carry a very high recommendation. After all, someone cared enough to think about you and take time to write a note. The specialness declines as the sender *CCs* more and more email addresses, though.

When a user posts a link to her Facebook or Twitter stream, that carries other implications: "I thought this was cool, and it represents something about who I am." Followers are still likely to read these links, especially if they trust that the poster has good taste. Furthermore, followers may repost or retweet it themselves, as will their followers, ad infinitum. This is how memes start, content goes viral, and the social web rolls on.

Chapter 2

Organizing the Content: Information Architecture and Application Structure

At this point, you know what your users want out of your application or site. You're targeting a chosen platform: the Web, the desktop, a mobile device, or some combination. You know which idiom or interface type to use—a form, an e-commerce site, an image viewer, or something else—or you may realize that you need to combine several of them. If you're really on the ball, you've written down some typical scenarios that describe how people might use high-level elements of the application to accomplish their goals. You have a clear idea of what value this application adds to people's lives.

Now what?

You could start making sketches of the interface. Many visual thinkers do that at this stage. If you're the kind of person who likes to think visually and needs to play with sketches while working out the broad strokes of the design, go for it.

But if you're not a visual thinker by nature (and sometimes even if you are), hold off on the interface sketches. They might lock your thinking into the first visual designs you put on paper. You need to stay flexible and creative for a little while, until you work out the overall organization of the application.

It can be helpful to think about an application in terms of its underlying data and tasks. What objects are being shown to the users? How are they categorized and ordered? What do users need to do with them? And now that you're thinking abstractly about them, how many ways can you design a presentation of those things and tasks?

These lines of inquiry may help you think more creatively about the interface you're designing.

Information architecture (IA) is the art of organizing an information space. It encompasses many things: presenting, searching, browsing, labeling, categorizing, sorting, manipulating, and strategically hiding information. Especially if you're working with a new product, this is where you should start.

The Big Picture

Let's look at the very highest level of your application first. From the designer's perspective, your site or application probably serves several functions: a software service—maybe several services—sharing information, selling a product, branding, social communication, or any number of other goals. Your home page or opening screen may need to convey all of these. Via text and imagery, users should be directed to the part of your site or app that accomplishes *their* purposes.

At this level, you'll make decisions about the whole package. What interaction model will it use? The desktop metaphor? The simpler model of a traditional website? Or a richly interactive site that splits the difference? Is it a self-contained device such as a mobile phone or digital video recorder, for which you must design the interactions from scratch? The interaction model establishes consistency throughout the artifact, and it determines how users move through and among the different pieces of functionality. I won't go into more detail at this level, because almost all of the patterns in this book apply at smaller scales.

Now let's look at a smaller unit within an application or site: pages that serve single important functions. In an application, this might be a main screen or a major interactive tool; in a richly interactive website, it might be a single page, such as Gmail's main screen; in a more static website, it might be a group of pages devoted to one process or function.

Any such page will primarily do one of these things:

1. Show one single thing, such as a map, book, video, or game

2. Show a list or set of things

3. Provide tools to create a thing

4. Facilitate a task

Most apps and sites do some combination of these things, of course. A website might show a feature article (1), a list of additional articles (2), with a wiki area for members to create pages (3), and a registration form for new members (4). That's fine. Each of these parts of the site should be designed using patterns and tools to fit that particular organizing principle.

This list mirrors some of the work done by Theresa Neil with application structures in the context of rich Internet applications (RIAs). She defines three types of structures based on the user's primary goal: information, process, and creation.[*]

This list gives us a framework within which to fit the idioms and patterns we'll talk about in this and other chapters.

---

[*] "Rich Internet Screen Design," in *UX Magazine*: *http://www.uxmag.com/design/rich-internet-application-screen-design*.

Show One Single Thing

Is this really what your page does? The whole point of the page's design is to show or play a single piece of content, with no list of other pieces that users could also see, no comments, and no table of contents or anything like that?

Lucky you!

All you really need, then, is to manage the user's interaction with this one thing. The IA is probably straightforward. There might be small-scale tools clustered around the content—scrollers and sliders, sign-in box, global navigation, headers and footers, and so forth—but they are minor and easily designed. Your design might take one of these shapes:

- A long, vertically scrolled page of flowed text (articles, books, and similar long-form content).

- A zoomable interface for very large, fine-grained artifacts, such as maps, images, or information graphics. Map sites such as Google Maps provide some well-known examples.

- The "media player" idiom, including video and audio players.

As you design this interface, consider the following patterns and techniques to support the design:

- Alternative Views, to show the content in more than one way.

- Many Workspaces, in case people want to see more than one place, state, or document at one time.

- Deep-linked State, in Chapter 3. With this, a user can save a certain place or state within the content so that he can come back to it later or send someone else a URL.

- Sharing Widget and other social patterns, in Chapter 9.

- Some of the mobile patterns described in Chapter 10, if one of your design goals is to deliver the content on mobile devices.

Show a List of Things

This is what most of the world's digital artifacts seem to do. Lists are everywhere! The digital world has converged on many common idioms for showing lists, most of which are familiar to you—simple text lists, menus, grids of images, search results, lists of email messages or other communications, tables, trees. There are more, of course.

Lists present rich challenges in information architecture. How long is the list? Is it flat or hierarchical, and if it is a hierarchy, what kind? How is it ordered, and can the user change that ordering dynamically? Should it be filtered or searched? What information or operations are associated with each list item, and when and how should they be shown?

Because lists are so common, a solid grasp of the different ways to present them can benefit any designer. It's the same theme again—by learning and formalizing these techniques, you can expand your own thinking about how to present content in different and interesting ways.

A few patterns for designing an interface around a list are described in this chapter (others are in Chapter 5). You can build either an entire app or site, or a small piece of a larger artifact, around one of these patterns. They set up a structure that other display techniques—text lists, thumbnail lists, and so on—can fit into. Other top-level organizations not listed here might include calendars, full-page menus, and search results.

- Feature, Search, and Browse is the pattern followed by countless websites that show products and written content. Searching and browsing provide two ways for users to find items of interest, while the front page features one item to attract interest.

- Blogs, news sites, email readers, and social sites such as Twitter all use the News Stream pattern to list their content, with the most recent updates at the top.

- Picture Manager is a well-defined interface type for handling photos and other pictorial documents. It can accommodate hierarchies and flat lists, tools to arrange and reorder documents, tools to operate directly on pictures, and so on.

Once you've chosen an overall design for the interface, you might look at other patterns and techniques for displaying lists. These fit into the patterns mentioned earlier; for instance, a Picture Manager might use a Thumbnail Grid, a Pagination, or both to show a list of photos—all within a Two-Panel Selector framework. See Chapter 5 for a thorough discussion.

Provide Tools to Create a Thing

Builders and editors are the great dynastic families of the software world. Microsoft Word, Excel, PowerPoint, and other Office applications, in addition to Adobe Photoshop, Illustrator, In Design, Dreamweaver, and other tools that support designers are all in this category. So are the tools that support software engineers, such as the various code editors and integrated development environments. These have long histories, large user bases, and very well established interaction styles, honed over many years.

Most people are familiar with the idioms used by these tools: text editors, code editors, image editors, editors that create vector graphics, and spreadsheets.

Chapter 8 of the previous edition of this book discusses how to design different aspects of these tools. But at the level of application structure or IA, the following patterns are often found:

- Canvas Plus Palette describes most of these applications. This highly recognizable, well-established pattern for visual editors sets user expectations very strongly.

- Almost all applications of this type provide Many Workspaces—usually windows containing different documents, which enable users to work on them in parallel.

- Alternative Views let users see one document or workspace through different lenses, to view various aspects of the thing they're creating.

- "Blank Slate Invitation" is named and written about in *Designing Web Interfaces* (*http://oreilly.com/catalog/9780596516253/*) by Bill Scott and Theresa Neil (O'Reilly), and is a profoundly useful pattern for builders and editors. It is closely related to the Input Hints pattern in Chapter 8.

Facilitate a Single Task

Maybe your interface's job isn't to show a list of anything or create anything, but simply to get a job done. Signing in, registering, posting, printing, uploading, purchasing, changing a setting—all such tasks fall into this category.

Forms do a lot of work here. Chapter 8 talks about forms at length and lists many controls and patterns to support effective forms. Chapter 6 defines another useful set of patterns that concentrate more on "verbs" than "nouns."

Not much IA needs to be done if the user can do the necessary work in a small, contained area, such as a sign-in box. But when the task gets more complicated than that—if it's long, or branched, or has too many possibilities—part of your job is to work out how the task is structured.

- Much of the time, you'll want to break the task down into smaller steps or groups of steps. For these, a Wizard might work well for users who need to be walked through the task.

- A Settings Editor is a very common type of interface that gives users a way to change the settings or preferences of something—an application, a document, a product, and so on. This isn't a step-by-step task at all. Here, your job is to give users open access to a wide variety of choices and switches and let them change only what they need, when they need it, knowing that they will skip around.

The Patterns

Several of the patterns in this chapter are large-scale, defining the interactions for large sections of applications or sites (or sometimes the entire thing). Some of these, including Picture Manager, Canvas Plus Palette, and Feature, Search, and Browse, are really clusters of other patterns that support each other in well-defined ways—they are "guilds" of smaller-scale patterns.

1. Feature, Search, and Browse

2. News Stream

3. Picture Manager

4. Dashboard

5. Canvas Plus Palette

6. Wizard

7. Settings Editor

The last three patterns are more "meta," in the sense that they can apply to the other patterns in the preceding list. For instance, almost any content, document, or list can be shown in more than one way, and the ability to switch among those Alternative Views can empower users.

8. Alternative Views

Likewise, a user may want to instantiate the interface more than once, to maintain several trains of thought simultaneously—consider the tabs in a browser window, all showing different and unrelated websites. Offer the Many Workspaces pattern to these users.

9. Many Workspaces

Many patterns, here and elsewhere in the book, contribute in varying degrees to the learnability of an interface. Multi-Level Help sets out ways to integrate help into the application, thus supporting learnability for a broad number of users and situations.

10. Multi-Level Help

Feature, Search, and Browse

Figure 2-1. *EMS*

What

Put three elements on the main page of the site or app: a featured article or product, a search box, and a list of items or categories that can be browsed.

Use when

Your site offers users long lists of items—articles, products, videos, and so on—that can be browsed and searched. You want to engage incoming users immediately by giving them something interesting to read or watch.

Why

These three elements are found together on many, many successful sites. Once you are attuned to them, you can find them just about everywhere.

Searching and browsing go hand in hand as two ways to find desired items: some people will know what they're looking for and zero in on the search box, while others will do more open-ended browsing through the lists and categories you show them.

Featured items are how you "hook" the user. They're far more interesting than just category lists and search boxes, especially when you use appealing images and headlines. A user who lands on your page now has something to read or experiment with, without doing any additional work at all—and he may find it more interesting than whatever he originally came for.

How

Place a search box in a prominent location, such as an upper corner, or in a banner across the middle top of the site. Demarcate it well from the rest of the site—use whitespace to set it off, and use a different surrounding background color if necessary.

Try to eliminate all other text fields above the fold (except the sign-in box, if you have one), to make sure users don't confuse those with the search box. People looking for a search box tend to zero in on the first text field they come across. Make sure they find the right one!

Set aside Center Stage (see Chapter 4) for the featured article, product, or video. Very near it, and still above the fold, place an area for browsing the rest of the site's content. Most sites show a list of topics or product categories. These might be links to pages devoted to those categories. Or they might change the current page's content, replacing the feature with a list of items in that category; see the Two-Panel Selector pattern in Chapter 5.

If the category labels open in place to show subcategories, the list behaves like a tree. Some sites, such as Amazon, turn the category labels into menus: when the pointer rolls over the label, a menu of subcategories appears.

Choose the features well. Features are a good way to sell items, advertise specials, and call attention to breaking news. However, they also define what your site is about. The items you choose to feature say a lot about the site's values. Features that talk about altruistic or charitable efforts have a very different appeal from those that advertise specific products. As always, know your users. What will they want to know about? What will capture their attention and hold them at your site?

As the user browses through categories and subcategories, help him "stay found" with the Breadcrumbs pattern (Chapter 3).

Examples

This pattern applies well to websites such as news outlets (CNET, Figure 2-2), publishers (Lulu), knowledge bases (About.com, Figure 2-3), and, of course, e-commerce sites (Amazon, Figure 2-4; and EMS, at the top of the pattern in Figure 2-1).

Figure 2-2. *CNET*

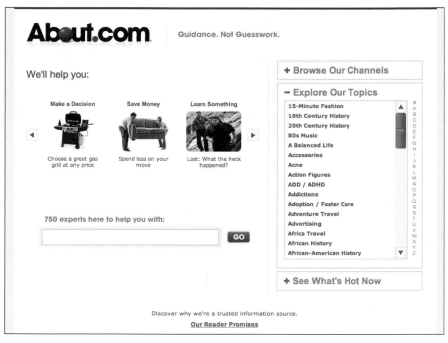

Figure 2-3. *About.com*

Figure 2-4. *Amazon*

News Stream

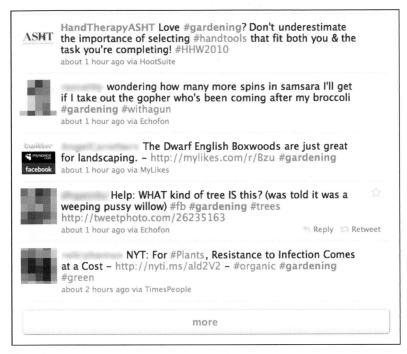

Figure 2-5. *Twitter*

What

Show time-sensitive items in a reverse chronological list, with the latest items at the top. Update it dynamically, and combine the items from different sources or people into one single stream.

Use when

Your site or app uses one or more communication channels, such as blogs, email, social site updates, or news sites, to deliver timely content to users.

This channel may be personal—a user "owns" it, like an email client or Facebook friends list—or public, such as a website or public Twitter stream.

Why

People can keep up with a news stream easily, since the latest items reliably appear on top with no effort on the part of the user. They can check in often and be assured of seeing what they need to see.

People go to many sites or apps each day to keep up with their friends' activities, engage in conversations, or follow topics or blogs of interest. When multiple "news" sources can be blended in one place, it's easier to keep track of it all.

This pattern supports the Microbreaks behavior pattern in Chapter 1. A glance at a News Stream application can give a user lots of useful information (or entertainment) with very little time or effort.

From the perspective of a publisher, such as a website, having a News Box (Chapter 9) or the equivalent on your main page lets visitors see what's new and noteworthy at your organization. Large organizations in particular may have many initiatives going on that would interest visitors: new products, blog entries, videos, news articles, charity work, and other content.

How

List incoming items in reverse chronological order. If the technology permits, "push" new items onto the top of the list without waiting for the user to request an update, but offer a way for the user to get an immediate update or refresh anyway.

Very busy streams can be split up into manageable substreams by topic, sender, source, search terms, or other factors—you could let the user choose which one(s) to show. Services such as Facebook, FriendFeed, Twitter, and some RSS readers show clickable lists of these substreams to the left or right of the incoming content (thus implementing the Two-Panel Selector pattern). Others, such as Tweetdeck, use Many Workspaces to show multiple parallel panels of incoming content.

Information shown with each item might include:

What

> For short micro-updates, show the whole thing. Otherwise, show a title, a teaser that's a few words or sentences long, and a thumbnail picture if one is available.

Who

> This might be the person who wrote an update, the blog where an article was posted, the author of said article, or the sender of an email. Actual person names humanize the interface, but balance this against recognition and authoritativeness—the names of news outlets, blogs, companies, and so forth are important, too. Use both if that makes sense.

When

> Give a date or timestamp; consider using relative times, such as "Yesterday" and "Eleven minutes ago."

Where

> If an item's source is a website, link to that website. If it comes from one of your organization's blogs, link to that. (But here's another interpretation of "where": can you get geolocation data about the item, and show it on a map?)

When there's more to an item than can be shown easily in the list display, show a "More" link or button. You might design a way to show the entire contents of an item within the News Stream window. The News Stream is a list, so you can choose among Two-Panel Selector, One-Window Drilldown, and List Inlay. Examples abound of each model.

Give the user ways to respond immediately to incoming items. Stars, thumbs-up, liking, and favoriting are available in some systems—these all provide low-effort feedback and "handshaking" among people who don't have time to write out long replies. But allow those long replies to be written, too! By placing controls and text fields immediately next to an item in a News Stream, you encourage responsiveness and interaction. This is usually a good thing in social systems.

Sharing of items, either privately via email or semipublicly via a provided social service, is also common in these interfaces. See the Sharing Widget pattern in Chapter 9.

News Stream designs for mobile devices are fairly straightforward as of this writing. Almost all of them devote the full screen to a single list—often a Thumbnail-and-Text List (Chapter 10) with richly formatted text—and users can drill down to an item by simply tapping or clicking it in the list.

Many News Stream services, including Twitter and Facebook, use the Infinite List pattern (see Chapter 10) for both their mobile and full-screen designs. This pattern lets users load a page or two of the most recent updates, and gives the option of loading more to go "backward in time."

Some resources use the term *activity stream* for a very closely related concept: the time-ordered stream of actions (usually social actions) performed by a single entity such as an individual, system, or organization. This is a useful concept, and it doesn't really conflict with the News Stream pattern, which talks about the stream of activities that are *of interest to* an individual or group of users, not *generated by* them. News Streams will usually have multiple diverse sources.

Examples

Digg (Figure 2-6) and Google News (Figure 2-7) are both public News Streams. Their purposes and designs are very different, but they share some of the features talked about in this pattern. Digg shows all incoming items in one large list; Google News splits them into topics, within which the most recent news articles are shown first. (Drilling down into the topic shows a page with a single list.) Both show comparable item information: title, teaser, linked source, and a relative timestamp. They use human names: Digg shows the submitter's name, while Google News shows the article author's name. And on both sites, you can mark items of interest—with a "digg" in one, a star in the other—and share them via email.

Figure 2-6. *Digg*

Figure 2-7. *Google News*

The previous two examples show public News Streams; the next two show personal News Streams.

Social networking services, news aggregators, and private communications (such as email) provide plenty of examples of personal News Streams. In Figures 2-8 and 2-9 we see Facebook and Google Reader, which is an RSS-based aggregator. They both use a single reverse chronological list of items, each of which shows a linked source, title and teaser (when appropriate), author name, and relative timestamp. Users can "like" items, share them, and follow links to read more.

But note the differences, too. Google Reader lets the user split a potentially huge combined stream into substreams, based on source and topic; these are displayed in a selectable tree list on the left, thus making the window a Two-Panel Selector. Facebook doesn't give the user this option by default, as of this writing. Instead, it automatically (and unpredictably) switches between a filtered "Top Stories" view, and a "Most Recent" view that shows everything. However, Facebook excels at the immediate response. Posting a short comment to a Facebook entry is almost as easy as thinking about it.

Figure 2-8. *Facebook*

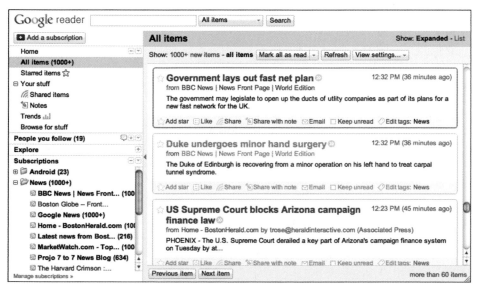

Figure 2-9. *Google Reader*

Picture Manager

Figure 2-10. *Two views of iPhoto*

What

Use thumbnails, item views, and a browsing interface to create a familiar structure for managing photos, videos, and other pictorial items.

Use when

People use your software to work with lists or collections of pictorial things: photos, drawings, video clips, and so on. The list might be in a web page, or in an application, or both. It might allow editing by the owner of the content, or it might simply show the content to the public for browsing, viewing, and comments.

Why

This is a distinct style of application that many people recognize. It is also a *guild* of patterns— a set of patterns linked together and supporting each other in predictable ways. Once someone sees a Thumbnail Grid of images or videos in the right context, she knows what to expect: browse, click to view, set up slideshows or playlists, and so on.

Patterns and other components that often play parts in this guild include:

- Thumbnail Grid
- One-Window Drilldown
- Two-Panel Selector
- Pyramid
- Tabs and Collapsible Panels
- Button Groups

- Trees or outlines
- Keyboard Only
- Sharing Widget
- Search box
- Social comments and discussion

Set up two principal views: a Thumbnail Grid of the items in the list, and a large view of a single item. Users will go back and forth between these. Design a browsing interface and associate it with the Thumbnail Grid to let users explore a large collection easily.

The Thumbnail Grid

Use this pattern to show a sequence of items. Many Picture Managers show a small amount of metadata with each item, such as its filename or author, but do this with care, as it clutters the interface. You might offer a control to adjust the size of the thumbnails. There may also be a way to sort the items by different criteria, such as date, label, or rating, or to filter it and show only the starred items (for instance).

When a user clicks on an item, show it immediately in the single-item view. Applications often let the user traverse the grid with the keyboard—for example, with the arrow keys and space bar. (See the Keyboard Only pattern in Chapter 1.)

If the user owns the items, offer ways to move, reorder, and delete items at this level in the interface. This implies having a multiple-selection interface, such as Shift-select, checkboxes, or lassoing a group of items with the pointer. Cut, copy, and paste should also work in applications.

You can offer slideshow or playlist functionality to all users at the Thumbnail Grid level.

The single-item view

Show a large view of the selected image (or a player, for a video). Display metadata—information about the item—next to it. This view can be next to the Thumbnail Grid if the window is large, or it might replace the area used by the grid. In practice, this means choosing between a Two-Panel Selector and a One-Window Drilldown. See Chapter 5 for these list-related patterns.

If the interface is a website or is otherwise web-connected, you might choose to offer social features at this level. Comments, liking or thumbs-up, and sharing might be here; see the Sharing Widget and other patterns in Chapter 9. Likewise, tagging or labeling can also be done here, either privately or publicly. An "other items you may like" feature is sometimes found in web-based public collections.

Editing features for individual items will live here, also. For instance, a photo manager might offer simple functionality such as cropping, color and brightness adjustment, and red-eye reduction. Metadata properties could be edited here, too. If a full editor is too complex to present here, give the user a way to launch a "real" editor. (Adobe Bridge, for example, lets the user launch Photoshop on a photo.) Use Button Groups to maintain a simple, comprehensible visual grouping of all these features.

Link the item to the previous and next items in the list by providing "previous" and "next" buttons, especially if you use One-Window Drilldown to display the single-item view (which also requires a "back" button). See the Pyramid navigational pattern in Chapter 3.

The browsing interface

The contents of the Thumbnail Grid should be driven by a browsing interface that might be complex, simple, or nearly nonexistent, depending on the nature of the application.

At minimum, most interfaces should offer a search box, either to search an individual user's items or to search all public items (or both).

Private photo and video management interfaces—especially desktop apps such as Picasa and iPhoto—should let the user browse the filesystem for images stored in different directories. If users can group items into albums, sets, projects, or other types of collections, these should be available in a browsing interface, too. Most also permit favoriting or starring of items.

Most apps and sites show the browsing interface above or to the left of the Thumbnail Grid. For highly interactive software, they relate to each other as a Two-Panel Selector: when the user selects a category or folder (or enters a search term), the contents immediately show up in the Thumbnail Grid next to the browsing interface.

Filters are sometimes found here. Adobe Bridge puts filters into its browsing interface; more than 10 properties can be used to slice through a large collection of items, including keywords, modification date, camera type, and ISO.

Websites that host public collections, such as YouTube and Flickr, sometimes use the entire home page as a browsing interface. Sites such as these are faced with an interesting choice: when a signed-in user who "owns" content visits the home page, should she see her own personal collections, or the featured content that the rest of the public sees? Or both?

Examples

Picasa and Adobe Bridge, along with iPhoto (shown in Figure 2-10), are desktop applications for managing personal collections of images. Their browsing interfaces—all Two-Panel Selectors—vary in complexity from iPhoto's very simple design to Adobe Bridge's numerous panels and filters. Picasa (Figure 2-11) and iPhoto use One-Window Drilldown to reach the single-item view, while Adobe Bridge (Figure 2-12) puts all three views together on one page.

Figure 2-11. *Two views of Picasa*

Figure 2-12. *Adobe Bridge, which contains all views in one complex window*

Flickr's design (Figure 2-13) has been mimicked by many other web-based image and video collections. Browsing images at Flickr is different from browsing in a private, desktop-based application—sets, pools, groups, and users' public collections are the means by which one explores the Flickr universe. Social elements are critical to Flickr's vitality, too. But you can still see a Thumbnail Grid, a single-item view reached via One-Window Drilldown, item details, and a Pyramid navigational pattern (previous, next, up).

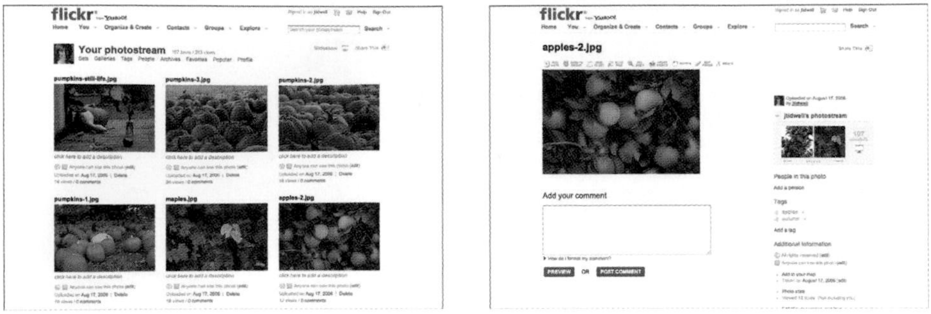

Figure 2-13. *Flickr*

Even video sites fit this pattern. When you view someone's YouTube channel, you can choose to see either a Thumbnail Grid, or a list beside a video player (the default). (Both options are shown in Figure 2-14.) Clicking a thumbnail brings you to the page for that video, where detailed information and discussion are shown. Visitors can browse by looking at playlists, the latest videos added, the most-viewed videos, and the top-rated videos; a search box is also provided, as it is everywhere.

Figure 2-14. *The Sesame Street channel on YouTube*

TED's browsing interface is more complex (see Figure 2-15). Its home page offers a dynamically changeable infographic made up of thumbnails of different sizes. By toggling fields on and off, visitors can narrow down the field of videos and find the ones they want. Rolling over a thumbnail gives item details. Clicking on it brings you to a single-item view, which looks a lot like YouTube's.

Figure 2-15. *TED*

In other libraries

The Image Browser pattern at Welie.com describes some aspects of a Picture Manager:

http://welie.com/patterns/showPattern.php?patternID=image-browsing

Dashboard

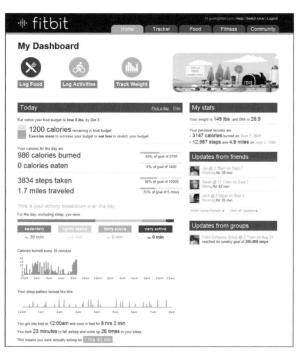

Figure 2-16. *Fitbit*

What

Arrange data displays into a single information-dense page, updated regularly. Show users relevant, actionable information, and let them customize the display as necessary.

Use when

Your site or application deals with an incoming flow of information from something—web server data, social chatter, news, airline flights, business intelligence information, or financials, for example. Your users would benefit from continuous monitoring of that information.

Why

This is a familiar and recognizable page style. Dashboards have a long history, both online and in the physical world, and people have well-established expectations about how they work: they show useful information, they update themselves, they usually use graphics to display data, and so on.

A dashboard is also a guild of interlocking patterns and components. Many online dashboards use these in predictable ways:

- Titled Sections
- Tabs and Collapsible Panels
- Movable Panels
- One-Window Drilldown

- Lists and tables of various kinds (see Chapter 5)
- Row Striping
- Information graphics (see Chapter 7)
- Datatips

How

Determine what information users need or want to see. This isn't as simple as it sounds, because you need an editorial eye—you can't just splatter the screen with confusing or unimportant data, or people won't be able to pick out the parts that matter. Remove, or at least deemphasize, information that doesn't help the user.

Use a good visual hierarchy (see Chapter 4) to arrange lists, tables, and information graphics on the page. Try to keep the main information on one page, with little or no scrolling, so people can keep the window on-screen and see everything at a glance. Group related data into Titled Sections, and use tabs only when you're confident that users won't need to see the tab contents side by side.

Use One-Window Drilldown to let users see additional details about the data—they should be able to click on links or graphics to find out more. Datatips work well to show individual data points when the pointer rolls over an information graphic.

Choose appropriate and well-designed information graphics for the data you need to show. Gauges, dials, pie charts, and 3D bar charts look nice, but they are rarely the best way to show comparative information at a glance—simple line and bar charts express data better, especially time-based data. When numbers and text are more relevant than graphics, use lists and tables. Row Striping is a common pattern for multicolumn data tables.

People will try to get actionable information from the dashboard at a glance, without looking hard at every element on the page. So, when you show text, consider highlighting keywords and numbers so that they stand out from surrounding text.

Should your users be able to customize their dashboard displays? Many dashboards do offer customization, and your users may expect it. One way to customize a dashboard page is to rearrange the sections—iGoogle and My Yahoo! both offer Movable Panels to users, in addition to choosing which gadgets get shown.

Examples

My Yahoo! is a portal-style dashboard, showing weather, news, email, and other personalized information to a signed-in user (see Figure 2-17). This is the kind of window that someone would check frequently throughout the day or week. It can be rearranged via Movable Panels, and a user can decide which sections and widgets to show.

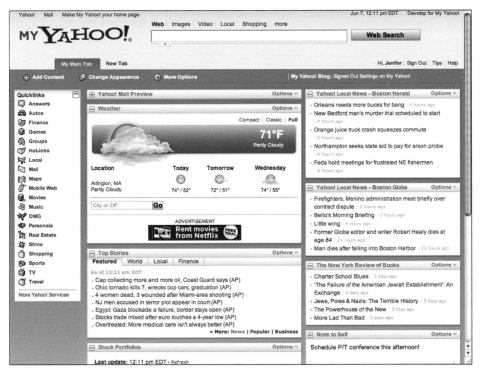

Figure 2-17. *My Yahoo!*

Netvibes offers fully customizable dashboards that can be hooked up to a broad-based web search (see Figure 2-18). With this, someone can stay abreast of conversations, pictures, and articles about a fast-moving topic. A tool tip shows the first few words of an article, which can help the user to decide whether to click through or not.

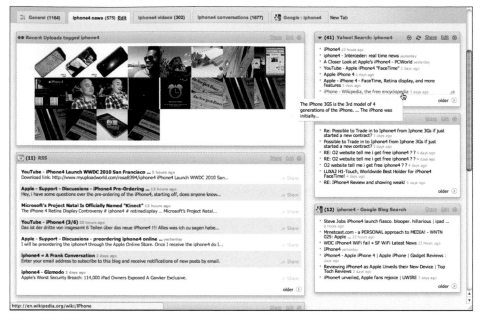

Figure 2-18. *Netvibes*

Google Analytics is more like the Fitbit example in Figure 2-16 at the top of the pattern—it uses information graphics to show a visual snapshot of a system. In Figure 2-19, the system is a website, and the dashboard illustrates log data.

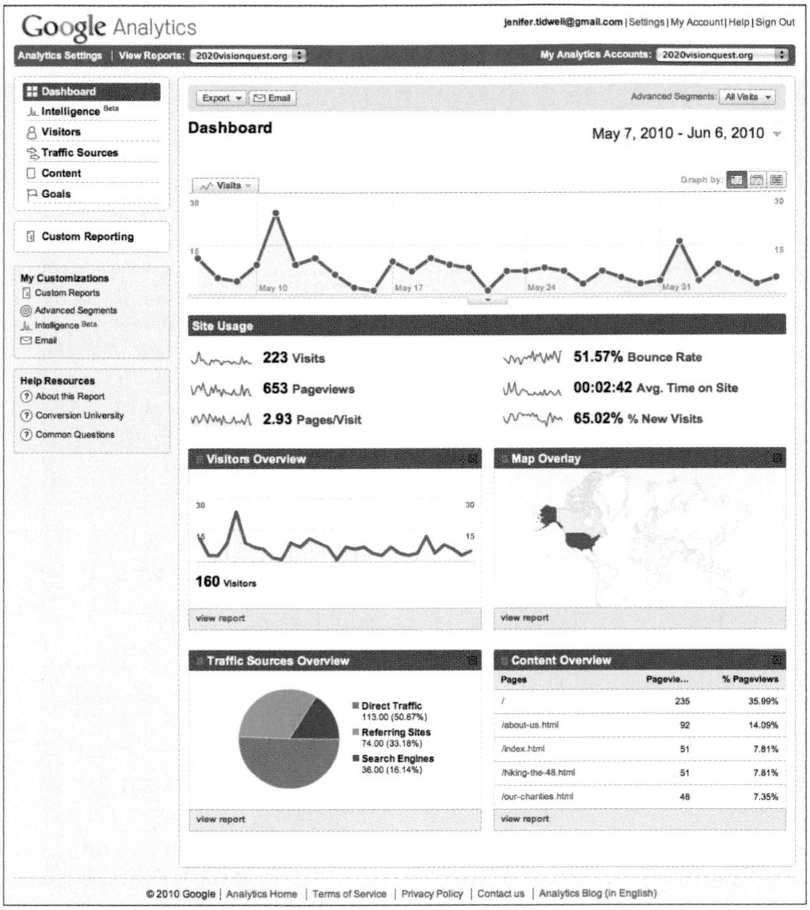

Figure 2-19. *Google Analytics*

In other libraries

http://quince.infragistics.com/Patterns/Dashboard.aspx

http://patternry.com/p=information-dashboard/

Dashboard is one of the canonical RIA screen layouts described by Bill Scott and Theresa Neil. An article in *UX Magazine* explains these layouts:

http://www.uxmag.com/design/rich-internet-application-screen-design

Finally, you may be interested in Stephen Few's book, *Information Dashboard Design: The Effective Visual Communication of Data* (O'Reilly, *http://oreilly.com/catalog/9780596100162/*).

Canvas Plus Palette

Figure 2-20. *Photoshop CS5*

Place an iconic palette next to a blank canvas; the user clicks on the palette buttons to create objects on the canvas.

You're designing any kind of graphical editor. A typical use case involves creating new objects and arranging them on some virtual space.

This pair of panels—a palette with which to create things, and a canvas on which to put them—is so common that almost every user of desktop software has seen it. It's a natural mapping from familiar physical objects to the virtual on-screen world. And the palette takes advantage of visual recognition: the most common icons (paintbrush, hand, magnifying glass, etc.) are reused over and over again in different applications, with the same meaning each time.

Present a large empty area to the user as a canvas. It might be in its own window, as in Photoshop (Figure 2-20), or embedded in a single page with other tools. The user just needs to see the canvas side by side with the palette. Place additional tools—property panels, color swatches, and so on—to the right or bottom of the canvas, in small palette-like windows or panels.

The palette itself should be a grid of iconic buttons. They can have text in them if the icons are too cryptic; some GUI-builder palettes list the names of GUI components alongside their icons, for instance. So does Visio, with its palettes of complex visual constructs tailored for specific domains. But the presence of icons is necessary for users to recognize the palette for what it is.

Place the palette to the left or top of the canvas. It can be divided into subgroups, and you may want to use Module Tabs or Collapsible Panels to present those subgroups.

Most palette buttons should create the pictured object on the canvas. But many builders have successfully integrated other things, such as zoom mode and lassoing, into the palette. This started early; MacPaint mixed its modes into its palette (see Figure 2-24) and people have learned what the arrow, hand, and other icons do.

The gestures used to create items on a palette vary from one application to another. Some use drag-and-drop only; some use a single click on the palette and a single click on the canvas; and some use One-off Modes, Spring-Loaded Modes (see the previous edition of this book for both of these patterns), and other carefully designed gestures. I have always found that usability testing in this area is particularly important, since users' expectations vary greatly.

The Raven vector editor (Figure 2-21), by Aviary, and Sumo Paint (Figure 2-22) are two web-based graphic editors that follow this pattern faithfully.

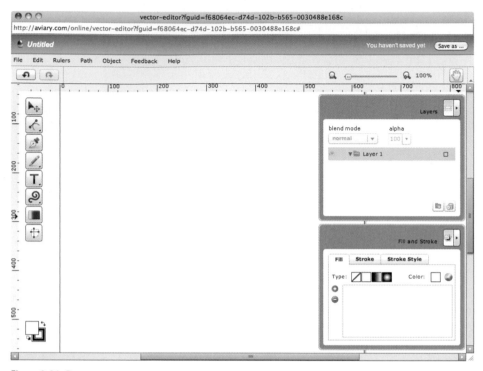

Figure 2-21. *Raven*

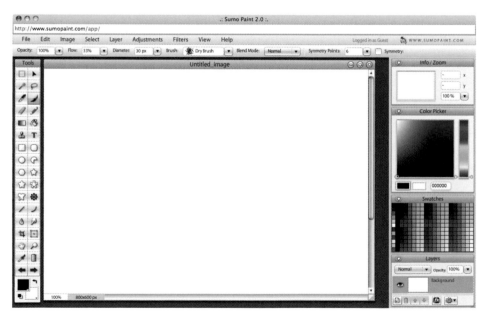

Figure 2-22. *Sumo Paint*

Adobe Flash Builder places its palette of Flex UI components at the lower left, as shown in Figure 2-23. Next to the icons, the palette shows text labels that clarify exactly what kind of component will be created for each palette item. Users of this application are assumed to be skilled enough to know the approximate names of the components they need. (Also shown is a drag operation from the palette to the canvas.)

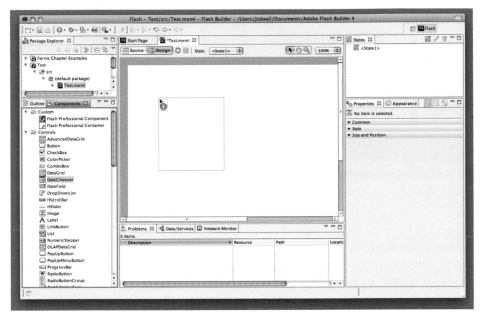

Figure 2-23. *Flash Builder*

Taking a trip back in time, let's look at one of the interfaces that popularized this pattern: MacPaint (see Figure 2-24). The pattern hasn't changed much since 1984—the basic elements are all there, in the same spatial configuration used by contemporary software such as Photoshop. Photoshop and other visual builders, in fact, still use many of MacPaint's icons more than 20 years later.

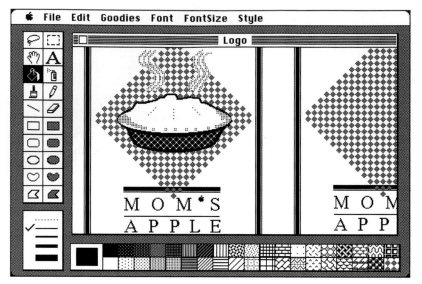

Figure 2-24. *MacPaint, circa 1984*

In other libraries

Palette/Canvas is one of the canonical RIA screen layouts described by Bill Scott and Theresa Neil. An article in *UX Magazine* explains these layouts:

http://www.uxmag.com/design/rich-internet-application-screen-design

Wizard

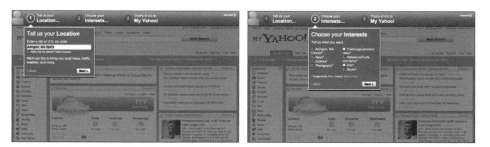

Figure 2-25. *The first two steps of the My Yahoo! setup Wizard*

What

Lead the user through the interface step by step to do tasks in a prescribed order.

Use when

You are designing a UI for a task that is long or complicated, and that will usually be novel for users—not something that they do often or want much fine-grained control over (such as the installation of a software package). You're reasonably certain that the designer of the UI will know more than the user does about how best to get the task done.

Tasks that seem well suited for this approach tend to be either branched or very long and tedious—they consist of a series of user-made decisions that affect downstream choices.

The catch is that the user *must* be willing to surrender control over what happens when. In many contexts, that works out fine, since making decisions is an unwelcome burden for people doing certain things: "Don't make me think, just tell me what to do next." Think about moving through an unfamiliar airport—it's often easier to follow a series of signs than it is to figure out the airport's overall structure. You don't get to learn much about how the airport is designed, but you don't care about that.

But in other contexts, it backfires. Expert users often find Wizards frustratingly rigid and limiting. This is particularly true for software that supports creative processes such as writing, art, or coding. It's also true for users who actually *do* want to learn the software; Wizards don't show users what their actions really do, or what application state gets changed as choices are made. That can be infuriating to some people. Know your users well!

Why

Divide and conquer. By splitting up the task into a sequence of chunks, each of which can be dealt with in a discrete "mental space" by the user, you effectively simplify the task. You have put together a preplanned road map through the task, thus sparing the user the effort of figuring out the task's structure—all he needs to do is address each step in turn, trusting that if he follows the instructions, things will turn out OK.

But the very need for a Wizard indicates that a task may be too complicated. If you can simplify a task to the point where a short form or a few button clicks can do the trick instead, that's a better solution. (Keep in mind, too, that Wizards are considered a bit patronizing in some Asian cultures.)

"Chunking" the task

Break up the operations constituting the task into a series of chunks, or groups of operations. You may need to present these groups in a strict sequence, or not; sometimes there is value in breaking up a task into steps 1, 2, 3, and 4 just for convenience.

A thematic breakdown for an online purchase may include screens for product selection, payment information, a billing address, and a shipping address. The presentation order doesn't much matter because later choices don't depend on earlier choices. Putting related choices together just simplifies things for people filling out those forms.

You may decide to split up the task at decision points so that choices made by the user can change the downstream steps dynamically. In a software installation Wizard, for example, the user may choose to install optional packages that require yet more choices; if she chooses not to do a custom installation, those steps are skipped. Dynamic UIs are good at presenting branched tasks such as this, because the user never has to see anything that's irrelevant to the choices she made.

In either case, the hard part of designing this kind of UI is striking a balance between the sizes of the chunks and the number of them. It's silly to have a 2-step Wizard, and a 15-step Wizard is tedious. On the other hand, each chunk shouldn't be overwhelmingly large, or you've lost some benefits of this pattern.

Physical structure

Wizards that present each step in a separate page, usually navigated with Back and Next buttons, are the most obvious and well-known implementation of this pattern. They're not always the right choice, though, because now each step is an isolated UI space that shows no context—the user can't see what went before or what comes next. But an advantage of such Wizards is that they can devote each page to that step completely, including illustrations and explanations.

If you do this, allow the user to move back and forth at will through the task sequence. Offer a way for the user to step backward, or to otherwise change her mind about an earlier choice. Additionally, many UIs show a selectable map or overview of all the steps, getting some of the benefits of a Two-Panel Selector. (In contrast to that pattern, a Wizards implies a prescribed order—even if it's merely suggested—as opposed to completely random access.)

If you instead choose to keep all the steps on one page, you could use one of several patterns from Chapter 4:

- Titled Sections, with prominent numbers in the titles. This is most useful for tasks that aren't heavily branched, since all steps can be visible at once.

- Responsive Enabling, in which all the steps are present on the page, but each one remains disabled until the user has finished the previous step.

- Responsive Disclosure, in which you wait to show a step on the UI until the user finishes the previous one. Personally, I think this is the most elegant way to implement a short Wizard. It's dynamic, compact, and easy to use.

Good Defaults (from Chapter 8) are useful no matter how you arrange the steps. If the user is willing to turn over control of the process to you, odds are good she's also willing to let you pick reasonable defaults for choices she may not care much about, such as the location of a software installation.

The My Yahoo! example in Figure 2-25 illustrates many good features of a contemporary Wizard. It uses a "lightbox" technique to focus attention on the modal dialogs; it lays out a clear Sequence Map (Chapter 3) of steps to show the user what will happen; it's short, easy to use, and visually interesting; and it has a Cancel button in the upper right, as an Escape Hatch from the whole thing.

Mint's add-a-bank dialog (see Figure 2-26) doesn't use a numbered sequence of steps, nor does it use a permanent Next button. But it still has the quintessential Wizard quality of leading the user through a relatively complex series of steps, one screen at a time. Also, the list of steps on the lefthand side (which can't be clicked) gives the user an overview of what to expect.

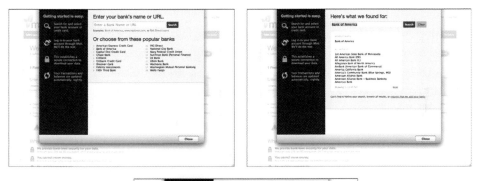

Figure 2-26. *Mint's add-a-bank Wizard*

The Microsoft Office designers have done away with many of its Wizards, but a few remain—and for good reason. Importing data into Excel is a potentially bewildering task. The Import Wizard (see Figure 2-27) is an old-school, traditional application Wizard with Back/Next buttons, branching, and no sequence map. But it works. Each screen lets you focus on the step at hand, without worrying about what comes next.

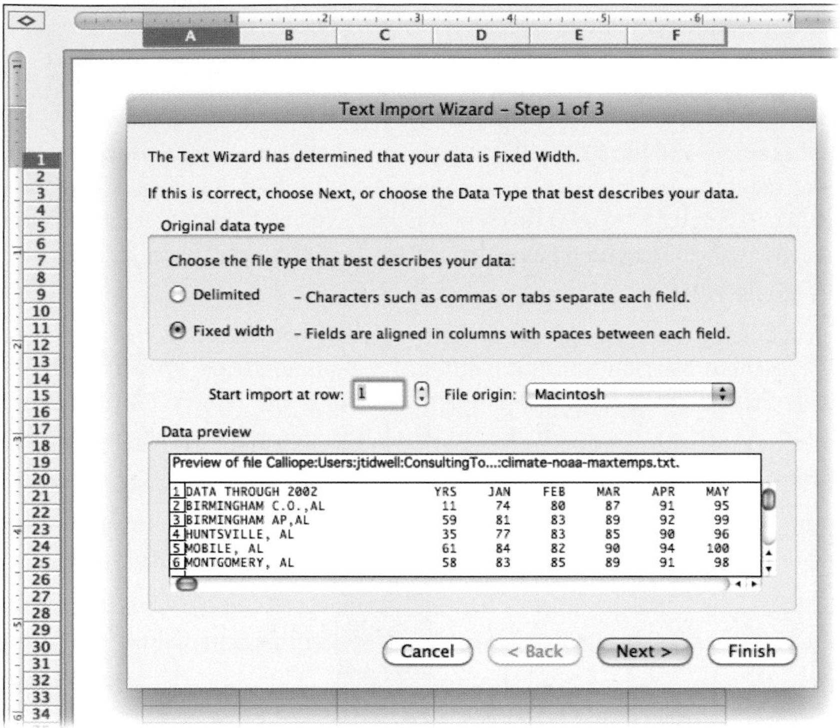

Figure 2-27. *Excel data import Wizard*

In other libraries

http://ui-patterns.com/patterns/Wizard

http://www.welie.com/patterns/showPattern.php?patternID=wizard

http://patternry.com/p=one-page-wizard/

http://patternry.com/p=multiple-page-wizard/

http://quince.infragistics.com/Patterns/Wizard.aspx

Wizard is one of the canonical RIA screen layouts described by Bill Scott and Theresa Neil. An article in *UX Magazine* explains these layouts:

http://www.uxmag.com/design/rich-internet-application-screen-design

Settings Editor

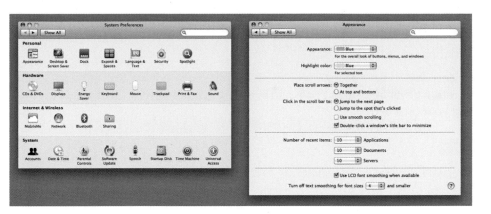

Figure 2-28. *Mac OS system preferences*

What

Provide an easy-to-find, self-contained page or window where users can change settings, preferences, or properties. Divide the content into separate tabs or pages, if you need to manage large numbers of settings.

Use when

You are designing any of the following applications or tools, or something similar:

- An application that has app-wide preferences.

- An operating system, mobile device, or platform that has system-wide preferences.

- A site or app for which a user must sign in—users will need to edit their accounts and profiles.

- An open-ended tool to create documents or other complex work products. Users may need to change a document's properties, an object within a document, or another item.

- A *product configurator*, which allows people to customize a product online. (This is really a different pattern, however, with slightly different requirements and constraints. See the Product Configurator pattern at *http://www.welie.com/patterns/showPattern.php?patternID=product-configurator.*)

Why

Though both use forms, a Settings Editor is distinct from a Wizard, and it has very particular requirements. A user must be able to find and edit a desired property without being forced to walk through a prescribed sequence of steps—random access is important.

To aid findability, the properties should be grouped into categories that are well labeled and make immediate sense.

Another important aspect of Settings Editor design is that people will use it for viewing existing settings, not just changing them. The design needs to communicate the values of those settings at a glance.

Experienced users have strong expectations for preference editors, account settings, and user profiles being in familiar places and behaving in familiar ways. Break these expectations at your own peril!

How

First, make it findable. Most platforms, both mobile and desktop, have a standard place to find application-wide preferences—follow the conventions, and don't try to be overly clever. Likewise, websites where people sign in usually put links to account settings and profiles where the username is shown, often in the upper-right or -left corner.

Second, group the properties into pages, and give those pages names that make it easy to guess what's on them. (Sometimes all the properties or settings fit on one page, but not often.) Card-sorting exercises with representative users can help you figure out the categories and their names. An outrageously large number of properties may require a three- or four-level hierarchy of groups, but be careful that users don't get frustrated at having to click 53 times to reach commonly needed properties.

Third, decide how to present these pages. Tabs, Two-Panel Selector, and One-Window Drilldown (Chapter 5) with an extensive page "menu" on the top page seem to be the most common layouts for Settings Editors.

The design of the forms themselves deserves an entire chapter. See Chapter 8 for patterns and techniques used in forms.

Finally, should you immediately apply changes that the user makes, or offer Save and Cancel buttons? That may depend on the type of settings you're working with. Platform-wide settings seem to be applied immediately when changed; settings on websites mostly use Save buttons; and application settings and preferences can go either way. It may not be a huge usability issue in any case. Follow an established convention if there is one, or see what the underlying technology requires; test it with users if you still have open questions.

Examples

Windows 7 offers the "outrageously large number of properties" that require a deep hierarchy of pages. The screenshots in Figure 2-29 illustrate the journey from the top of the Settings Editor down to the page that lets you change the desktop theme. (There's one more level, too—if you want to change the desktop icons or some other obscure thing, you need to launch a dialog from a link on the last screen.)

The designers mitigated some of the problems with a deep hierarchy, however. For instance, they put a list of shortcuts on the top-level page; these are probably the items users look for most often. They put a search box on the top and clickable Breadcrumbs beside it. And by putting lists of items on the top two levels, they show users which items fall into which categories.

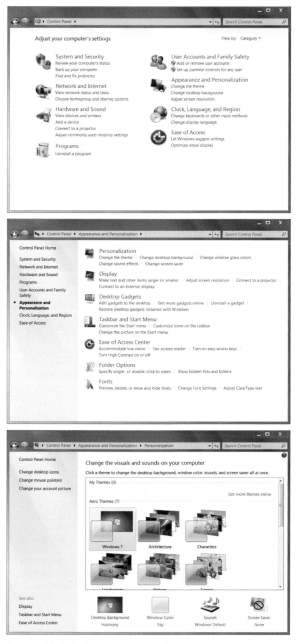

Figure 2-29. *Windows 7 settings editor*

Yahoo! (Figure 2-30) and Facebook (Figure 2-31) both use tabs to present the pages of their profile editors. The Yahoo! example is actually two-level; see the tabs across the top.

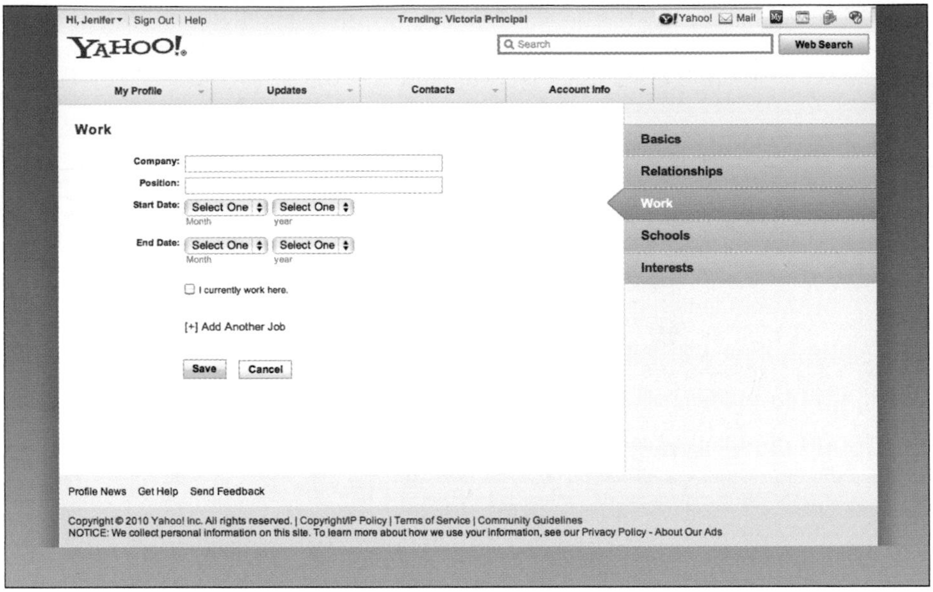

Figure 2-30. *Yahoo! profile settings*

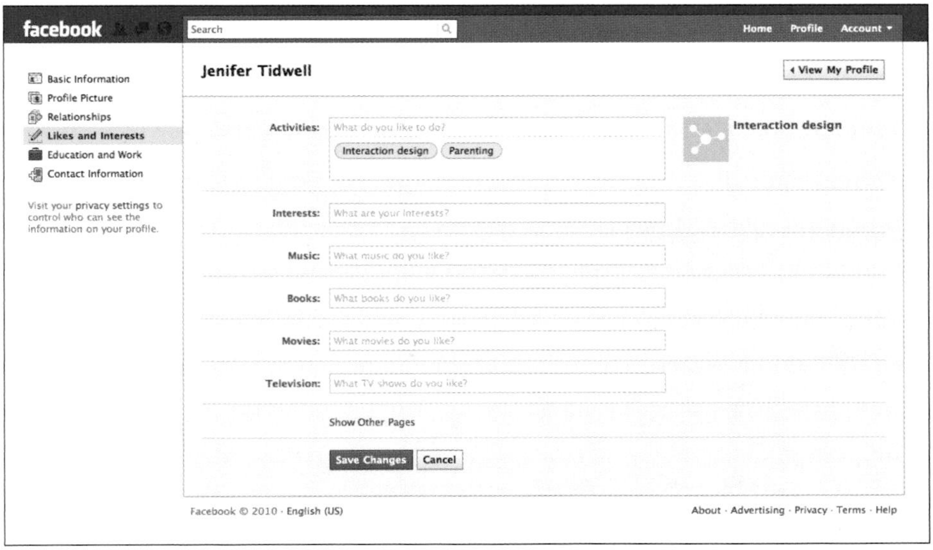

Figure 2-31. *Facebook profile settings*

Amazon has one single link for all account-related information: "Your Account" (see Figure 2-32). This Menu Page (Chapter 3) lists account settings alongside order information, credit card management, digital content, and even community and wish-list activity. The clean, tight page organization is terrific—if I have any questions about what's going on with my relationship to Amazon, I know I can find it somewhere on this page. (Contrast this to Facebook, which habitually obscures certain profile information behind complicated design.)

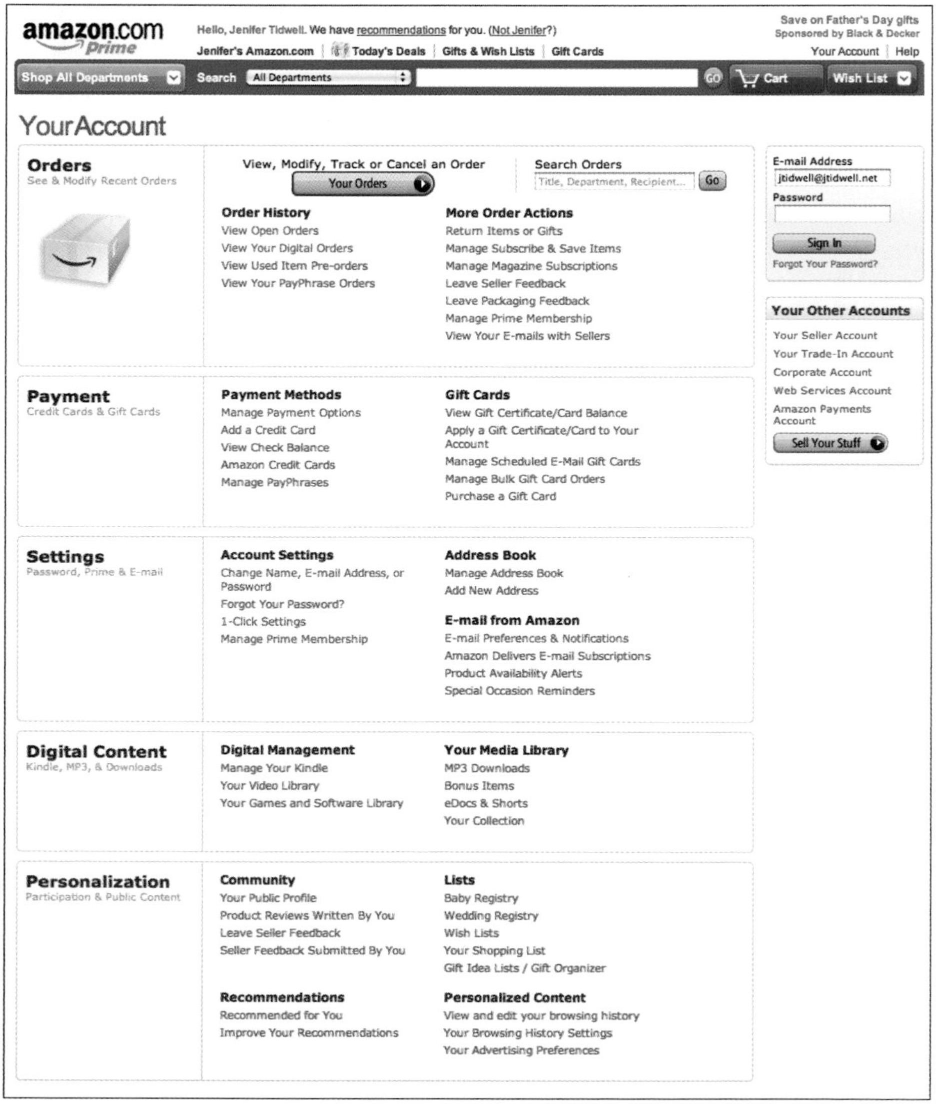

Figure 2-32. *Amazon account settings*

Alternative Views

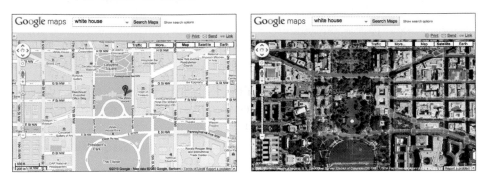

Figure 2-33. *Google Maps*

Let the user choose among alternative views that are substantially different from the default view.

You're building something that views or edits a complex document, list, website, map, or other content. Maybe you already provide some customizability—font size, language, sort order, zoom level, and so forth—but those lightweight changes don't go far enough to accommodate all the things people typically do with it.

You may face design requirements that directly conflict with each other. You can't find a way to show both feature set A and feature set B at the same time, so you need to design both separately and let the user choose between them.

Try as you might, you can't always accommodate all possible usage scenarios in a single design. For instance, printing is typically problematic for websites because the information display requirements differ—navigation and interactive gizmos should be removed, for instance, and the remaining content reformatted to fit the printer paper.

There are several other reasons for Alternative Views:

- Users have preferences with regard to speed, visual style, and other factors.

- A user might need to temporarily view data through a different "lens" or perspective in order to gain insight into a problem. Consider a map user switching between views of street information and topographic information (see Figure 2-33 at the top of the pattern).

- If a user is editing a slideshow or website, for instance, he may do most of his editing while using a "structural" view of the document, containing editing handles, markers for invisible content, layout guides, private notes, and so on. But sometimes he will want to see the work as an end user would see it.

How

Choose a few usage scenarios that cannot easily be served by the application's or site's normal mode of operation. Design specialized views for those scenarios, and present them as alternatives within the same window or screen.

In these alternative views, some information might be added and some might be taken away, but the core content should remain more or less the same. A common way to switch views is to change the rendering of a list; file finders in both Windows and Mac OS let users switch from lists to Thumbnail Grids to Tree Tables to Cascading Lists to Carousels, for instance.

If you need to strip down the interface—for use by a printer or screen reader, for instance—consider removing secondary content, shrinking or eliminating images, and cutting out all navigation but the most basic.

Put a "switch" for the mode somewhere on the main interface. It doesn't have to be prominent; PowerPoint and Word used to put their mode buttons in the lower-left corner, which is an easily overlooked spot on any interface. Most applications represent the alternative views with iconic buttons. Make sure it's easy to switch back to the default view, too. As the user switches back and forth, preserve all of the application's current state—selections, the user's location in the document, uncommitted changes, undo/redo operations, and so on—because losing them will surprise the user.

Applications that "remember" their users often retain the user's alternative-view choice from one use to the next. In other words, if a user decides to switch to an alternative view, the application will just use that view by default next time. Websites can do this by using cookies; desktop applications can keep track of preferences per user; an app on a mobile device can simply remember what view it used the last time it was invoked. Web pages may have the option of implementing Alternative Views as alternative CSS pages. This is how some sites switch between ordinary pages and print-only pages, for example.

Examples

In Figures 2-34 and 2-35, two graphic editors, Microsoft PowerPoint and Adobe Illustrator, show different views of a work product. In the slideshow, the user normally edits one slide at a time, along with its notes, but sometimes the user needs to see all the slides laid out on a virtual table. (Not shown is a third view, in which PowerPoint takes over the screen and actually plays the slideshow.) In the website example, Illustrator shows an "outline" view of the graphic objects in the document—most useful if you have a lot of complex and layered objects—and the normal, fully rendered view of the artwork. The outline view speeds up work considerably.

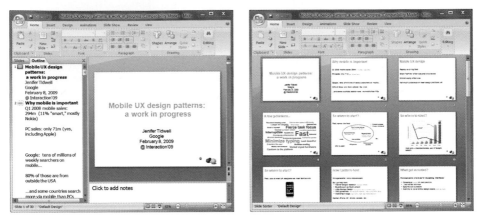

Figure 2-34. *PowerPoint alternative views*

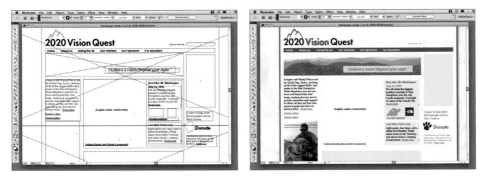

Figure 2-35. *Illustrator alternative views*

News sites and blogs often show lots of "extras" in the margins around an article, many of which are animated or interactive. But some sites considerately provide a print view—a version of the article that has none of that extra stuff. The formatting is simple, and the branding is minimal. The example in Figure 2-36 is from CNN.

Figure 2-36. *CNN web and print views of an article*

In other libraries

http://quince.infragistics.com/Patterns/Alternative%20Views.aspx

Many Workspaces

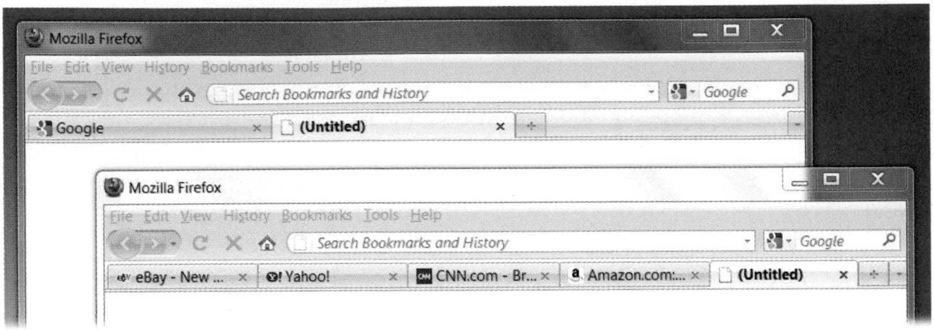

Figure 2-37. *Firefox windows and tabs*

What

Use multiple top-level tabs, tab groups, and windows so that users can view more than one page, project, file, or context at a time. Let users place these workspaces side by side if possible.

Use when

You're building an application that views or edits any type of content—websites, documents, images, or entire projects that include many files.

Designers of conventional websites don't generally need to think about this. All the common browsers supply perfectly good implementations of this pattern, using tabs and browser windows (as shown in Figure 2-37 at the top of the pattern).

Applications whose central organizing structure is a personal News Stream may not need Many Workspaces, either. Email clients, personal Facebook pages, and so forth only show the one News Stream that matters to the user; multiple windows don't add much value. That being said, email clients often let a user launch multiple email messages in different windows. Some Twitter applications can show several filtered streams side by side—they might show a search-based feed, then a feed from a custom list, then a feed of popular retweets, for instance. (See the TweetDeck example in Figure 2-38.)

Why

People multitask. They go off on tangents, abandon trains of thought, stop working on task A to switch to task B, and eventually come back to something they left hanging. One way or the other, they will multitask, so you might as well support it directly with a well-designed interface for doing so.

Side-by-side comparisons between two or more items can help people learn and gain insight. Let users pull up pages or documents next to each other without having to laboriously switch context from one to another.

This pattern directly supports some Chapter 1 patterns, such as Prospective Memory (a user may leave a window open as a self-reminder to finish something) and Safe Exploration (because there's no cost in opening up an additional workspace while leaving the original one where it is).

Choose one or more ways to show multiple workspaces. Many well-known applications use the following:

- Tabs

- Separate operating-system windows

- Columns or panels within a window

- Split windows, with the ability to adjust the splitters interactively

If you deal with fairly simple content in each workspace—such as text files, lists, or News Streams—split windows or panels work fine. More complex content might warrant entire tab pages or windows of their own so that a user can see a larger area at once.

The most complicated cases that I've seen involve development environments for entire coding projects. When a project is open, a user might be looking at several code files, stylesheets, command windows (where compilers and other tools get run), output or log-files, or even visual editors. This means that many, many windows or panels can be open at once.

(And then, perhaps, the user might temporarily switch to another project, with another set of open files and editors! Some development environments can support that.)

When users close some web browsers, such as Chrome, the set of workspaces (all open web pages, in tabs and windows) gets automatically saved for later use. Then when the user restarts the browser, her entire set of previously opened web pages is restored, almost as she left it. This is especially nice when the browser or machine has crashed. Consider designing in this feature, as it would be a kindness to your users.

Examples

TweetDeck is a News Stream–type application that can show many streams at once: filtered Twitter feeds, non-Twitter sources, and so on. The example in Figure 2-38 shows several typical TweetDeck columns. This maintains the spirit of a News Stream by keeping all the updates visible at once; had these columns been in different tabs or windows, a user wouldn't be able to see all the updates as they happen.

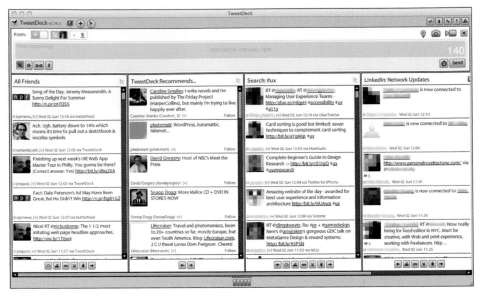

Figure 2-38. *TweetDeck*

On tiny mobile screens, you don't have room to show anything side by side. Safari on the iPhone has solved this problem by letting the user open up to eight websites at a time, then using a Carousel to shuffle between them (see Figure 2-39). A user swipes to the right and left to reach the other windows.

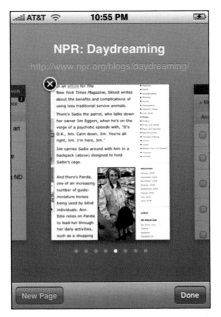

Figure 2-39. *Safari's browser windows on the iPhone*

Multi-Level Help

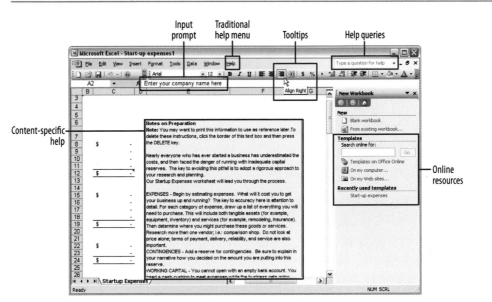

Figure 2-40. *Many types of help in Excel*

What

Use a mixture of lightweight and heavyweight help techniques to support users with varying needs.

Use when

You're designing a complex application. Some users may need a full-fledged help system, but you know most users won't take the time to use it. You want to support the impatient or occasional user too, to the extent you can. In particular, you might need to tailor your design for intermediate-to-expert users—but how will you help beginners become experts?

Why

Users of almost any software artifact need varying levels of support for the tasks they're trying to accomplish. Someone approaching it for the first time ever (or the first time in a while) needs different support than someone who uses it frequently. Even among first-time users, enormous differences exist in commitment level and learning styles. Some people want to read a tutorial, some won't; most find tool tips helpful, but a few find them irritating.

Help texts that are provided on many levels at once—even when they don't look like traditional "help systems"—reach everyone who needs them. Many good help techniques put the help texts within easy reach, but not directly in the user's face all the time, so users don't get irritated. However, the techniques need to be familiar to your users. If they don't notice or open a Collapsible Panel, for instance, they'll never see what's inside it.

How

Create help on several levels, including some (but not necessarily all) of the help types in the following list. Think of it as a continuum: each requires more effort from the user than the previous one, but can supply more detailed and nuanced information.

- Captions and instructions directly on the page, including patterns such as Input Hints and Input Prompt (both found in Chapter 8). Be careful not to go overboard with them. If done with brevity, frequent users won't mind them, but don't use entire paragraphs of text—few users will read them.

- Tool tips. Use them to show very brief, one- or two-line descriptions of interface features that aren't self-evident. For icon-only features, tool tips are critical; users can take even nonsensical icons in stride if a rollover says what the icon does! (Not that I'd recommend poor icon design, of course.) Tool tips' disadvantages are that they hide whatever's under them and that some users don't like them popping up all the time. A short time delay for the mouse hover—for example, one or two seconds—removes the irritation factor for most people.

- Hover Tools (Chapter 6). These can display slightly longer descriptions, shown dynamically as the user selects or rolls over certain interface elements. Set aside areas on the page itself for this, rather than using a tiny tool tip.

- Longer help texts contained inside Collapsible Panels (see Chapter 4).

- Introductory material, such as static introductory screens, guided tours, and videos. When a new user starts the application or service for the first time, these materials can immediately orient him toward his first steps (see the Instant Gratification pattern in Chapter 1). Users might also be interested in links to help resources. Offer a toggle switch to turn off the introduction—users will eventually stop finding it useful—and offer a way back to it elsewhere in the interface, in case a user wants to go back and read it later.

- Help shown in a separate window, often in HTML via browsers, but sometimes in WinHelp or Mac Help. The help resource is often an online manual—an entire book—reached via menu items on a Help menu, or from Help buttons on dialog boxes and HTML pages.

- "Live" technical support, usually via email, the Web, Twitter, or telephone.

- Informal community support. This applies only to the most heavily used and invested software—the likes of Photoshop, Linux, Mac OS X, or MATLAB—but users may consider it a highly valuable resource. Use social networking resources for these, or more traditional online forums.

Firefox is "merely" a web browser, and a free one at that, but its help systems are stellar. Help is offered at most of the levels described in the preceding list, so both beginners and experts are well supported. All of the following examples come from Firefox so that you can see the range of help that can be offered for one product.

When you visit Firefox's site in order to download the browser, you are greeted by an outline of the install process and a very clear call to action, as shown in Figure 2-41.

Figure 2-41. *Firefox download page*

When you launch it for the first time, you see an introductory screen that may intrigue the user: easy ways to customize the Firefox look, connections to social media, and links to help resources (see Figure 2-42). The page also confirms for the user that the install was successful; if the user needs to do anything more, such as get security updates, the introductory page will say so.

![Firefox startup page screenshot showing Firefox 3.6 update page with Choose Your Persona, Stay Connected, and Rock Your Firefox sections]

Figure 2-42. *Firefox startup page*

Each tool on the browser window has a tool tip (see Figure 2-43). The basic buttons—back, next, reload, home—will be familiar to almost all users, but the more obscure items may need to be explained.

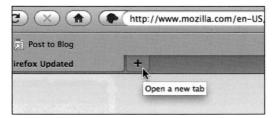
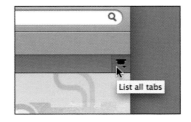

Figure 2-43. *Firefox tool tips*

The main text fields use Input Prompts to describe themselves (see Figure 2-44). This is a more appropriate choice than Input Hints (which would be displayed beside the text fields) because it keeps the window clean and uncluttered. Furthermore, not much knowledge is lost when a user starts typing into the text field, erasing the prompt. See the pattern descriptions for Input Hints and Input Prompt in Chapter 8.

Figure 2-44. *Firefox input prompts*

Some dialogs attempt to describe themselves, as shown in Figure 2-45.

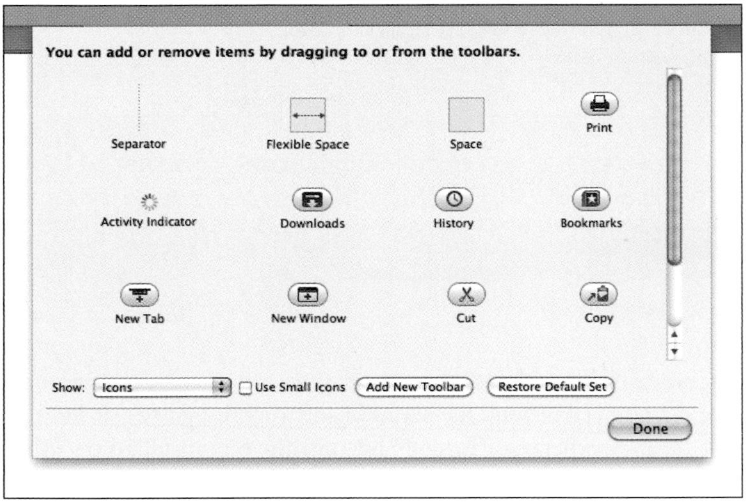

Figure 2-45. *Firefox toolbars dialog*

Other dialogs offer links to the formal help system; an appropriate help page is displayed in a browser window when the user clicks the round purple button in the lower-left corner (see Figures 2-46 and 2-47).

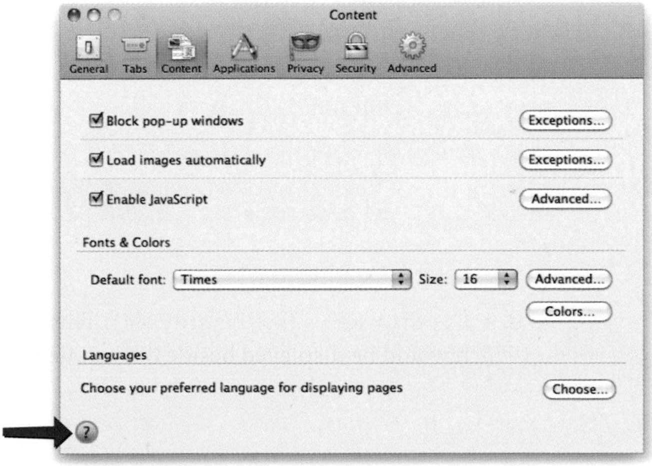

Figure 2-46. *Firefox preferences dialog*

Figure 2-47. *Firefox preferences dialog help page*

Finally, if all other sources of help are exhausted, a user can turn to the wider user community for advice. We've now moved beyond the realm of software design per se, but this is still product design—the user experience extends beyond the bits installed on users' computers. It includes the interactions they have with the organization, its employees or other representatives, and its website (see Figure 2-48).

Community building like this happens only for products in which users become deeply invested, perhaps because they use the product every day at work or at home—as is the case with Firefox—or because they have some emotional attachment to it.

Figure 2-48. *Firefox support forums*

Chapter 3

Getting Around:
Navigation, Signposts, and Wayfinding

The patterns in this chapter deal with the problem of navigation. How do users know where they are now, where to go next, and how to get there from here?

I call navigation a "problem" because navigating around a website or application is like commuting. You have to do it to get where you need to go, but it's dull, it's sometimes infuriating, and the time and energy you spend on it just seems wasted. Couldn't you be doing something better with your time, such as playing a game or getting some actual work done?

The best kind of commuting is none at all. Having everything you need right at your fingertips without having to travel somewhere is pretty convenient. Likewise, keeping most tools "within reach" on an interface is handy, especially for intermediate-to-expert users (i.e., people who have already learned where everything is). Sometimes you do need to put lesser-used tools on separate screens, where they don't clutter things up; sometimes you need to group content onto different pages so that the interface makes sense. All this is fine, as long as the "distances" that a user must travel remain short.

So, less is better. Let's talk terminology for a minute and come back to this concept.

Staying Found

Let's say you've built a large website or application that you've had to break up into sections, subsections, specialized tools, pages, windows, wizards, and so forth. How do you help users navigate?

Signposts are features that help users figure out their immediate surroundings. Common signposts include page and window titles, web page logos and other branding devices, tabs, and selection indicators. Patterns and techniques such as good global and local navigation links, Sequence Map, Breadcrumbs, and Annotated Scrollbar—all described in this chapter—tell users where they currently are, and often where they can go with only one more jump. They help a user to stay "found" and to plan his next steps.

Wayfinding is what people do as they find their way toward their goal. The term is pretty self-explanatory. But how people actually do it is quite a research subject—specialists from cognitive science, environmental design, and website design have studied it. These common-sense features help users with wayfinding:

Good signage

Clear, unambiguous labels anticipate what you're looking for and tell you where to go; signs are where you expect them to be, and you're never left standing at a decision point without guidance. You can check this by walking through the artifact you're designing and following the paths of all the major use cases. Make sure that each point where a user must decide where to go next is signed or labeled appropriately. Use strong "calls to action" on the first pages that a user sees.

Environmental clues

You'd look for restrooms in the back of a restaurant, for instance, or a gate where a walkway intersects a fence. Likewise, you would look for an "X" close button at the top right of a modal dialog and logos in the upper-left corner of a web page. Keep in mind that these clues are often culturally determined, and someone new to the culture (e.g., someone who's never used a given operating system before) will not be aware of them.

Maps

Sometimes people go from sign to sign or link to link without ever really knowing where they're going in a larger frame of reference. (If you've ever found your way through a strange airport, that's probably what you did.) But some people might prefer to have a mental picture of the whole space, especially if they're there often. Also, in badly signed or densely built spaces, such as urban neighborhoods, maps may be the only navigational aids people have.

In this chapter, the Clear Entry Points pattern is an example of careful signage combined with environmental clues—the links should be designed to stand out on the page. A Sequence Map, obviously, is a map; you can use Overview Plus Detail (Chapter 7) to show maps for virtual spaces, too. Modal Panel sort of qualifies as an environmental clue, since the ways out of a modal panel take you right back to where you just were.

I've compared virtual spaces to physical ones here. But virtual spaces have the unique ability to provide a navigational trump card, one that physical spaces can't (yet) provide: the Escape Hatch. Wherever you are, click on that link, and you're back to a familiar page. It's like carrying a wormhole with you. Or a pair of ruby slippers.

The Cost of Navigation

When you walk into an unfamiliar room, you look around. In a fraction of a second, you take in the shape of the room, the furnishings, the light, the ways out, and other clues; very quickly, you make some assumptions about what this room is and how it relates to why you walked in. Then you need to do what you came in to do. Where? How? You might be able to answer immediately—or not. Or maybe you're just distracted by other interesting things in the room.

Similarly, bringing up a web page or opening a window incurs a cognitive cost. Again, you need to figure out this new space: you take in its shape, its layout, its contents, its exits, and how to do what you came to do. All of this takes energy and time. The "context switch" forces you to refocus your attention and adjust to your new surroundings.

Even if you're already familiar with the window (or room) you just went into, it still incurs a cost. Not a large cost, but it adds up—especially when you figure in the actual time it takes to display a window or load a page.

This is true whether you're dealing with web pages, application windows, dialog boxes, or device screens. The decisions that users make about where to go are similar—labels still need to be read or icons decoded, and the users will still make leaps of faith by clicking on links or buttons they're not sure about.

Furthermore, loading time affects people's decisions. If a user clicks through to a page that takes too long to load—or fails to load altogether—he may be discouraged, and may just close the page before he finds what he came for. (So, how many viewers is that sidebar video player costing you?) Also, if a site's pages take a chronically long time to load, users will be less likely to explore that site.

There's a reason that companies like Google work very hard to keep page loads as fast as possible: latency costs viewers.

Keep Distances Short

Knowing that there's a cost associated with jumping from page to page, you can understand now why it's important to keep the number of those jumps down. When a common task requires many page jumps, try to reduce it to one or two.

But the real efficiency gains come from the structure of the application. One of the nastiest things a designer can do is force a user to go into multiple levels of subpages, dialogs, and so forth every time he needs to accomplish a simple and everyday task. (Worse is to lead him there, tell him he can't accomplish it because of some missing precondition, and send him back to square one.)

Can you design your application so that the most common 80% of use cases can be done in one page, without any context switches? (Or perhaps only one?)

This is hard to do with some kinds of applications. Is a certain tool too big to put on your main page? Try shrinking it: eliminate controls, shorten labels, turn words into pictures, or use specialized form controls that save space. Is it too distracting when combined with everything else on the main page? Again, try shrinking it, isolating it with whitespace, or putting it in an out-of-the-way spot. Can you use progressive disclosure to gradually show more content on the same page? Can you use Module Tabs or an Accordion to hide some content by default?

Sometimes it's appropriate to bury functionality inside pages that take more than one jump to get to, such as that extra 20% of tasks left over from the 80% you made easily available. It could also be that on your application, simplicity of presentation is more important than saving one or two jumps. You could put little-used functionality behind an extra "door" (also using the 80/20 rule). As always, experiment with different designs, and usability-test them if you have any doubts.

Navigational Models

What is the *navigational model* for your site or app? In other words, how do the different screens (or pages, or spaces) link to each other, and how do users move between them?

First, some more terminology.

Global navigation is what's found on every main screen. It usually takes the form of menus, tabs, and/or sidebars, and this is how users move around the formal navigational structure of the site. (In an earlier version of this book, global navigation was defined as a pattern. But by now, it's so common and well understood that it really doesn't need to be called out as such anymore.)

Utility navigation, also found on every main screen, contains links and tools related to noncontent aspects of the site or application: sign-in, help, print, Settings Editors (see Chapter 2), language tools, and so on.

Associative and *inline navigation* embed links in or near the actual content. As the user reads or interacts with the site, these links present options that might be immediately relevant to the user. They tie content together thematically.

Now let's look at a few models found in typical sites and apps:

Hub and spoke
> Most often found on mobile devices, this architecture (Figure 3-1) lists all the major parts of the site or app on the home screen, or "hub." The user clicks or taps through to them, does what she needs to do, and comes back to the hub to go somewhere else. The "spoke" screens focus tightly on their jobs, making careful use of space—they may not have room to list all the other major screens. The iPhone home screen is a good example; the Menu Page pattern found on some websites is another.

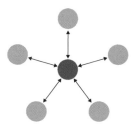

Figure 3-1. *Hub and spoke*

Fully connected

Many websites follow this model. There's a home page or screen, but it and every other page link to all the others—they each have a global navigation feature, such as a top menu. The global navigation may be a single level (as shown in Figure 3-2, with only five pages), or it might be deep and complex, with multiple levels and deeply buried content. As long as the user can reach any page from any other with a single jump, it's fully connected.

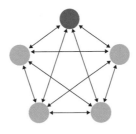

Figure 3-2. *Fully connected*

Multi-level

This is also common among websites (see Figure 3-3). The main pages are fully connected with each other, but the subpages are only connected among themselves (and usually to the other main pages, via global navigation). You've seen this on sites that have subpages listed only in sidebars or subtabs—users see these on menus that only show up after they've clicked the link for the main page or category. It takes two or more jumps to get from one arbitrary subpage to another. Using drop-down menus, the Fat Menus pattern, or the Sitemap Footer pattern with a multi-level site converts it to a fully connected one, which is preferable.

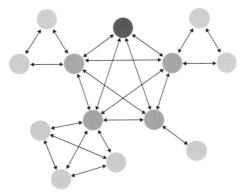

Figure 3-3. *Multi-level*

Stepwise

Slideshows, process flows, and Wizards (see Chapter 2) lead the user step by step through the screens in a prescribed sequence (see Figure 3-4). Back/Next links are prominent on the page.

Figure 3-4. *Stepwise*

Pyramid

A variant on the stepwise model, a pyramid uses a hub page or menu page to list an entire sequence of items or subpages in one place (see Figure 3-5). The user picks out any item, jumps to it, and then has the option to use Back/Next links to step through other items in order. He can go back to the hub page anytime. See the Pyramid pattern in this chapter for more.

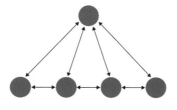

Figure 3-5. *Pyramid*

Pan-and-zoom

Some artifacts are best represented as single large spaces, not many small ones. Maps, large images, large text documents, information graphics, and representations of time-based media (such as sound and video) fall into this category. Chapter 7 discusses these in more detail. Panning and zooming are still navigation—so offer controls for panning (moving horizontally or vertically), zooming in and out, and resetting to a known position and state. Figure 3-6 shows an example of pan-and-zoom.

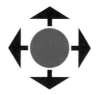

Figure 3-6. *Pan-and-zoom*

Flat navigation

Some types of applications need little or no navigation at all. Consider Canvas Plus Palette applications such as Photoshop, or other complex apps such as Excel—these offer tons of tools and functions that are easily reached via menus, toolbars, and palettes. Tools that don't act immediately upon the work may be accessible via Modal Panels or step-by-step progressions. These types of applications seem to be qualitatively different from the other navigation styles listed here: the user always knows where he is, but he may not easily find the tools he needs because of the sheer number of features available at one time.

Modal panel

This brings a user to a screen with no navigation options other than acknowledging its message, completing its form, or clicking the panel away (Figure 3-7). Modal panels often show up layered on top of a full screen or page, and are used for small, focused tasks that require the user's full attention. See the Modal Panel pattern for more discussion.

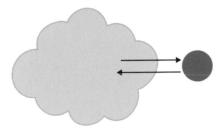

Figure 3-7. *Modal panel*

Clear entry points

How does a user know where to start in a complex site or app? The Clear Entry Points pattern shows him where to go first (see Figure 3-8). For first-time and infrequent users, it removes some of the burden of learning the site.

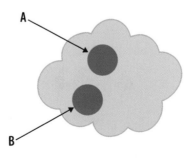

Figure 3-8. *Clear entry points*

Bookmarks

Bookmarks (Figure 3-9), permalinks, deep links, and Deep-linked State are all ways for a user to conveniently navigate to a point of his choice, anytime he wants, even if it's deep inside a navigational structure. These give him a way to avoid traversing many links to get to a desired page or state.

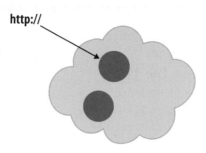

Figure 3-9. *Bookmarks*

Escape hatch

When a user is hopelessly entangled in an app, reaches an error state, or gets deep-linked into a page that he has no context for understanding, he needs an escape hatch (Figure 3-10), a well-labeled link to get back to a known place. See the Escape Hatch pattern.

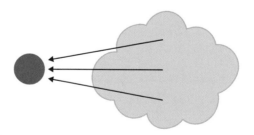

Figure 3-10. *Escape hatch*

There are three things to notice about these navigational models. The first is that they're mix-and-match—an app or site might combine several of these, especially Modal Panel, Clear Entry Points, bookmarks, and Escape Hatch, which are very local and don't affect the site-wide navigation strategy.

The second thing is that some of these mechanisms actually restrict a user's navigation options. Most of the time, open access and short jumps are good things. But when a user is in the middle of a full-screen slideshow, she doesn't want to see a complicated global navigation menu! She would rather just focus on the slideshow itself, so Back/Next controls and an Escape Hatch are all that's necessary. The presence of full navigation options is not without cost: it takes up space, clutters the screen, incurs cognitive load, and signals to the user that leaving the page doesn't matter.

Third, all these mechanisms and patterns can be rendered on-screen in different ways. A complex site or app might use tabs, or menus, or a sidebar tree view to show the global navigation on each page—that's something you don't need to decide until you start laying out the page. Likewise, a modal panel might be done with a lightbox or an actual modal dialog—but you can postpone that until you know what needs to be modal and what doesn't.

Visual design can come later in the design progression, after the information architecture and navigational models.

Design Conventions for Websites

It's a fine thing to separate the navigational model from its visual design. Doing so can help you think more flexibly and deliberately about how to design the pages themselves. But websites have certain conventions regarding visual placement of navigational features, and it's probably unwise to ignore them.

Global navigation is almost always shown at the top or left of a web page, sometimes both. Rarely, it can be found on the right—this placement can cause problems with page size and horizontal scrolling, unless the designer uses a Liquid Layout (see Chapter 4).

Two relatively new approaches to global navigation are found in the Fat Menus and Sitemap Footer patterns. In these, the whole structure of a hierarchical site is laid out for the user to see, at the cost of screen space in the header or footer. As explained earlier, these patterns turn a multi-level navigational model into a fully connected one.

When a site's visitors are typically signed-in members, that site may offer a set of utility navigation links in its upper-right corner. Users tend to look there for tools related to their presence on the site: account settings, user profile, logout, help, and so on. See the Sign-in Tools pattern for more.

A common form of *associative navigation*—when links are embedded in or near the content itself, linking items together thematically—is a "Related Articles" section or panel. News sites and blogs use this a lot: when a user reads an article, a sidebar or footer shows other articles that talk about similar topics or are written by the same author.

Tags, both user-defined and system-defined, can help support associative navigation and related articles or links. Tag clouds support topical findability on some sites, especially where the number of articles is very large and the topics fine-grained. (On smaller sites and blogs, they don't work as well.) A more common navigational technique is to list an article's tags at the end; each tag is a link leading to a whole set of articles that share that tag.

When a site takes advantage of social media, even more navigation options come into play. The front of a site may have a News Box, which links users to the items posted most recently. Content Leaderboards show the most frequently shared or commented pieces, while Recent Chatter directs users to ongoing conversations. And Social Links and Sharing Widgets connect users directly to social media services. See Chapter 9 for these patterns.

The Patterns

To recap, this chapter talks about several aspects of navigation: overall structure or model, knowing where you are, figuring out where you're going, and getting there efficiently.

The first set of patterns address the navigational model, and are more or less independent of screen layout:

1. Clear Entry Points

2. Menu Page

3. Pyramid

4. Modal Panel

5. Deep-linked State

6. Escape Hatch

Combining layout and model on conventional websites, we get these patterns:

7. Fat Menus

8. Sitemap Footer

9. Sign-in Tools

The next few patterns work well as "You are here" signposts (as can a well-designed global navigation). Sequence Map, Breadcrumbs, and Annotated Scrollbar also serve as interactive maps of the content. Annotated Scrollbar is intended more for pan-and-zoom models than for multiple interconnected pages.

10. Sequence Map

11. Breadcrumbs

12. Annotated Scrollbar

Animated Transition helps users stay oriented as they move from one place to another. It's a visual trick, nothing more, but it's very effective at preserving a user's sense of where he is and what's happening.

13. Animated Transition

Clear Entry Points

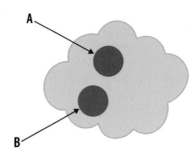

Figure 3-11. *Clear Entry Points schematic*

What

Present only a few main entry points into the interface; make them task-oriented and descriptive. Use clear calls to action.

Use when

You're designing a site or app that has a lot of first-time or infrequent users. Most of these users would be best served by reading a certain piece of introductory text, doing an initial task, or choosing from a very small number of frequently used options.

However, if the purpose is clear to basically everyone who starts it, and if most users might be irritated by one more navigation step than is necessary (like applications designed for intermediate-to-expert users), this may not be the best design choice.

Why

Some applications and websites, when opened, present the user with what looks like a morass of information and structure: lots of tiled panels, unfamiliar terms and phrases, irrelevant ads, or toolbars that just sit there disabled. They don't give the hesitant user any clear guidance on what to do first. "OK, here I am. Now what?"

For the sake of these users, list a few options for getting started. If those options match a user's expectations, he can confidently choose one and begin working—this contributes to immediate gratification. If not, at least he knows now what the site or app actually does, because you've defined the important tasks or categories up front. You've made the application more self-explanatory.

When the site is visited or the application started, present these entry points as "doors" into the main content. From these starting points, guide the user gently and unambiguously into the application until he has enough of a context to continue by himself.

Collectively, these entry points should cover most of the reasons most users would be there. There might only be one or two entry points, or many; it depends on what fits your design. But you should phrase them with language first-time users can understand—this is not the place for application-specific tool names.

Visually, you should show these entry points with emphasis proportional to their importance.

On the home page or starting page, most sites will additionally list other navigation links—global navigation, utility navigation, and so on—and these should be smaller and less prominent than the Clear Entry Points. They're more specialized, and don't necessarily lead you directly into the heart of the site, any more than a garage door leads you directly into the living room. The Clear Entry Points should serve as the "front doors."

Examples

The top of Apple's main iPad page (Figure 3-12) needs to do only a few things: identify itself, make the iPad look inviting, and direct the user toward resources for buying one or learning more. The global navigation recedes visually, compared to the strong, well-defined entry points. On the rest of the page, more text and links make the page denser, but this is all the user sees above the fold.

Figure 3-12. *iPad page on Apple's site*

Fireworks and other applications show a startup dialog when the application is started (see Figure 3-13). This orients a new or infrequent user to the possibilities for action; creating something new, opening an existing document, or reading help resources are the most common items to be found here. (Appropriately, this startup dialog has a checkbox that lets the user turn it off for future startups. Expert users may not want to bother with such a dialog, since it adds one more step—and no value—to the process of getting started on their work.)

Figure 3-13. *Fireworks startup dialog*

http://quince.infragistics.com/Patterns/Clear%20Entry%20Points.aspx

Menu Page

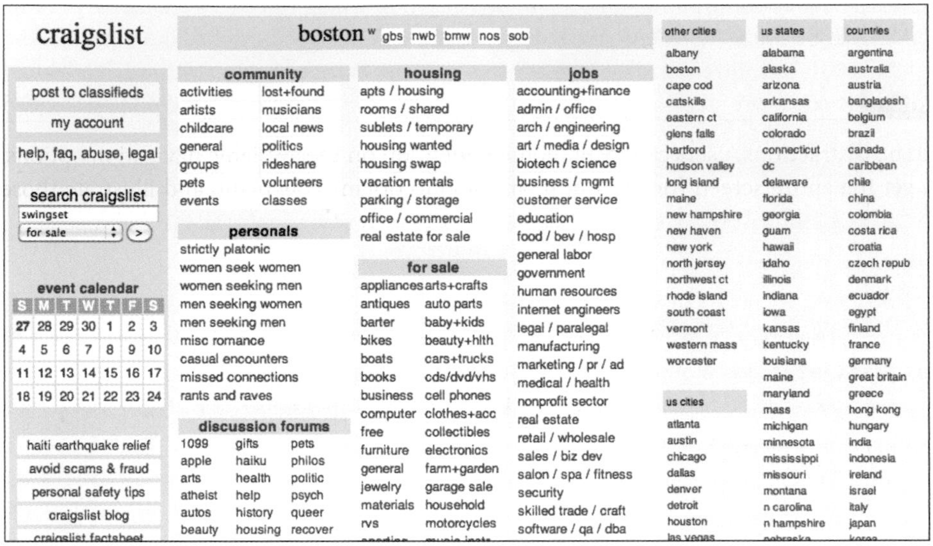

craigslist   boston W gbs nwb bmw nos sob

community

post to classifieds

my account

help, faq, abuse, legal

search craigslist
swingset
for sale

event calendar
S M T W T F S
27 28 29 30 1 2 3
4 5 6 7 8 9 10
11 12 13 14 15 16 17
18 19 20 21 22 23 24

haiti earthquake relief
avoid scams & fraud
personal safety tips
craigslist blog
craigslist factsheet

activities   lost+found
artists   musicians
childcare   local news
general   politics
groups   rideshare
pets   volunteers
events   classes

personals
strictly platonic
women seek women
women seeking men
men seeking women
men seeking men
misc romance
casual encounters
missed connections
rants and raves

discussion forums
1099   gifts   pets
apple   haiku   philos
arts   health   politic
atheist help   psych
autos   history   queer
beauty   housing   recover

housing
apts / housing
rooms / shared
sublets / temporary
housing wanted
housing swap
vacation rentals
parking / storage
office / commercial
real estate for sale

for sale
appliances arts+crafts
antiques   auto parts
barter   baby+kids
bikes   beauty+hlth
boats   cars+trucks
books   cds/dvd/vhs
business   cell phones
computer   clothes+acc
free   collectibles
furniture electronics
general   farm+garden
jewelry   garage sale
materials household
rvs   motorcycles

jobs
accounting+finance
admin / office
arch / engineering
art / media / design
biotech / science
business / mgmt
customer service
education
food / bev / hosp
general labor
government
human resources
internet engineers
legal / paralegal
manufacturing
marketing / pr / ad
medical / health
nonprofit sector
real estate
retail / wholesale
sales / biz dev
salon / spa / fitness
security
skilled trade / craft
software / qa / dba

other cities
albany
boston
cape cod
catskills
eastern ct
glens falls
hartford
hudson valley
long island
maine
new hampshire
new haven
new york
north jersey
northwest ct
rhode island
south coast
vermont
western mass
worcester

us cities
atlanta
austin
chicago
dallas
denver
detroit
houston
las vegas

us states
alabama
alaska
arizona
arkansas
california
colorado
connecticut
dc
delaware
florida
georgia
guam
hawaii
idaho
illinois
indiana
iowa
kansas
kentucky
louisiana
maine
maryland
mass
michigan
minnesota
mississippi
missouri
montana
n carolina
n hampshire
nebraska

countries
argentina
australia
austria
bangladesh
belgium
brazil
canada
caribbean
chile
china
colombia
costa rica
croatia
czech repub
denmark
ecuador
egypt
finland
france
germany
great britain
greece
hong kong
hungary
india
indonesia
ireland
israel
italy
japan
korea

Figure 3-14. *Craigslist*

What

Fill the page with a list of links to content-rich pages in your site or app. Show enough information about each link to enable the user to choose well. Show no other significant content on the page.

Use when

You're designing a home page, starting screen, or any other screen whose purpose is to be just a "table of contents"—to show where users can go from here. You may not have room for featured content (such as an article, video, or promotion), or you may simply want to let the user pick a link with no distractions.

Mobile apps and sites especially need Menu Pages to make the best use of their small screens.

If your (full-size) site needs to "hook" visitors into staying on the page, it may be better to use some of the page space for promotional items or other interesting content, and a Menu Page wouldn't be the right design choice. Likewise, a site that needs to explain its value and purpose should use the space to do that instead.

It takes some audacity to design a Menu Page, because you must be very confident that:

- Visitors know what the site or app is about.

- They know what they came for and how to find it.

- They wouldn't be interested in news, updates, or features.

Why

With no distractions, users can focus all their attention on the available navigation options. You get the entire screen (or most of it, anyway) to organize, explain, and illustrate those links, and can thus direct users to the most appropriate destination page for their needs.

How

If you're creating a mobile design, Menu Pages are one of your principal tools for designing sites or apps with many levels of functionality. Keep list labels short, make targets large enough to tap easily (for touch screens), and try not to make hierarchies too deep.

The rest of this applies to full-size sites and apps.

First, label the links well, and provide just enough contextual information for users to decide where to go. This isn't necessarily easy. Visitors may find it very helpful to have a description or teaser with each link, but that could take up a lot of space on the page. Likewise for thumbnail images—they can look great, but how much value do they add?

Look at Figures 3-15 and 3-16. Visitors to the MIT site already know the meanings of these links—they're the names of academic programs—so extra information is unnecessary. The designer is thus able to pack in more links above the fold. The result is an information-dense, useful page.

On the other hand, the articles in the AIGA resources page do benefit from descriptive text and images. The titles alone aren't necessarily enough to persuade a visitor to click through. (Keep in mind, too, that a user who clicks through and finds that the destination page isn't what he wanted will get frustrated quickly. Make sure your descriptions are accurate and fair!)

Second, consider the visual organization of the list of links. Do they come in categories, or perhaps a two- or three-level hierarchy? Is it ordered by date? Express that organizational scheme in the list. See Chapter 5 for more discussions on this topic.

Third, don't forget a search box.

Finally, reconsider whether you have anything else to say on this page. Home page space, in particular, is quite valuable for drawing in users. Is there an interesting article teaser you can put there? A work of visual art? A News Box (see Chapter 9)? If such things would annoy more than intrigue, continue designing a pure Menu Page.

In the website for MIT (Figure 3-15), the "Education" page shows very little explanatory text and a whole lot of links. When a user reaches this point in the website, she's probably looking for a specific department or resource, and she isn't looking for, say, an explanation of what MIT is about. The whole point of this page is to move the visitor along to a page that answers a well-defined need. (The same is true of the Craigslist example in Figure 3-14 at the top of the pattern.)

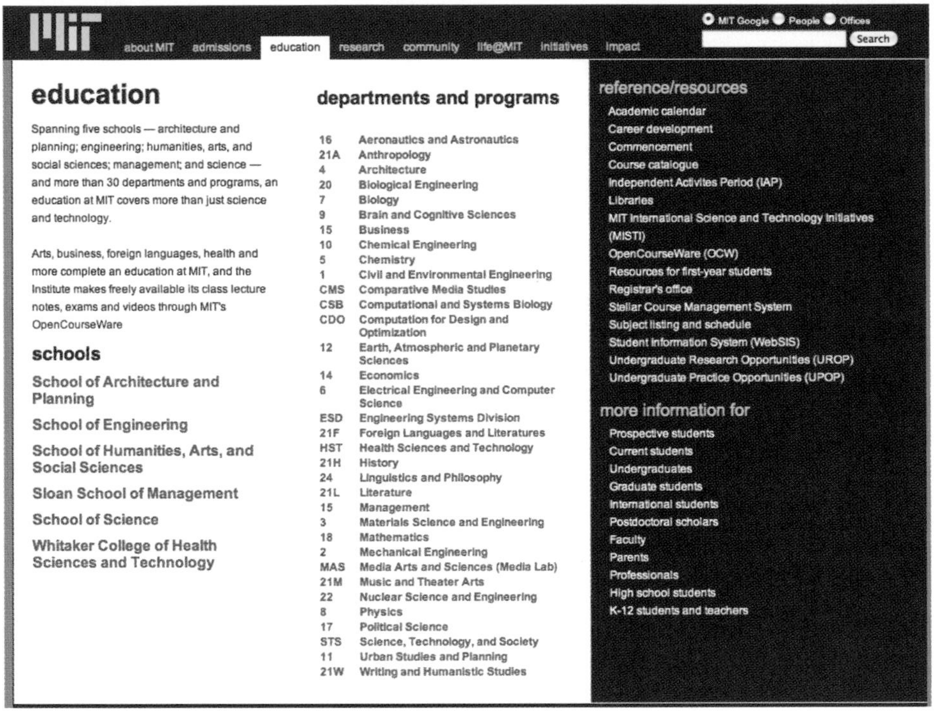

Figure 3-15. *A menu page from MIT's website*

The AIGA website contains many resources for design professionals. The site presents several top-level categories for those resources, as shown in the global navigation, but the landing page for each of those categories is a Menu Page (Figure 3-16). The articles are shown with thumbnail images and summary text; the rich format gives the viewer enough of a context to decide whether to invest time in clicking through to the article.

Figure 3-16. *A Menu Page from AIGA's website*

Last, the Museum of Modern Art uses large images and little text on this Menu Page (see Figure 3-17). This page is intriguing enough to hook a user on its own, without featuring any particular content at all.

Figure 3-17. *A Menu Page from MoMA's website*

In other libraries

The Directory Navigation pattern at the following URL describes one specialized use of a Menu Page:

http://welie.com/patterns/showPattern.php?patternID=directory

Pyramid

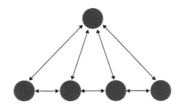

Figure 3-18. *Pyramid schematic*

What

Link together a sequence of pages with Back/Next links. Create a parent page that links to all of the pages in this sequence, and let the user view them either in sequence or out of order.

Use when

The site or application contains a sequence of items that a user would normally view one after another, such as a slideshow, a wizard, chapters in a book, or a set of products. Some users would rather view them one at a time and out of order, however, and they need to be able to pick from a full list of the items.

Almost all Picture Managers (see Chapter 2) use a Pyramid navigational model. Sometimes people need to look at pictures individually; sometimes they would rather browse by walking through the whole sequence. Pyramids support both use cases.

Why

This pattern reduces the number of clicks it takes to get around. It improves navigation efficiency, and it expresses a sequential relationship among the pages.

Back/Next (or Previous/Next) links or buttons are all well and good. People know what to do with them. But a user doesn't necessarily want to be locked into a page sequence that he can't easily get out of: having gone seven pages in, will he need to click the Back button seven times to get back where he started? Not fun!

By putting a link back to the parent page on each sequence page, you increase the user's options. You've now got three main navigation options instead of two—Back, Next, and Up. You haven't made it much more complex, but a casually browsing user (or one who's changed his mind in midstream) will need far fewer clicks to go where he wants to go. It's more convenient for users.

Likewise, chaining together a set of unconnected pages is kind to users who actually want to see all the pages. Without the Back/Next links, they would be "pogo sticking" to the parent page all the time; they might just give up and leave.

List all the items or pages, in order, on the parent page. Render the list in a way that suits the types of items you're dealing with (see Chapter 5), such as a Thumbnail Grid for photos, or a rich text list for articles. A click on an item or link brings the user to that item's page.

On each item page, put Back/Next links. Many sites show a small preview of the next item, such as its title or a thumbnail (Flickr does this, as shown in Figure 3-19). In addition, put in an Up link to bring the user back to the parent page, and label it with "Back to <Page Title Here>" or something similar.

One Pyramid variation turns a static linear sequence into a loop by linking the last page back to the first without going back to the parent. This can work, but does the user know she's looped all the way back around? Does she recognize the first page in the sequence? Not necessarily. If the order of a sequence is important, you should link the last page to the parent page, since it tells the user that she's seen all there is to see.

Flickr's item page is a classic Pyramid example. This Picture Manager shows pictures in a sequence called a *photostream*, which can be seen in its entirety by clicking the labeled link at the top of this widget (see Figure 3-19). The two thumbnails show the previous and next pictures in the photostream.

Figure 3-19. *Flickr*

The *New York Times* interactive feature shown in Figure 3-20 is another Picture Manager. The parent page shows an irregular Thumbnail Grid of clickable pictures; the item page (shown in Figure 3-21) contains arrow buttons to traverse the series of photos. Note that this shows the user where she is in the sequence—"121 of 176"—which is a nice touch. There is no "Up" button, but the only other control in that panel, "Close," returns the user to the parent page. (It thus makes an interesting use of a Modal Panel.)

Figure 3-20. *A New York Times interactive feature; this is the parent page, where all the photos are shown*

Figure 3-21. *A child page from the same feature, showing Back, Next, and Close buttons near the photo*

Modal Panel

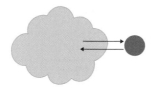

Figure 3-22. *Modal Panel schematic*

Show only one page, with no other navigation options, until the user finishes the immediate task.

The app or site has gotten into a state from which it shouldn't or can't proceed without input from the user. In a document-centric application, for instance, a "save" action might need the user to supply a filename if one wasn't already given. In other contexts, the user may need to sign in before proceeding, or acknowledge an important message.

If the user simply initiates a minor action that may need further input, try to find a way to ask for that input without a modal panel. You could show a text field right below the button that the user clicked, for example, and leave it "hanging" there until the user comes back to it—there's no need to hold up the whole site or app until that input is given. Let the user do something else, and then return to the question at a later time.

A modal panel cuts off all other navigation options from the user. He can't ignore it and go somewhere else in the app or site: he must deal with it here and now. When that's done, he gets sent back to where he was before.

It's an easy model to understand—and to program—though it was overused in applications of past years. A modal panel is disruptive. If the user isn't prepared to answer whatever the modal panel asks, it interrupts his workflow, possibly forcing him to make a decision about something he just doesn't care about. But when used appropriately, a modal panel channels the user's attention into the next decision that he needs to make. There are no other navigation possibilities to distract him.

In the same space on the screen where the user's attention lies, place a panel, dialog box, or page that requests the needed information. It should prevent the user from bringing up other pages in that application. This panel ought to be relatively uncluttered, in keeping with the need to focus the user's attention onto this new task with minimal distractions.

Remember that this is a navigation-related pattern. You should carefully mark and label the ways out, and there shouldn't be many of them; one, two, or maybe three. In most cases, they are buttons with short, verbish labels, such as "Save" or "Don't save." There is usually a "Close" or "X" button in the upper right. Upon clicking a button, the user should be taken back to the page he came from.

The lightbox effect is a very effective visual presentation of a modal panel. By dimming most of the screen, the designer highlights the bright modal panel and focuses attention on it. (For this to work, the modal panel needs to be large enough for the user to find it effortlessly. I've seen modal panels that were so small and off-center that it was hard to find them in a large browser window.)

Instead of layering a modal panel on top of another page, some websites simply use pages with extremely limited navigation. Sign-in and registration screens are commonly done this way: global and local navigation are stripped out, and all that's left are the exits (Cancel, Continue, etc.) and an Escape Hatch.

Operating systems and GUI platforms usually offer OS-level modal dialog boxes. These are best used in traditional desktop applications—websites should avoid them in favor of lighter-weight overlay techniques, which are easier for the designer to control and less disruptive to the user.

Examples

SlideShare uses a lightbox to draw attention to its login dialog. If you try to do something on SlideShare that requires you to be signed in, the modal panel in Figure 3-23 appears. There are only three ways to deal with it: sign in, register, or click the familiar "X" button in the upper-right corner. This is very typical of many lightbox-highlighted modal panels on the Web.

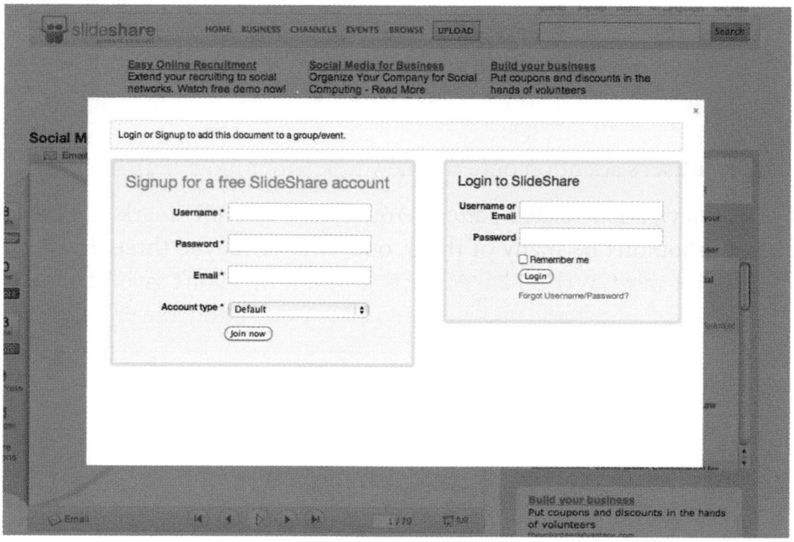

Figure 3-23. *SlideShare's login modal panel*

Likewise, Kayak uses a similar lightbox for a modified search—but this one actually points to the link that launched it, which helps the user connect her gesture with the resultant modal panel (see Figure 3-24). It's a nice touch.

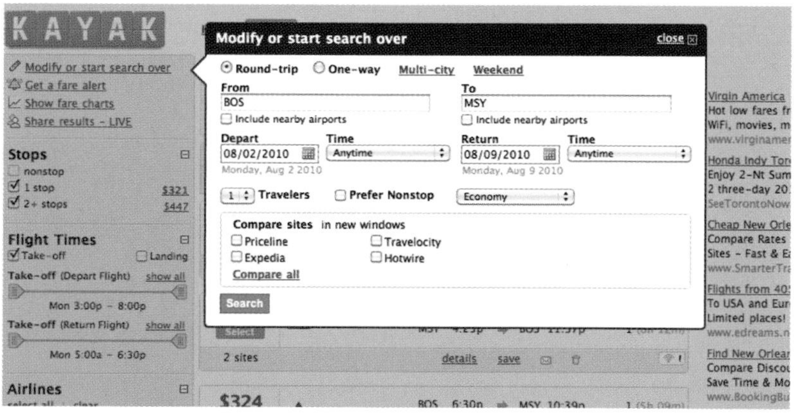

Figure 3-24. *Kayak's modal panel for modifying searches*

The "shade" form of a Mac modal dialog box draws attention to itself as it drops down from the window title bar (animated, of course). These and other application-level modal dialogs actually prevent the user from interacting with the rest of the application, so the user is forced to finish or dismiss this thread of work before doing anything else (see Figure 3-25).

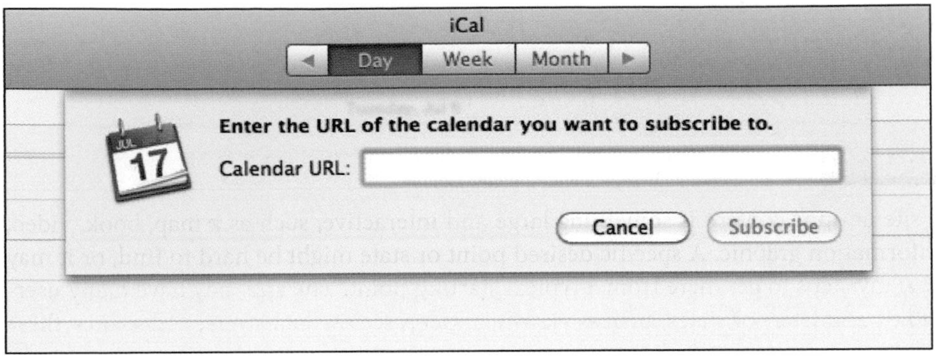

Figure 3-25. *A modal panel in a Mac application*

In other libraries

http://quince.infragistics.com/Patterns/Modal%20Panel.aspx

http://patternry.com/p=overlay/

See also the Dialog Overlay pattern in *Designing Web Interfaces* by Bill Scott and Theresa Neil (O'Reilly, *http://oreilly.com/catalog/9780596516253/*). Other types of overlays are described in that chapter as well.

Deep-linked State

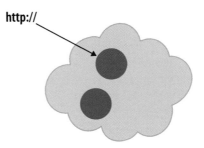

Figure 3-26. *Deep-linked State schematic*

What

Capture the state of a site or app in a URL that can be saved or sent to other people. When loaded, it restores the state of the app to what the user was seeing.

Use when

The site or app's content is something large and interactive, such as a map, book, video, or information graphic. A specific desired point or state might be hard to find, or it may take many steps to get there from a typical starting point. The app may have many user-settable parameters or states, such as viewing modes, scales, data layers, and so on—these may add to the complexity of finding a particular point and seeing it in the "right" way.

Why

Deep-linked State gives the user a way to jump directly to a desired point and application state, thus saving time and work. It behaves like a "deep link" directly into a piece of content on a conventional site—or a permalink to a blog entry—in the sense that you end up with a URL pointing directly to the desired content. But it can be more complex than a permalink, because it can capture both application state and content position.

This pattern is useful for saving a state that the user might want to re-create later, especially if he can "bookmark" it using well-known mechanisms (like browser bookmarks, sites such as Delicious, etc.). It's also handy for sharing with other people, and that's where it really shines. A URL representing a Deep-linked State can be emailed, tweeted, posted to a social network, discussed in a forum, published in a blog entry, and talked about in any number of ways. It might make a statement, or go viral, or become a "socially mediated object."

How

Track the user's position in the content, and put that into a URL. Track supporting data there as well—comments, data layers, markers, highlighting, and so on—so that reloading the URL will bring it all back.

Consider what other parameters or interface states you might want users to save: zoom levels, magnification, viewing modes, search results, and so on. Not all of these should necessarily be captured, since loading the Deep-linked State shouldn't trample on settings that a user doesn't want changed. Work carefully through some usage scenarios to figure this out.

URLs are the best format for saving Deep-linked States: they are universally understood, portable, short, and supported by a vast variety of tools, such as bookmarking services. (If you're dealing with nonweb applications, you may need to be more creative.) Other formats can also be used, such as XML; a text-based format is generally much easier to manage than a binary format.

As a user moves through the content and changes various parameters, immediately put the updated URL in the browser's URL field so that it can be easily seen and captured. Not everyone will think to find it there, so you might also design a "Link" feature whose existence tells the user, "Here's how you create a link to this screen." Some sites offer to generate a JavaScript fragment that not only captures position and state, but also lets users embed the whole thing into another website.

Examples

Google Books captures a large amount of state in its URLs (see Figure 3-27): the position in the book, the viewing mode (single page, two-up, thumbnails), the presence of toolbars, and even search results. It does not capture magnification level, which makes sense, as that's a very individual setting. The URL as seen in the "Link" tool is actually redundant—the URL shown by the browser itself is exactly the same.

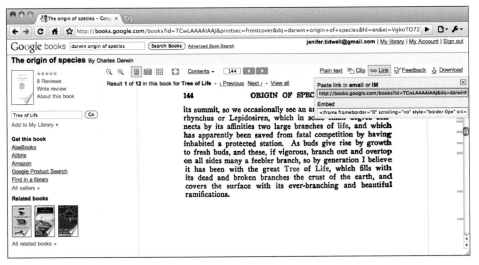

Figure 3-27. *Deep-linked State in Google Books, found in two places: the browser's URL field, and the "Link" feature*

Many Eyes, the visualization tools published by IBM, gives visitors the ability to put together their own custom information graphics, based on plot types and data sets offered by the site (see Figure 3-28). They're highly interactive and rich. To share one of these visualizations, you can either generate JavaScript for it (for embedding), or create a snapshot image.

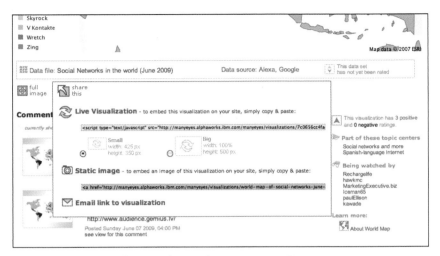

Figure 3-28. *Capturing the state of a visualization at Many Eyes*

Its interface doesn't advertise it, but YouTube lets you put a timestamp into the URL for a video. When loaded, this brings the viewer directly to the specified time in the video. The site *http://youtubetime.com* explains how to do it (see Figure 3-29): add #t=*X*m*Y*s to the end of the URL, where *X* is the number of minutes and *Y* the number of seconds.

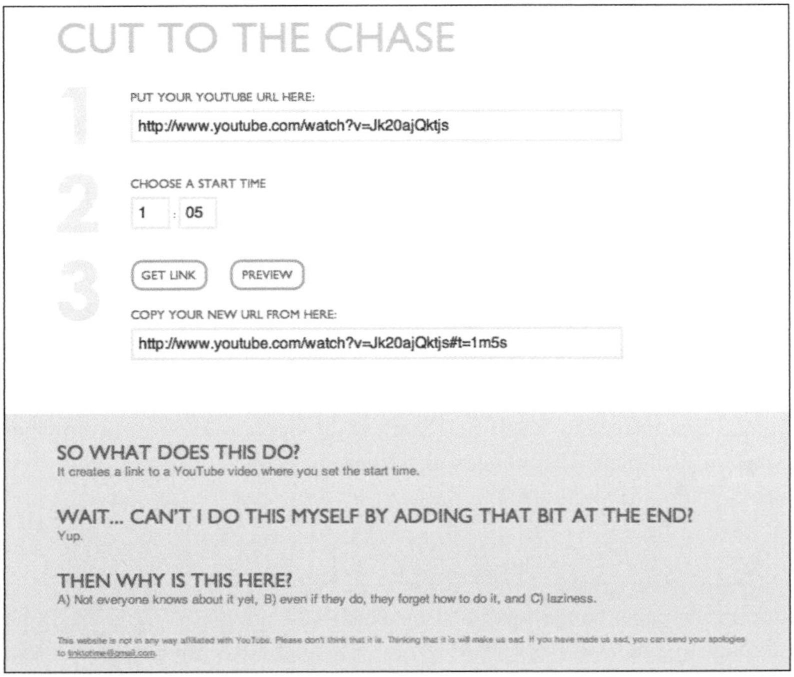

CUT TO THE CHASE

1
PUT YOUR YOUTUBE URL HERE:

http://www.youtube.com/watch?v=Jk20ajQktjs

2
CHOOSE A START TIME

1 : 05

3
(GET LINK)   (PREVIEW)

COPY YOUR NEW URL FROM HERE:

http://www.youtube.com/watch?v=Jk20ajQktjs#t=1m5s

SO WHAT DOES THIS DO?
It creates a link to a YouTube video where you set the start time.

WAIT... CAN'T I DO THIS MYSELF BY ADDING THAT BIT AT THE END?
Yup.

THEN WHY IS THIS HERE?
A) Not everyone knows about it yet, B) even if they do, they forget how to do it, and C) laziness.

This website is not in any way affiliated with YouTube. Please don't think that it is. Thinking that it is will make us sad. If you have made us sad, you can send your apologies to tinktotime@gmail.com.

Figure 3-29. *YouTubeTime's explanation of how to use the URL to deep-link into the middle of a video*

Escape Hatch

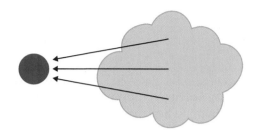

Figure 3-30. *Escape Hatch schematic*

What

On each screen that has limited navigation options, place a button or link that clearly gets the user out of that screen and back to a known place.

Use when

You've got pages that constitute some sort of serial process, such as a wizard, or any pages that lock the user into a limited navigation situation, such as a Modal Panel. These might be pages that users can reach out of context, as they could do via search results.

(Escape Hatches sometimes aren't necessary when you have Sequence Maps or Breadcrumbs on a page. Users who understand them can use those to get back to some known place.)

Why

Limited navigation is one thing, but having no way out is quite another! If you give the user a simple, obvious way to escape from a page, no strings attached, he's less likely to feel trapped there.

This is the kind of feature that helps people feel like they can safely explore an app or site. It's sort of like an undo feature—it encourages people to go down paths without feeling like they're committing to them. See the Safe Exploration pattern in Chapter 1.

Now, if these are pages that users can reach via search results, it's doubly important that Escape Hatches be put on each page. Visitors can click these to get to a "normal" page that tells them more about where they actually are.

How

Put a button or link on the page that brings the user back to a "safe place." This might be a home page, a hub page in a hub-and-spoke design, or any page with full navigation and something self-explanatory on it. Exactly what it links to will depend upon the application's design.

Websites often use clickable site logos as home-page links, usually in the upper left of a page. These provide an Escape Hatch in a familiar place, while helping with branding.

In some dialogs, a Cancel button or the equivalent can serve this purpose. These also let the user say, "I'm done with this; forget I ever started it."

Have you ever called a company—say, your bank—and had to work your way through a set of phone menus? They can be long, confusing, and time-consuming. If you find yourself in the wrong menu, you may just hang up and try again from the top. But many phone menu systems have a hidden Escape Hatch that they don't tell you about: if you dial "0" at any point, you might be connected to a human operator.

Many websites have certain pages that limit navigation options, such as Modal Panels and pages without global navigation. The Netflix login screen is one example. If a user finds herself here and doesn't want to log in, she can click on the Netflix logo to go back to the home page (see Figure 3-31).

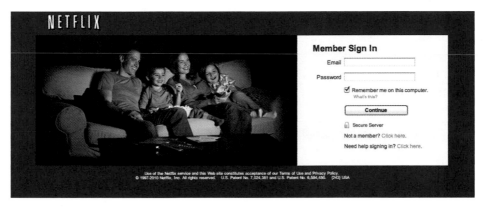

Figure 3-31. *Netflix sign-in page, with the logo as an Escape Hatch*

Sometimes literalism works. Google Labs offers features that aren't ready for release, and they occasionally break. In the example shown in Figure 3-32, Google Maps gives the user an explicit "escape hatch" URL to use when things go wrong.

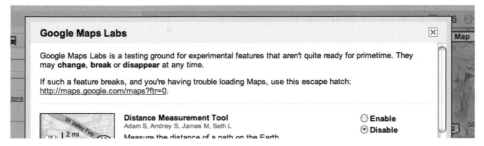

Figure 3-32. *Google Maps Labs Escape Hatch*

In other libraries

These two patterns are named "Home Link." The concept is very similar to Escape Hatch.

http://ui-patterns.com/patterns/HomeLink

http://welie.com/patterns/showPattern.php?patternID=home

Fat Menus

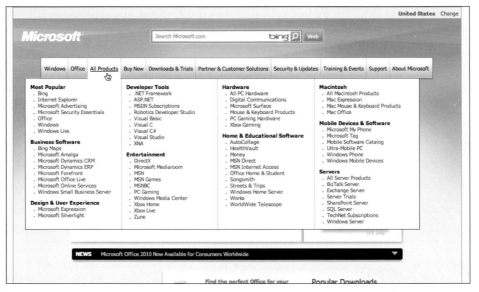

Figure 3-33. *Microsoft's All Products menu*

What

Display a long list of navigation options in drop-down or fly-out menus. Use these to show all the subpages in site sections. Organize them with care, using well-chosen categories or a natural sorting order, and spread them out horizontally.

Use when

The site or app has many pages in many categories, possibly in a hierarchy with three or more levels. You want to expose most of these pages to people casually exploring the site, so they can see what's available. Your users are comfortable with drop-down menus (click to see them) or fly-outs (roll over them with the pointer).

Why

Fat Menus make a complex site more discoverable. They expose many more navigation options to visitors than they might otherwise find.

By showing so many links on every page, you make it possible for a user to jump directly from any subpage to any other subpage (for most subpages, anyhow). You thus turn a multi-level site—where subpages aren't linked to the subpages in other site sections—into a fully connected site.

Fat Menus are a form of *progressive disclosure*, an important concept in user interface design. Complexity is hidden until the user asks to see it. A visitor to a site that uses these can look over the menu headings to get a high-level idea of what's there, and when he's ready to dive in, he can open up a Fat Menu with a gesture. He isn't shown millions of subpages before he's ready to deal with them.

If you're already using menus in your global navigation, you might consider expanding them to Fat Menus if surfacing more links makes the content more attractive to casual browsers. People won't have to drill down into categories and subcategories of your site hierarchy in order to discover interesting pages—they'll see them there, right up front.

How

On each menu, present a well-organized list of links. Arrange them into Titled Sections (Chapter 4) if they fit into subcategories; if not, use a sorting order that suits the nature of the content, such as an alphabetical or time-based list.

Use headers, dividers, generous whitespace, modest graphic elements, and whatever else you need to visually organize those links. And take advantage of horizontal space—you can spread the menu across the entire page if you wish. Many sites make excellent use of multiple columns to present categories. If you make the menu too tall, it might go right off the end of the browser page. (The user controls how tall the browser is; guess conservatively.)

The best sites have Fat Menus that work stylistically with the rest of the site. Design them to fit well into the color scheme, grid, and so on of the page.

Some menu implementations don't work well with accessibility technology such as screen readers. Ensure that your Fat Menus can work with these. If they can't, consider switching to a more static strategy, such as a Sitemap Footer.

Examples

The Fat Menus on the Starbucks website are very well designed (see Figure 3-34). Each menu is a different height but the same width, and follows a strict common page grid (they're all laid out the same way). The style blends in with the site, and the generous whitespace makes it easy to read. Ads are worked into the design, but not obnoxiously. The nonrectangular shape adds a polished look.

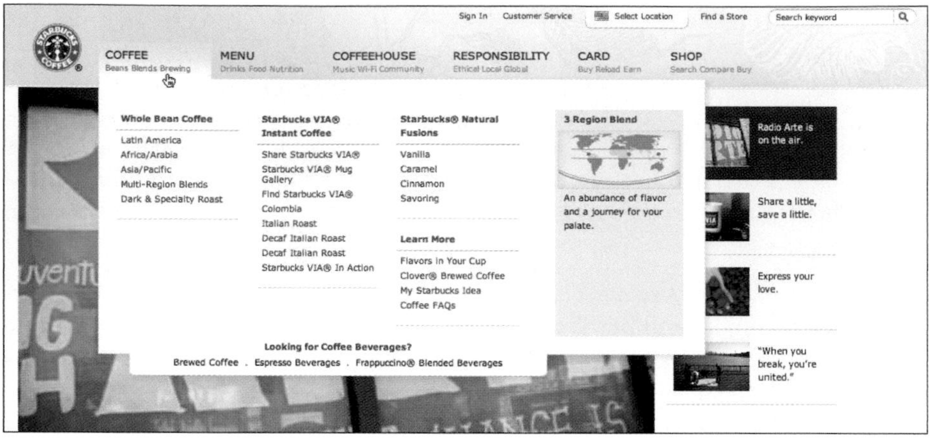

Figure 3-34. *Starbucks coffee menu*

As shown in Figure 3-35, Slate's menus are less readable and more crowded (in keeping with the overall style of the site). These don't take full advantage of horizontal space, either. But the idea of using them to show featured articles is clever—the knowledgeable user can skim a large number of headlines by rolling over the menus.

Figure 3-35. *Slate's News & Politics menu*

The American Red Cross doesn't merely float its menus over the top of the page (see Figure 3-36). When the user rolls over any top-level menu item, the resultant Fat Menu actually replaces a carousel-style rotating news panel, taking its space in the page. The menu is the same for all the top-level menu items, so all the subpages in every category are visible at once.

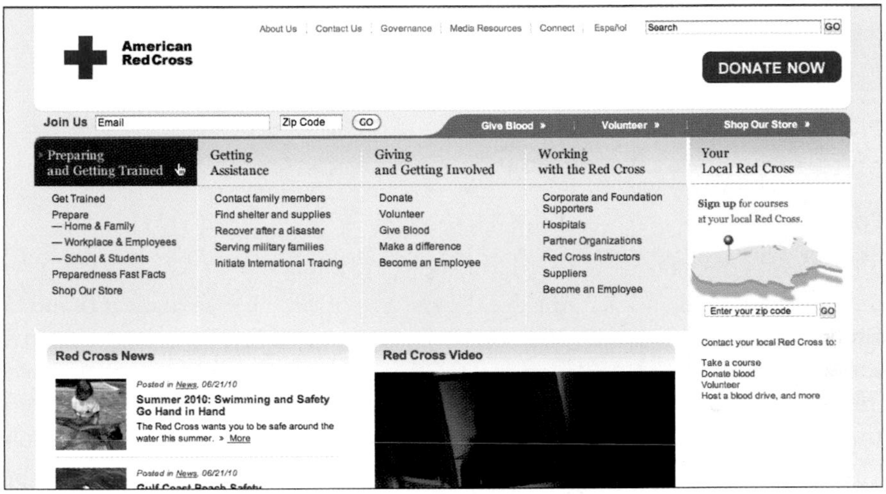

Figure 3-36. *The American Red Cross menus (all of them)*

WebMD uses an alphabetical sorting order for its long, flat list of health topics, as shown in Figure 3-37.

Figure 3-37. *WebMD's Health A–Z menu*

Sitemap Footer

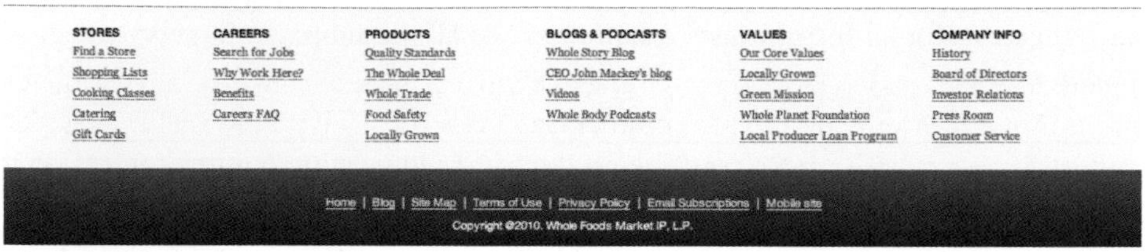

Figure 3-38. *Whole Foods footer*

What

Place a site map into the footer of every page in a site. Treat it as part of the global navigation, complementary to the header. Abridge the site map if you need to make it fit into a compact space.

Use when

The site you're designing uses a generous amount of space on each page, and you don't have severe constraints on page size or download time. You don't want to take up too much header or sidebar space with navigation.

The site has more than a handful of pages, but not an outrageously large number of categories and "important" pages (things that users will look for). You can fit a reasonably complete site map—at least for pages that aren't in the header—into a strip no taller than about half of a browser window.

There may be a global navigation menu in the page header, but it doesn't show all levels in the site hierarchy—maybe it only shows the top-level categories. You prefer a simple, well-laid-out footer instead of Fat Menus, perhaps because of implementation ease or accessibility issues.

Why

Sitemap Footers make a complex site more discoverable. They expose many more navigation options to visitors than they might otherwise have.

By showing so many links on every page, you make it possible for a user to jump directly from any subpage to any other subpage (or major page, anyhow). You thus turn a multilevel site—where subpages aren't linked to the subpages in other site sections—into a fully connected site. The footer is where the user's attention lands when she reads to the end of a page. By placing interesting links there, you entice the user to stay on the site and read more.

Finally, showing users the whole site map gives them a strong sense of how the site is constructed and where they might find relevant features. In complex sites, that could be valuable.

You may find yourself trying to choose between a Sitemap Footer design and a Fat Menus design. In conventional websites, a Sitemap Footer would be easier to implement and debug because it doesn't depend on anything dynamic: instead of showing fly-out menus when the user rolls over items or clicks on them, a Sitemap Footer is just a set of static links. It's also easier to use with screen readers and it doesn't require fine pointer control, so it wins on accessibility as well.

On the other hand, the footer may be ignored by busy or casual users who focus only on the page content and the headers. Usability-test if you have any doubts, and watch the click metrics to see if anyone even uses the Sitemap Footer.

How

Design a page-wide footer that contains the site's major sections (categories) and their most important subpages. Include utility navigation, tools such as language choice or Social Links (Chapter 9), and other typical footer information such as copyright and privacy statements.

This might constitute a complete site map for your site, or it might not. The idea is to cover most of what visitors need to find, without overloading the header or sidebar navigation.

In practice, what often happens is that the global navigation options at the top of the page reflect a more task-oriented design—it tries to answer visitors' immediate questions regarding "What is this about?" and "Where do I find *X* right this second?" Meanwhile, the Sitemap Footer shows the actual hierarchical structure of the site itself. This two-part arrangement appears to work well.

If your site deals with content that itself requires complex navigation—such as a large set of products, news articles, music, videos, books, and so on—you could use the top of the page for content navigation and the Sitemap Footer for almost everything else.

Here are some features that can often be found in Sitemap Footers:

- Major content categories
- Information about the site or organization
- Partner or sister sites—for example, sites or brands owned by the same company
- Community links, such as forums
- Help and support
- Contact information
- Current promotions
- Donation or volunteer information, for nonprofits

REI's website demonstrates the difference between task-oriented top-of-page global navigation and an effective Sitemap Footer (see Figure 3-39). Shopping, learning, and travel dominate the header, as they should—these are what most site visitors come for. The footer handles secondary tasks that are nevertheless important: "about" information, customer support, membership, and so on.

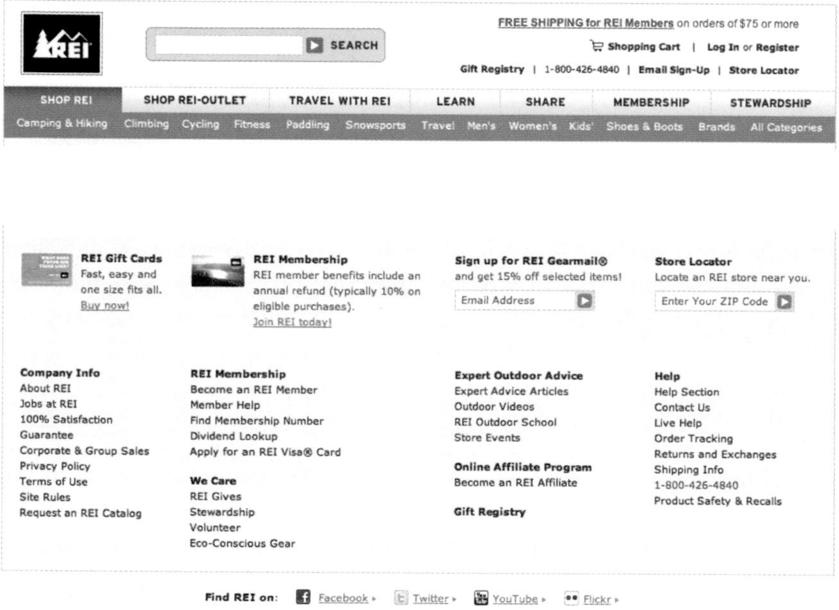

Figure 3-39. *REI header and footer*

The *Los Angeles Times* footer shows much of the same content as the double tab in the header, but flattened and organized somewhat differently (see Figure 3-40).

Figure 3-40. *Los Angeles Times header and footer*

The *Wall Street Journal* has an immense footer (see Figure 3-41). This is probably larger than you'll want to make yours.

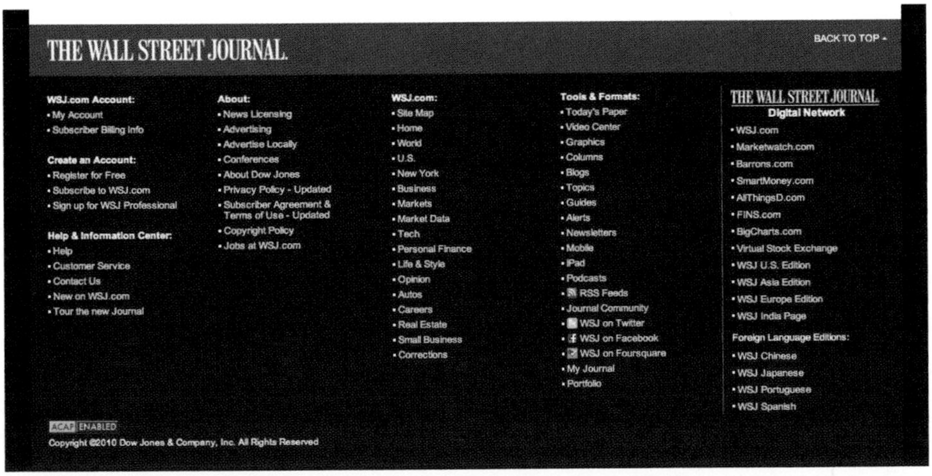

Figure 3-41. *Wall Street Journal footer*

Flickr, as always, is minimalist (see Figure 3-42). It eschews the column structure that most other sites use for their Sitemap Footers, and uses rows instead. MapQuest uses columns, but it also does a lovely job in a small amount of space (see Figure 3-43).

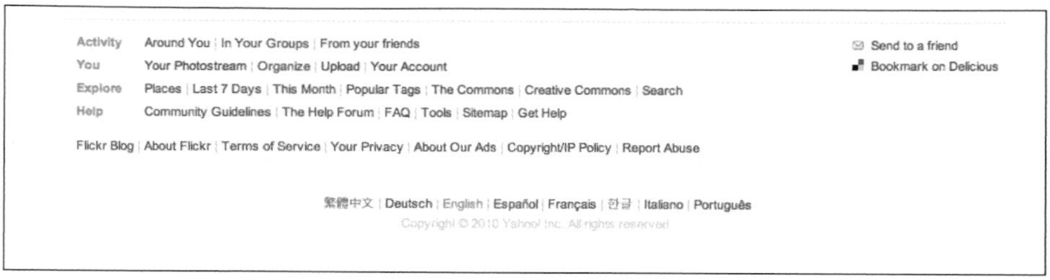

Figure 3-42. *Flickr footer*

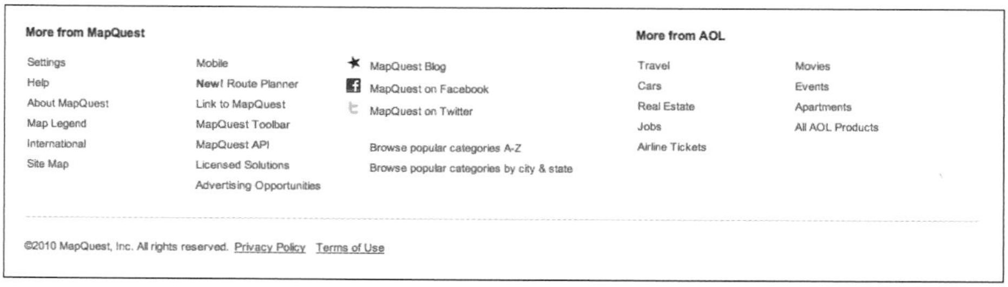

Figure 3-43. *MapQuest footer*

In other libraries

http://welie.com/patterns/showPattern.php?patternID=sitemap-footer

http://ui-patterns.com/patterns/FatFooter

The name "Fat Footer" has sometimes been used for this pattern, with a slightly expanded definition. For some wonderful examples, see the *Smashing Magazine* article titled "Informative and Usable Footers in Web Design":

http://www.smashingmagazine.com/2009/06/17/informative-and-usable-footers-in-web-design/

Sign-in Tools

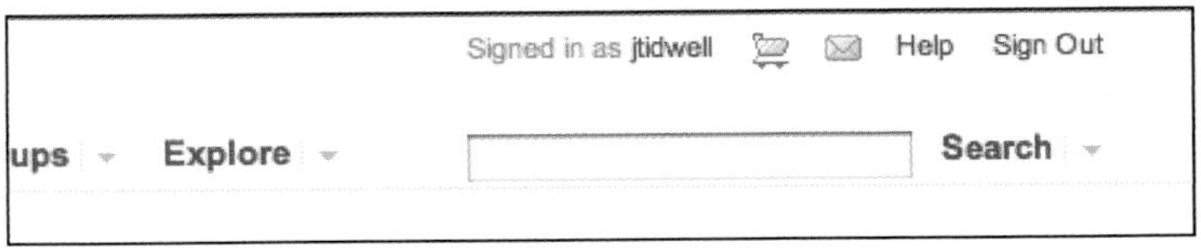

Figure 3-44. *Flickr sign-in tools*

Place utility navigation related to a signed-in user's site experience in the upper-right corner. Show tools such as shopping carts, profile and account settings, help, and sign-out buttons.

Sign-in Tools are useful for any site or service where users often sign in.

This pattern is purely convention; the upper-right corner is where many people expect such tools to be, so they will often look there. Give users a successful experience by putting these tools where they expect them to be.

Reserve space near the upper-right corner of each page for Sign-in Tools. Place the user's sign-in name there first (and possibly a small version of her avatar, if it exists), unless the name and avatar are already present elsewhere on the page. Make sure each tool works exactly the same on every page in the site or app.

Cluster together tools such as the following:

- Sign-out button or link (this is important, so make sure it's here)
- Account settings
- Profile settings
- Site help

- Customer service
- Shopping cart
- Personal messages or other notifications
- A link to personal collections of items (e.g., image sets, favorites, or wish lists)
- Home

Don't make this space too large or loud, lest it dominate the page—it shouldn't. This is utility navigation; it's there when a user needs it, but is otherwise "invisible" (well, not literally). For some items, you can use small icons instead of text—shopping carts, messages, and help all have standard visuals you can use, for instance. See the examples in this pattern for some of them.

The site search box is often placed near the Sign-in Tools, although it needs to be in a consistent spot regardless of whether anyone is signed in.

When no user is signed in, this area of the page can be used for a sign-in box—name, password, call to action, and possibly tools for retrieval of forgotten passwords.

Examples

Figure 3-45 shows an assortment of Sign-in Tools from Mint, Twitter, Amazon, and Gmail. These are visually unobtrusive, but findable simply because they're in the correct corner of the page or window.

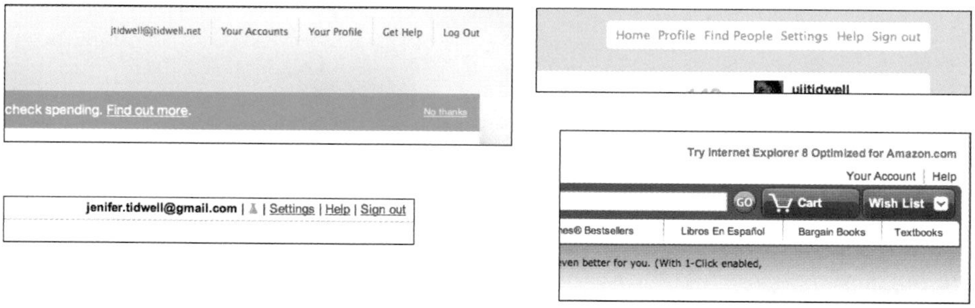

Figure 3-45. *Clockwise from top left: Mint, Twitter, Amazon, and Gmail*

Scribd uses almost all of the tools listed in this pattern (see Figure 3-46). Since there are so many of them, a drop-down menu seems appropriate to keep them from cluttering the corner of the page. iTunes also uses a drop down (see Figure 3-47).

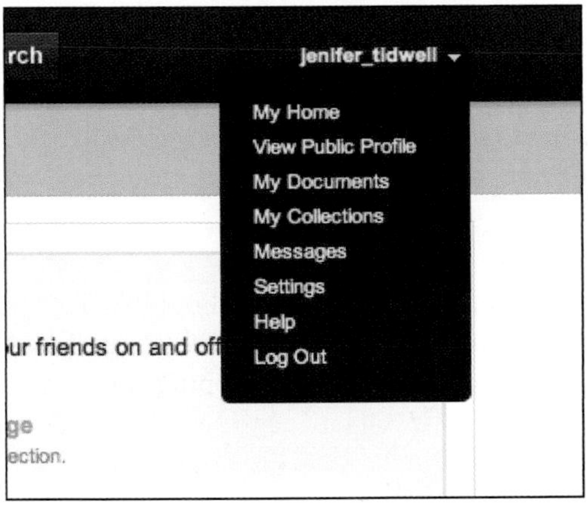

Figure 3-46. *Scribd sign-in tools*

Figure 3-47. *iTunes sign-in tools*

Sequence Map

Figure 3-48. *Hanna Andersson order sequence map*

What

On each page in a sequence, show a map of all the pages in order, including a "You are here" indicator.

Use when

You design a written narrative, a process flow, a Wizard, or anything else through which a user progresses page by page. The user's path is mainly linear.

If the navigation topology is large and hierarchical (as opposed to linear) you may want to consider using Breadcrumbs instead. If you have a large number of steps or items and their order doesn't matter much, this morphs into a Two-Panel Selector (Chapter 5) or Overview Plus Detail (Chapter 7).

Why

Sequence Maps tell a user how far he's come through a series of steps—and, more importantly, how far he has yet to go before he's finished. Knowing this helps him decide whether to continue, estimate how long it will take, and stay oriented.

Sequence Maps also serve as navigational devices. If someone wants to go back to a previously completed step, he can do so by clicking that step in the map.

How

Near an edge of the page, place a small map of the pages in the sequence. Make it one line or column if you can, to keep it from competing visually with the actual page content. Give the current page's indicator some special treatment, such as making it lighter or darker than the others; do something similar with the already-visited pages.

For the user's convenience, you might want to put the map near or next to the main navigation controls, usually Back and Next buttons.

How should you label each page's indicator on the map? If the pages or steps are numbered, use the numbers—they're short and easy to understand. But you should also put the page titles in the map. (Keep the titles short, so the map can accommodate them.) This gives the user enough information to know which pages to go back to, and anticipate what information he'll need in upcoming pages.

The slideshow shown in Figure 3-49 has a Sequence Map at the bottom. It allows viewers to move somewhat randomly through the images, though most users will probably use the Prev and Next buttons at the top.

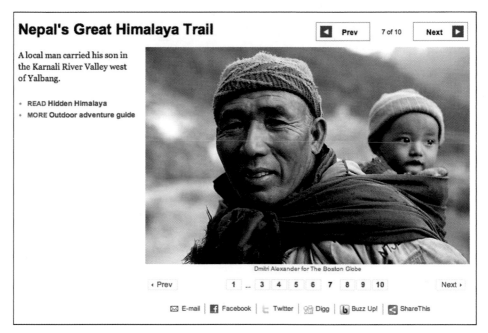

Figure 3-49. *Boston Globe slideshow, with sequence map under photo*

The Mini Cooper product configurator (see Figure 3-50) is a cross between a Settings Editor and a Wizard in that it lets the user move back and forth at will, but organizes the pages in a numbered sequence. The Sequence Map at the top is a critical control for "playing" with the app, for moving among the various pages and exploring different options.

Installation wizards usually require a lot of steps. The one shown in Figure 3-51, from Adobe, has a typical Sequence Map on the lefthand side. Its steps are disabled when they're irrelevant or bypassed, such as this trial installation that has no Adobe ID.

Figure 3-50. *Mini Cooper product configurator, with sequence map in upper left*

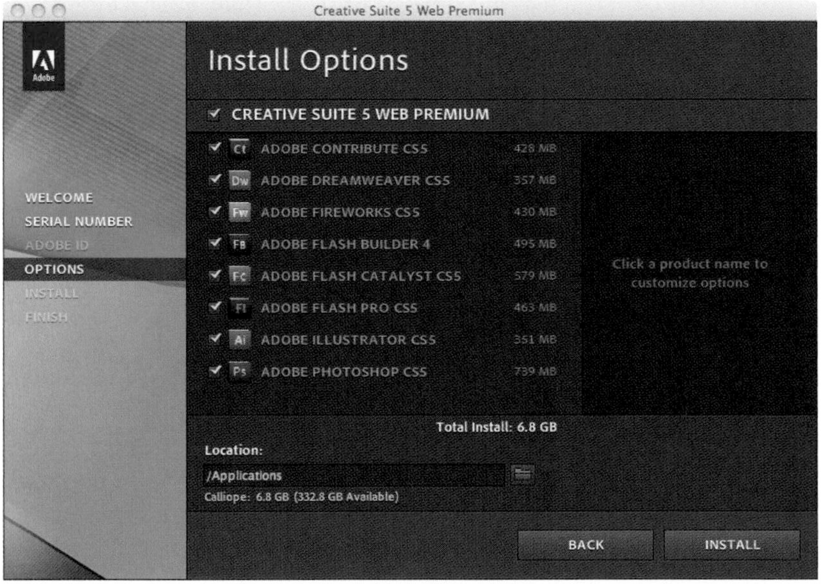

Figure 3-51. *Adobe CS5 installer, with sequence map at left*

In other libraries

http://ui-patterns.com/patterns/StepsLeft

http://developer.yahoo.com/ypatterns/navigation/bar/progress.html

Breadcrumbs

Target : Kitchen : Kitchen Appliances : Stand Mixers : KitchenAid Artisan 5-qt. Stand Mixer - Cobalt Blue (KSM150)

‹‹ Previous Page

Similar Categories

KitchenAid Appliances
Mixers
Appliances
Cooking Appliances

KitchenAid A
Stand Mixer -
(KSM150)
★★★★★ (61 reviews)

Figure 3-52. *Target breadcrumbs*

What

On each page in a deep navigational hierarchy, show a list of all the parent pages, up to the main or home page.

Use when

Your application or site has a hierarchical structure with two or more levels. Users move around via direct navigation, browsing, filtering, searching within the site, or deep-linking into it from elsewhere. Global navigation alone isn't sufficient to show a "You are here" signpost, because the hierarchy is too deep or large.

Alternatively, your site or app may have a set of browsing and filtering tools for a large data set, such as products being sold online. The products are categorized in a hierarchy, but that categorization doesn't necessarily match the way people will look for those products.

Why

Breadcrumbs show each level of hierarchy leading to the current page, from the top of the application all the way down. In a sense, they show a single linear "slice" of the overall map of the site or app.

So, like a Sequence Map, Breadcrumbs help a user figure out where he is. This is especially handy if he's jumped abruptly to somewhere deep in the tree, as he would by following search results or a faceted browsing tool. Unlike a Sequence Map, though, Breadcrumbs don't tell the user where he's headed next. They deal only with the present.

Some texts tell you that Breadcrumbs—so named for the Hansel and Gretel story, in which Hansel drops breadcrumbs on a forest trail to mark his way home—are most useful for telling the user how he got to where he is from the top of the site or app. But that's only true if the user has drilled straight down from the top, with no sidetracking, or following other branches, or dead ends, or searching, or linking directly from other pages…not likely.

Instead, Breadcrumbs are best for telling you where you are relative to the rest of the app or site—it's about context, not just history. Look at the Target example in Figure 3-52. Faceted browsing—searching for items with certain characteristics—brought me to this page deep in the Target website. (A keyword search could have done the same.) But now that I'm here, I can see where I am in the product hierarchy and I know what else I can look at. I can use the Breadcrumbs to look at all of Target's stand mixers and do some comparison shopping.

Finally, Breadcrumbs are usually clickable links or buttons. This turns them into a navigational device in their own right.

How

Near the top of the page, put a line of text or icons indicating the current level of hierarchy. Start with the top level; to its right, put the next level and so on down to the current page. Between the levels, put a graphic or text character to indicate the parent/child relationship between them. This is usually a right-pointing arrow, triangle, greater-than sign (>), slash (/), or right angle quotes (»).

The labels for each page should be the page titles. Users should recognize them if they've been to those pages already; if not, the titles should at least be self-explanatory enough to tell the user what those pages are about. The labels should be links to those pages.

Some Breadcrumbs show the current page as the last item in the chain; some don't. If yours do, make them visually different from the rest of the items, since they're not links.

Examples

The Windows 7 control panel is a hierarchical Settings Editor that can be three levels deep. The screenshot in Figure 3-53 shows the Personalization settings within the Appearance and Personalization category (which has at least six subcategories in addition to Personalization).

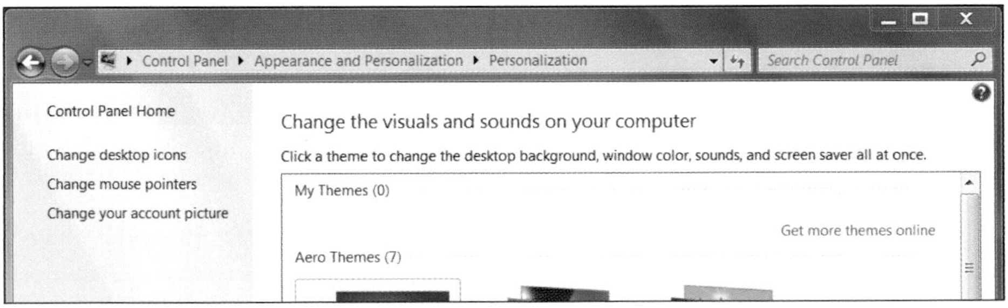

Figure 3-53. *Windows 7 control panel*

Online communities such as the one shown in Figure 3-54 often have deep hierarchies: forum categories, forums, subforums, yet more subforums, and threads. Breadcrumbs help users understand and traverse this hierarchy.

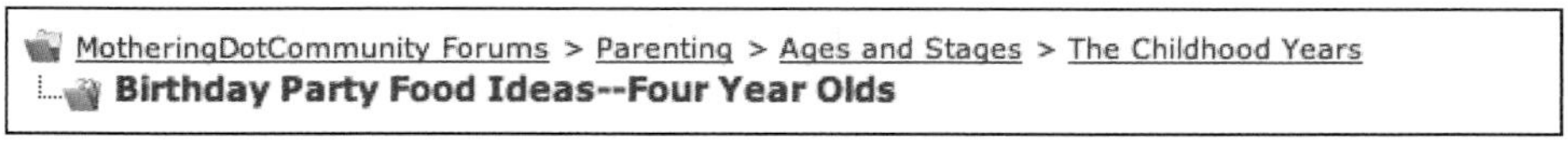

Figure 3-54. *Mothering.com forums*

Figure 3-55 shows an example of Breadcrumbs used outside a "page" context. The Chrome developer tools, among many other such tools for software developers, provide a way for users to manage very deep hierarchical structures (in this case, nested structural tags in an HTML page). Breadcrumbs are invaluable here for keeping track of where one is in that structure.

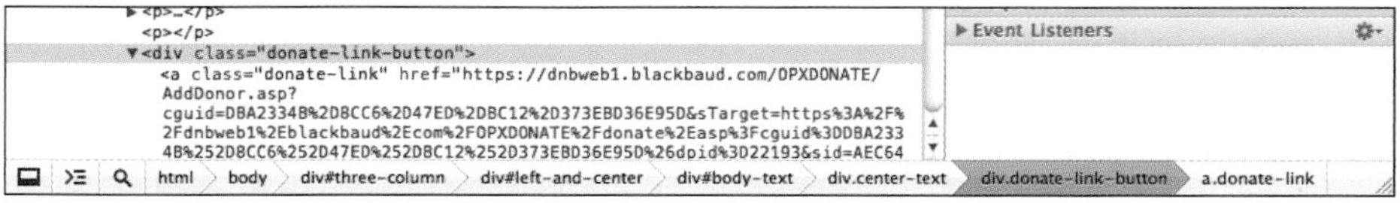

Figure 3-55. *Chrome developer tools*

In other libraries

http://developer.yahoo.com/ypatterns/navigation/breadcrumbs.html

http://ui-patterns.com/patterns/Breadcrumbs

http://www.welie.com/patterns/showPattern.php?patternID=crumbs

http://patternry.com/p=breadcrumbs/

http://quince.infragistics.com/Patterns/Breadcrumbs.aspx

http://www.smashingmagazine.com/2009/03/17/breadcrumbs-in-web-design-examples-and-best-practices-2/

Annotated Scrollbar

Figure 3-56. *MSNBC scrollbar showing page sections*

What

Make the scrollbar serve double-duty as a map of the content, or as a "You are here" indicator.

Use when

You're designing either a document-centric application or a pan-and-zoom interface, such as a map or large visualization. Users will scan this document or graphic for items of note, such as specific page numbers or landmarks. They might have trouble keeping track of where they are and where to go next as they scroll.

Even though the user remains within one navigational space as she scrolls through the content, signposts are still useful. When scrolling quickly, it's really hard to read the text flying by (or impossible, if the screen can't refresh quickly enough), so some other indicator of position is necessary. Even if she stops briefly, the part of the document she can see may not contain anything she can orient herself by, like headers.

Why a scrollbar? Because that's where the user's attention is focused. If you put signposts there, the user will see them and use them as she scrolls, rather than trying to look at two different screen areas at once. You can put signposts close to the scrollbar and still get the same effect; the closer, the better.

When the scrollbar shows indicators in the scrollbar track itself, you get something that behaves just like a one-dimensional Overview Plus Detail (Chapter 7). The track is the overview; the scrolled window is the detail.

Put a position indicator on or near the scrollbar. Either static or dynamic indicators might work—static indicators are those that don't change from second to second, such as blocks of color in the scrollbar track (see the tkdiff screenshot in Figure 3-57). Make sure their purpose is clear, though; such things can baffle users that aren't used to seeing graphics in the scrollbar track!

Dynamic indicators change as the user scrolls, and they are often implemented as tool tips. As the scroll position changes, the tool tip shown next to the scroll thumb changes to show information about the content there. This will vary with the nature of the application. Microsoft Word, for instance, puts page numbers and headers in these tool tips.

In either case, you'll need to figure out what a user will most likely be looking for, and thus what you need to put into the annotations. The content structure is a good starting point. If the content is code, you might show the name of the current function or method; if it's a spreadsheet, show the row number, and so on. Also consider whether the user is currently performing a search—the scrollbar annotation should show where the search results are in the document.

The tkdiff application shown in Figure 3-57 visually highlights the differences between two versions of a text file: newly added sections are marked in green, changed sections are in blue, and deleted sections are in red. An Annotated Scrollbar serves as an overall map, thus making large file "diffs" easier to comprehend.

```
.size() > 1) &&                              2087    } else if ((index == 0) &&
.get(1) instanceof BrowserSeparator)) {      2088              (fProxies.size() > 1) &&
the top and had a separator after it, remove that too:  2089              (fProxies.get(1) instanceof BrowserS
veElementAt (1);                             2090         // if it was at the top and had a separato
veElementAt (0);                             2091         fProxies.removeElementAt (1);
sDeleted (0, 1);                             2092         fProxies.removeElementAt (0);
                                             2093         fireTableRowsDeleted (0, 1);
                                             2094    } else {
veElementAt (index);                         2095         fProxies.removeElementAt (index);
sDeleted (index, index);                     2096         fireTableRowsDeleted (index, index);
                                             2097    }
                                             2098  }
                                             2099
                                             2100 +  public void removeContiguousElements (int st
                                             2101 +    if ((startIndex < 0) || (startIndex >= fProxies
                                             2102 +       (endIndex  < 0) || (endIndex  >=
                                             2103 +       (startIndex > endIndex))
                                             2104 +       return;
```

Figure 3-57. *tkdiff*

Chrome annotates its scrollbar with search results (see Figure 3-58). When you search for a word on a web page, Chrome highlights the found words on the page with yellow, and places a yellow indicator in the scrollbar wherever they are found. This way, the user can scroll directly to those points in the document.

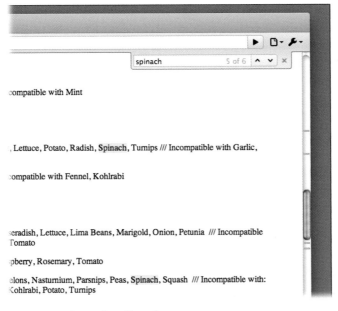

Figure 3-58. *Chrome "Find" results*

In other libraries

http://quince.infragistics.com/Patterns/Annotated%20Scrollbar.aspx

Animated Transition

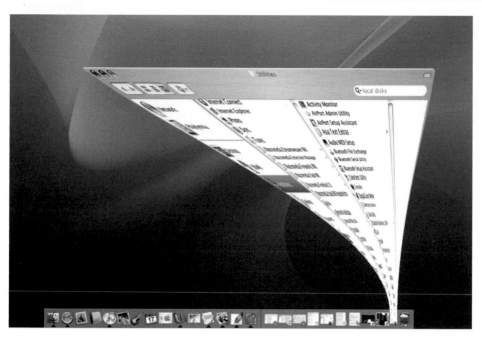

Figure 3-59. *Mac OS dock transition*

What

Smooth out a startling or dislocating transition with an animation that makes it feel natural.

Use when

Users move through a large virtual space, such as an image, spreadsheet, graph, or text document. They might be able to zoom in to varying degrees, pan or scroll, or rotate the whole thing. This is especially useful for information graphics, such as maps and plots. (See Chapter 7 for more about information graphics.)

Alternatively, the interface might have sections that can be closed and opened again, either by the system or by the user—such as trees with closable parent nodes, standalone windows that open and close, or an interface built with Collapsible Panels (Chapter 4). Animated Transition might also be used when users jump from one separate page to another.

All of these transformations can disrupt a user's sense of where she is in the virtual space. Zooming in and out, for instance, can throw off her spatial sense when it's done instantaneously, as can rotation and the closing of entire sections that prompts a re-layout of the screen. Even scrolling down a long page of text, when it's jumpy, can slow down the reader.

But when the shift from one state to another is visually continuous, it's not so bad. In other words, you can animate the transition between states so that it looks smooth, not discontinuous. This helps keep the user oriented. We can guess that it works because it more closely resembles physical reality—when was the last time you instantly jumped from the ground to 20 feet in the air? Less fancifully, an animated transition gives the user's eyes a chance to track a location while the view changes, rather than trying to find the location again after an abrupt change.

When done well, Animated Transitions bolster your application's cool factor. They're fun.

For each type of transformation that you use in your interface, design a short animation that "connects" the first state with the second state. For zoom and rotate, you might show the in-between zoom or rotate levels; for a closing panel, you might show it shrinking while the other panels expand to take up the space it leaves behind. To whatever extent possible, make it look like something physical is happening.

But this pattern is a double-edged sword. Beware of making the user motion-sick! The animations should be quick and precise, with little or no lag time between the user's initiating gesture and the beginning of the animation. Limit it to the affected part of the screen; don't animate the whole window. And keep it short. My preference would be to keep it well under a second, and research shows that 300 milliseconds might be ideal for smooth scrolling. Test it with your users to see what's tolerable.

If the user issues multiple actions in quick succession, such as pressing the down arrow key many times to scroll, combine them into one animated action. Otherwise, the user might sit there through several seconds' worth of animation as the punishment for pressing the down arrow key 10 times. Again: keep it quick and responsive.

Some of the types of transitions listed by the Yahoo! pattern library (*http://developer.yahoo.com/ypatterns/richinteraction/transition/*) and *Designing Web Interfaces* are as follows:

- Brighten and dim
- Expand and collapse
- Fade in, fade out, and cross-fade
- Self-healing
- Slide
- Spotlight

In other libraries

For more discussion and tons of great examples of the Animated Transitions in the preceding list, see the Transition cluster of patterns at the Yahoo! Design Pattern Library:

http://developer.yahoo.com/ypatterns/richinteraction/transition/

In addition, Scott and Neil's *Designing Web Interfaces* contains an entire chapter on transitions. It covers some of the same ground as the Yahoo! site, but it's worth reading.

Chapter 4

Organizing the Page: Layout of Page Elements

Page layout is the art of manipulating the user's attention on a page to convey meaning, sequence, and points of interaction.

If the word *manipulating* sounds unseemly to you, think about it this way. Film and television directors make their living by manipulating your attention on the movie or TV screen, and you are presumably a willing participant. It is the same for editors who arrange articles, headlines, and ads in a newspaper. If all this content were presented in a drab monotone, with no graphic emphasis to grab and move your attention, you would find it harder to extract meaning—what's supposed to be important, and what's not?

Even though it is ultimately an art, there is more rationality to good page layout than you might think there is. Some important ideas from graphic design are explained in this chapter introduction; each can guide you in the layout of pages, screens, and dialog boxes. We'll talk about visual hierarchy, visual flow and focal points, and grouping and alignment—all predictable and rational approaches to page design. This chapter's patterns describe concrete ways to apply those high-level concepts to interface design.

But the changeable, interactive nature of computer displays makes layout easier in some ways, harder in others. We'll talk about why that's true. Some of these patterns work as well in print as they do on-screen, but most of them would be useless in print—they presume that the user will interact with the page.

The Basics of Page Layout

This section discusses several elements of page layout: visual hierarchy, visual flow, and how to use dynamic displays.

Visual Hierarchy: What's Important? What's Related?

The concept of visual hierarchy plays a part in all forms of graphic design. Put simply, the most important content should stand out the most, and the least important should stand out the least. Also, titles ought to look like titles, subtitles ought to look like subtitles, and lists ought to look like lists—in other words, a reader should be able to deduce the informational structure of the page from its layout.

What is the most important thing on the page you're designing? Make that the center of attention. Can you rank other things in declining order of importance? Arrange them on the page in ways that draw progressively less attention; make them look less interesting.

In short, a good visual hierarchy gives instant clues about:

- The relative importance of page elements
- The relationships among them

How to make things look important

For short but large text—such as headlines and short phrases—use font size, contrasting color, and visual weight (see Figure 4-1). You can also make text look very dramatic by setting it off with generous whitespace or background color. Use two or more of these characteristics at a time on emphasized text to differentiate it from body text.

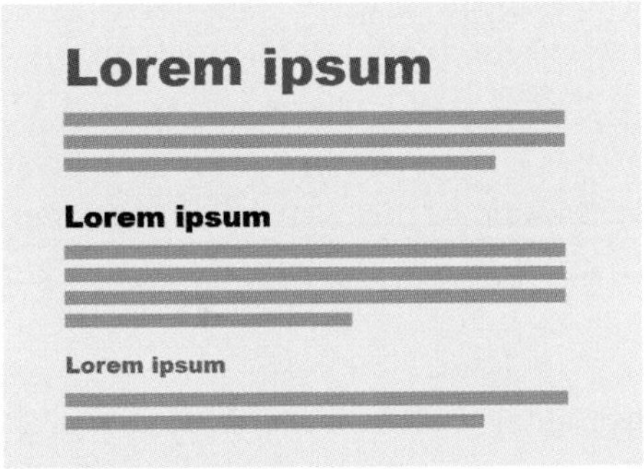

Figure 4-1. *Large text in a hierarchy*

Blocks of smaller items—such as body text, links, or interactive tools—can be emphasized or deemphasized with these tools. See Figure 4-2 for examples of each.

Density

A dense, heavy-looking block has stronger contrast with the surrounding page; an open look has less contrast.

Background color

Contrast draws attention. Black on white, or vice versa, is the strongest contrast possible.

Position and size

A medium or large text block, roughly in the center of the page, calls attention to itself as the primary content (like an article or blog post). But a small strip of text at the bottom of the page says quietly, "I'm just a footer" and begs to be ignored!

Rhythm

Lists, grids, alternating elements such as headlines and summaries, and whitespace separation can create a strong visual rhythm that irresistibly draws the eye.

Figure 4-2. *Ways to emphasize blocks of text or small items (clockwise from upper left): density, background color, rhythm, and position and size*

Put small but important items at the top of the page, along the left side, or in the top-right corner (see Figure 4-3). Give them high contrast and visual weight, and set them off with whitespace. But note that in a text-heavy screen, like most websites, certain controls—especially search fields, sign-in fields, and large buttons—tend to stand out anyway! This is less about raw visual characteristics than meaning: if someone is looking for a search box, for instance, her eyes will go straight to the text fields on the page. (She may not even read the labels for those text fields.)

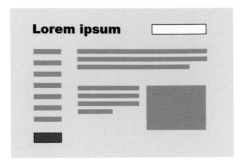

Figure 4-3. *Emphasizing small items*

High-contrast, dramatic images draw attention; so do pictures of faces. But much of the time, images on websites get ignored by viewers motivated to get information out of a page or to get a task done. Pictures are a wildcard in a visual hierarchy. Use them thoughtfully, and refer to Chapter 11 for a discussion on using visual elements to communicate branding, emotion, and other nonrational attributes.

One more thing: don't discount "ad blindness." Users may consciously ignore elements that look like ads, even if those elements carry important information! Again, this is about meaning, not visuals. If you've ever brought up an ad-filled web page and pointedly ignored the brightly colored moving ads (so you could read the monotonous blocks of text that you went there to read), you know that we're not merely slaves to our hardwired visual systems! We can choose to ignore things that we think we don't need to look at, and zero in on what we think is the important part of the page.

How to show relationships among page elements

Grouped items look related (see Figure 4-4). Conversely, isolation implies distinction—in the previous section, I recommended that small but important items be set off with whitespace for this reason. This uses the Gestalt principles of *proximity* and *closure* (see the sidebar "Four Important Gestalt Principles" on page 139).

Similar items look like peers (see Figure 4-5). If you have a few things "of a type" and you want viewers to see them as equally interesting alternatives, give them an identical (and distinctive) graphic treatment.

Is one item more "special" than the others like it? Give it a slightly different treatment, such as a contrasting background color, but otherwise keep it consistent with the others (see Figure 4-6). Or use a graphic element to disrupt the line along which the items are aligned, such as a bump-out, overlap, or something at an angle.

A list of many similar items, arranged in a strong line or column, becomes a set of peer items to be viewed in a certain order (see Figure 4-7). Align these items very precisely with each other to create a visual line (see the Gestalt principle of *continuity* in the upcoming sidebar). Examples include bulleted lists, navigation menus, text fields in a form, row-striped tables, and lists of headline/summary pairs. Note the alternating repetition used in the latter two examples. Alternating repetition can look beautiful when done well, and can set up a nice visual rhythm on the page.

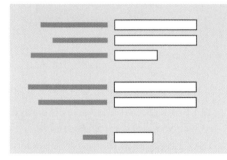

Figure 4-4. *Grouping related items*

Figure 4-5. *Peer items*

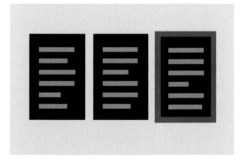

Figure 4-6. *Distinguishing one item among peers*

Figure 4-7. *Lists of items*

Indented and shrunken text tucked under a stronger element modifies that stronger element. Image captions, secondary text, comments, and so forth all behave this way (see Figure 4-8).

Containment implies a parent/child relationship (see Figure 4-9). Use boxes, blocks of background color, Module Tabs, Accordions, and text blocks or tool groups surrounded by whitespace to contain and nest related items (see the Gestalt principle of *closure* in the upcoming sidebar). Indenting also implies parent/child relationships in the context of an outline or a hierarchical menu.

Figure 4-8. *Captions and comments*   **Figure 4-9.** *Containment*

Visual Flow: What Should I Look at Next?

Visual flow deals with the tracks that readers' eyes tend to follow as they scan the page. It's intimately related to visual hierarchy, of course—a well-designed visual hierarchy sets up focal points on the page wherever you need to draw attention to the most important elements, and visual flow leads the eyes from those into the less important information. As a designer, you want to be able to control visual flow on a page so that people follow it in approximately the right sequence.

Several forces can work against each other when you try to set up a visual flow. One is our tendency to read top to bottom and left to right. When faced with a monotonous page of text, that's what you'll do naturally; but if there are strong focal points on the page, they can distract you from the usual progression, for better or for worse.

Focal points are the spots your eyes can't resist going to. You tend to follow them from strongest to weakest, and skillfully designed pages have only a few—too many focal points dilute the importance of each one. A good visual hierarchy uses focal points to pull eyes to the right places in the right order.

The next time you pick up a magazine, look at some well-designed ads, and notice what your eyes gravitate toward. The best commercial graphic artists are masters at setting up focal points to manipulate what you see first.

So how do you create a good visual flow? One simple way is to use implied lines, either curved or straight, to connect elements on the page (see Figure 4-10). This creates a visual narrative for the viewer to follow.

Figure 4-10. *Implied lines for visual flow*

Put calls to action after the text you want viewers to read first. If you don't care whether they read it or not, you can isolate the calls to action with whitespace (see Figure 4-11).

Figure 4-11. *Calls to action, both in the flow and out of it*

Likewise, if you're designing a form, arrange the controls along a continuous path and put "I'm finished" buttons (OK, Cancel, Submit, Buy, etc.) at the end of that line (see Figure 4-12). See the patterns Right/Left Alignment and Diagonal Balance for two concrete approaches to form layout, and Prominent "Done" Button in Chapter 6.

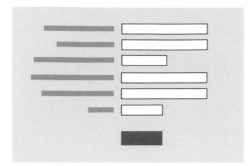

Figure 4-12. *OK button at the end of a form*

It's not hard to set up a layout that flows well, but be on your guard against layout choices that work counter to flow. If you want viewers to read a site's story and value proposition, arrange the critical pieces of that narrative along a continuous line, and don't interrupt it with eye-catching extras. If you're designing a form or set of interactive tools, don't scatter controls all over the page—that just forces the user to work harder to find them.

Figure 4-13 shows a distinctly poor example of visual flow and visual hierarchy. How many focal points are there, and how do they compete with one another? Where does your eye want to go first, and why? What does this page say is important?

Figure 4-13. *Weather Underground's jumbled visual hierarchy*

Four Important Gestalt Principles

The theory behind grouping and alignment was developed early in the 20th century by the Gestalt psychologists. They described several layout properties that seem to be hardwired into our visual systems. Among them are the following:

Proximity
> Put things close together, and viewers will associate them with one another. This is the basis for strong grouping of content and controls on a UI.

Similarity
> If two things are the same shape, size, color, or orientation, for instance, viewers will also associate them with each other.

Continuity
> Our eyes want to see continuous lines and curves formed by the alignment of smaller elements.

Closure
> We also want to see simple closed forms, such as rectangles and blobs of whitespace, that aren't explicitly drawn for us. Groups of things often appear to be closed forms.

Figure 4-14 depicts these four layouts and shows how you can combine them to create an effective overall design.

As important as they are individually, these principles are best used in combination with one another. Once again, redundancy is helpful; the fifth grouping looks more like an actual page layout than a retro-styled mosaic.

Continuity and closure, then, explain alignment. When you align things, you form a continuous line with their edges, and the users will follow that line and (perhaps subconsciously) assume a relationship. If the aligned items are coherent enough to form a shape—or to form one out of the whitespace or "negative space" around it—closure is also at work, adding to the effect.

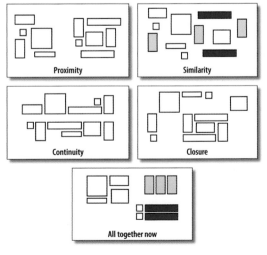

Figure 4-14. *Four Gestalt principles*

Using Dynamic Displays

Everything I've discussed so far applies equally to UIs, websites, posters, billboards, and magazine pages. They deal with static aspects of layout. Ah, but you have a dynamic computer display to work with—and suddenly time becomes another dimension of design! Just as importantly, computers permit user interaction with the layout to an extent that most printed things can't.

There are many, many ways you can take advantage of the dynamic nature of computer displays. Consider space usage, for example—even the biggest consumer-grade computer screens have less usable space than, say, a poster or a newspaper page. That's life. If you design for mobile devices, you've got an especially tiny space to work in. There are many dynamic techniques for using that space to present more content than you can show at one time.

Scrollbars, of course, are one very common way of presenting a small "viewport" onto a large thing, such as text, an image, or a table. Scrollbars let the user move around at will, in one or two dimensions (but refrain from using horizontal scrolling with text, please).

Or, if you can carve up the content into coherent sections, you have several options—Module Tabs, Accordions, Collapsible Panels, and Movable Panels all put some layout control into the user's hands, unlike the more static Titled Sections. (You can also split up content over multiple virtual pages and let the user navigate between them; see Chapter 3.) These patterns invoke time by letting the user see different content at different times of his choosing.

If you want to direct the user through a sequence of steps, Responsive Enabling and Responsive Disclosure are two time-honored ways of doing so.

The Patterns

This chapter's patterns give you specific ways to put all these layout concepts into play.

The first three address the visual hierarchy of the whole page, screen, or window, regardless of the type of content you put into that page. You should consider Visual Framework fairly early in a project, since it affects all the major pages and windows in an interface.

1. Visual Framework

Do you have a single important thing to show on the page, or several features or options of similar importance? Center Stage applies to pages that contain a single main item or task with other lesser items around it, whereas Grid of Equals makes several "peer" items look similar. (You could use both in separate sections of a large page, of course.)

2. Center Stage

3. Grid of Equals

The next group of patterns represents alternative ways of "chunking" content on a page or window. They're useful when you have more content than you can comfortably put on the page at one time. Should the different sections all be visible at once, or can they be viewed independently? Is it OK for users to manipulate those sections on the page, or maybe overlook the hidden ones? These patterns deal with visual hierarchy too, but they also involve interactivity, and they can help you choose among the specific mechanisms available in UI toolkits.

4. Titled Sections

5. Module Tabs

6. Accordion

7. Collapsible Panels

8. Movable Panels

Right/Left Alignment and Diagonal Balance draw on the concepts of visual flow, alignment, and other things discussed in the chapter introduction. They deal with the spatial relationships among the smaller, more static elements on a page, such as text and controls.

9. Right/Left Alignment

10. Diagonal Balance

The last three patterns deal with the dynamic aspects of content layout. Responsive Disclosure and Responsive Enabling are two ways of directing a user through a series of steps or a set of options; they indicate what can be done at any point in time, while preventing the user from straying into areas that will get her into trouble. Liquid Layout is a technique for arranging a page that can change size and shape at the user's whim.

11. Responsive Disclosure

12. Responsive Enabling

13. Liquid Layout

Visual Framework

Figure 4-15. *JAQK*

What

Design each page to use the same basic layout, colors, and stylistic elements, but give the design enough flexibility to handle varying page content.

Use when

You're building a website with multiple pages, or a UI with multiple windows—in other words, almost any complex software. You want it to "hang together" and look like one thing, deliberately designed; you want it to be easy to use and navigate.

Why

When a UI uses consistent color, font, and layout, and when titles and navigational aids—signposts—are in the same place every time, users know where they are and where to find things. They don't have to figure out a new layout each time they switch context from one page or window to another.

Have you ever seen a book in which the page numbers and headings were in a different place on each page?

A strong visual framework, repeated on each page, helps the page content stand out more. That which is constant fades into the background of the user's awareness; that which changes is noticed. Furthermore, adding enough character to the design of the visual framework helps with the branding of your website or product—the pages become recognizable as yours.

How

Draw up an overall look-and-feel that will be shared among all pages or windows. Home pages and main windows are "special" and are usually laid out differently from inner pages, but they should still share certain characteristics with the rest of the site. For example:

Color
　　Backgrounds, text colors, accent colors, and other colors

Fonts
　　For titles, subtitles, ordinary text, callout text, and minor text

Writing style and grammar
　　Titles, names, content, short descriptions, any long blocks of text, and anything else that uses language

All other pages or windows should also share the following, as appropriate:

- "You are here" signposts, such as titles, logos, Breadcrumb trails, global navigation with indicators of the current page, and Module Tabs

- Navigational devices, including global and utility navigation, OK/Cancel buttons, Back buttons, Quit or Exit buttons, and navigational patterns such as Sequence Map and Breadcrumbs (all in Chapter 3)

- Techniques used to define Titled Sections

- Spacing and alignment, including page margins, line spacing, the gaps between labels and their associated controls, and text and label justification

- Overall layout, or the placement of things on the page, in columns and/or rows, taking into account the margins and spacing issues listed previously

If you're familiar with graphic design concepts, you may recognize some of these techniques as comprising a *layout grid*. A layout grid is a structural template for a set of pages or layouts. Each individual page is different, but all use specified margins and align their contents along invisible gridlines. A good Visual Framework does indeed include a layout grid, but it also includes other aspects of look-and-feel such as colors, visual details, and writing style.

Implementation of a Visual Framework should force you to separate stylistic aspects of the UI from the content. This isn't a bad thing. If you define the framework in only one place—such as a CSS stylesheet or a Java class—it lets you change the framework independently from the content, which means you can tweak it and get it right more easily. (It's also good software engineering practice.)

Examples

JetBlue's site employs a restricted color palette, a strong header, and consistent use of fonts and curved rectangles in its Visual Framework (see Figure 4-16). Even the login page and modal dialogs use these elements; they don't look out of place.

In the same way, TED's site uses limited color and a layout grid to maintain consistency (see Figure 4-17). It has an interesting problem that's more common than it might appear: its subsidiary or related sites (such as its blog and its conference site) must look somewhat like the main TED site, but still have distinct visual identities. In this case, the two related sites share most of their framework elements with the TED site, with some key differences (see Figure 4-18).

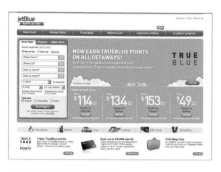

Figure 4-16. *JetBlue website*

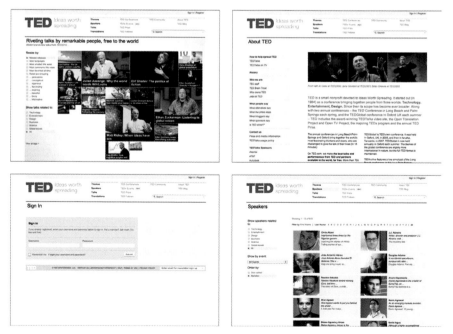

Figure 4-17. *TED website*

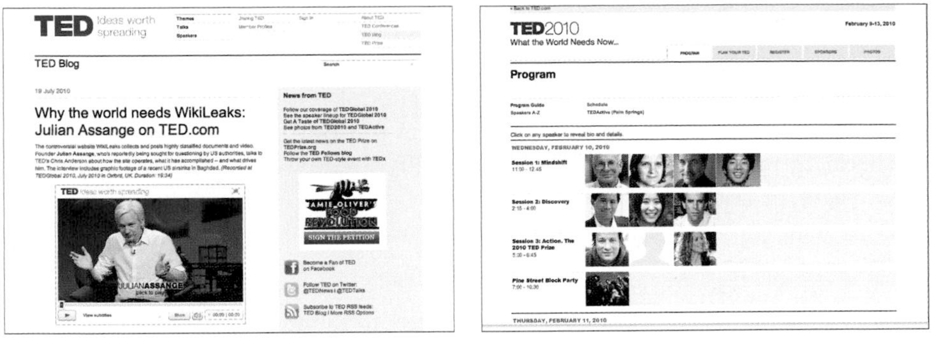

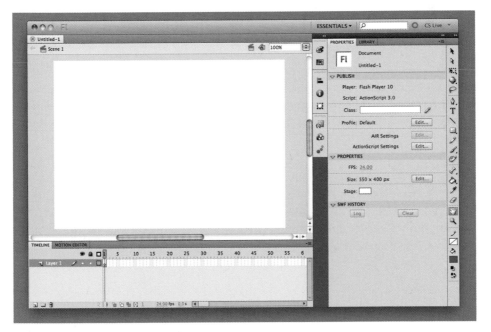

Figure 4-18. *TED-associated websites, with related but slightly different visual frameworks*

Center Stage

Figure 4-19. *Flash editor*

Put the most important part of the UI into the largest subsection of the page or window; cluster secondary tools and content around it in smaller panels.

Use when

The page's primary job is to show a single unit of coherent information to the user, let him edit a document, or enable him to perform a certain task. Other content and functions are secondary to this one. Many types of interfaces can use a Center Stage—tables and spreadsheets, forms, and graphical editors all qualify. So do web pages that show single articles, images, or features.

Why

The design should guide the user's eyes immediately to the start of the most important information (or task) rather than have them wandering over the page in confusion. An unambiguous central entity anchors the user's attention. Just as the lead sentence in a news article establishes the subject matter and purpose of the article, so the entity in Center Stage establishes the purpose of the UI.

Once that's done, the user will assess the items in the periphery in terms of how they relate to what's in the center. This is easier for the user than repeatedly scanning the page, trying to figure it out. What comes first? What's second? How does this relate to that? And so on.

How

Establish a visual hierarchy with the primary content or document dominating every-thing else. See the chapter introduction for a discussion of visual hierarchy. When design-ing a Center Stage, consider these particular factors, though none of them are absolutely required:

Size

> The Center Stage content should be at least twice as wide as whatever's in its side margins, and twice as tall as its top and bottom margins. (The user may change its size in some UIs, but this is how it should be when the user first sees it.) Keep the *fold* in mind—when a small screen is used, where does the content get cut off at the bottom? Make sure the Center Stage still takes up more of the above-the-fold space than anything else.

Color

> Use a color that contrasts with the items in the margins. In desktop UIs, white works well against Windows gray, especially for tables and trees. As it happens, white often works in web pages too, since ads and navigation bars usually use other colors as their backgrounds; also, web users have been "trained" by convention to look for the plain text on a white background.

Headlines

> Big headlines are focal points, and can draw the user's eye to the top of the Center Stage. That happens in print media too, of course. See the chapter introduction and Titled Sections for more.

Context

What does the user expect to see when she opens up the page? A graphic editor? A long text article? A map? A filesystem tree? Work with her preconceptions; put that in Center Stage and make it recognizable. The user will look for it—this trumps all other rules about visual perception. (But it doesn't mean you can frustrate her by hiding what she's looking for! Some websites put their main content so far down the page that it's below the fold in short windows, requiring the user to scroll down to find it. That's just sadistic.)

Notice that I didn't mention one traditional layout variable: position. It doesn't much matter where you put the Center Stage—top, left, right, bottom, center, any can be made to work. If it's big enough, it ends up more or less in the center anyway. Note that well-established genres have conventions about what goes into which margins, such as toolbars on top of graphic editors, or navigation bars on the left sides of web pages. Be creative, but with your eyes open. If you're in doubt, take a screenshot of the layout, shrink it, blur it, and ask someone where he thinks the main content should start. Again, see the chapter introduction for an example.

Examples

The Google Docs text editor devotes almost all of its horizontal space to the document being edited; so does its spreadsheet editor. Even the tools at the top of the page don't take up a huge amount of space. The result is a clean and balanced look (see Figure 4-20).

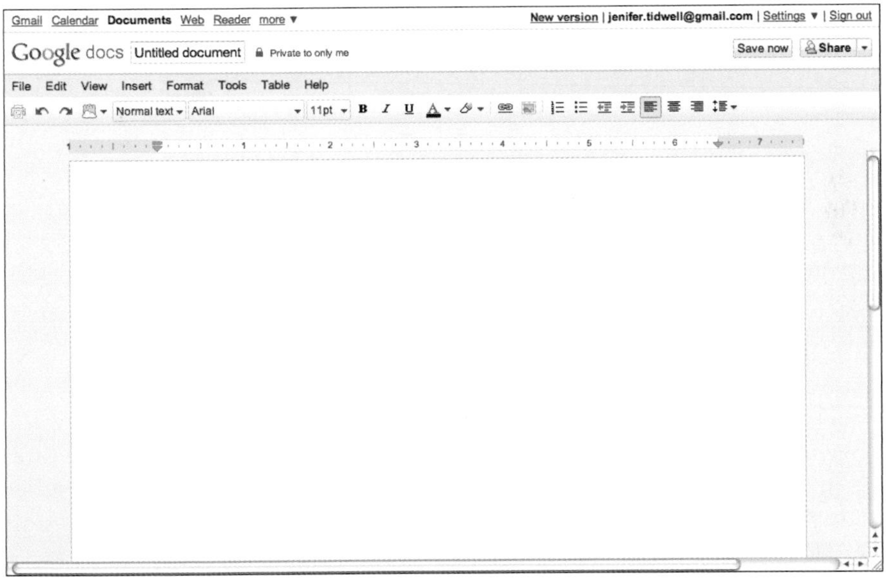

Figure 4-20. *Google Docs text editor*

Text-based content such as blog articles is often crowded with too many items in the margins. The sites for Newfangled (Figure 4-21) and Steepster (Figure 4-22) give their main content enough space to compete with the navigation and other peripheral features.

Notice the percentage of space devoted to the main article for both of these sites, and how high on the page the article starts.

Figure 4-21. *Newfangled article*

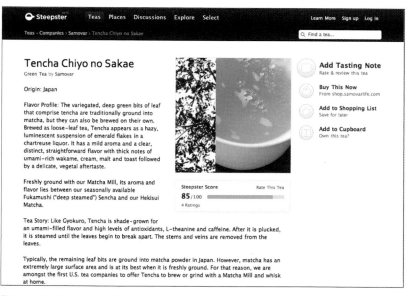

Figure 4-22. *Steepster article*

In other libraries

http://www.welie.com/patterns/showPattern.php?patternID=center-stage

Grid of Equals

Figure 4-23. *Nike*

What

Arrange content items in a grid or matrix. Each item should follow a common template, and each item's visual weight should be similar. Link to jump pages as necessary.

Use when

The page contains many content items that have similar style and importance, such as news articles, blog posts, products, or subject areas. You want to present the viewer with rich opportunities to preview and select these items.

Why

A grid that gives each item equal space announces that they have equal importance. The common template for items within the grid tells the user that the items are similar to each other. Together, these techniques establish a powerful visual hierarchy that should match the semantics of your content.

Grids look neat, ordered, and calming. That may suit the style of your site or app.

How

Figure out how to lay out each item in the grid. Do they have thumbnail images or graphics? Headlines, subheads, summary text? Links to jump pages (e.g., a page with the full story)? Render them with more than just blocks of body text: make headlines of different colors, be creative with whitespace, and use images if you can do so evenly across all items. Experiment with ways to fit all the right information into a relatively small space— tall, wide, or square—and apply that template to the items you need to display.

Now arrange the items in a grid. You could use a single row, or a matrix that's two, three, or more items wide. Consider page width as you do this design work—what will your design look like in a narrow window? Will most of your users have large browser windows? What happens on tiny mobile devices?

You may choose to highlight grid items, either statically (to emphasize one item over others) or dynamically, as a user hovers over those grid items. Use color and other stylistic changes, but don't change the positions, sizes, or other structural elements of the grid items—you don't want content jumping around as the user hovers over different items!

A related pattern is Thumbnail Grid, in Chapter 5. This is a way of rendering a list in a 2D matrix of small pictures, perhaps with a small amount of text with each one. See also the Thumbnail-and-Text List pattern for mobile design (Chapter 10). It's about a single column, not a grid, but the idea is the same: use a consistent, richly styled template for all the items in a list.

Examples

Hulu (Figure 4-24), CNN (Figure 4-25), and Nike (Figure 4-23, shown at the top of the pattern) use a rigid template for each item. The overall effect is rhythmic and calming. Note how each site uses a different balance of text and imagery.

Figure 4-24. *Hulu*

Figure 4-25 (CNN)

U.S. »
- New Orleans asking BP for $75M grant
- Tornado rips through Montana
- AZ wildfire forces evacuations
- Florida county to feds: Stay out
- Hot rods, pinup models fill CA fest
- Beachgoers stunned by murky oil
- Chicago subway fire injures 12

More

World »
- Santos declares victory in Colombia
- One year since Neda's death
- Sweden's crown princess marries
- Xe subsidiary gets Afghan contract
- Accused Sudanese rebels surrender
- Elton John performs in Israel
- Toll in China flood rises to 147

More

Business »
- Wall Street's push into China
- B&N slashes Nook price to $150
- Is the Fed out of bullets?
- China loosens currency chokehold
- Bill Gates' very full life after Microsoft
- Foreclosure crisis hits minorities hard
- How to lower credit card debt

More

Quick vote
Would you donate time or money to help fight the Gulf oil disaster?
○ Yes   ○ No

VOTE or view results

SPONSORED BY EQUIFAX

Politics »
- Obama plans bipartisan energy talks
- Kagan e-mails often brassy side
- Barton BP apology argued
- Part-time recovery chief defended
- Netanyahu to visit U.S. July 6
- Tea Party Express chair resigns
- U.S., Cuba talk migration

More

Entertainment »
- 'Toy Story' breaks box-office records
- Perez: no regrets over Miley pic
- Man held in actor's kidnapping
- Michael Jackson estate to repay L.A.
- More ballpark drama for Lady Gaga
- Amanda Bynes quits acting via Twitter
- Chris Klein checks into rehab

More

Health »
- Why do we need Bigfoot?
- Do women need a sex pill?
- Long goodbye of Alzheimer's
- Men's voices may predict strength
- Breast best for newborns, study says
- Study: Cartoons pull kids to junk food
- Chemicals found to affect thyroid

More

Sponsored Links
Obama Helps Homeowners Refinance
If you owe less than $729k you probably qualify for Obamas Refi...

Mom Wins iPad for $23.74?
Special Report: Apple iPads are being auctioned for an incredible 80% off!

Get Your Own Debt Bailout
See if You Too Qualify for The Govt's Personal Credit Reform Bailout!

Buy a link here

Tech »
- It's not just teens who text and drive
- A look at winners and losers from E3
- Is AT&T ready for the iPhone 4?
- How to get TV on the Internet
- Microsoft school gets back to basics
- World Cup vuvuzelas buzz online
- Why you won't pay for Facebook

More

Living »
- Warhol, Hendrix, grandma got rejected
- Your pilot dies, lions are circling
- Newlyweds lose $3,000 wedding gift
- Taking action against job burnout
- Florida tourism biz fights back
- School of future focuses on basics
- 10 things my father was right about

More

Justice »
- Van der Sloot: I was 'tricked'
- Man fights to be Jaycee Dugard's dad
- Six trials, then a 30-minute verdict
- Cops want info on Kyron's stepmom
- Man charged with killing family
- Killer, 13, locked up until he turns 21
- Young gymnast still missing

More

CNN Challenge »
Take our new online news trivia quiz hosted by your favorite CNN anchors.

Play

Figure 4-25. *CNN*

The examples from MapQuest (Figure 4-26) and IBM (Figure 4-27) show how to do this with only a single row of items. (Technically it's still a "grid.") The consistent visual treatment marks these items as peers of each other. Each item ends with one or more links—and that's true of the Hulu and CNN examples, too. Most of the examples I've seen of this pattern use it to showcase linked content.

Figure 4-26. *MapQuest*

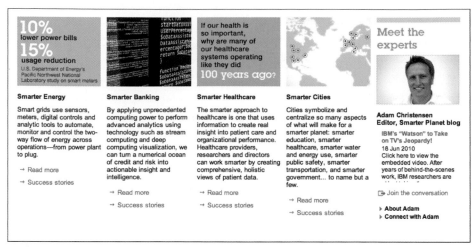

Figure 4-27. *An inner page at IBM's website*

In other libraries

For some wonderful examples, see "15 Tips for Designing Terrific Tables," by Joshua Johnson:

http://designshack.co.uk/articles/css/15-tips-for-designing-terrific-tables

Titled Sections

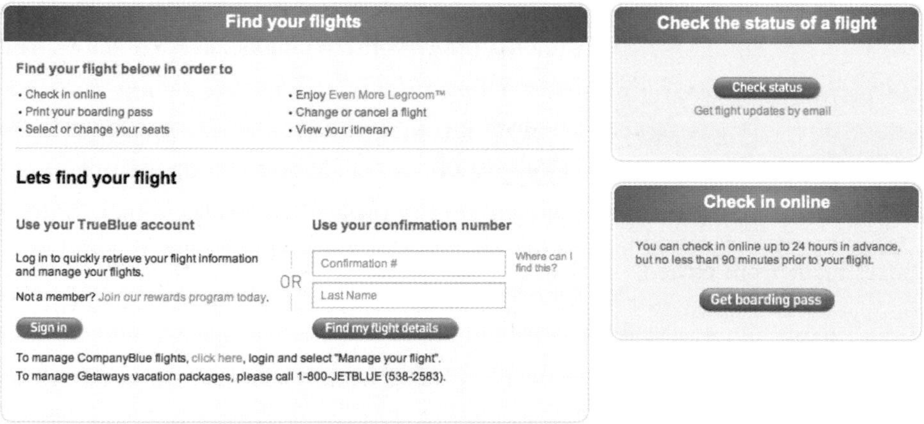

Figure 4-28. *JetBlue's titled sections*

What

Define separate sections of content by giving each one a visually strong title, separating the sections visually, and arranging them on the page.

Use when

You have a lot of content to show, but you want to make the page easy to scan and understand, with everything visible. You can group the content into thematic or task-based sections that make sense to the user.

Why

Well-defined and well-named sections structure the content into easily digestible chunks, each of which is now understandable at a glance. This makes the information architecture obvious. (See this chapter's introduction for a discussion of visual hierarchy, which is basically about rendering content in a way that communicates its actual structure. See also Chapter 2 for a definition of information architecture.)

When the user sees a page sectioned neatly into chunks like this, her eye is guided along the page more comfortably. The human visual system always looks for bigger patterns, whether they're deliberate or not. So, put them in deliberately!

How

First, get the information architecture right—split up the content into coherent chunks, if it hasn't already been done for you, and give them short, memorable names. Next, choose a presentation:

- For titles, use typography that stands out from the rest of the content—bolder, wider, larger point size, stronger color, different font family, outdented text, and so on. See the chapter introduction for more on visual hierarchy.

- Try reversing the title against a strip of contrasting color.

- Use whitespace to separate sections.

- Use blocks of contrasting background color behind the entire section.

- Boxes made from etched, beveled, or raised lines are familiar on desktop UIs. But they can get lost—and just become visual noise—if they're too big, too close to each other, or deeply nested.

If the page is still too overwhelming, try using Module Tabs, an Accordion, or Collapsible Panels to hide some of the content.

If you're having trouble giving reasonable titles to these chunks of content, that may be a sign that the grouping isn't a natural fit for the content. Consider reorganizing it into different chunks that are easier to name and remember. "Miscellaneous" categories may also be a sign of not-quite-right organization, though sometimes they're genuinely necessary.

Examples

In its account settings page, Amazon shows three levels of titles corresponding to three levels of the visual hierarchy: the page title, section titles (Orders, Payment, Settings), and subtitles atop lists of links (see Figure 4-29). Note the use of whitespace, boxes, and alignment to structure the page.

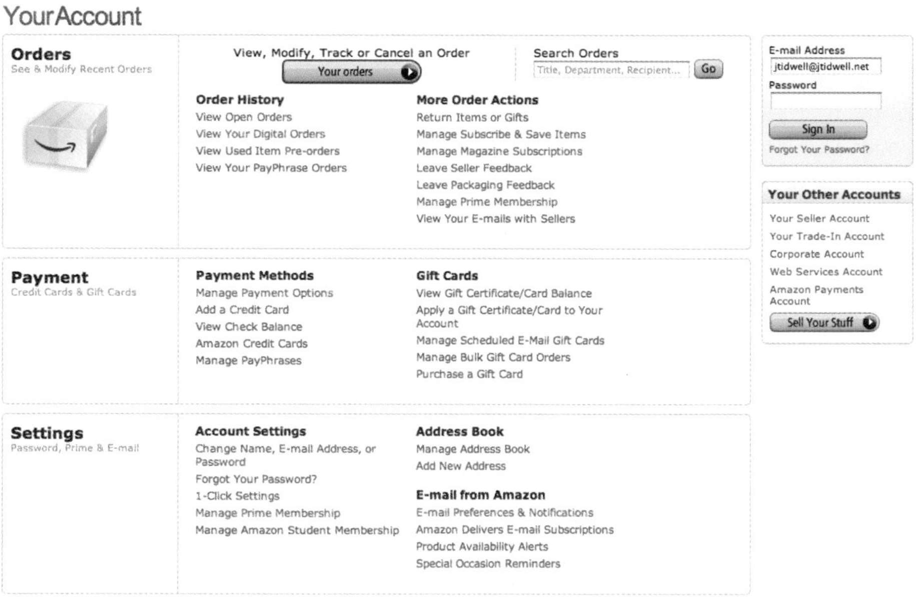

Figure 4-29. *Amazon account settings*

The iPhone sync utility shown in Figure 4-30 shows one nice-looking way to put very different kinds of content into titled boxes. These sections show very little internal consistency (other than typography)—they share no mutual grid, alignment, or layout plan. But the boxes and whitespace break up the page so much that this doesn't really matter.

Figure 4-30. *iPhone sync utility*

In other libraries

http://quince.infragistics.com/Patterns/Titled%20Sections.aspx

http://patternry.com/p=content-groups/

Module Tabs

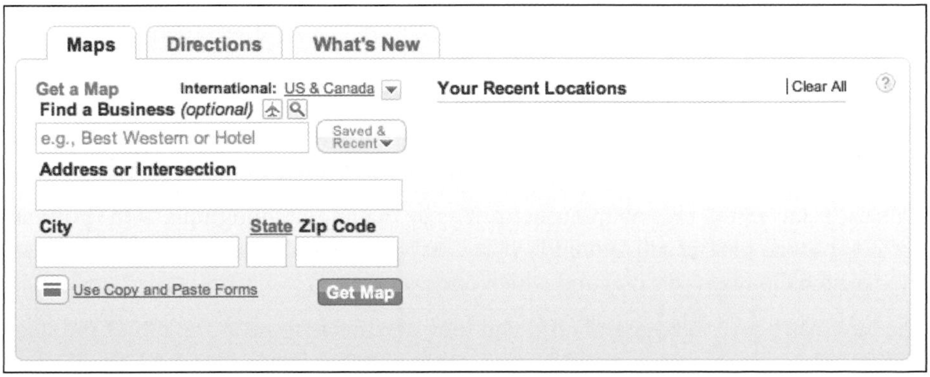

Figure 4-31. *MapQuest*

What

Put modules of content into a small tabbed area so that only one module is visible at a time. The user clicks on tabs to bring different modules to the top.

Use when

You have a lot of heterogeneous content to show on the page, possibly including text blocks, lists, buttons, form controls, or images. You don't have room for everything.

Some of the page content comes in groups or modules (or can be sorted into coherent groups). Those modules have the following characteristics:

- Users only need to see one module at a time.

- They are of similar length and height.

- There aren't many modules—fewer than 10, and preferably a small handful.

- The set of modules is fairly static; new pages won't be added frequently, nor will existing pages be changed or removed frequently.

- The modules' contents may be related or similar to each other.

Why

Tabs are now ubiquitous in desktop interfaces and websites. No one is going to be confused by how they work.

In general, grouping and hiding chunks of content can be a very effective technique for decluttering an interface. Tabs work well; so do Accordions, Movable Panels, Collapsible Panels, and simply arranging things into a clean grid of Titled Sections.

How

First, get the information architecture right. Split up the content into coherent chunks, if it hasn't already been done for you, and give them short, memorable titles (one or two words, if possible). Remember that if you split up the content incorrectly, users will be forced to switch back and forth between tabs as they compare them or look for information they can't find. Be kind to your users and test the way you've organized it.

Indicate the selected tab unambiguously, such as by making it contiguous with the panel itself. (Color alone isn't usually enough. If you have only two tabs, make sure it's abundantly clear which one is selected and which one isn't.)

But the tabs don't have to be literal tabs, and they don't have to be at the top of the stack of modules. You can put them in a lefthand column, or underneath, or even turned 90 degrees with the text read sideways.

When deployed on web pages, Module Tabs tend to be distinct from navigational tabs (those used for global navigation, or separate documents, or for loading new pages). Tabs are useful there too, of course, but this pattern is more about giving the user a lightweight way to see alternative modules of content within a page.

If there are too many tabs to fit in a narrow space, you could do one of several things: shorten the labels with an ellipsis (and thus make each tab narrower), or use Carousel-like arrow buttons to scroll the tabs. You could also put the tab labels in a lefthand column, instead of putting them on top. Never double-row the tabs.

(In the first edition of this book, this pattern was named Card Stack. Most people now know this concept as simply "tabs," however, and Module Tabs is a name used by at least two other pattern libraries.)

Examples

Microsoft Office for Windows 7 uses a "ribbon" atop documents, instead of the traditional menu and toolbars (see Figure 4-32). The ribbon is essentially a set of Module Tabs.

Figure 4-32. *Two tabs on the Excel ribbon*

Some Module Tabs in Mac OS don't look like tabs—they look like buttons. They behave exactly like tabs, however. The tabs are across the top, labeled "Audio," "Photos," "Movies," and "Widgets," as shown in Figure 4-33.

Figure 4-33. *iWeb*

Tabs can work along the sides of a module too, as shown in Figure 4-34.

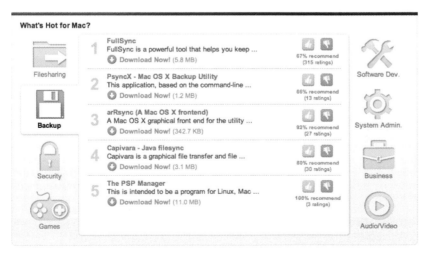

Figure 4-34. *SourceForge*

In other libraries

http://developer.yahoo.com/ypatterns/navigation/tabs/moduletabs.html

http://ui-patterns.com/patterns/ModuleTabs

http://www.welie.com/patterns/showPattern.php?patternID=tabbing

http://patternry.com/p=horizontal-module-tabs/

Accordion

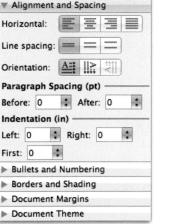

Figure 4-35. *Word palette*

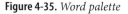

Put modules of content into a collinear stack of panels that can be closed and opened independently of each other.

Use when

You have a lot of heterogeneous content to show on the page, possibly including text blocks, lists, buttons, form controls, or images. You don't have room for everything.

Some of the page content comes in groups or modules (or can be sorted into coherent groups). Those modules have the following characteristics:

- Users may want to see more than one module at a time.

- Some modules are much taller or shorter than others, but they're all of similar width.

- The modules are part of a tool palette, a two-level menu, or some other coherent system of interactive elements.

- The modules' contents may be otherwise related or similar.

- You may want to preserve the linear order of the modules.

Also note that when large modules are open or many modules are open, the labels on the bottom of the Accordion may scroll off the screen or window. If that's a problem for your users, consider using a different solution.

Why

Accordions have become a familiar interactive element on web pages, almost as familiar as Module Tabs and drop-down menus. (They aren't quite as straightforward to use, however.) Many websites use Accordions in their menu systems to manage very long lists of pages and categories.

In general, grouping and hiding chunks of content can be a very effective technique for decluttering an interface. Accordions are part of a toolkit that includes Module Tabs, Movable Panels, Collapsible Panels, and Titled Sections to do so.

Accordions may be useful in web page navigation systems, but they really shine in desktop applications. Tool palettes in particular work well with Accordions (and Movable Panels as well, for similar reasons). Because users can open any set of modules and leave them open, Accordions help users modify their "living space" in a way that suits them. Yet it's easy to reopen a rarely used module when it becomes needed.

How

Arrange the modules vertically, in an order that makes sense for your particular application or site. Give each module a short and descriptive title, and put that title into a horizontal bar that the user can click to toggle the module open and closed. You could indicate the "openability" of a module title bar with a rotating triangle icon: point it rightward when closed, and downward when open.

Allow more than one module to be open at a time. There are differing opinions on this—some designers prefer only one module to be open at a time, and some implementations only allow one (or have a switch that developers can set, at least). But in my experience, especially in applications, it's better to let users open multiple modules at a time. It avoids the abrupt and unexpected disappearance of a previously open module: "Hey, where'd that other menu go? It was right here!"

When used in an application or when the user is signed in to a website, an Accordion ought to preserve its state of opened and closed modules between sessions. This isn't as important for navigation menus as it is for tool palettes.

Accordions can be nested if the module contents need further subdivision, but they tend to look confusing. Users find it hard to tell the difference between an "outer" accordion panel and an "inner" accordion panel; with everything all in one column, there's no clarity to the containment hierarchy. It's better to use just one flat set of accordion modules, and to use some other structuring pattern inside a module (e.g., tabs) if necessary.

This technique has existed since at least 1993, and possibly earlier. The Motif-based GUI builder called UIM/X used closable panels—even with the twist-down arrows—for its widget palettes.

(In the first edition of this book, this pattern was named Closable Panels. During the years since then, the user experience community seems to have settled on the name Accordion instead.)

Examples

Picasa's browsing window uses an Accordion to show several different ways of viewing a person's images. Within each pane, content might be further subdivided or organized, which Picasa does in the example in Figure 4-36 with Titled Sections. Chrome's developer tools, on the other hand, nest Accordions inside each other (see Figure 4-37). You can figure out the nesting scheme if you stare at it hard enough, but it's not easy.

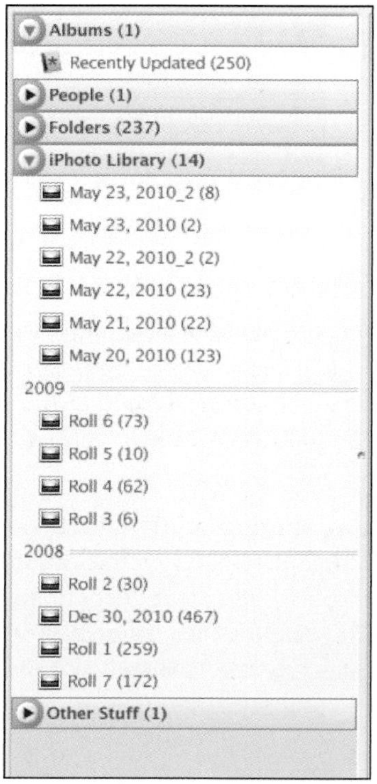

Figure 4-36. *Picasa lefthand sidebar*

Figure 4-37. *Chrome righthand sidebar, with nested accordions*

CNN uses an Accordion to show personalized material (see Figure 4-38). Only one panel can be open at once in this implementation. If it were up to me, I'd want to see both of these panels open at the same time, but maybe CNN had a very limited amount of vertical space to work with.

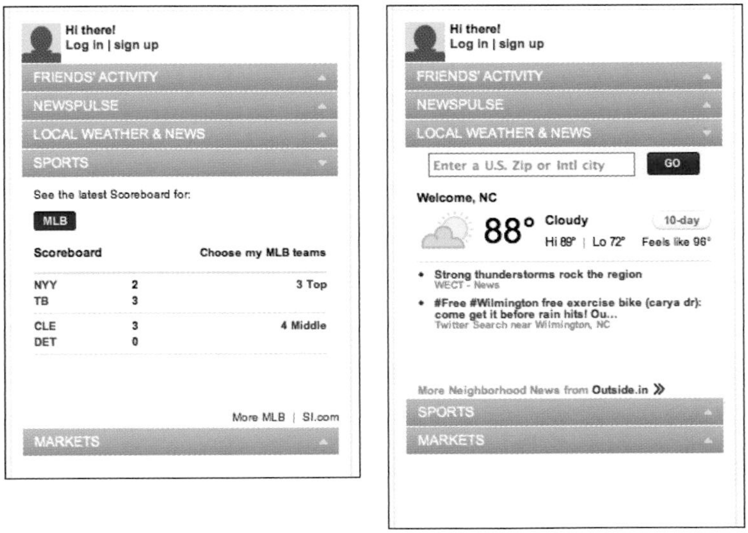

Figure 4-38. *CNN sidebar*

As shown in Figure 4-39, the Yahoo! Developer Network uses an Accordion in its footer to let users hide and show sections that they care about (or don't). Note the use of a Sitemap Footer, described in Chapter 3.

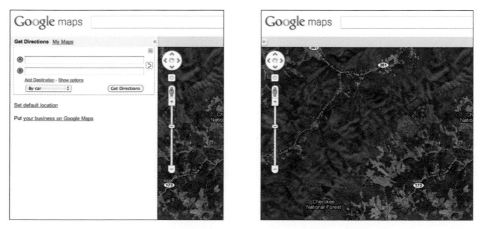

Figure 4-39. *Yahoo! Developer Network page footer*

http://developer.yahoo.com/ypatterns/navigation/accordion.html

http://ui-patterns.com/patterns/AccordionMenu

http://www.welie.com/patterns/showPattern.php?patternID=accordion

Designing Web Interfaces by Bill Scott and Theresa Neil (O'Reilly, *http://oreilly.com/ catalog/9780596516253/*) also describes an Accordion pattern.

Collapsible Panels

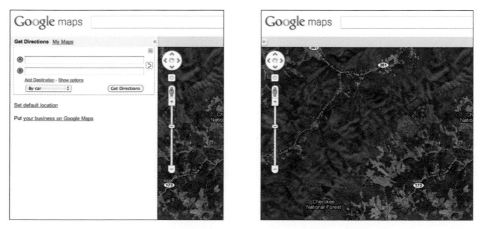

Figure 4-40. *Google Maps*

What

Put secondary or optional material into panels that can be opened and closed by the user.

Use when

You have a lot of heterogeneous content to show on the page, possibly including text blocks, lists, buttons, form controls, or images. You don't have room for everything. You might, however, have Center Stage content that needs to take visual priority.

Some of the page content comes in groups or modules (or can be sorted into coherent groups). Those modules have the following characteristics:

- Their content annotates, modifies, explains, or otherwise supports the content in the main part of the page.

- The modules may not be important enough for any of them to be open by default.

- Their value may vary a lot from user to user. Some will really want to see a particular module, and others won't care about it at all.

- Even for one user, a module may be useful sometimes, but not other times. When it's not open, its space is better used by the page's main content.

- Users may want to open more than one module at the same time.

- The modules have very little to do with each other. When Module Tabs or Accordions are used, they group modules together, implying that they are somehow related; Collapsible Panels do not group them.

Why

Hiding noncritical pieces of content helps to simplify the interface. When a user hides a module that supports the main content, it simply collapses, giving its space back over to the main content (or to whitespace). This is an example of the principle of *progressive disclosure*—show hidden content "just in time," when and where the user needs it.

In general, grouping and hiding chunks of content can be a very effective technique for decluttering an interface. Collapsible Panels are part of a toolkit that includes Module Tabs, Accordions, Movable Panels, and Titled Sections to do so.

How

Put each supporting module into a panel that the user can open and close via a single click. Label the button or link with the module's name or simply "More," and consider using a chevron or rotating triangle to indicate that more content is hidden there. When the user closes the panel, collapse the space used by that panel and devote it to other content (such as by moving up the content below it on the page).

Consider animating the panels as they open and close. It appears less dislocating when they smoothly zip open and closed again.

If you have more than one module to hide in this way, you could either put the modules together on one panel with Module Tabs or an Accordion, or put them in separate places on the main page.

If you find that most users are opening up a Collapsible Panel that's closed by default, switch it to being open by default.

Examples

Google Maps, shown in Figure 4-40 at the top of the pattern, demonstrates how useful it can be to collapse a panel that's outlived its usefulness—the visible map area is significantly bigger without the sidebar.

Some discussion forums, such as that shown in Figure 4-41, place long comments into Collapsible Panels. A visitor can skim the page's short and truncated comments to get a sense of the discussion, and if a long comment attracts her attention, she can open the truncated comment to read the whole thing.

Figure 4-41. *MSNBC article comments*

Many applications show optional sidebars attached to their Center Stage windows. Firefox's sidebar, shown in Figure 4-42, is closed by a single click on the "X" button, and a user can bring it back by selecting a menu item (or by using a keyboard shortcut). Note the asymmetry—it's much easier to hide it than to show it, at least until the user memorizes the keyboard sequence! With a web page, or with an app that isn't frequently used, a visible button to bring back the panel would be a better choice.

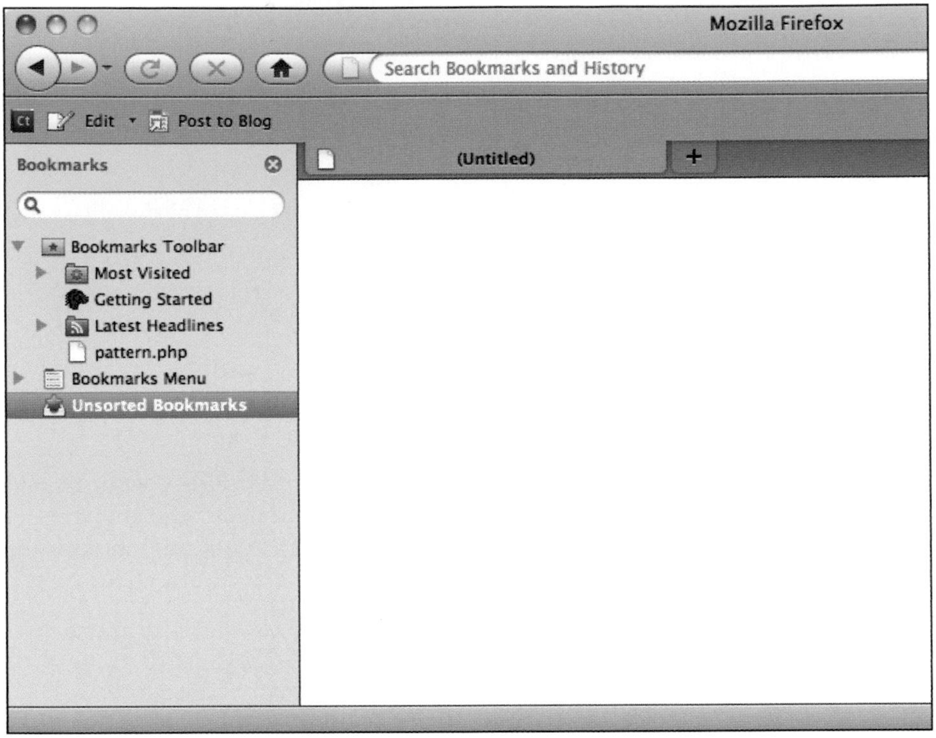

Figure 4-42. *Firefox bookmarks sidebar*

At the time of this writing, YouTube places many Collapsible Panels on a video's page (see Figure 4-43). They contain extra content such as the video description, viewing statistics, and more videos from this poster (not shown in the figure). The page draws attention to these expandable areas by highlighting them in blue on rollover. They're all closed by default, and they close themselves when the page is reloaded. The resultant page is less cluttered than it would otherwise be, while still providing interesting information to users inspired enough to open these panels.

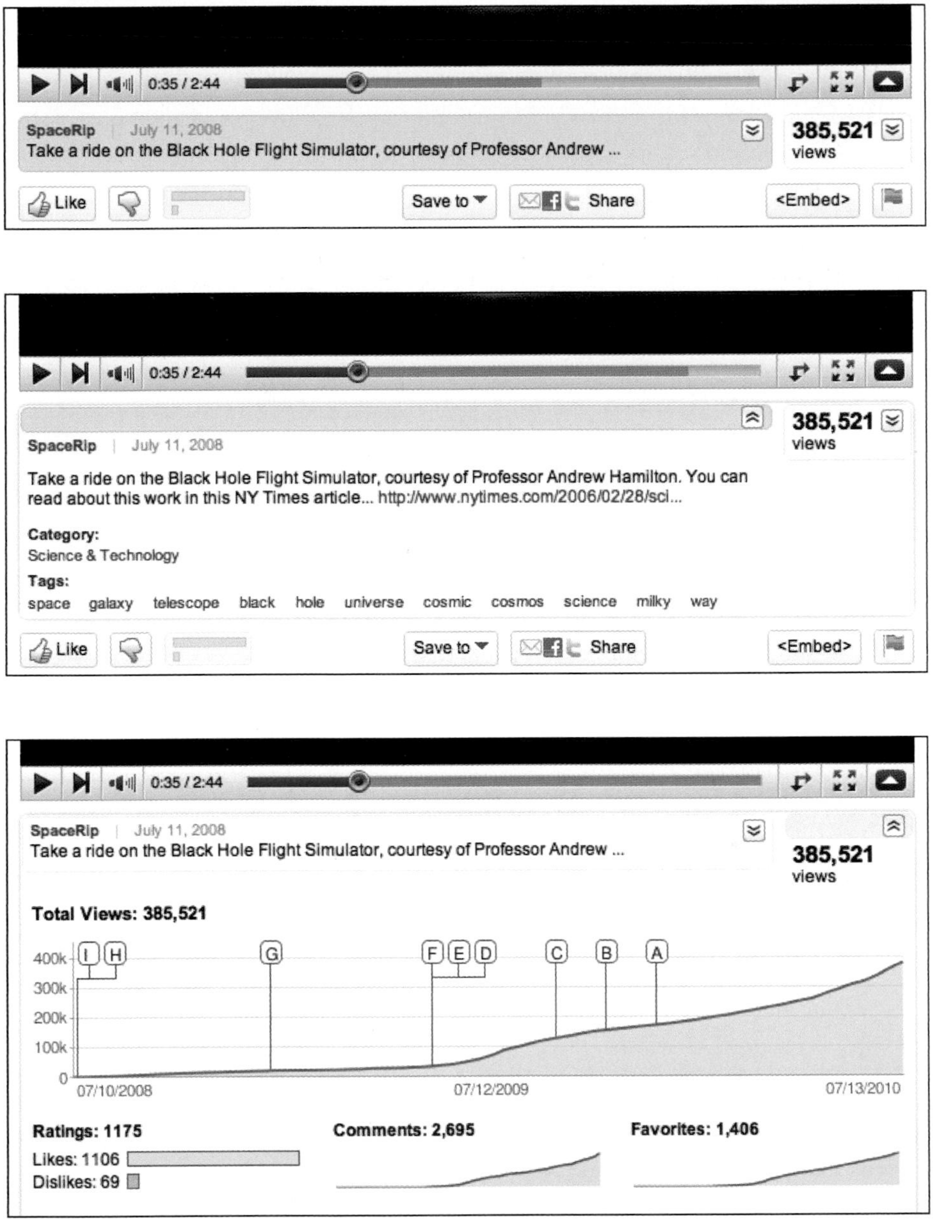

Figure 4-43. *YouTube's collapsible panels; three states are shown: neither panel open, video description panel open, and statistics panel open (both cannot be open at once)*

In other libraries

http://www.welie.com/patterns/showPattern.php?patternID=collapsible-panels

http://www.welie.com/patterns/showPattern.php?patternID=details-on-demand

http://quince.infragistics.com/Patterns/Closable%20Panels.aspx

Movable Panels

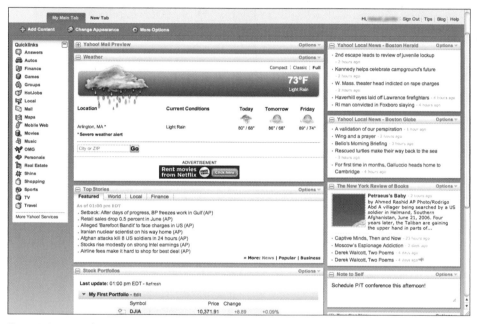

Figure 4-44. *My Yahoo!*

What

Put modules of content into boxes that can be opened and closed independently of each other. Arrange the boxes freely on the page, and let the user move them around into a custom configuration.

Use when

You're designing either a desktop application, or a website that most users sign in to. News portals, Dashboards, and Canvas Plus Palette apps often use Movable Panels. You want users to feel a sense of ownership of the software, or at least have fun playing with it.

The page in question is a major part of the app or site—something that users see often or for long periods of time. You have a lot of heterogeneous content to show on the page, possibly including text blocks, lists, buttons, form controls, or images. You don't have room for everything.

Some of the page content comes in groups or modules (or can be sorted into coherent groups). Those modules have some of the following characteristics:

- Users will almost certainly want to see more than one module at a time.

- Their value may vary a lot from user to user. Some people want modules A, B, and C, while others don't need those at all and only want to see D, E, and F.

- The modules vary a lot in size.

- Their position on the page isn't terribly important to you, but it might be to users. (By contrast, a page of static Titled Sections ought to be arranged with thought given to the importance of page position; important things go to the top, for instance.)

- There are many modules—possibly so many that if all were shown at once, a viewer would be overwhelmed. Either you or the user should pick and choose among them.

- You're willing to let users hide some modules from view altogether (and offer a mechanism to bring them back).

- The modules may be part of a tool palette or some other coherent system of interactive elements.

Why

Different users have different interests. Websites such as dashboards and portals are most useful to people when they can choose the content they see.

When they'll be working on something for a while in a desktop application, people like to rearrange their environment to suit their working style. They can place needed tools close to where they work; they can hide things they don't need; they can use Spatial Memory (Chapter 1) to remember where they put things. Rationally speaking, Movable Panels help users get things done more efficiently and comfortably (in the long run—once they've spent time rearranging their environment the way they like it!).

But this kind of personalization seems to appeal to people on some other level, too. They may do this on infrequently visited websites that provide some kind of entertainment, for instance. Personalization can increase engagement and buy-in.

Finally, a Movable Panels design easily accommodates new modules introduced over time, such as those contributed by third parties.

How

Give each module a name, a title bar, and a default size, and arrange them on the page in a reasonable default configuration. Let the user move modules around the page at will, via drag-and-drop if possible. Permit each module to be opened and closed with a simple gesture, such as a mouse click on a title bar button.

Depending upon the design you've chosen, you may want to give the user freedom to place these pieces anywhere at all, even if they overlap. Or you may want a predefined layout grid with "slots" where pieces can be dragged and dropped—this lets the page maintain alignment (and some sense of dignity!) without making the user spend too much time fiddling with windows. Some designs use *ghosting*—big drop targets that appear dynamically; for example, dotted rectangles—to show where a dragged module would go when dropped.

Consider letting users remove modules altogether. An "X" button in the title bar is the familiar way to remove one. Once a module is gone, how does a user bring it back? Let users add modules—including brand-new ones, perhaps—from a list of available modules that can be browsed and searched.

Modules may individually allow customization; they might offer Settings Editors (Chapter 2) to adjust various parameters for content or viewing. (A weather widget might ask the user to set a desired location, for instance.) Some designs make this available via another button or drop-down menu on the module title bar.

When used in an application or when the user is signed in to a website, Movable Panels must preserve the state of opened and closed modules between sessions. People will expect that, and they will be startled if it doesn't work. (You may also put a "revert to defaults" function somewhere, in case a user gets tangled up in the customization and wants to start anew.)

Examples

iGoogle, shown in Figures 4-45 and 4-46, demonstrates the mechanics of dragging and dropping a Movable Panel around a page. A user grabs the title bar of a panel; at the beginning of the drag operation, a dotted-line "ghost" shows the place where the panel had been. As the panel is dragged near another drop zone between panels, another "ghost" appears there—if the user lets go of the panel now, that's where it will land.

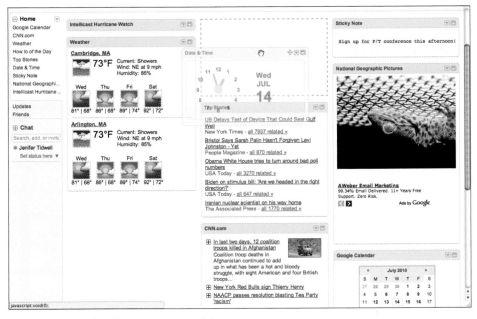

Figure 4-45. *iGoogle, after starting a panel drag*

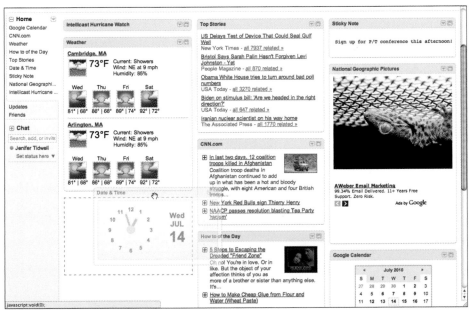

Figure 4-46. *iGoogle, about to finish a panel drag*

Desktop applications might use Movable Panels in a couple of ways: to show all the major tool windows in a complex application such as MATLAB, or to arrange small palette windows around a document, as Photoshop and other Canvas Plus Palette applications do. MATLAB (Figure 4-47) tiles the panels within one window, much like My Yahoo! and iGoogle—but each panel can be set to a custom size. Photoshop (Figure 4-48) puts the palette windows out on the desktop, where a user can freely move them, resize them, and stack them in Module Tabs.

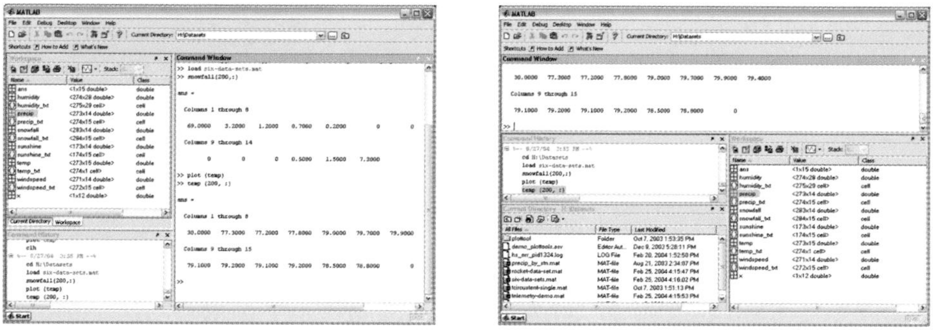

Figure 4-47. *MATLAB desktop*

Figure 4-48. *Photoshop desktop*

In other libraries

http://quince.infragistics.com/Patterns/Movable%20Panels.aspx

http://www.welie.com/patterns/showPattern.php?patternID=customization-window

http://patternry.com/p=drag-and-drop-modules/

http://developer.yahoo.com/ypatterns/richinteraction/dragdrop/modules.html

In developer-oriented references, the term *portlet* is commonly used to describe the actual components that go into Movable Panels and thus compose a portal page.

Right/Left Alignment

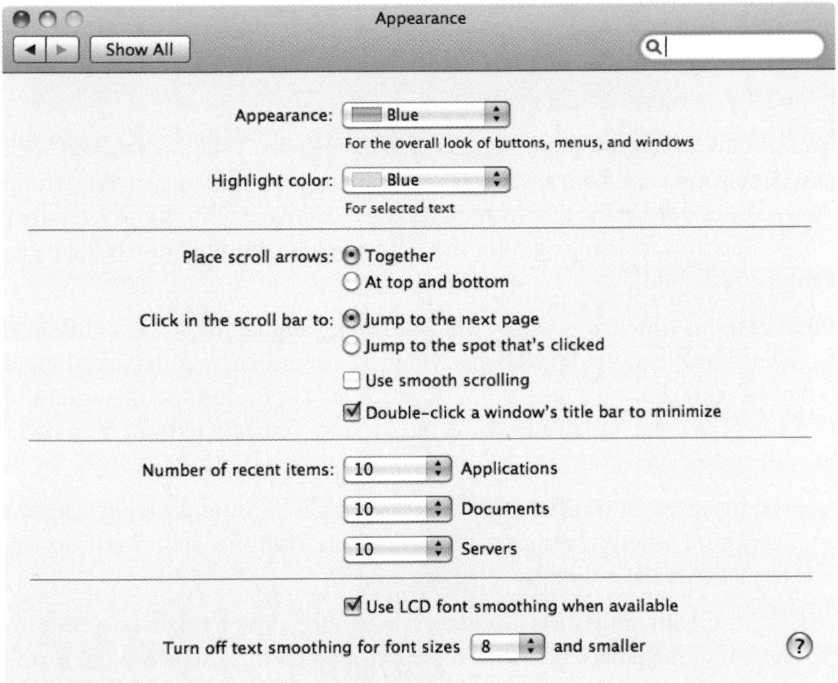

Figure 4-49. *Mac OS system preferences*

What

When designing a two-column form or table, right-align the labels on the left and left-align the items on the right.

You're laying out a form or any other set of items that have text labels in front of them. This could also apply to the internal structure of tables, or any other two-column structure in which the rows should be read left to right.

The labels come in many lengths—some are short, some long, some line-wrapped. Left-aligning the labels would put some of them too far away from their associated fields, leaving a gap too large for users' eyes to span easily.

When you put text right next to the thing it labels, you form a strong perceptual grouping of that pair—much more so than if they were separated by a large amount of space. If you align variable-length labels along their left sides, the short labels won't be close enough to their controls, and the side-to-side grouping is broken. (This is the Gestalt principle of *proximity* at work.) In short, people will more easily connect each label to its associated control when the UI uses right/left alignment.

Meanwhile, you should always left-align the controls themselves. When combined with the right-aligned labels and a uniform spacing between them, they help form a nice strong double edge down the middle of the whole thing (taking advantage of *continuity*, another Gestalt principle). This powerful edge guides the viewer's eyes smoothly down the page, supporting a good visual flow.

There are several cases in which you would not want right-aligned labels. For instance, there is good evidence that reading right-aligned labels is harder than reading left-aligned labels (which makes sense, because the eye has to work harder to find the beginning of the line). If your labels are long and need to be carefully read, consider left-aligning them instead.

If the labels will be localized into different languages, they'll become different lengths. Layout becomes awkward when labels sit to the left of the controls—put them on top instead. (This is harder to read, and makes the page longer.)

In some layouts, right-aligning the labels just doesn't look good. There might be a column of items just to the left of the labels, or perhaps the left-aligned titles separate the form's sections—all of these, and more, can ruin a right/left alignment. Go with what works.

Instead of left-aligning each text label, right-align it. Bring it right up close to its control, separated by only a few pixels. The net effect will probably be a ragged (unaligned) left edge—that's usually OK. If some labels are too long to make this work, try breaking them into multiple lines, or resort to putting the labels above the control, in which case this pattern becomes irrelevant.

Then left-align the controls against an imaginary line a few pixels away from the right edges of the labels. Make them precisely aligned, pixel-perfect—if they're not, the controls will look messy. (The human visual system is really good at picking out slight misalignments!)

Again, the other edge of the control column may be ragged. That's not so good if you're dealing with text fields, combo boxes, and other visually "heavy" objects, as in Figure 4-49. Try to stretch them so that their right edges are aligned too, to whatever extent you can. You can try to align the short ones with one another, and the long ones with one another.

Examples

Right/Left Alignment also works with layouts that have no input controls at all. The Mac OS address book entry shown in Figure 4-50 has very little whitespace between the two columns, but the difference in color helps to separate them visually. Notice that the label "home page" is much longer than the others; this would have made a lefthand label alignment less pleasing to the eye and harder to read.

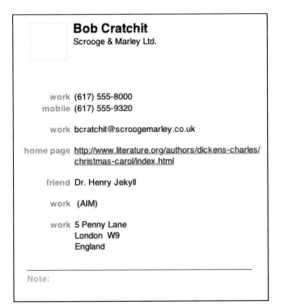

Figure 4-50. *Mac OS address book entry*

In other libraries

http://quince.infragistics.com/Patterns/Right%20Aligned%20Labels.aspx

http://www.uxmatters.com/mt/archives/2006/07/label-placement-in-forms.php

Diagonal Balance

Figure 4-51. *Windows 7 control panel*

What

Arrange page elements in an asymmetric fashion, but balance it by putting visual weight into both the upper-left and lower-right corners.

Use when

You're laying out a page or dialog box that has a title or header at the top, and some links or action buttons—such as OK and Cancel, or Submit, or Back and Next—at the bottom. The page is short enough to fit on the screen without scrolling.

Why

Visually prominent features such as titles, tabs, and buttons should contribute to a balanced composition on the screen. They're already at opposite ends of the page; when you put them on opposite sides, too, they often balance one another out. (Think of them as weights—the bigger or more "contrasty" the features are, the heavier they are; the closer to the edge they get, the more you need to put on the other side to compensate.)

Besides being nicer to look at, a diagonal balance also sets up the page so that the user's eye moves easily from the top left to the bottom right—an ideal visual flow for users who speak left-to-right languages. (See the chapter introduction for a discussion of visual flow.) The rest of the page should support this visual flow, too. The eye finally comes to rest on elements representing actions that the user might do next, such as close this UI or go somewhere else.

How

Place the title, tabs, or some other strong element at the upper left of the page; place the button(s) at the lower right. Content of any width goes in between. If the content itself contributes to the balance of the page, so much the better—don't put too much whitespace on only one side, for instance.

Consider what the dialog box in Figure 4-51 would look like if you placed the OK and Cancel buttons to the left edge instead of the right edge. The whole dialog would feel left-weighted and precarious.

In Windows, the placement of the title in the upper left and the conventional placement of buttons in the lower right do this for you automatically. In Mac OS, elements such as title bars, tabs, and action buttons are centered, so Diagonal Balance is much less common there.

Kevin Mullet and Darrell Sano's classic pre-Web book *Designing Visual Interfaces* (Sun Microsystems) describes the ideas of diagonal balance:

> *Symmetrical layouts provide…visual equilibrium automatically. Asymmetrical layouts can achieve equilibrium as well, but their tenser, more dramatic form of balance, depends on careful manipulation to compensate visually for differences in the size, position, and value of major elements.*

The following are examples of how you can achieve this balance.

Examples

The simple screen shown in Figure 4-52 directs the viewer's attention to the lower right, where the call to action sits.

Figure 4-52. *Starbucks WiFi screen*

The focal points in the site shown in Figure 4-53 are the logo, the moving car, the "Let's Motor" tag line, and the dealer-locator text field at bottom right—all in a diagonal line (approximately). The motion of the photograph pushes the eye down and right even more forcefully than the other examples. Undoubtedly, the designers of the site wanted to encourage people to use the text field. If it were at the bottom left instead, the page would lose much of its punch, and the text field might get lost in the page.

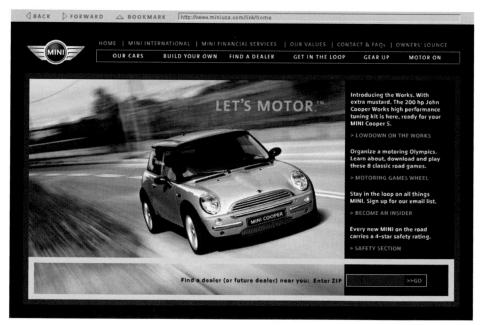

Figure 4-53. *Mini Cooper website from 2005*

Responsive Disclosure

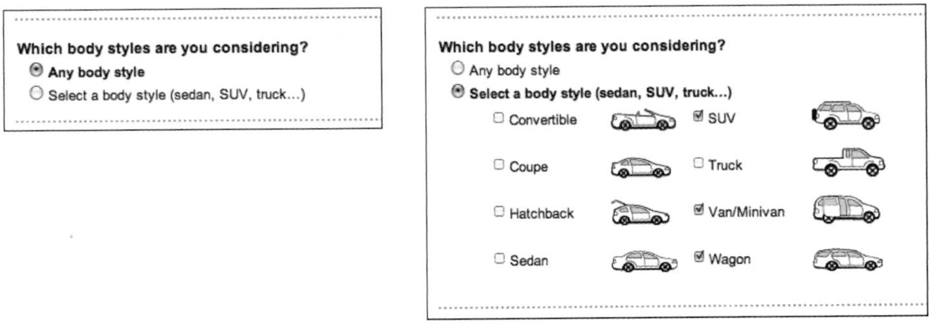

Figure 4-54. *AutoTrader*

What

Starting with a very minimal UI, guide a user through a series of steps by showing more of the UI as he completes each step.

Use when

The user should be walked through a complex task step by step, perhaps because the task is novel, rarely done, or outside the user's domain knowledge. But you don't want to force the user to go page by page at each step—you'd rather keep the whole interface on one single page.

Alternatively, the task may be branched, with different types of information required "downstream" depending on a user's earlier choices.

Why

In this pattern, the interface actually appears to be "created" in front of the user, one step at a time. At first, the user sees only those elements that are necessary for the first step. When the user takes that step, the next set of elements is displayed in addition to the first ones, then the next, and so on.

As the user sees the task unfolding directly in front of him via a dynamically growing UI, he can form a correct mental model of the task more quickly and easily. None of the awkward context switches that separate wizard screens impose exist here: when a user is yanked out of his workflow into a rigid set of modal screens shown one at a time, it feels like more of an imposition than if the UI had stayed within the user's working context.

Furthermore, since the UI is kept together on one page, the user can easily go back and change his mind about earlier choices. As each step is redone, he immediately sees the effect on subsequent steps. This is better than jumping from one content-starved wizard screen to another.

For occasional tasks, Responsive Disclosure can work better than presenting a complex and interlinked set of controls all at once, because it's always obvious what the first step is—and the next, and the next. The user never has to think too hard.

How should you choose between this pattern and Responsive Enabling? If you use Responsive Enabling, you will have to put all the controls for all choices on the UI—you'll just disable the irrelevant ones until they become relevant (again, in response to the user's choices). Sometimes that can make the UI too cluttered or complicated-looking. It's a judgment call: if you need to fit the UI into a very small space, or if you think too many controls on the UI might look bad or make users nervous, use Responsive Disclosure instead.

How

Start by showing the controls and text for only the first step. When the user completes that step, show the controls for the next step, and so on. Leave the previous steps' controls visible to let the user go backward if necessary. Keep it all on one page or dialog box so that the user isn't abruptly pushed into a separate "UI space."

In many such step-by-step designs, the choices the user makes at one step alter the rest of the task (i.e., the task is branched, not linear). For instance, an online order form asks whether the billing address is the same as the shipping address. If the user says yes, the UI doesn't even bother showing entry fields for it. Otherwise, there's one more step in the process, and the UI shows the second set of entry fields when appropriate.

The concept of responsive disclosure isn't new. It was used in 1981 in the first commercial WIMP interface, the Xerox Star. Its designers considered "progressive disclosure," a more general concept that includes responsive disclosure, to be a major design principle: "Progressive disclosure dictates that detail be hidden from users until they ask or need to see it. Thus, Star not only provides default settings, it hides settings that users are unlikely to change until users indicate that they want to change them."[*] Indeed.

In the Star's property sheets, for instance, blank space was reserved for controls that would appear as needed, in response to user choices. When a user chose from a set of values including the word *Other*, for instance, an extra text field would appear for the user to enter a number.

---

[*] Johnson, J.A., et al. 1989. "The Xerox 'Star': A Retrospective." *IEEE Computer* 22(9), 11–29. See also *http://www.digibarn.com/friends/curbow/star/retrospect/*.

The Kayak example in Figure 4-55 hides the calendar and comparison box until the user has filled out enough of the form. Once they appear, the user will shift attention to them.

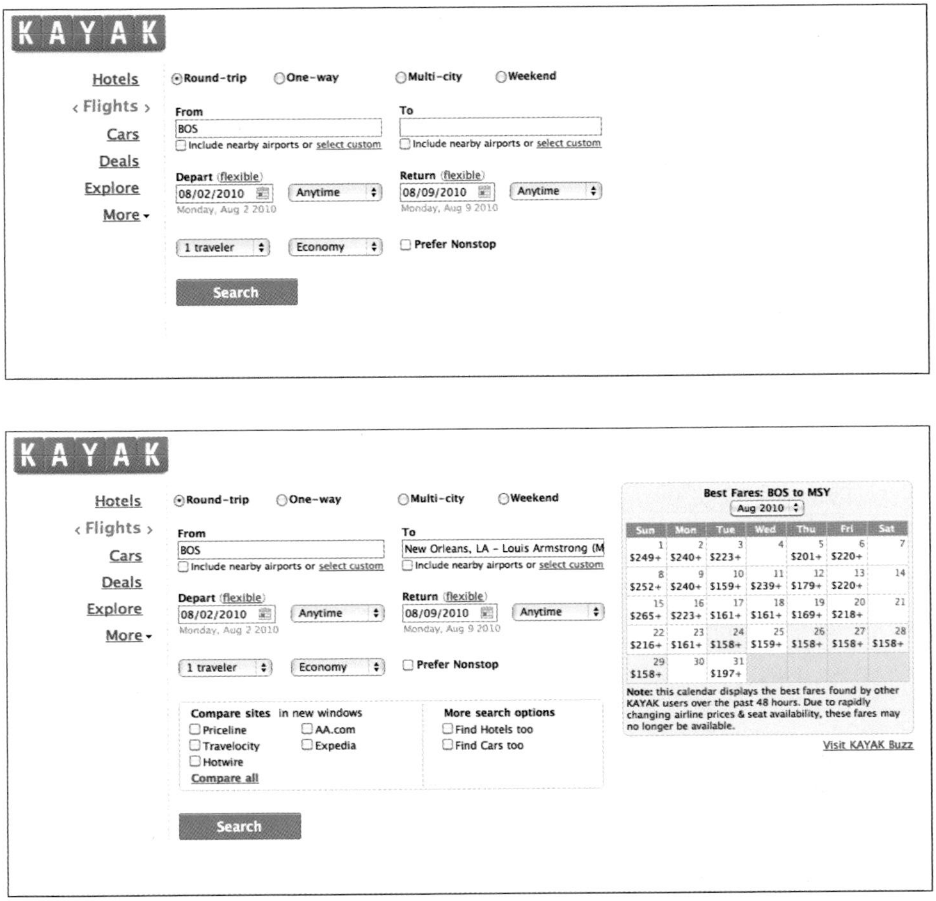

Figure 4-55. *Kayak*

Another way to use Responsive Disclosure is to swap out a piece of a UI depending on the selection made in a drop-down or other limited-choice control. The examples in Figure 4-56, from Google Docs, do this: when the user changes the "Question Type" selection, the follow-on questions change accordingly. (So does the AutoTrader example, at the top of the pattern in Figure 4-54.)

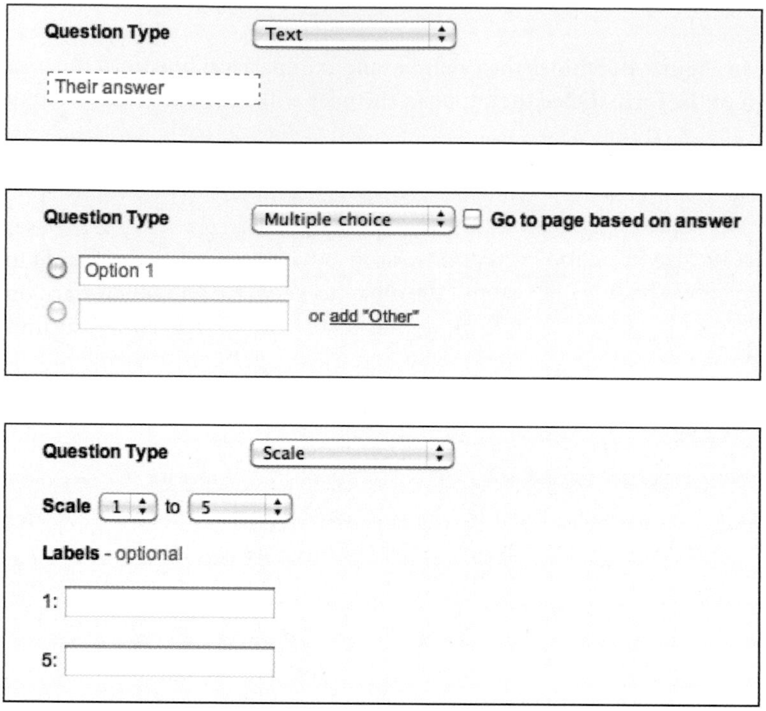

Figure 4-56. *Google Docs form field creation*

In other libraries

http://patternry.com/p=inline-input-adder/

http://quince.infragistics.com/Patterns/Responsive%20Disclosure.aspx

Responsive Enabling

Figure 4-57. *TurboTax*

What

Starting with a UI that is mostly disabled, guide a user through a series of steps by enabling more of the UI as each step is done.

Use when

The user should be walked through a complex task step by step, perhaps because the user is computer-naive or because the task is rarely done (as in a Wizard). But you don't want to force the user to go page by page at each step—you'd like to keep the whole interface on one page. Furthermore, you want to keep the interface stable; you'd rather not dynamically reconfigure the page at each step, as you would with Responsive Disclosure.

Why

Like Responsive Disclosure, this pattern takes advantage of the malleability of computer displays to interactively guide the user through the interface. The user thus gets a chance to form a correct mental model about cause and effect. The UI itself tells her the consequences of some choices: if I turn this checkbox on, I have to fill in these four text fields that just got enabled.

Furthermore, the user can't do things that would get her into trouble, since the UI has "locked out" those actions by disabling them. Unnecessary error messages are thus avoided.

How

In some applications, most actions on the UI start off disabled—only the actions relevant to the user's first step are available. As the user makes choices and performs actions, more disabled items should be enabled and brought into play. In this respect, it's remarkably like Responsive Disclosure, in that the machine specifies a particular sequence through the interface.

A similar, less sequence-based technique is much more common in desktop UIs. As the user does things on the interface, certain actions or settings become irrelevant or impossible, and those actions get disabled until the user does whatever is necessary to reenable them. Overall sequence isn't as important.

Whenever possible, put the disabled items in close proximity to whatever enables them. That helps users find the magic enabling operation and understand the relationship between it and the disabled items. The examples in Figures 4-57 and 4-58 place that text field (or checkbox, respectively) at the top or left of the disabled items, which follows the natural top-to-bottom and left-to-right "flow" of the interface.

When you design an interface that uses Responsive Enabling or Responsive Disclosure, be sure to disable only things that really can't or shouldn't be used. Be wary of overconstraining the user's experience in an attempt to make the interface friendlier or easier to understand. When you decide what to disable, carefully consider each item. Is it being disabled for a really good reason? Can that functionality be enabled all the time? As usual, usability testing gives users a chance to tell you that you've done it wrong.

Another usability problem to avoid is what Bruce Tognazzini once called the "Mysteriously Dimmed Menu Items"—when the design offers no clue as to why a given item is disabled. Again, minimize the set of things that *have* to be disabled, especially when they're far away from whatever operation turns them on. Also, somewhere in the interface or its help system, tell the user what causes a feature to be unavailable. Again, this whole problem can be avoided more easily when the disabled controls aren't menus on a menu bar, but instead sit out on the main UI, collocated with whatever switches them on. Spatial proximity is an important clue.

Examples

The Mac OS System Preferences, shown in Figure 4-58, provide a typical example of disabling based on a binary choice: should the desktop show the date and time on the menu bar, or not? If the user chooses to show it, she gets a panoply of choices about how it ought to be shown. If not, the choices are irrelevant, so they're disabled. This behavior (plus the indenting of the options under the checkbox) tells the user that these choices affect the date/time display which the checkbox toggled—and nothing else.

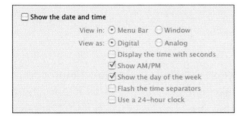 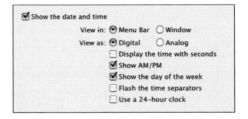

Figure 4-58. *Mac OS system preferences*

You can also reverse the sense of this pattern and do "responsive disabling." The navigation system used in Toyota's Prius and Lexus cars employs this technique when a user enters a destination address (see Figure 4-59). Knowing what streets exist in a given search area, the system narrows down the possible street names with each successive letter entered by the user. It then disables the letters that can't possibly follow the currently typed string; the user has fewer buttons to think about, plus some assurance that the system "knows" what she's trying to type. Address entry is thus made easier and more pleasant. (When only a few streets match, the system takes away the keyboard altogether and shows the streets as a list of choices—see the Autocompletion pattern in Chapter 8.)

Figure 4-59. *Lexus hybrid navigation system*

In other libraries

http://quince.infragistics.com/Patterns/Responsive%20Enabling.aspx

Liquid Layout

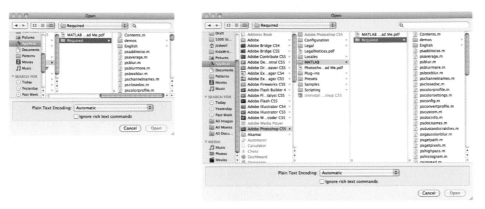

Figure 4-60. *Mac OS open dialog*

What

As the user resizes the window, resize the page contents along with it so that the page is constantly "filled."

Use when

The user might want more space—or less—in which to show the content of a window, dialog box, or page. This is likely to happen whenever a page contains a lot of text (as in a web page), a high-information control such as a table or tree, or a graphic editor. This pattern doesn't work as well when the visual design requires a certain amount of screen real estate, neither more nor less.

Why

Unless you're designing a "closed" UI such as a kiosk or a full-screen video game, you can't predict the conditions under which users will view your UI. Screen size, font preferences, other windows on the screen, or the importance of any particular page to the user—none of this is under your control. How, then, can you decide the one optimal page size for all users?

Giving the user a little control over the layout of the page makes your UI more flexible under changing conditions. It may also make the user feel less antagonistic toward the UI, since he can bend it to fit his immediate needs and contexts.

If you need more convincing, consider what happens to a fixed-layout "nonliquid" UI when the language or font size changes. Do columns still line up? Do pages suddenly become too wide or even clipped at the margins? If not, great; you have a simple and therefore robust design. But pages engineered to work nicely with window size changes generally also accommodate language or font size changes.

How

Make the page contents continuously "fill" the window as it changes size. Multiline text should wrap at the right margin until it becomes 10 to 12 words wide (more on that later). Text, trees, tables, graphs, and editors at "center stage" should enlarge generously while their margins stay compact. If the page has anything form-like on it, horizontal stretching should cause text fields to elongate—users will appreciate this if they need to type in anything longer than the text field's normal length. Likewise, anything scrolled (such as lists or tables) should lengthen, and possibly widen, too.

Web pages and similar UIs should allow the body content to fill the new space, while keeping navigational devices and signposts anchored to the top and left margins. Background colors and patterns should always fill the new space, even if the content itself cannot.

What happens when the window gets too small for its content? You could put scrollbars around it. Otherwise, whitespace should shrink as necessary; outright clipping may occur when the window gets really tiny, but the most important content should hang in there to the end.

If the interface shows paragraphs of text, remember that they become nearly illegible when they're too wide. Graphic designers target an optimal line length for easy reading of text; one metric is 10 to 12 average English words per line. Another metric is 30 to 35 em widths—that is, the width of your font's lowercase *m*. When your text gets much wider than that, users' eyes have to travel too far from the end of one line to the beginning of the next one; if it gets narrower, it's too choppy to read easily.

(That being said, there is evidence that text with a longer line length, such as 100 characters per line, is faster to read than shorter lines, even though users prefer to read lines fewer than 55 characters long.[*])

Examples

Mac OS allows you to resize the standard Open dialog box, which uses a Liquid Layout. This is good because the user can see as much of the filesystem hierarchy as he wants, rather than being constrained to a tiny predetermined space. See Figure 4-60 at the top of the pattern.

---

[*] "Use Reading Performance or User Preference," from *http://usability.gov/guidelines/*.

When a Liquid Layout is used on text in a browser, the floated elements should handle the resize gracefully, as in the Drupal.org example shown in Figure 4-61. Note also that the text in this article never gets so wide as to be unreadable, even when the window itself is very wide.

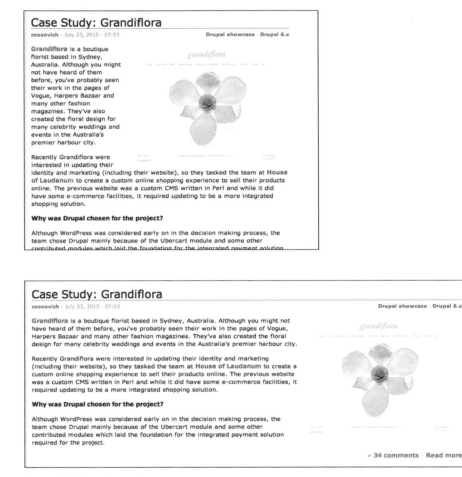

Figure 4-61. *From Drupal.org*

Google Docs allows the user to shrink the window to a very narrow size (see Figure 4-62). Though it places long toolbars across the top of the document, those toolbars wrap around and collapse gracefully as the window shrinks. (The user can't resize it to be smaller than the smallest size shown here.)

Figure 4-62. *Google Docs slideshow editor*

In other libraries

http://www.welie.com/patterns/showPattern.php?patternID=liquid-layout

http://quince.infragistics.com/Patterns/Liquid%20Layout.aspx

http://www.designofsites.com/designing-effective-page-layouts/expanding-screen-width

Chapter 5

Lists of Things

This chapter covers only one topic: how to display lists of items in an interactive setting. Just items. Actual data—complex and highly structured data sets—isn't covered until Chapter 7.

Why do lists merit their own chapter, you may ask?

Consider the many types of items that get shown in lists: articles, pages, photos, videos, maps, books, games, movies, TV shows, songs, products, email messages, blog entries, status updates, forum posts, comments, search results, people, events, files, documents, apps, links, URLs, tools, modes, actions. (Add your own!)

Practically every moderately complex interface or website ever designed includes lists. This chapter will help you think about them logically and clearly, understand different design aspects, and make good trade-offs when designing interfaces that use lists.

Since so many other interface design topics overlap with this one, this chapter will often refer to other chapters and patterns. Menus are handled in Chapter 6, complicated data in Chapter 7, and links and other navigational mechanisms in Chapter 3. Mobile platforms have very specific design constraints, so Chapter 10 will be referred to as well. But there's still a lot left over.

Use Cases for Lists

Before jumping into a design, it's useful to analyze the use cases for a list. What will people need to do with it? Which of these scenarios apply?

Getting an overview

> What impression will someone get from the list as a whole? In some cases, a user should be able to skim down the list and understand what it's about. Sometimes that requires more than just words; it may require images or careful visual organization to convey that impression.

Browsing item by item

> Will the user peruse items, either randomly or in order? Does he need to click on items to open them? If so, it should be easy to go back to the list and find another item, or move directly to the next one.

Searching for a specific item

> Is the user looking for something in particular? He should be able to find it quickly, with a minimum of clicks, scrolling, and back-and-forth.

Sorting and filtering

> If someone is looking for an item or group of items with a specific characteristic (e.g., "anything with a date between X and Y") or is looking for general insight into a set of data, sorting and filtering functions might help. This is addressed in more detail in Chapter 7.

Rearranging, adding, deleting, or recategorizing items

> Consider a Picture Manager containing the user's photos: the user owns the list and the items within it. Most apps and sites that show personal collections permit direct manipulation of those lists so that the user can drag items around into a desired order or grouping scheme. He should also be able to select multiple items at a time for moving, editing, or deleting; a design should either use the platform standards for multiple selection (e.g., Shift-select), or supply checkboxes beside each item to permit the user to select an arbitrary subset.

Back to Information Architecture

We discussed information architecture—the design of information, independent of its visual representation—in Chapter 2. Let's return to it for a minute. If you have a list of things to show in a page, what are the salient nonvisual characteristics of that list?

Length

- How long is the list? Can it fit in the space you've designed for it?

- Could the list sometimes be "bottomless"? For example, web search results often constitute such a long list that the user will never reach the end; likewise for items taken from a very large and deep archive.

Order

- Does the list have a natural order, such as alphabetical or by time?

- Would it make sense for a user to change the sorting order of the list? If so, what would the user sort on?

- If you choose to put a list into an order, would it actually make more sense as a grouping scheme, or vice versa? As an example, think about a blog archive: the articles are naturally ordered by time, and most blogs categorize them by month and year, rather than offering a flat ordered list. Someone looking for a particular article might remember that "it was before article X but after article Y," but not remember exactly which month it was published. A monthly grouping thus makes it hard to find that article; a time-ordered flat list of titles might work better.

Grouping

- Do the items come in categories? Is it a natural categorization that users will immediately understand? If not, how can you explain it, either verbally or visually?

- Do these categories come in larger categories? More broadly, do the items fit into a multi-level hierarchy, such as files in a filesystem?

- Are there several potential categorizations? Would they fit different use cases or user personas? And can users create their own categories for their own purposes?

Item types

- What are the items like? Are they simple, or are they rich and complex? Are they just stand-ins for larger things, such as headlines for articles or thumbnails for video clips?

- Are the items in a list very different from each other (e.g., some are simple and some are complex)? Or are they homogeneous?

- Does each item have an image or picture associated with it?

- Does each item have a strict field-like structure? Would it help the user to know that structure, or possibly even sort the list based on different fields? (Email messages typically have a strict and sortable structure—timestamp, from field, subject, and so on—and this structure typically is shown in lists of messages.)

Interaction

- Should you show the whole item at once in the list, or can you just show a representation of the item (such as its name or the first few sentences) and hide the rest?

- What is the user supposed to do with those items? Should they be looked at? Should they be selected for inspection, or for performing tasks on them? Or are they links or buttons to be clicked on?

- Does it make sense for the user to select multiple items at a time?

Dynamic behavior

- How long does it take to load the whole list? Can it be more or less immediate, or will there be a noticeable delay as the list is put together somewhere and finally shown to the user?

- Will the list change on the fly? Should you show the updates as they happen? Does this mean inserting new items at the top of the list automatically?

The answers to these questions may suggest a variety of design solutions to you. Of course, a solution should also take into account the type of content (blogs should look different from, say, contact lists), the surrounding page layout, and implementation constraints.

Some Solutions

The interaction questions listed in the preceding section set the tone for almost all the other decisions. For instance, a fully interactive list—multiple selection, drag-and-drop, editing items, and so on—tends to dominate the interface. You may be building a Picture Manager, an email client, or some other full-fledged application that people use to manage and enjoy content that they own.

In this and other types of interfaces, a common requirement is to show only item names or thumbnails in a list—just a representation of each item—and then display the whole item when the user selects one from the list. There are at least three ways to do this.

"When the user selects an item from a list, where should I show the details of that item?"

- Two-Panel Selector shows the item details right next to the list. It supports the overview and browsing use cases quite well because everything's visible at once; the surrounding page stays the same, so there's no awkward context switch or page reload.

- List Inlay shows the item details embedded in the list itself. The details only open up when the user requests them with a click or tap. This pattern supports the overview and browsing use cases, too—though an overview is harder if lots of items are open—and searching on item contents can be done smoothly by automatically opening matched items.

- One-Window Drilldown replaces the list's space with the item details. This is often used for small spaces that cannot accommodate a Two-Panel Selector, such as mobile screens or small module panels. It does lead to "pogo sticking" between the list screen and the item screen, though, so browsing and searching are not so easy.

Now let's shift our attention to the items themselves. How much detail should you show with each item, assuming the user will click through to see the whole thing? Again, you have three main use cases to serve: get a quick overview, browse the list, and find items of interest. For really focused tasks, such as finding a person's phone number in a long contact list, all that's needed is the item name. But for a broader, more browsing-oriented experience—news articles on a web page, for instance—more information makes an item more interesting (up to a point, anyway). And if you have visuals associated with each item, show thumbnails!

"How can I show a list with heavy visuals?"

- Use fat rows. Instead of just one line per item, give each item row several lines' worth of text. Enhance it with a small graphic or image thumbnail, if available, and use rich text formatting to express a miniature visual hierarchy within each row. See the Grid of Equals pattern in Chapter 4 for the basis of this pattern.

- Thumbnail-and-Text List, in Chapter 10, is a specialization of fat rows for a mobile device.

- Thumbnail Grid is a common pattern for pictorial objects. A 2D grid of small pictures is visually powerful; it dominates the page and draws attention. Text data is often shown with the thumbnails, but it tends to be small and less important than the pictures. Again, see the Grid of Equals pattern for a generalization.

- Carousel is an alternative to Thumbnail Grid that can use less space on the page. It is strictly linear, not 2D, and the user must actively scroll through it to see more than a few objects. Depending on its design, a Carousel implementation might actually give you more space to show the selected or center object than a Thumbnail Grid.

Highly structured, homogeneous sets of items work well in a table layout, with a column for each field of interest to users. Such a table might offer sorting via a Sortable Table, or a "Sort by" drop down for a simpler implementation. Row Striping can help a viewer's eyes travel across a single item's row, from left to right and back again. Tables are lists, but they're also complex data graphics that can be filtered and visualized with sophisticated tools. So for other table-related patterns, I refer you to Chapter 7.

Very long lists can be difficult to design, especially on web pages. Certainly there are technical challenges around loading times and page length, but interaction design might be even harder—how does a user browse and move through such a list? How can he find something specific, especially if a text search doesn't behave as desired? The following techniques and patterns apply to all the previously listed ways to show a list and its items (except maybe a Carousel, which has tighter constraints):

"How can I manage a very long list?"

- Pagination lets you load the list in sections, putting the onus on the user to load those sections as needed. This is, of course, quite common in websites—it's easy to design and implement. Pagination is most useful when the user is likely to find the desired item(s) in the first page, since many people won't bother going to subsequent pages anyway. You could also resort to Pagination when loading the whole list will result in a ridiculously long page or take a ridiculously long time. A good Pagination control shows the user how many pages of items there are, as well as letting a user jump among those pages.

- Infinite List is a single-page alternative to Pagination. The first section of a long list gets loaded, and at the bottom the user finds a button that loads and appends the next section. The user stays on one page. Common in mobile designs, this pattern can be found in Chapter 10. Don't discount it for regular web pages, however! This pattern is useful when you don't actually know how long the list will be, or when it's "bottomless."

- A variant on Infinite List has the list automatically loading itself as the user scrolls down. See the Continuous Scrolling pattern at the following page:

  http://ui-patterns.com/patterns/ContinuousScrolling

- When a very long alphabetized list is kept in a scrolled box, consider using an Alphabet Scroller. Related to Annotated Scrollbar (Chapter 3), this device shows the alphabet arrayed along the scrollbar itself; the user can then jump directly to a desired letter.

- Direct searching via a "Find" field may be critical for helping your users to find specific items. Also, filtering a list—screening out entire classes of items that don't meet certain criteria—can help shorten a list to a manageable size.

So far, this section has talked mostly about flat lists: those that have no categories, containment, or hierarchy. However a list might be rendered, you may still want to break it up into categories for clarity.

"How can I show a list that's organized into categories or hierarchies?"

- Titled Sections (Chapter 4) work well for a single level of containment. Just separate the list into sections with titles, and perhaps allow the user to sort the list within a single section so as not to disrupt the categorization. If you only have a few sections, try an Accordion—this lets the user close list sections that she doesn't need.

- For two or more levels of hierarchy, basic trees are the standby solution. These are normally presented with indented hierarchy levels, and with icons such as pluses and minuses (commonly found on Windows) or rotating triangles. The levels can be closed and opened by the users or automatically by the interface as needed. Many UI toolkits offer tree implementations.

- Cascading Lists take a tree's vertically oriented hierarchy and turn it on its side, with a series of columns that list all the possibilities at every level of the hierarchy. Popularized by Mac OS, this pattern allows very effective browsing and overviews of hierarchies at the cost of large amounts of space. (It does not work in a small window or screen.)

- When the items are heavily structured and you want to present them in a table but they come organized in a hierarchy, consider a Tree Table. Literally, it combines a tree with a table, and it's exactly what it sounds like.

The Patterns

First are the three patterns that place item details next to, inside, or on a different page from the list itself:

1. Two-Panel Selector
2. One-Window Drilldown
3. List Inlay

The next few patterns cover ways to show lists of various sorts—image-based lists (Thumbnail Grid and Carousel), tables (Row Striping), long lists (Pagination, Jump to Item, Alphabet Scroller), and hierarchies (Cascading Lists and Tree Table). If you're using a table or Tree Table, consider making it a Sortable Table (see Chapter 7).

4. Thumbnail Grid
5. Carousel
6. Row Striping
7. Pagination
8. Jump to Item
9. Alphabet Scroller
10. Cascading Lists
11. Tree Table

Finally, New-Item Row lets a user add items to a list however that list may be rendered.

12. New-Item Row

Two-Panel Selector

Figure 5-1. *Mac OS system preferences*

What

Put two side-by-side panels on the interface. In the first one, show a list of items that the user can select at will; in the second one, show the content of the selected item.

Use when

You have a list of items to show. Each item has interesting content associated with it, such as the text of an email message, a long article, a full-sized image, contained items (if the list is a set of categories or folders), or details about a file's size or date.

You want the user to see the overall structure of the list and keep that list in view all the time, but you also want him to be able to browse through the items easily and quickly. People won't need to see the details or content of more than one item at a time.

Physically, the display you're working with is large enough to show two separate panels at once. Very small cell phone displays cannot cope with this pattern, but many larger mobile devices can.

Why

This is a learned convention, but it's an extremely common and powerful one. People quickly learn that they're supposed to select an item in one panel to see its contents in the other. They might learn it from their email clients, or from Windows Explorer, or from websites; whatever the case, they apply the concept to other applications that look similar.

When both panels are visible side by side, users can quickly shift their attention back and forth, looking now at the overall structure of the list ("How many more unread email messages do I have?"), and now at an object's details ("What does this email say?"). This tight integration has several advantages over other physical structures, such as two separate windows or One-Window Drilldown:

- It reduces physical effort. The user's eyes don't have to travel a long distance between the panels, and he can change the selection with a single mouse click or key press rather than first navigating between windows or pages (which can take an extra mouse click).

- It reduces visual cognitive load. When a window pops to the top, or when a page's contents are completely changed (as happens with One-Window Drilldown), the user suddenly has to pay more attention to what he's now looking at; when the window stays mostly stable, as in a Two-Panel Selector, the user can focus on the smaller area that did change. There is no major "context switch" on the page.

- It reduces the user's memory burden. Think about the email example again: when the user is looking at just the text of an email message, there's nothing on-screen to remind him of where that message is in the context of his inbox. If he wants to know, he has to remember, or navigate back to the list. But if the list is already on-screen, he merely has to look, not remember. The list thus serves as a "You are here" signpost (see Chapter 3 for an explanation of signposts).

- It's faster than loading a new page for each item, as can happen with One-Window Drilldown.

How

Place the selectable list on the top or left panel, and the details panel below it or to its right. This takes advantage of the visual flow that most users who read left-to-right languages will expect (so try reversing it for right-to-left language readers).

When the user selects an item, immediately show its contents or details in the second panel. Selection should be done with a single click. But while you're at it, give the user a way to change his selection from the keyboard, particularly with the arrow keys—this helps reduce both the physical effort and the time required for browsing, and contributes to keyboard-only usability (see Keyboard Only in Chapter 1).

Make the selected item visually obvious. Most GUI toolkits have a particular way of showing selection (e.g., reversing the foreground and background of the selected list item). If that doesn't look good, or if you're not using a GUI toolkit with this feature, try to make the selected item a different color and brightness than the unselected ones—that helps it stand out.

What should the selectable list look like? It depends—on the inherent structure of the content, or perhaps on the task to be performed. For instance, most filesystem viewers show the directory hierarchy, since that's how filesystems are structured. Animation and video editing software use interactive timelines. A GUI builder may simply use the layout canvas itself; selected objects on it then show their properties in a property editor next to the canvas.

A Two-Panel Selector has identical semantics to tabs: one area for the selectors, and one area next to it for the content of the selected thing. Likewise, a List Inlay is like an Accordion (Chapter 4), and One-Window Drilldown is like a Menu Page (Chapter 3).

When the select-and-show concept is extended through multiple panels to facilitate navigation through a hierarchical information architecture, you get the Cascading Lists pattern.

Examples

Many email clients use this pattern to show a list of email messages next to the currently selected message (see Figure 5-2). Such listings benefit from being nearly as wide as the whole window, so it makes sense to put the listing on top of the second panel, not to its left. (Also, this example shows the use of a third selector panel on the left that lets the user choose which mailbox to work in.)

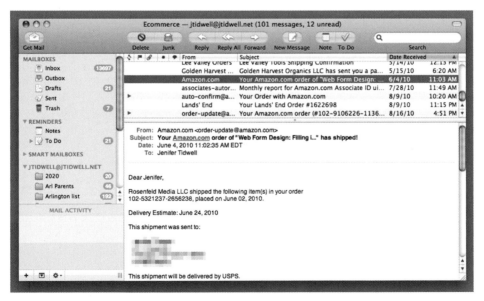

Figure 5-2. *Mac Mail on a desktop*

Like many other Picture Managers, Picasa (Figure 5-3) lists the various image folders and categories in its Two-Panel Selector. The result is a second list, of images. When the user selects an image, the whole window is replaced; see One-Window Drilldown.

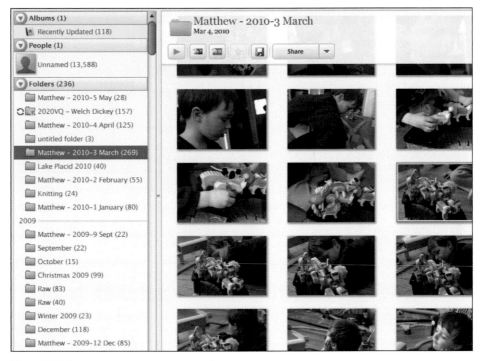

Figure 5-3. *Picasa*

In other libraries

http://quince.infragistics.com/Patterns/Two-Panel%20Selector.aspx

http://www.welie.com/patterns/showPattern.php?patternID=overview-detail

One-Window Drilldown

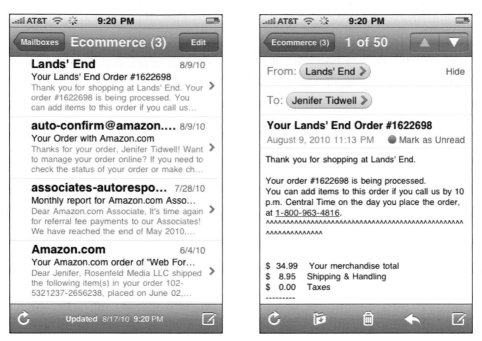

Figure 5-4. *Mac Mail on iPhone*

What

Show a list or menu of items in a single window. When the user selects an item from the list, show the details or contents of that item in the window, replacing the list.

Use when

You have a list of items to show. Each item has interesting content associated with it, such as the text of an email message, a long article, a full-size image, or details about a file's size or date.

You have very little space to work with—not enough for a Two-Panel Selector or a List Inlay. For instance, the design might be intended for a very small mobile screen, or for a self-contained web page sidebar or widget.

Alternatively, the list items and contents might just be large. You might need the entire screen or window to show the list, and again to show the contents of an item. Online forums tend to work this way, requiring the whole width of the page to list conversation topics and a separate scrolled page to show the conversations themselves.

Why

In a very constrained space, this may be the only reasonable option for presenting a list and item details. It gives each view the entire available space to "spread out" on the page.

Like Menu Page in Chapter 3, however, this pattern has the benefit of simplicity. A list of items (or links) is easy to understand: to see more of an item, you click or tap on it and thus "drill down" one level. Then you can come back up to the main list or menu to go to another item.

How

Create the list using whatever layout or format you find best—simple text names, multi-line "fat rows" with text formatting, trees or outlines, and Thumbnail Grids all work fine, as do other formats. Vertically scroll it if necessary to fit it into the available space.

When the user clicks, taps, or otherwise selects one of the list items, replace the list display with a display of the item details or contents. On it, place a Back or Cancel button that brings the user back to the list screen (unless the platform supplies hardware buttons for such).

The item screen may offer additional navigational possibilities, such as drilling down further into the item details, stepping down into an item contained within that item (as in a hierarchy), or going "sideways" to the previous or next item in the list (as discussed in the next paragraph). In each case, replace the previous screen with the new one, and make sure the user can easily step back to the previous screen.

One disadvantage of this pattern is that to go from item to item, the user must "pogo-stick" between the list page and the item page. It takes a lot of clicks or taps to see more than a few items, and the user certainly can't flick between them quickly (as with Two-Panel Selector) or compare them easily (as with List Inlay). You can mitigate this problem by using Back and Next links to connect the user directly to the previous and next items in the list—see the Pyramid pattern in Chapter 3.

Examples

Examples abound in mobile designs, as shown in Figure 5-4. Contrast this mobile version of a mail client with its desktop counterpart shown in the Two-Panel Selector pattern. For instance, the One-Window Drilldown approach requires more text to be shown in the list, so the user has enough context to identify messages and triage them.

You can find One-Window Drilldown in full-size applications and web pages, too. Forums and communities tend to use it a lot—topics are listed on one page, and discussion threads are on their own pages. Ravelry demonstrates this approach, as do about six million other online forums (see Figure 5-5).

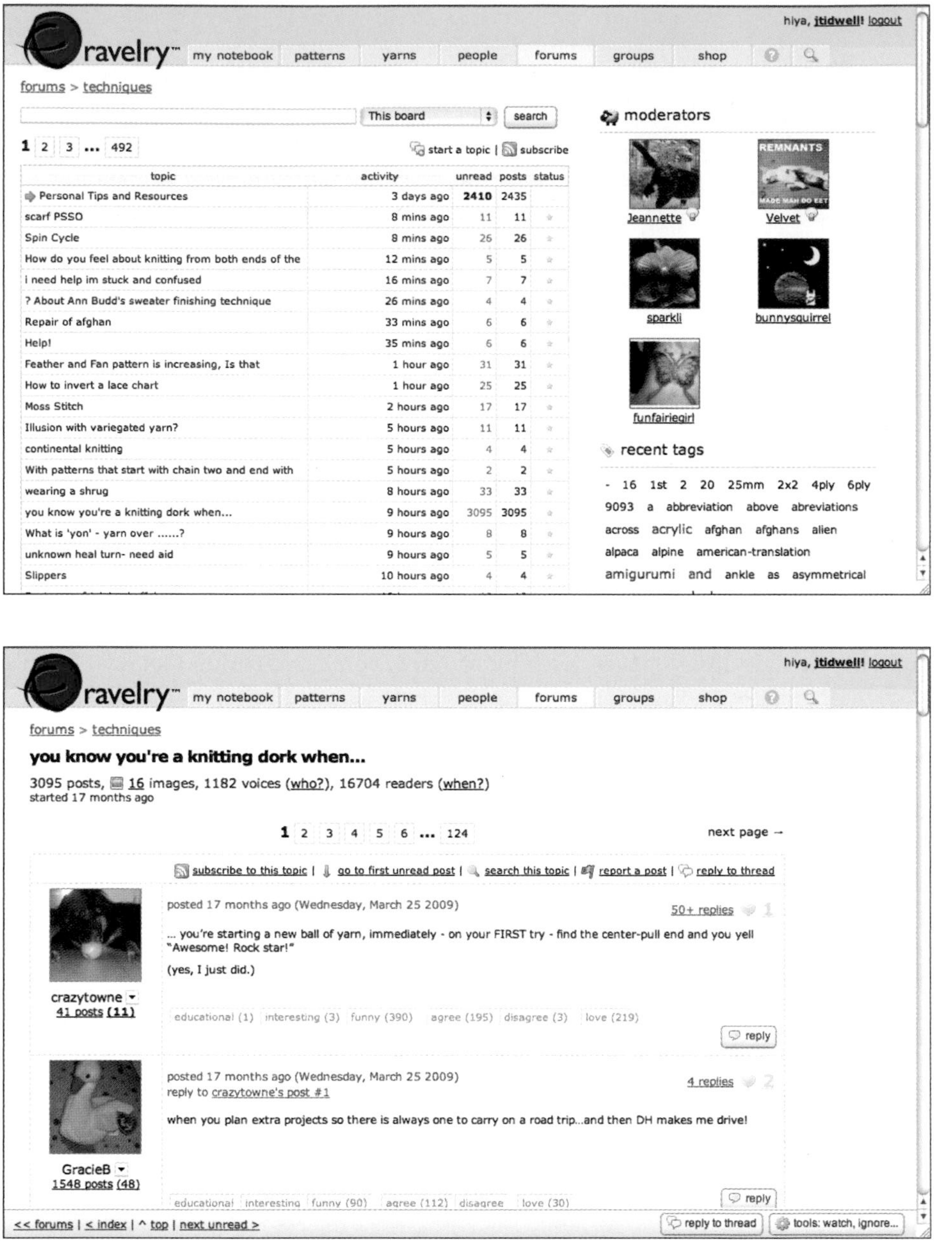

Figure 5-5. *Ravelry forums*

The Picasa desktop application, a Picture Manager, uses a Two-Panel Selector beside a Thumbnail Grid for its browsing interface (see Figure 5-6). But once the user clicks a photo, Picasa replaces the entire contents of the window (except the bottom toolbar) with a new layout—one that shows the photo itself in Center Stage, with a set of tools next to it.

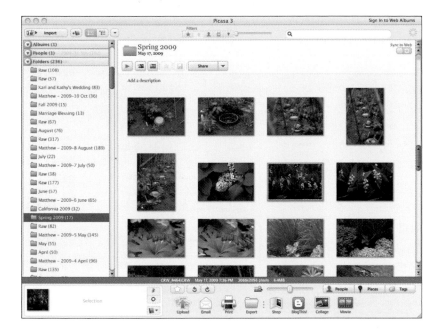

Figure 5-6. *Picasa*

In other libraries

http://quince.infragistics.com/Patterns/One-Window%20Drilldown.aspx

List Inlay

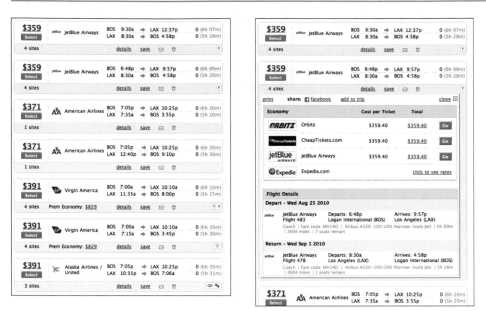

Figure 5-7. *Kayak's expanding list items*

Show a list of items as rows in a column. When the user selects an item, open that item's details in place, within the list itself. Allow items to be opened and closed independently of each other.

You have a list of items to show. Each item has interesting content associated with it, such as the text of an email message, a long article, a full-size image, or details about a file's size or date. The item details don't take up a large amount of space, but they're not so small that you can fit them all in the list itself.

You want the user to see the overall structure of the list and keep that list in view all the time, but you also want her to browse through the items easily and quickly. Users may want to see two or more item contents at a time, for comparison.

The list of items has a vertically oriented, columnar structure.

Why

A List Inlay shows an item's details within the context of the list itself. The user can see the surrounding items, which might help in understanding and using the item contents.

Also, a user can see the details of multiple items at once. This is not possible in Two-Panel Selector, One-Window Drilldown, rollover windows, or most other ways of displaying item details. If your use cases call for frequent comparison of two or more items, this might be the best option.

Because a List Inlay is neatly contained within a vertical column, it can be combined well with a Two-Panel Selector to present a three-level containment hierarchy. Consider an email client or RSS reader, for instance—the messages or articles might be viewed in a List Inlay, while the item containers (mailboxes, groupings, filters, etc.) are shown next to it in a Two-Panel Selector structure.

How

Show list items in a column. When the user clicks on one, open the item in place to show the details of that item. A similar gesture should close the item back up again.

When an item is opened, enlarge the item's space downward, pushing the subsequent items down the page. Other items do the same when opened. A scrolled area should be used to contain this ever-changing vertical structure, since it could get very tall indeed!

To close the details panel, use a control that clearly indicates its purpose (e.g., "Close" or "X"). Some implementations of List Inlay only put that control at the end of the details panel, but users may need it at the top if the panel is long and they don't want to move down the whole thing. Put a closing control very near the original "open" control (or replace one with the other). This at least ensures that the user's pointer won't move very far if she wants to open an item, glance at it, close it, and move on.

Use an Animated Transition as the item opens and closes, to keep the user oriented and to focus attention on the newly opened item.

If your application permits the user to edit items, you could use a List Inlay to open an editor instead of item details (or in addition to them).

A list that uses List Inlays works the same way as an Accordion: everything lies in a single column, with panels opening and closing *in situ* within it. Likewise, a Two-Panel Selector works like a set of tabs, and One-Window Drilldown is like a Menu Page (Chapter 3).

Examples

Google Reader (Figure 5-8) uses a List Inlay within the context of a Two-Panel Selector. It has a multi-level hierarchy of containers to present; the containers are shown in the tree selector on the left, but the list of articles takes up Center Stage and the user can then open them in place to read them.

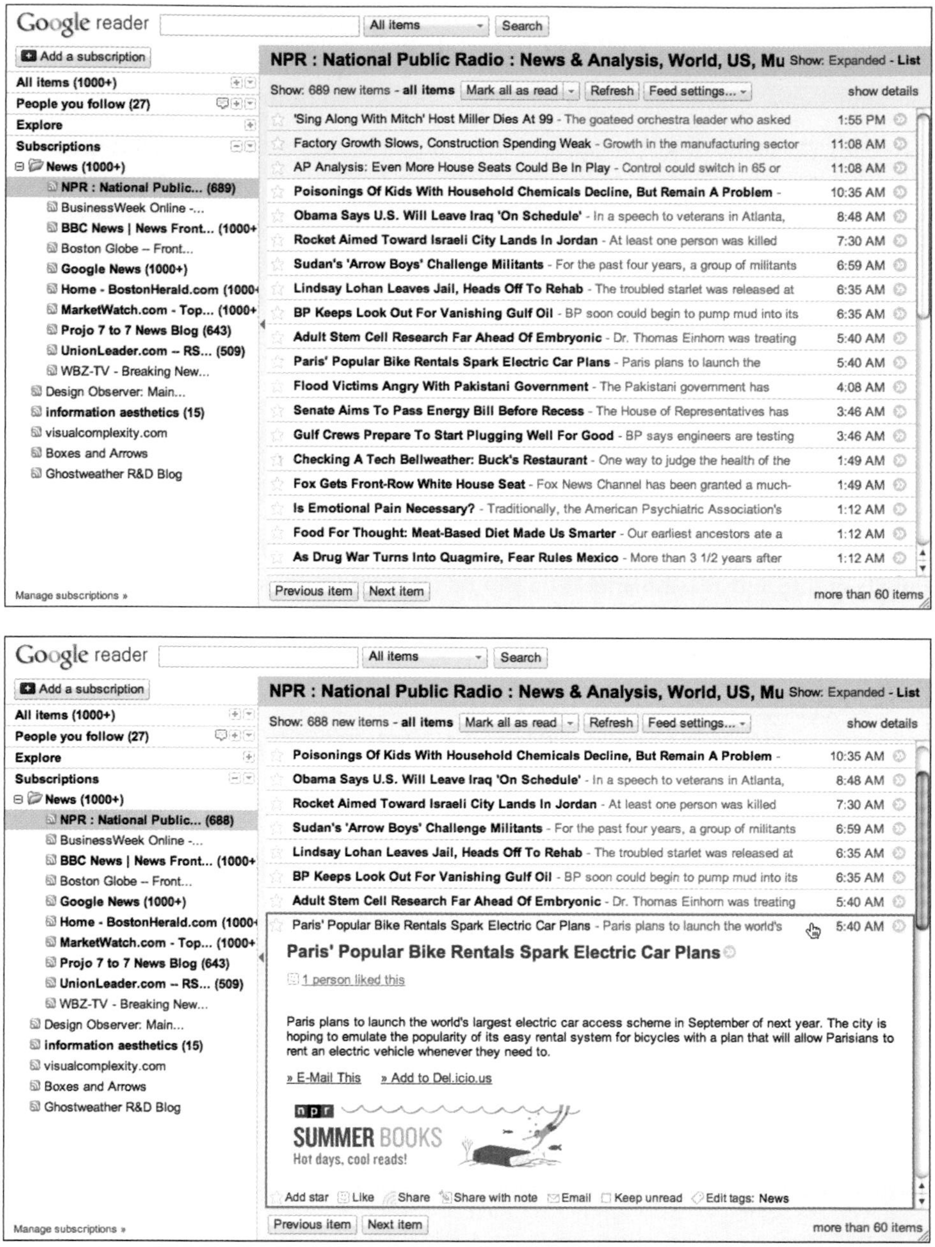

Figure 5-8. *Google Reader*

Rather than forcing the user to pogo-stick back and forth from the list of book reviews to the actual text of each review, Amazon's mobile site lets users read them in a List Inlay. The list of items on the left tempts the user with short teasers from each review, and when a user is interested enough to keep reading, she can tap the title to read the whole thing (Figure 5-9). The existence of plus and minus controls signals to the user that these items expand.

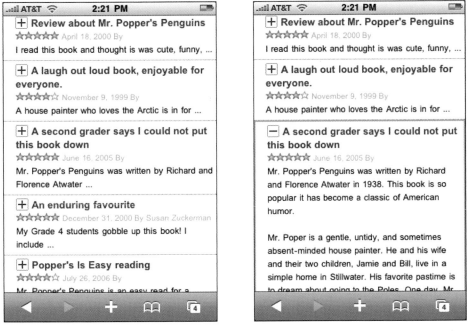

Figure 5-9. *Amazon reviews on the iPhone*

http://www.patternry.com/p=inline-expand/

Bill Scott and Theresa Neil identified this technique in their book, *Designing Web Interfaces* (O'Reilly, *http://oreilly.com/catalog/9780596516253/*). List Inlays are one of a set of inlay techniques that includes Dialog Inlays and Detail Inlays.

The Accordion pattern exists in many pattern libraries, including this one. Much of the design advice proffered for Accordion can apply equally well to List Inlay. (There really isn't a huge practical difference between them.)

Thumbnail Grid

Figure 5-10. *Hanna Andersson product listing*

What

Arrange a list of visually interesting items into a "small multiples" grid of thumbnail images. Let the user select one or more thumbnails to view or manage those items.

Use when

The list items have small visual representations that uniquely identify them: images, logos, screen captures, reduced photos, and so forth. These tend to be similar in size and style. The list may be long, and it may be divided into Titled Sections (Chapter 4).

You want to show a little bit of metadata (information about the item) with each one, such as its name and date, but you don't need to show a lot of that—the picture should take up most of the space devoted to the item.

Users will want an overview of the whole list, and they may need to scan it quickly to find a particular item of interest. Users may also need to select one or more items at a time for moving, deleting, or viewing.

Why

A Thumbnail Grid is a dense, attractive presentation of large numbers of items. Related to Grid of Equals (Chapter 4), this pattern creates a visual hierarchy that shows the list items as peers, and a strong grid tends to draw the eye to that part of the page.

It might be easier to show the list items in text form, but sometimes pictures can be recognized and differentiated more easily than text.

Thumbnails that are roughly square make easy targets for fingertips (on touch screens) and for indirect pointing devices as well. This pattern works well on mobile devices with relatively high-resolution touch screens, such as iPhones.

How

Arrange the item thumbnails into a 2D grid. Scale the thumbnails so that they're approximately the same size, to keep the grid tidy. Place the text metadata close to the thumbnail, but in small print in order to maintain the thumbnail's visual prominence.

Some Thumbnail Grids look much nicer when the thumbnails all have similar width and height. If you're working with graphics that come in different sizes or aspect ratios (the ratio of width to height), or if they're large, some image processing will need to be done to construct thumbnails. Try to find a size and aspect ratio that works reasonably well with all of them, even if some images will be cropped to fit it. (Reducing image size is easy; cropping appropriately is not. Be careful to preserve the image's integrity by choosing the most relevant piece of the image to show, when possible.)

An exception is if you're dealing with images whose size and proportion are useful information to the viewer. For instance, a set of personal photos will contain some that are in a landscape format and some in a portrait (vertical) format. There's no need to crop these to match an idealized thumbnail—the user will want to see which photos are which!

On the other hand, a thumbnail gallery of products (such as shoes or shirts) should all have the same height and width, with the products presented consistently within those photos.

Mac OS Finder displays a variety of thumbnail types for a file directory listing (see Figure 5-11). When a file is an image, a shrunken version of that image is shown; for directories, a simple folder; for files without an available visual, just the file type (e.g., "DOC") over a generic icon. The thumbnail grid is not at all uniform, so it doesn't look as clean as the others in this pattern, but the size and style variations communicate useful information to the user.

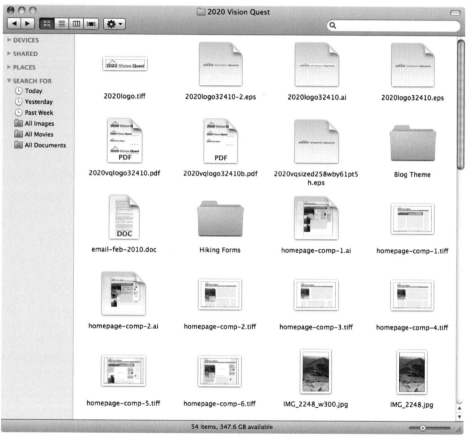

Figure 5-11. *Mac OS Finder*

AIGA's design archives (Figure 5-12) and YouTube (Figure 5-13) are two Picture Managers that show no text information and lots of text information, respectively.

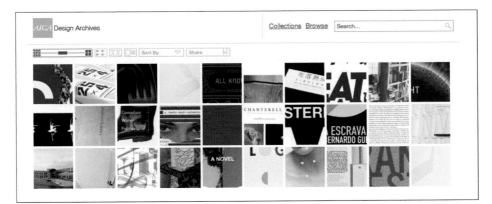

Figure 5-12. *AIGA design archives*

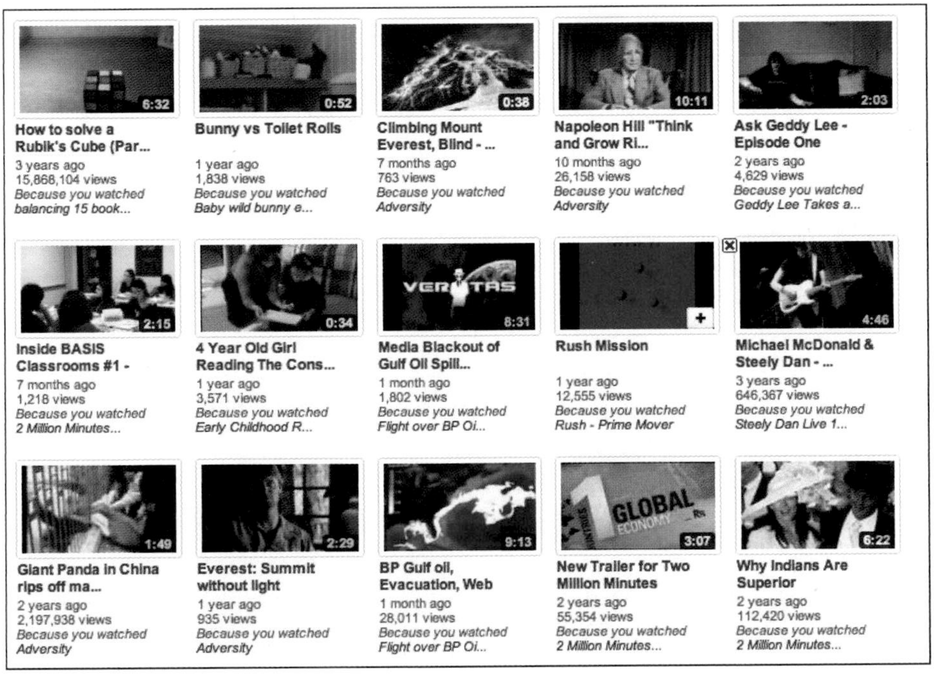

Figure 5-13. *YouTube*

Zappos (Figure 5-14) and Hanna Andersson (Figure 5-10, at the top of the pattern) demonstrate nicely designed Thumbnail Grids for product galleries. Uniformity is beautiful here—the similarities and differences between products show up with stunning clarity, and a strong visual rhythm exists on the page.

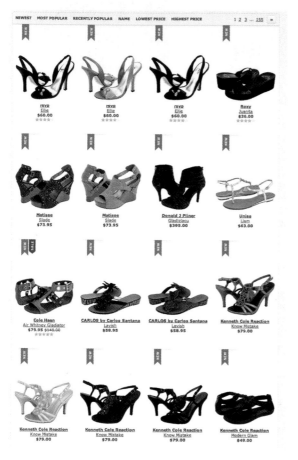

Figure 5-14. *Zappos*

Mobile devices need Thumbnail Grids in many contexts: to show applications, features, and images themselves. Note the relative sizes of the thumbnails in Figure 5-15; the Google Images and iPhone home screen examples are just big enough to be touched easily by human fingertips. The Facebook example is more relaxed, with more space around each item.

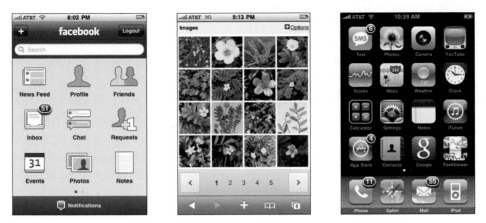

Figure 5-15. *Thumbnail Grids on the iPhone: Facebook, Google Images, and the home screen*

In other libraries

http://ui-patterns.com/patterns/Thumbnail

Carousel

Figure 5-16. *Marriott*

What

Arrange a list of visually interesting items into a horizontal strip or arc, and let the user scroll or swipe the image thumbnails back and forth to view them. Enlarge the center item, if appropriate.

The list items have visual representations that uniquely identify them: images, logos, screen captures, reduced photos, and so forth. These tend to be similar in size and style. The list is *flat* (i.e., not divided into categories or containers).

You want to show a little bit of metadata (information about the item) with each one, such as its name and date, but you don't need to show a lot of that—the picture should take up most of the space devoted to the item.

Each item is potentially of interest. Users will browse the items casually; they won't normally search for a specific item, or need to get an overall look at the entire list at once. If someone does look for a specific item, he won't mind moving past many items before finding the one he's looking for. You may be able to order the items with the most interesting ones first, or in chronological order.

You don't have enough vertical space for a Thumbnail Grid, and you may not have a lot of horizontal space either, but you need to make this list look interesting and attractive.

A Carousel offers an engaging interface for browsing visual items, encouraging the user to inspect the items that are in view and to see what's next. A user can't easily jump to a certain point deep in the list, so he has to scroll through everything—this pattern thus encourages browsing and serendipity.

Carousels are compact vertically, so they may be a better solution than a Thumbnail Grid for a small space. Horizontally, they can be either compact or spread out.

If a particular implementation focuses attention on a central item or selection, such as by enlarging it, this pattern delivers "focus plus context"—users get a detailed view of one item, while also seeing the ones immediately around it. See Chapter 7 for more discussion of this principle.

First, create thumbnails for each item shown in the Carousel. See the Thumbnail Grid pattern for issues related to thumbnail size and proportion (keeping in mind that Carousels impose even stricter restraints—thumbnails of different size or aspect ratio tend to look more awkward in Carousels than in Thumbnail Grids). Place the text metadata close to the thumbnail, but in small print in order to maintain the thumbnail's visual prominence.

In a horizontal scrolling widget, arrange the thumbnails horizontally, either randomly or in an order that makes obvious sense to the user (such as by date). Show a small number of them—fewer than 10—and hide the rest on either side. Put large arrows on the left and right for paging through the Carousel; each click on an arrow should move more than one item. Animate this scrolling for extra visual interest.

If users will want to move quickly through a long list, as though they are looking for something in particular, put a scrollbar below the Carousel in addition to the arrows. You may find that users do this a lot; if so, consider restructuring the list as a more conventional vertical list, and add a "find" capability.

You may choose to enlarge the central item in the Carousel to draw attention to it. This gives the Carousel single-selection semantics—the enlarged item is clearly the selected one, and you can then do dynamic things based on that selection, such as showing text details about it, or offering video controls if the items are video thumbnails.

Some Carousels are straight; some are curved or circular. These usually use the trick of a 3D perspective, in which items shrink and are partially obscured as they drift farther away from the center.

In the mobile design space, the Filmstrip pattern (Chapter 10) is a variant on a Carousel. Only one item at a time is shown on the small screen, and the user swipes or scrolls back and forth to see other items.

Examples

Many websites use a basic, linear Carousel for browsing products. Amazon and Google Books show book covers this way (see Figure 5-17); note the different amounts of text metadata and the implications for design. How much information should be provided with each book? How tightly packed should the book covers be?

Figure 5-17. *Amazon and Google Books*

Apple and Flickr (Figures 5-18 and 5-19) provide horizontal scrollbars along with their Carousels. These may contain a lot of items, so a scrollbar is needed for fast progress through them. Note that Apple's Carousel uses an Annotated Scrollbar (Chapter 3) to help users find product categories. The horizontal aspect of this list makes for a graceful presentation of the product names, but it wouldn't scale much beyond a small handful of categories—it's quite unusual to present a categorized list in a Carousel. Flat lists usually work better.

Figure 5-18. *Apple product carousel*

Figure 5-19. *Flickr organizational tools*

Cover Flow (Figure 5-20) is essentially a media Carousel that enlarges the central, selected item. Compare it to a curved Carousel in an Android app (Figure 5-21); these are similar in behavior, but very different in visual styling.

Figure 5-20. *Cover Flow in iTunes*

Figure 5-21. *Sherpa for Android (image courtesy of http://www.androidtapp.com/sherpa-discover-your-world/sherpa-nearest-dining-on-carousel/)*

The *New York Times* presents some of its feature articles in a Carousel (see Figure 5-22). These are the kinds of articles that may tempt a user to look at each one and browse slowly; it wouldn't work for all of the *Times'* countless daily articles, since people mostly skim the headlines and cherry-pick articles of interest. Features are different, however.

Figure 5-22. *New York Times feature articles*

In other libraries

http://developer.yahoo.com/ypatterns/selection/carousel.html

http://ui-patterns.com/patterns/Carousel

http://welie.com/patterns/showPattern.php?patternID=carrousel

Row Striping

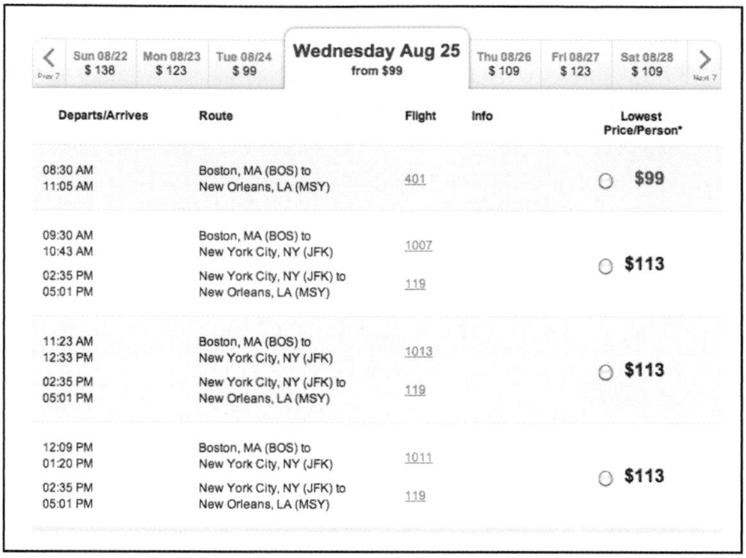

Figure 5-23. *JetBlue*

What

Use two similar shades to alternately color the backgrounds of the table rows.

Use when

Your interface presents data in a large multicolumn table, but the table's rows are difficult to separate visually. Users will need to look up specific data items in the table.

Why

Blocks of gentle color define and delineate the information contained inside them, even when you can't use whitespace to separate the data into "chunks." Cartographers and graphic designers have known this color-block technique for ages. (Remember that colored backgrounds are also effective for defining page sections and articulating a visual hierarchy. See Chapter 4 for more information.)

When someone looks at a large data table with a single background color, she will tend to see the columns as coherent objects due to proximity—the table entries in a column are closer to one another than they are to the other entries in their rows. But you want the viewer to read the table "row-wise" as well as column-wise. By coloring adjacent rows differently, you turn the rows into coherent visual objects, too. (This takes advantage of the Gestalt principles of *continuity* and *closure*; again, see Chapter 4.)

Specifically, Row Striping helps a user:

- Follow a row from left to right and back again, without confusing the rows
- See the "footprint" of the table itself, as separate from its containing page

However, Row Striping introduces more visual noise into the page. Some users in some contexts may find that it slows them down or that it makes the table harder to use.

Two studies on Row Striping, also known as *zebra striping*, indicate that it has a small but noticeable benefit for lookup speed and accuracy—under some conditions. The tables for which lookup improved were fairly large, with many rows and several widely spaced columns; a smaller table showed no benefit one way or the other. The researchers also noted that when asked about it, users said they preferred Row Striping! See the two articles at the following URLs for discussions of these studies, and for links to the original research performed by Formulate Information Design:

http://www.alistapart.com/articles/zebrastripingdoesithelp/
http://www.alistapart.com/articles/zebrastripingmoredataforthecase/

How

Pick a pair of quiet, low-saturation colors that are similar in value but not identical. (In other words, one needs to be a wee bit darker than the other.) Good choices are light blue and white, beige and white, or two similar shades of gray—assuming the text on top of them is dark. Generally, one of the colors is your page's background color.

Alternate the color from row to row. If the rows are thin, you could also experiment with grouping the rows—the first three are white, the next three are blue, and so on—but the research described a few paragraphs up found that users preferred single-line striping.

This pattern virtually eliminates the need for horizontal lines between the rows (though you could use them if they are very thin and inconspicuous). If your columns are aligned with one another, you don't need vertical lines between them, nor a heavy border around the table—the viewer's sense of visual closure will kick in, and the row colors will define the edges of the table for you. However, if row striping isn't working well for your users, you might try very thin horizontal lines instead, since they have a similar effect of forcing the eye to see horizontal groups instead of vertical groups.

Examples

The JetBlue example at the top of the pattern (Figure 5-23) shows several lines per row. The data itself is multiline and carefully formatted; some row separation other than whitespace was needed here. Lightweight horizontal rules may have worked too, but Row Striping makes coherent shapes out of the rows.

Single-row striping is more common. iTunes uses it to good effect, as shown in Figure 5-24.

	#	Name	Time	Artist	Album	Genre	Play Count	Last Played
☑	1	Slip Set	4:41	beòlach	beòlach	Celtic	1	7/19/05 5:30 PM
☑	2	Holly Bush	5:15	beòlach	beòlach	Celtic	1	7/19/05 5:35 PM
☑	3	Three Mile Bridge	5:11	beòlach	beòlach	Celtic	2	3/5/06 10:35 PM
☑	4	Superfly	4:59	beòlach	beòlach	Celtic	2	1/6/06 2:03 PM
☑	5	Rector	6:24	beòlach	beòlach	Celtic	1	7/20/05 9:24 AM
☑	6	Hen Party	6:38	beòlach	beòlach	Celtic	1	7/20/05 9:31 AM
☑	7	Blow My Chanter	3:19	beòlach	beòlach	Celtic	1	7/20/05 9:34 AM
☑	8	Scott Skinner's	6:18	beòlach	beòlach	Celtic	1	7/20/05 9:40 AM
☑	9	Bovaglies' Plaid	2:32	beòlach	beòlach	Celtic	2	7/20/05 9:48 AM
☑	10	Freddy's Set	4:24	beòlach	beòlach	Celtic	1	7/20/05 9:53 AM
☑	11	Hot Lunch Set	7:04	Beòlach	Variations	Celtic	3	3/3/06 5:16 PM
☑	12	Norman's	3:38	Beòlach	Variations	Celtic	3	3/3/06 5:19 PM
☑	13	Belle Lane	5:47	Beòlach	Variations	Celtic	1	3/3/06 5:25 PM
☑	14	Sweet Steevo Drover on the Golden Keyboard	4:09	Beòlach	Variations	Celtic	4	3/5/06 6:02 PM
☑	15	The Git Box Set	5:45	Beòlach	Variations	Celtic	4	3/5/06 6:07 PM
☑	16	Corporal AB	5:11	Beòlach	Variations	Celtic	3	3/5/06 6:13 PM
☑	17	Mrs. Crawford's	4:03	Beòlach	Variations	Celtic	2	3/5/06 6:17 PM
☑	18	The Watchmaker Set	5:17	Beòlach	Variations	Celtic	2	3/5/06 6:22 PM
☑	19	Memories of Father Charlie MacDonald	1:54	Beòlach	Variations	Celtic	2	3/5/06 6:24 PM
☑	20	David Rankin's	5:09	Beòlach	Variations	Celtic	2	3/5/06 6:29 PM
☑	21	Toss the Fiddles	6:02	Beòlach	Variations	Celtic	2	3/5/06 6:35 PM
☑	22	The West Mabou Set (Live)	2:56	Beòlach	Variations	Celtic	2	3/5/06 6:38 PM
☑	23	My Great Friend John Morris Rankin/The Flax ...	3:40	Kinnon Beaton	Heart Of Cape Breton	Celtic	1	8/25/10 10:23 PM
☑	24	Trad Strathspey/Stumpie/Primrose Lass/A Bri...	2:46	Jackie Dunn MacIsaac	Heart Of Cape Breton	Celtic	3	8/25/10 10:26 PM
☑	25	New Haven Reel/Mrs. Norman MacKeigan's R...	5:36	Kinnon Beaton	Heart Of Cape Breton	Celtic		
☑	26	In Memory Of Herbie MacLeod/Christy Camp...	7:13	Jerry Holland	Heart Of Cape Breton	Celtic		
☑	27	The Way To Judique/Compliments To The Bo...	5:17	Buddy MacMaster	Heart Of Cape Breton	Celtic		

Figure 5-24. *iTunes*

The Excel ledger spreadsheet shown in Figure 5-25 permits the user to change gridline styles, and Row Striping is among the possibilities. This sheet makes it fairly easy to follow the lines from left to right and back again.

Payee	Category	Date Paid ▼	Amount Paid ▼	Posted ▼
Whole Foods	Misc	6/17/2010	$67.20	☑
Trader Joe's	Misc	6/18/2010	$13.10	☐
Chestnut Farm	Meat, eggs	6/23/2010	$12.00	☐
Verrill Farm	Produce	6/23/2010	$18.72	☐
Whole Foods	Misc	6/27/2010	$43.10	☐
Stop & Shop	Paper goods	6/27/2010	$15.99	☐
Busa Farm	Produce	6/30/2010	$12.00	☐
Chestnut Farm	Meat, eggs	6/30/2010	$30.00	☐
Drumlin Farm	Produce	7/3/2010	$24.00	☐
Whole Foods	Misc	7/4/2010	$54.81	☐
Trader Joe's	Food	7/6/2010	$23.67	☐
Flora	Entertainment	7/7/2010	$56.61	☐
Trader Joe's	Misc	7/8/2010	$4.99	☐
Verrill Farm	Produce	7/9/2010	$14.00	☐
Springdell	Dairy	7/9/2010	$30.00	☐
Great Harvest	Bakery	7/9/2010	$5.99	☐
Whole Foods	Misc	7/12/2010	$78.12	☐
Busa Farm	Produce	7/14/2010	$22.00	☐
Wright-Locke Farm	Produce	7/14/2010	$5.00	☐
Kimball's Fruit Farm	Produce	7/14/2010	$7.50	☐
Swiss Bakers	Bakery	7/14/2010	$3.25	☐
Chestnut Farm	Meat, eggs	7/14/2010	$19.00	☐
Rancatore's	Desserts	7/14/2010	$14.00	☐

Figure 5-25. *Excel ledger, with stripes*

But look what happens when the gray row backgrounds are stripped away, as shown in Figure 5-26. The columns suddenly become much stronger visually, and each row is harder to read from left to right. Some designers, however, find this design to be cleaner and more pleasing. There's no absolutely correct answer about whether to use Row Striping or not.

Payee	Category	Date Paid ▼	Amount Paid ▼	Posted ▼
Whole Foods	Misc	6/17/2010	$67.20	☑
Trader Joe's	Misc	6/18/2010	$13.10	☐
Chestnut Farm	Meat, eggs	6/23/2010	$12.00	☐
Verrill Farm	Produce	6/23/2010	$18.72	☐
Whole Foods	Misc	6/27/2010	$43.10	☐
Stop & Shop	Paper goods	6/27/2010	$15.99	☐
Busa Farm	Produce	6/30/2010	$12.00	☐
Chestnut Farm	Meat, eggs	6/30/2010	$30.00	☐
Drumlin Farm	Produce	7/3/2010	$24.00	☐
Whole Foods	Misc	7/4/2010	$54.81	☐
Trader Joe's	Food	7/6/2010	$23.67	☐
Flora	Entertainment	7/7/2010	$56.61	☐
Trader Joe's	Misc	7/8/2010	$4.99	☐
Verrill Farm	Produce	7/9/2010	$14.00	☐
Springdell	Dairy	7/9/2010	$30.00	☐
Great Harvest	Bakery	7/9/2010	$5.99	☐
Whole Foods	Misc	7/12/2010	$78.12	☐
Busa Farm	Produce	7/14/2010	$22.00	☐
Wright-Locke Farm	Produce	7/14/2010	$5.00	☐
Kimball's Fruit Farm	Produce	7/14/2010	$7.50	☐
Swiss Bakers	Bakery	7/14/2010	$3.25	☐
Chestnut Farm	Meat, eggs	7/14/2010	$19.00	☐
Rancatore's	Desserts	7/14/2010	$14.00	☐

Figure 5-26. *Excel ledger, without stripes*

In other libraries

This technique is also known in many places as "alternating row colors" or "zebra striping." Descriptions abound on the Web:

http://ui-patterns.com/patterns/AlternatingRowColors

http://www.welie.com/patterns/showPattern.php?patternID=zebra-table

http://quince.infragistics.com/Patterns/Alternating%20Row%20Colors.aspx

Pagination

| ← Previous | 1 | … | 5 | 6 | **7** | 8 | 9 | … | 1046 | Next → |

Figure 5-27. *Songza pagination control*

What

Break up a very long list into pages, and load them one at a time. Provide controls for the user to navigate the list—next, previous, first, and last pages.

Use when

You're showing a list that might be very, very long. Most users will either look for a particular item or browse the top of the list for relevant items (e.g., with search results); in any case, they won't really want to see the entire list.

The technology you're using doesn't support loading the entire list into a single page or scrolled area, for any of the following reasons:

- Loading the whole list would take too much time, and you don't want to make the user wait. This might be the case over a slow Internet connection or with a slow backend server.

- Rendering the list would take too much time.

- The list is effectively "bottomless," and implementing an Infinite List or a continuously scrolling list (which both handle bottomless lists) isn't feasible for some reason.

Why

Pagination breaks a list into chunks that a user can easily take in without being overwhelmed. Furthermore, it puts the choice to see more into the user's hands—do you want to load more items from the list, or is this page of items enough for you?

This pattern also has the advantage of being very common on the Web, especially (though not exclusively) for search results. It's easy to implement, and may come prebuilt in some systems.

First, you'll need to decide how many items will be in each page. Base this on the amount of space each item takes up, the screen sizes users are likely to have (don't forget to consider mobile platforms), the time it takes to load or show the items, and the likelihood that the user will find one or more desired items in the first page.

This is fairly important: the first page should be enough! The odds are good that most users won't go beyond that first page of items, so if they can't find what they're looking for in that first page, they may get discouraged. (If you're dealing with a search facility, make sure that it returns high-quality results at the top of that first page.)

On pages that users may linger over, such as lists of products or videos, consider letting the user set the number of items per page. Some people are irritated by having to page back and forth to see all the items of interest.

Next, you'll need to decide how to present the pagination controls. They're usually found at the bottom of the page, but some designs also have them at the top—if a user really does need to go to a subsequent page of items, there's no need to make him scroll all the way down the page.

Consider these elements in the pagination control:

- Previous and Next links, with arrows or triangles for emphasis. Disable the Previous link when the user is on the first page and the Next link when the user is on the last page (if there is a known last page).

- A link to the first page. This should always be visible; remember that the first page is supposed to contain the most relevant items.

- A sequence of numbered links to pages. Don't link the page the user is on, of course; instead, show it in a contrasting color and type size to give the user a "You are here" navigational clue.

- Ellipses to cut out parts of the sequence if there are too many pages to reasonably show in the control—more than 20, for instance. Again, keep the first page, and the last page if the list isn't "bottomless." Keep the pages immediately before and after the user's current page. Elide the rest.

- Optionally, the total number of pages (if known). You could do this in several ways, such as showing text like "Page 2 out of 45," or simply showing the last page as a numbered link at the end of the pagination control. See the examples for some ideas.

Digg and Google both do an excellent job of including all the elements and cues from the preceding list. The screenshots in Figure 5-28 show the most interesting pagination control states: first and last pages for only a small number of items, and the first, middle, and last pages for a very large number of items. Note that Digg uses ellipses to manage large numbers, and Google simply omits the beginning and end of the range. Digg knows exactly how many pages of items there are, whereas Google's list is sometimes bottomless. (The last Google example shows the last page of a search that wasn't bottomless—it only returned 21 pages of results.)

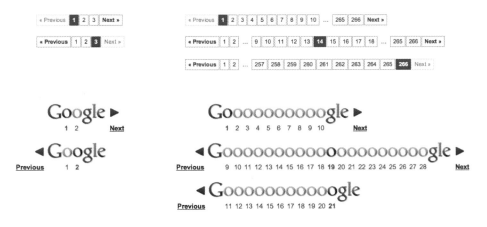

Figure 5-28. *Digg and Google examples*

Figure 5-29 shows a gallery of examples from all over the Web. Notice which ones are easier to parse visually—Which link is which? Where should I click next?—and which ones give you sufficient information about your location and the total number of pages. Also note the size of the click targets. How accurate does the user have to be with her mouse or fingertip?

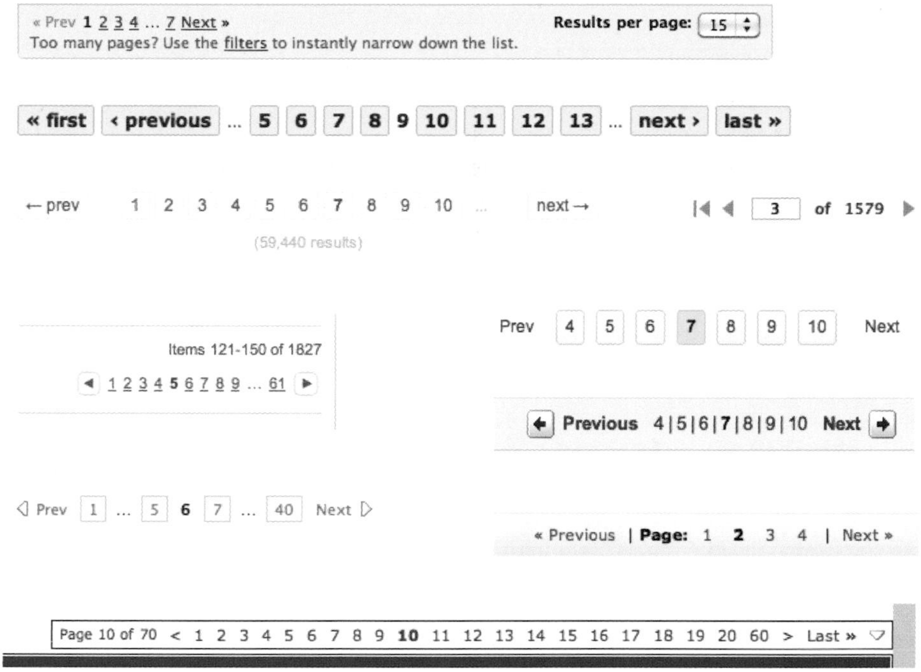

Figure 5-29. *Counterclockwise from top: Kayak, Drupal.org, Flickr, Target, Last.fm, Mothering.com, Amazon, eBay, YouTube, and Hulu*

In other libraries

http://www.welie.com/patterns/showPattern.php?patternID=paging

http://ui-patterns.com/patterns/Pagination

http://www.patternry.com/p=search-pagination/

http://quince.infragistics.com/Patterns/Paging.aspx

The Yahoo! pattern library has two versions of the Pagination pattern, one for search and one for other types of items:

http://developer.yahoo.com/ypatterns/navigation/pagination/item.html

http://developer.yahoo.com/ypatterns/navigation/pagination/search.html

Jump to Item

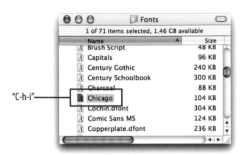

"C-h-i"————

Figure 5-30. *Font dialog on Mac OS*

What

When the user types the name of an item into a table or tree, jump straight to that item and select it.

Use when

The interface uses a scrolling list, table, drop down, combo box, or tree to present a long list of items. These items are sorted, either alphabetically or numerically. The user wants to select one particular item quickly and accurately, and preferably with the keyboard.

This pattern is often used in file finders, long lists of names, and drop-down boxes for state or country selection. You can also use it for numbers—such as years or dollar amounts— or even calendar time, such as months or days of the week.

Why

People aren't good at scanning down long lists of words or numbers for a particular item. But computers are. Let them do what they're good at!

Another nice thing about this technique is that it lets the user keep her hands on the keyboard. As she moves through a form or dialog box, she might find it nice to select from a list simply by typing the first few characters of the item she wants—the system then picks the item for her, and she can continue on to the next thing. No scrolling or clicking is necessary; the user's hand never has to move from the keyboard to the mouse.

How

When the user types the first letter or number of the item she's looking for, jump to the first item that matches what the user typed: automatically scroll the list so that the item is visible, and select it.

As the user types more characters in rapid succession, keep changing the selection to the first exact match for the whole user-typed string. If there is no match, stay put at the nearest match, and don't scroll back to the top of the list. You may want to beep at the user to tell her that there's no match—some applications do, some don't.

A variant of Jump to Item is used by GNU Emacs' incremental-search facility (see Figure 5-31). After the user enters i-search mode via Ctrl-S, each character typed brings the user to the first instance of that cumulative string in the document. It doesn't matter that the original material wasn't sorted.

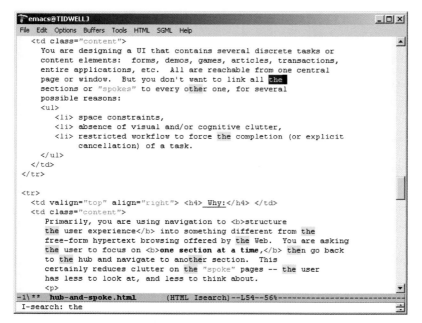

Figure 5-31. *Emacs*

Once an occurrence of the string has been found, the user can find subsequent ones by pressing Ctrl-S repeatedly. In some ways, this incremental search is more convenient—and certainly faster—than typical desktop "Find" dialog boxes, which don't update continuously as you type the search string.

Furthermore, Emacs can highlight all other instances of that string in the document in addition to scrolling to the first one. This gives the user lots of extra contextual information about the search she's conducting. Is it a common string, or not? Are they clustered together, or scattered?

Alphabet Scroller

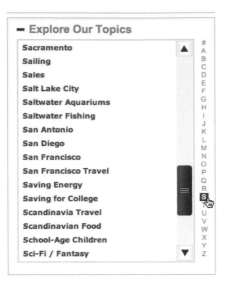

Figure 5-32. *About.com*

What

Show the letters of the alphabet arrayed along the scrollbar of an alphabetized list.

Use when

Users will be searching for very specific items in a long list, which is usually rendered as a scrolled list, table, or tree. You want to make item finding as easy and quick to achieve as possible.

Why

Alphabet scrollers are not common, but their use is self-explanatory. They provide an interactive map to the list content, in much the same way as an Annotated Scrollbar (Chapter 3). They're closely related to Jump to Item—both enable immediate jumping to a point in an ordered list.

This pattern probably arose from physical books (such as dictionaries) and notebooks (such as address books) that use tabs to mark points in the alphabet.

How

Place a long alphabetized list into a scrolled area. Along the scrollbar, show the letters of the alphabet; when the user clicks on a letter, scroll the list to that point (see Figure 5-32, at the top of the pattern).

There are multiple operational examples of alphabetized lists working this way, but there is no reason why another ordering—by number or by date, for example—couldn't also work well. Consider expanding this pattern beyond the alphabet!

Examples

The iPhone offers what is probably the best-known example of this pattern. Figure 5-33 shows its built-in Contacts app.

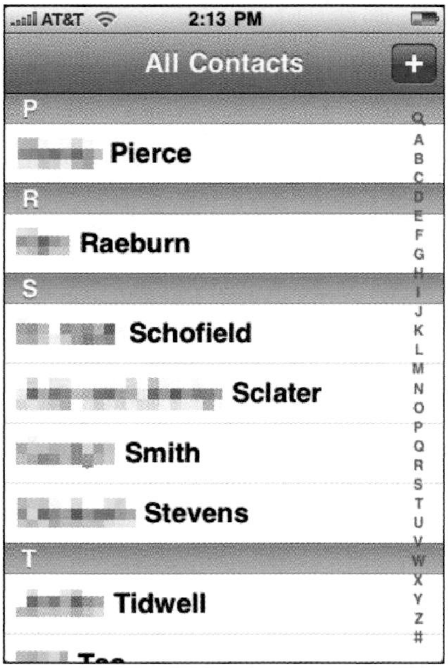

Figure 5-33. *iPhone contacts list*

Cascading Lists

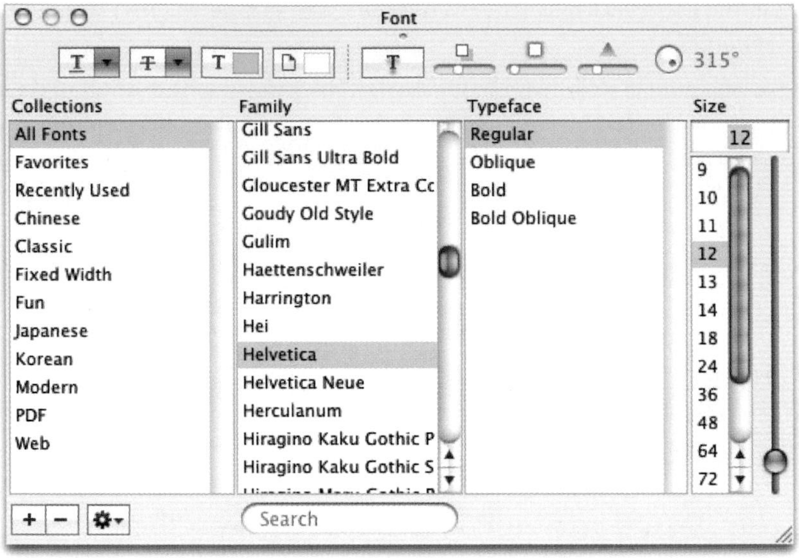

Figure 5-34. *Mac OS font dialog*

What

Express a hierarchy by showing selectable lists of the items in each hierarchy level. Selection of any item shows that item's children in the next list.

Use when

The list items are arranged in a hierarchy. The hierarchy might be deep, and it might have many items on each level. A tree (outline) would work, but the user would have to scroll up and down a lot to see all the items, and he wouldn't get a good overview of the items at higher levels in the hierarchy.

The hierarchy may be a literal one, such as a filesystem, or a conceptual one—this pattern is often used to let a user navigate and choose items within categories or make a series of interdependent choices, as with the fonts in the example in Figure 5-34 at the top of the pattern.

Why

By spreading the hierarchy out across several scrolled lists, you show more of it at once. It's that simple. Visibility is helpful when you're dealing with complex information structures. Also, laying the items out in lists organizes them nicely—a user can more easily keep track of what level he's dealing with than he could with an outline format, since the hierarchy levels are in nice, predictable, fixed-position lists.

How

Put the first level of the hierarchy in the leftmost list (which should use single-selection semantics). When the user selects an item in it, show that item's children in the next list to the right. Do the same with the child items in this second list; show its selected item's children in the third list. And so on.

Once the user reaches items with no children—the "leaf" items, as opposed to "branches"—you might want to show the details of the last-selected item at the far right. An image file typically displays a thumbnail; you might instead offer a UI for editing an item, reading its content, or whatever is appropriate for your particular application.

A nice thing about this pattern is that you can easily associate buttons with each list: delete the current item, move up, move down, and so on. Many toolkits will let you do this in tree controls via direct manipulation, but for those that don't have built-in tree controls, this is a viable alternative.

Examples

The Mac OS Finder screenshot shown in Figure 5-35 is an extreme example, with seven levels. But it shows that the pattern scales well, letting the user drill down into deep filesystem hierarchies while staying oriented. (Warning: this can be confusing for people who aren't familiar with this pattern and the concept of a hierarchy.)

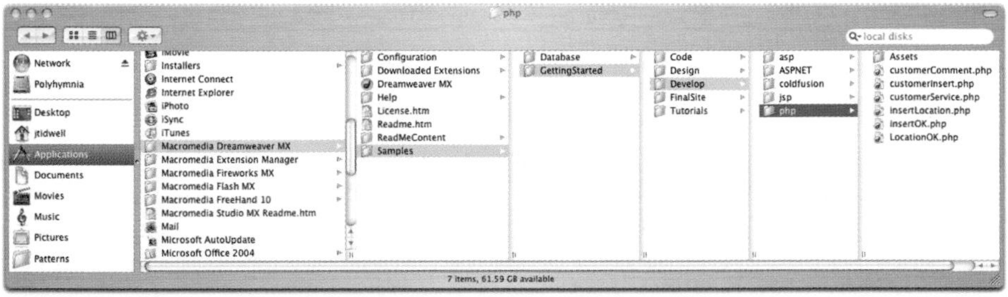

Figure 5-35. *Mac OS Finder*

NeXTSTEP originally used this technique in its own File Viewer, circa 1990 or so. The example in Figure 5-36 is from *http://www120.pair.com/mccarthy/nextstep/intro.htmld/ Workspace.html.*

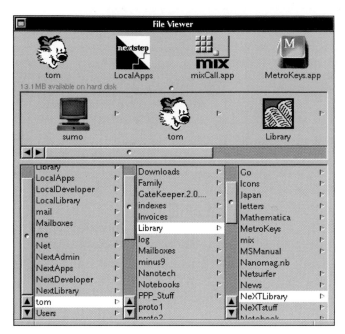

Figure 5-36. *NeXTSTEP File Viewer*

In other libraries

http://quince.infragistics.com/Patterns/Cascading%20Lists.aspx

Tree Table

Name	Date Modified	Size	Kind
▼ 📁 1000 Screenshots	Aug 17, 2010 2:40 PM	--	Folder
▼ 📁 Accordions	Jul 18, 2010 2:10 PM	--	Folder
📄 chrome-tools-2.tiff	Jun 29, 2010 2:08 PM	332 KB	TIFF image
📄 chrome-tools.tiff	Jun 29, 2010 2:07 PM	45 KB	TIFF image
📄 cnn-1.tiff	Jul 18, 2010 2:10 PM	41 KB	TIFF image
📄 cnn-2.tiff	Jul 18, 2010 2:10 PM	61 KB	TIFF image
📄 picasa.tiff	Jul 8, 2010 11:36 PM	57 KB	TIFF image
📄 word-1.tiff	Jul 18, 2010 1:56 PM	737 KB	TIFF image
📄 word-2.tiff	Jul 18, 2010 1:57 PM	770 KB	TIFF image
📄 word.tiff	Jul 8, 2010 11:24 PM	627 KB	TIFF image
📄 yahoo-devel.tiff	Jul 9, 2010 11:23 PM	152 KB	TIFF image
▶ 📁 Action Panel	Aug 17, 2010 2:42 PM	--	Folder
▼ 📁 Advanced Search	Feb 4, 2008 1:51 PM	--	Folder
📄 ebay.tiff	Jan 11, 2008 10:37 AM	135 KB	TIFF image
📄 gather.tiff	Feb 4, 2008 1:51 PM	143 KB	TIFF image
📄 lulu.tiff	Jan 10, 2008 12:37 PM	213 KB	TIFF image
▶ 📁 Alphabet Scroller	Aug 17, 2010 2:31 PM	--	Folder
▶ 📁 Alternative Views	Jun 23, 2010 12:51 PM	--	Folder
▶ 📁 Annotated Scrollbar	Jul 19, 2010 11:33 AM	--	Folder

Figure 5-37. *Mac OS Finder*

What

Put item fields in table-like columns, but use an indented outline structure in the first column to illustrate the tree structure.

Use when

The items in a list are highly structured, with specific attributes that are of interest to users. You can show them in a multicolumn list or table. But the items are primarily organized as a hierarchy, so you also want a tree to display them most of the time.

Your users are relatively sophisticated with respect to interface usage; this is not an easy pattern for naive computer users to understand (and the same can be said about most hierarchical views, including trees and Cascading Lists).

Why

Combining the two data-viewing approaches into one view gives you the best of both worlds, at the cost of some visual and programming complexity. You can show the hierarchy of items, plus a matrix of additional data or item attributes, in one unified structure.

How

The examples show what you need to do: put the tree (really an outline) in the first column, and the item attributes in the subsequent columns. The rows—one item per row— are usually selectable. Naturally, this can be combined with Sortable Tables to produce a more browsable, interactive structure. Sorting on the columns disrupts the tree ordering, so you'll need to provide an extra button or some other affordance to re-sort the table into the order required by the tree.

This technique seems to have found a home in email clients and news readers, where threads of discussion form tree-like structures.

Examples

The Firefox browser once used a distinctive-looking Tree Table in one of its dialog boxes. The separators—horizontal lines—help to visually group the items in different categories, which isn't a bad idea at all (see Figure 5-38).

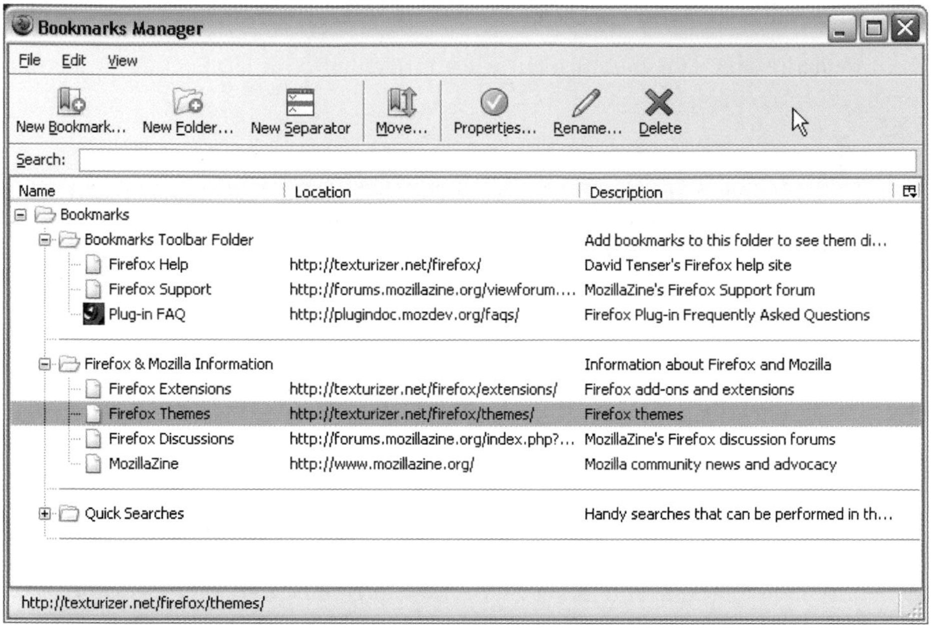

Figure 5-38. *Firefox Bookmarks Manager, from an early version of the browser*

In other libraries

http://quince.infragistics.com/Patterns/Tree-Table.aspx

New-Item Row

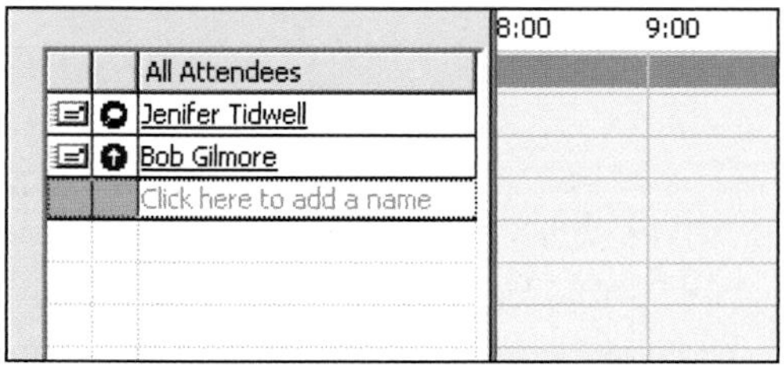

Figure 5-39. *Microsoft Outlook*

What

Use the last or first row in the list or table to create a new item in place.

Use when

The interface contains a table, list, tree view, or any other vertical presentation of a set of items (one item per row). At some point, the user needs to add new items to it. But you don't have a lot of room to spare on the UI for extra buttons or options, and you want to make item creation very efficient and easy for the user.

Why

By letting the user type directly into the end (or the beginning) of the table, you put the act of creation into the same place where the item will ultimately "live." It's conceptually more coherent than putting it in some other part of the UI. Also, it makes the interface more elegant than having an entirely different UI for item creation—it uses less screen real estate, it reduces the amount of navigation that needs to be done (thus eliminating a "jump" to another window), and it's less work for your users.

How

Give the user an easy and obvious way to initiate a new object from the first empty table row. A single mouse click in that row might start editing, for instance, or the row might contain a "New Whatever" pushbutton, or it might contain a dummy item as shown at the top of the pattern in Figure 5-39.

At that point, the UI should create the new item and put it in that row. Each column in the table (if it's a multicolumn table) should then be editable, thus letting the user set up the values of that item. The cells could have text fields in them, or drop-down lists, or whatever else is necessary to set the values quickly and precisely. As with any form-like user input, Good Defaults (Chapter 8) help save the user work by prefilling those values; the user doesn't have to edit every column.

There are still some loose ends to clean up, though. What happens if the user abandons the new item before finishing? You can establish a valid item right from the beginning—if the user abandons the edits at any time, the item exists until the user goes back and deletes it. Again, Good Defaults help by prefilling valid values if there are multiple fields.

Depending on how it's implemented, this pattern can resemble Input Prompt (Chapter 8). In both cases, a dummy value is set up for the user to edit into a real value, and that dummy value is worded as a "prompt" that shows the user what to do.

Examples

Excel's built-in spreadsheet templates, such as the one shown in Figure 5-40 for budgeting, mark the New-Item Row very clearly by putting a blue box around the entire row. The PowerPoint outline view shown in Figure 5-41 affords creation of new slides by typing into the bottom row, but the interface is subtler and hard to notice. (I went looking for this feature before I found it; I never knew beforehand that it existed.)

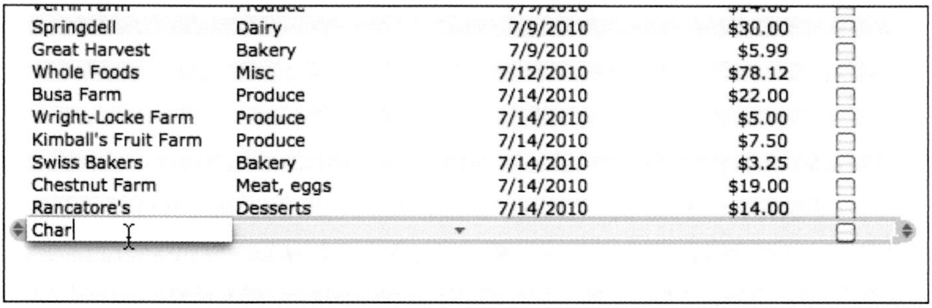

Figure 5-40. *New entry in an Excel ledger*

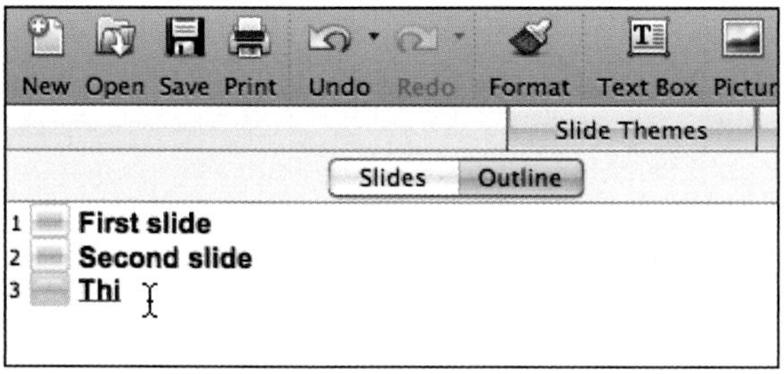

Figure 5-41. *New slide in a PowerPoint slideshow*

In other libraries

http://quince.infragistics.com/Patterns/New-Item%20Row.aspx

http://www.welie.com/patterns/showPattern.php?patternID=list-entry-view

Chapter 6

Doing Things: Actions and Commands

This chapter is devoted to the "verbs" in the interface. We've spent a lot of pages talking about overall structure and flow, visual layout, and "nouns"—such as windows, text, links, and static elements in pages. Chapter 7 spends even more pages on nouns, and Chapter 8 handles traditional (and a few nontraditional) controls and widgets: things that let users supply information and set state, but that don't actually *do* much.

So now let's talk about buttons and menus.

Sounds exciting, doesn't it? Probably not. Desktop interfaces have used menu bars as long ago as the first Macintosh, and buttons for even longer. What we think of as "buttons" are only a visual rendering of a physical device that long predated GUIs.

It's true that there is a lot of history here, and there are many best practices to follow. The standard platform style guides, such as those for Windows and Macintosh, will generally get you pretty close to a workable UI. Most users depend upon learned conventions to negotiate menus and find buttons, so it behooves you to follow those conventions, even when they feel restrictive or nonsensical.

Common functionality such as cut, copy, and paste also carries lots of historical baggage—if it could be reinvented now, it would probably work differently—but even moderately experienced desktop computer users have learned how it's "supposed to work." The same is true for pop-up menus (context menus), which some users seem to look for everywhere, and other users never think to look for at all. Drag-and-drop isn't as bound by history, but it absolutely has to work the way users intuitively expect it to, or the illusion of direct manipulation is broken.

That being said, you can do many things to make your interface less dull and more usable. Your goals should be to make the right actions available, label them well, make them easy to find, and support sequences of actions. There are a few creative ways to do it.

First, I'll list the common ways actions are rendered to the user:

Buttons

> Buttons are placed directly onto the interface, without requiring the user to perform any action to see them, and are usually grouped semantically. (See the Button Groups pattern.) They're big, readable, obvious, and extremely easy to use for even the most inexperienced computer users. But they take up a lot of space on the interface, unlike menu bars and pop-up menus. On landing pages, such as corporate home pages and product startup pages, calls to action are usually represented as single, large, eye-catching buttons—this is entirely appropriate for their purpose, which is to attract attention and say, "Click me!"

Menu bars

> Menu bars are standard on most desktop applications. They generally show an application's complete set of actions, organized in a mostly predictable way (such as File, Edit, or View). Some actions operate on the entire application, and some operate only on individually selected items. Menu bars often duplicate functionality found in context menus and toolbars because they are *accessible*—screen readers can read them, users can reach them via keyboard accelerators, and so on. (Accessibility alone makes menu bars indispensable in many products.) Menu bars appear in some web applications, especially productivity software, drawing programs, and other products that emulate desktop apps.

Pop-up menus

> Also known as context menus, pop-up menus are raised with a right-mouse click or some similar gesture on panels or items. They usually list context-specific, common actions, not all the actions that are possible on the interface. Keep them short.

Drop-down menus

> Users raise these menus by clicking on a drop-down control such as a combo box. However, drop-down controls are intended for selecting choices on a form, not for performing actions. Avoid using them for actions.

Toolbars

> The canonical toolbar is a long, thin row of iconic buttons. Often they have other kinds of buttons or controls on them too, such as text fields or Dropdown Choosers (see Chapter 8). Iconic toolbars work best when the portrayed actions have obvious visual renderings; when the actions really need to be described with words, try other controls, such as combo boxes or buttons with text labels. Cryptic icons are a classic source of confusion and unusability.

Links

> Buttons 9don't need borders. Thanks to the Web, everyone understands that colored text (especially blue text) usually indicates a clickable link. In a UI area where actions are expected but where you don't need to draw attention or clutter the page, you can

use simple clickable "link" text for actions instead of buttons. When the user rolls the mouse over the text, change the cursor and underline the text to reinforce the impression of clickability.

Action panels

These are essentially menus that the user doesn't need to post; they're always visible on the main interface. They are a fine substitute for toolbars when actions are better described verbally than visually. See the Action Panel pattern.

Hover tools

If you \want to show two or more actions for each item on an interface but you don't want to clutter the page with lots of repeated buttons, you can make those buttons invisible until the mouse hovers over the item. (This is great for mouse-driven interfaces, but it doesn't work well for touch screens.) See the Hover Tools pattern for more.

Then there are invisible actions, which don't have any labels at all to announce what they do. Users need to know (or guess) that they're there, unless you put written instructions on the UI. Therefore, they don't help with discovery at all, since users can't read over them to find out what actions are possible. With buttons, links, and menus, the UI actions are available for inspection, so users learn from those. In usability tests, I've seen many users look at a new product and methodically walk down the menu bar, item by item, just to find out what it can do.

That being said, you almost always need to use one or more of the following invisible actions. People often expect to be able to double-click on items, for example. However, the keyboard (or the equivalent) is sometimes the only means of access for visually impaired users and people who can't use a mouse. In addition, the expert users of some operating systems and applications prefer to work by typing commands into a shell and/or by using its keyboard actions.

Double-clicking on items

Users tend to view double-clicking as either "open this item" or "do whatever the default thing is with this item," depending on context. In a graphical editor, for instance, double-clicking on an element often means opening a property sheet or specialized editor for it. Double-clicking an application's icon in most operating systems launches that application. Double-clicking a piece of text might edit it in place.

Keyboard actions

Keyboard shortcuts, such as the well-known Ctrl-S to save, should be designed into most desktop applications for accessibility and efficient use. The major UI platforms, including Windows, Mac, and some Linux environments, each have style guides that describe the standard shortcuts—and they're all very similar. Additionally, menus and controls often have underlined access keys, which let users reach those controls without mouse-clicking or tabbing. (Press the Alt key, and then press the key corresponding to the underlined letter, to invoke these actions.)

Drag-and-drop

> Dragging and dropping items on an interface usually means either "move this here" or "do this to that." In other words, someone might drag a file onto an application icon to say, "Open this file in that application." Or she might drag that file from one place in a file finder to another place, thus moving or copying the item. Drag-and-drop is context-dependent, but it almost always results in one of these two actions.

Typed commands

> Command-line interfaces generally allow free-form access to all the actions in the software system, whether it's an operating system or an application. I consider these kinds of actions "invisible" because most command-line interfaces (CLIs) don't easily divulge the available commands. They're not very discoverable, though they're quite powerful once you learn what's available—much can be done with a single well-constructed command. As such, CLIs are best for users committed to learning the software very well.

Pushing the Boundaries

Some application idioms give you freedom to design nonstandard buttons and controls. Visual editors, media players, applications intended mostly for experts, instant messaging, games, and anything that's supposed to be fun and interesting all have users who might be curious enough to figure out how to use unusual but well-designed interface elements.

Where can you be more creative? Consider the items on the first list in the preceding section; visible buttons and menus are easier to use than invisible actions, such as keyboard shortcuts. Generalizing from that, actions could be:

- Clickable icons

- Clickable text that doesn't look like a button

- Something that reacts when the mouse pointer rolls over it

- Some object that looks like it may be manipulated by the user

- Something placed on almost any piece of screen real estate

But how much creativity can you get away with before the application becomes too hard to figure out?

For a real-life example, we'll look at the GarageBand application, shown in Figure 6-1. There's a lot going on in this interface. Some objects are obviously buttons, such as the player controls—rewind, play, fast forward, and so forth—and the scrollbar arrows. You will find some sliders and knobs, too.

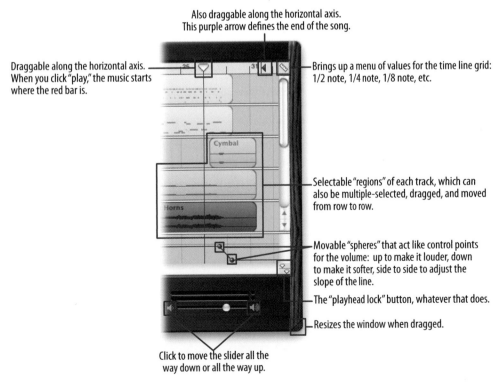

Figure 6-1. *GarageBand*

But look harder at the far right of the window, between the red line and the wood-grain edge. To your eyes, what pieces of the interface look clickable? Why? If you want, you can look ahead to Figure 6-2 and cheat. (And if you already know GarageBand, please bear with me.)

Figure 6-2. *GarageBand actions*

Figure 6-2 shows which objects on the interface perform actions. You clearly couldn't have known what they all do, since this book doesn't give you the benefit of tool tips, rollover cursors, or experimentation. But did you figure out that some of these objects could be clicked or manipulated? I'm guessing you did.

How? You probably know that interfaces that look like this offer a lot of functionality through direct manipulation, so you have good grounds for assuming that every interesting visual feature does something. You might know that sliders, such as the volume slider at the bottom, sometimes have "jump buttons" at the ends—and you might have recognized the volume slider itself from iTunes. You might guess that tiny squarish icons tend to be buttons, often for presentation-related actions; Word and PowerPoint use a lot of them. You might have seen a vertical line topped with an inverted triangle in some other context—maybe movable, maybe not. But didn't this triangle look like it was movable?

When an object looks like it might let you do something, such as click it or drag it, we say it "affords" performing that action. Traditional raised-edge buttons afford pushing; a slider thumb affords dragging; a text field affords typing; a blue underlined word affords clicking. And anything that reacts to the mouse cursor affords something, although you can't necessarily tell what!

Figure 6-2 points out the *affordances* in the GarageBand interface. This is an important concept. In software interfaces, the user doesn't get many sensory clues about what can be tweaked or handled: visuals give most of the clues, and mouse rollovers do the rest. Use them to communicate affordances well.

Here's some specific design advice:

- Follow conventions whenever possible. Reuse UI concepts and controls that people already know, such as the volume sliders in the example.

- Use pseudo-3D shading and drop shadows to make things look "raised."

- When the mouse pointer hovers over items that can be clicked or dragged, turn the pointer into something different, such as a finger or a hand.

- Use tool tips, or some other descriptive text, to tell the user what the objects under the mouse pointer do. If you don't need them, that's great—you have a self-describing design—but many users expect tool tips anyway.

The Patterns

The first patterns in this chapter talk about three of the many ways to present actions. When you find yourself reflexively putting actions on an application's menu bar or pop-up menu, stop for a moment and consider using one of these instead.

1. Button Groups

2. Hover Tools

3. Action Panel

Prominent "Done" Button improves the single most important button on many web pages and dialog boxes. Smart Menu Items is a technique for improving some of the actions you put on menus; this is a very general pattern, useful for many kinds of menus (or buttons or links).

4. Prominent "Done" Button

5. Smart Menu Items

We'd like it if all the user-initiated actions in an application could be completed instantly, but that's not reality. Preview shows the user what's going to happen before a time-consuming action is committed. Progress Indicator is a well-known technique for letting the user know what's going on while an operation proceeds, while Cancelability refers to a UI's ability to stop an operation when the user asks it to.

6. Preview

7. Progress Indicator

8. Cancelability

The last three patterns—Multi-Level Undo, Command History, and Macros—all deal with sequences of actions. These three interlocking patterns are most useful in complex applications, especially those whose users are committed to learning the software well and using it extensively. (That's why the examples come from complex software such as Linux, Photoshop, Word, and MATLAB.) Be warned that these patterns are not easy to implement. They require the application to model a user's actions as discrete, describable, and sometimes reversible operations, and such a model is very hard to retrofit into an existing software architecture. The Command pattern in the classic book *Design Patterns* (Addison-Wesley Professional) is one good place to look for implementation advice.

And that's as close as this book gets to implementation details. We'll now return to the realm of interface design.

9. Multi-Level Undo

10. Command History

11. Macros

Button Groups

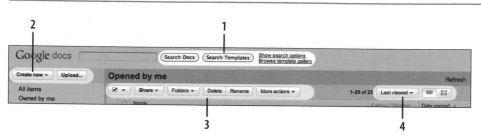

Figure 6-3. *Google Docs main screen header, with four button groups highlighted*

What

Present related actions as a small cluster of buttons, aligned and with similar graphic treatments. Create multiple groups if there are more than three or four actions.

Use when

There are many actions to show on the interface. You want to make sure they are all visible all the time, but you need to visually organize them so that they're not chaotic or hard to sort out. Some of these actions are similar to each other—they have similar or complementary effects, for instance, or they operate with similar semantics—and they can thus be assembled into groups of two to five.

Button Groups can be used for app-wide operations (such as Open or Preferences), item-specific actions (Save, Edit, Delete), or any other scope. Actions with different scope ought not to be grouped together, however.

Why

Button Groups help make an interface self-describing. Well-defined clusters of buttons are easy to pick out of a complex layout, and because they're so visible, they instantly communicate the availability of those actions. They announce, "These are the actions you've got to work with in this context."

The Gestalt principles discussed in Chapter 4 apply here. Proximity hints at relatedness; if the buttons are all together, they probably do similar things. So does visual similarity; if you make all the buttons the same dimensions, for instance, they look like they belong together. Conversely, button groups that are separated in space—or that are different in shape—imply unrelated groups of actions.

Proper sizing and alignment help the Button Group form a larger composite visual shape (this is the principle of *closure*).

Make a group out of the buttons in question. Label them with short but unambiguous verbs or verb phrases, and don't use jargon unless users expect it. Do not mix buttons that affect different things or have different scope; separate them into different groups.

All buttons in the group should have the same graphic treatment: borders, color, height and/or width, icon style, dynamic effects, and so on. You can line them up in a single column, or arrange them in a single row if they aren't too wide.

(However, treat them differently if one action is a "primary" action, such as a Submit button on a web form. A primary action is an action that you want most users to take, or that most users will expect to take. Give that button a stronger graphic treatment to make it stand out among the others.)

If all the buttons in a group act on the same object or objects, put the Button Group to the left or right of those objects. You could put them below the objects instead, but users often have a "blind spot" at the bottom of complex UI elements such as multicolumn lists and trees—the buttons may not be seen at all. To make them more visible, keep the rest of the interface clean and uncluttered. If you have a specific design that works better with the buttons at the bottom, usability-test it and find out. If there are enough buttons and if they have icons, you could also put them on a toolbar or toolbar-like strip at the top of the page.

By using Button Groups, you're trying to avoid a crowded mess of buttons and links, or perhaps a long and plodding list of actions with no apparent differentiation at all. With this pattern, you create a miniature visual hierarchy of actions: the user can see at a glance *what's related* and *what's important*.

Standard tools for WYSIWYG editors are often grouped by function. The two examples shown in Figure 6-4, from Word and Flash Builder, show some common tools in groupings that actually aid recognition.

As shown in Figure 6-5, iTunes places Button Groups at each of the four corners of the main window, plus the standard title bar buttons (such as close and minimize). When the user browses the Music Store, even more actions are contained in the web-page-like third panel (not shown)—links constitute many of the actions there—and a button for each song in the table.

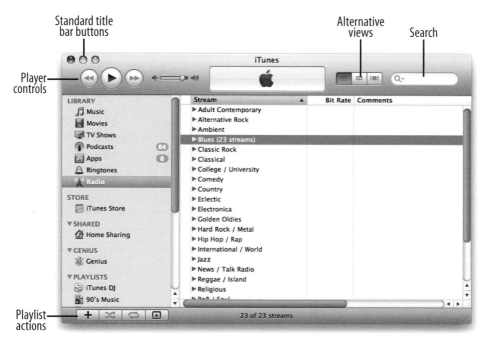

Figure 6-4. *Microsoft Word and Adobe Flash Builder*

There are no fewer than 13 buttons on this interface, and I'm not even counting the four
scrollbar buttons or the three clickable table headers. There's a lot to do here, but thanks to
careful visual and semantic organization, the interface is never overwhelming.

Figure 6-5. *iTunes*

http://quince.infragistics.com/Patterns/Button%20Groups.aspx

Hover Tools

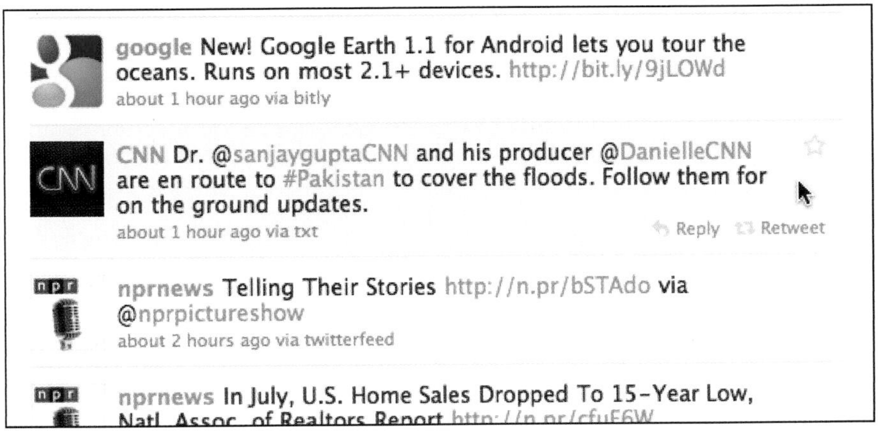

Figure 6-6. *Twitter*

What

Place buttons and other actions next to the items they act upon, but hide them until the user hovers the pointer over them.

Use when

There are many actions to show on the interface. You want a clean, uncluttered look most of the time, but you have to put those actions somewhere, preferably on or next to the items they act upon. You've already allocated the space to show those actions, but they just make things too crowded and busy if they're all visible all the time.

Hover Tools are commonly used in list interfaces, in which many small items—photos, messages, search results, and so on—are displayed in a column or list. The user can perform a number of actions on each one.

You don't intend the interface to be used with fingertips, as with a touchpad device—you're certain that almost all users will interact with your UI via a mouse. (If your UI is a web page, consider carefully whether it should behave differently on a touchpad versus a desktop or laptop platform.)

Why

Hover Tools reveal themselves exactly when and where they're needed. They stay out of sight otherwise, allowing the UI to remain clean and uncluttered. They appear when the user requests them, and by appearing in response to the user's gesture, they draw attention to themselves.

Pop-up (right-click) menus, pull-down menus, and menu bars also meet these criteria, but they are not discoverable enough for some kinds of interfaces—they're best used on traditional desktop applications, not web-based interfaces. (And sometimes they're not the best choice on traditional applications, either.) Hover Tools are more easily discoverable because the gesture that produces them—a rollover—is so simple and natural.

Unfortunately, Hover Tools currently don't work so well on touch devices. A rollover with a mouse is an easy, natural act that leads to discovery; but on a touchpad, the only way a user can see the Hover Tools is if she actually touches the hover area, which is a more committing act. It doesn't help much with discovery at all.

How

Design each item or hover area with enough space to show all the available actions. Hide the ones that clutter the interface too much, and show them only when the user hovers the mouse pointer over the area in question.

Respond quickly to the hover, and don't use an Animated Transition—simply show the tools immediately, and hide them immediately when the user moves the pointer away. Likewise, never enlarge the hover area or otherwise rearrange the page when the user hovers the pointer over it. The idea is to make the hover action as lightweight and quick as possible so that the user can easily reach the necessary tools.

If the hover area is an item in a list, you may wish to highlight the item by changing its background color or drawing a border around it. The act of showing tools will draw the user's eyes to that area, but highlighting the item will do so even more.

Consider Hover Tools as an alternative to a drop-down menu, a pop-up menu, an Action Panel, a List Inlay with buttons in it, or a set of buttons repeated in each item.

Examples

Grooveshark uses Hover Tools to show per-song actions (see Figure 6-7). The alternatives would have been to show all the tools all the time—busy, but not terrible—or to move the tools to the top toolbar, where they would only operate on songs selected in the list. That's rather complicated for the designer, the programmer, and especially the user: she would have to figure out how to select a song, and then make the spatial and logical connection between the selected song(s) and the tools at the top of the table. In contrast, the Hover Tools are right there and self-explanatory.

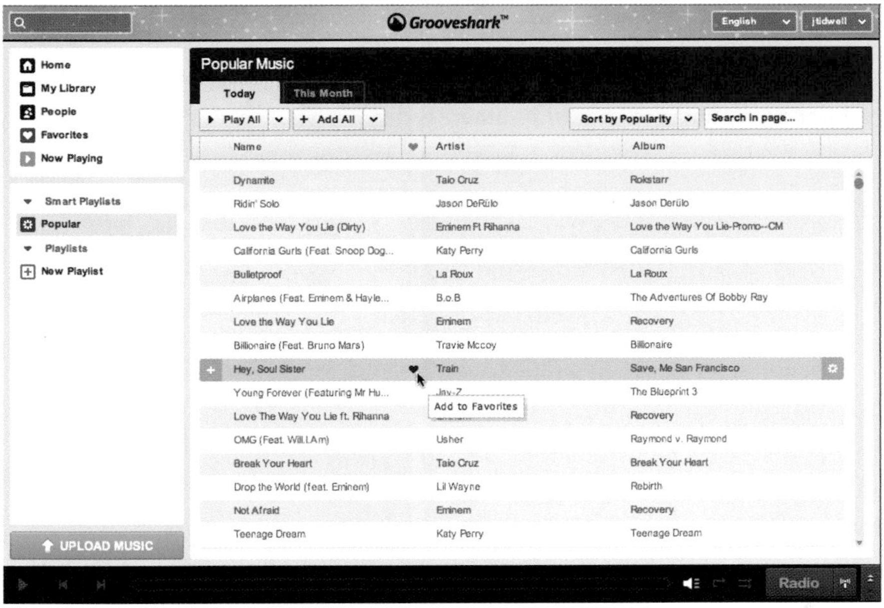

Figure 6-7. *Grooveshark*

The benefit of the Hover Tools pattern is a cleaner interface, but one drawback is that the user can't immediately see the available actions. Zillow's search results page, shown in Figure 6-8, shows one possible compromise: "gray out" the tools normally, and show them more strongly when the mouse hovers over the item.

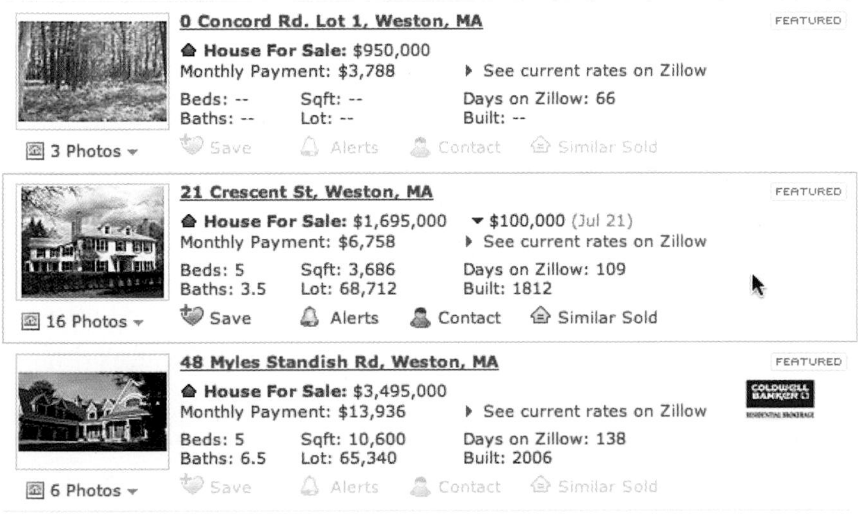

Figure 6-8. *Zillow*

Some implementations of Hover Tools use a lightweight overlay to show buttons or controls such as sliders. This is similar to the Dropdown Chooser pattern in Chapter 8, the only difference being your intent to use it for actions and not settings. In Figure 6-9, the YouTube player uses a hover to show the volume slider.

Figure 6-9. *YouTube player*

http://patternry.com/p=hover-reveal-tools/

http://www.flickr.com/photos/designingwebinterfaces/tags/hoverrevealtools/

Action Panel

Figure 6-10. *iPhoto*

What

Instead of using menus, present a group of related actions on a UI panel that's richly organized and always visible.

Use when

You have a list of items, and a set of actions that can be performed on each one—too many to show all the actions for each item, and too many for Hover Tools. You could put them into a menu, but you may not have a menu bar at all, or you'd rather make the actions more discoverable than they would be on menu bars. Same for pop-up menus; they're just not visible enough. Your users may not even realize the pop-up menus exist.

Or maybe your set of possible actions is too complex for a menu. Menus are best at showing a flat set of actions (since pull-right menus, or cascading menus, are hard for some users to manipulate) in a very simple, linear, one-line-per-item presentation. If your actions need to be grouped, and especially if those groups don't fit the standard top-level menu names—such as File, Edit, View, Tools, and so on—you might want a different presentation altogether.

This pattern can take up a lot of screen space, so it's not usually a good choice for small devices.

Why

There are three main reasons to use Action Panels instead of menus or per-item buttons: visibility, available space, and freedom of presentation.

By placing the actions out on the main UI and not hiding them inside a traditional menu, you make those actions fully visible to the user. Really, Action Panels *are* menus in the generic sense; they just aren't found in menu bars, drop downs, or pop ups. Users don't have to do anything to see what's on an Action Panel—it's right there in front of them—so your interface is more discoverable. This is particularly nice for users who aren't already familiar with the traditional document model and its menu bars.

There are many, many ways to structure objects on an interface: lists, grids or tables, hierarchies, and just about any custom structure you can devise. But Button Groups and traditional menus only give you a list (and not a very long one at that). An Action Panel is free-form—it gives you as much freedom to visually organize verbs as you have for nouns. Use it wisely!

How

Putting the Action Panel on the UI

Set aside a block of space on the interface for the Action Panel. Place it below or to the side of the target of the action. The target is usually a list, table, or tree of selectable items, but it might also be a document in Center Stage (Chapter 4). Remember that proximity is important. If you place the Action Panel too far away from whatever it acts on, users may not grasp the relationship between them.

The panel could be a simple rectangle on the page. It could be one of several tiled panels on the page, perhaps a Movable Panel (see Chapter 4), a "drawer" in Mac OS X, or even a separate window. If it's closable, make it very easy to reopen, especially if those actions are present only on the Action Panel and aren't duplicated on a menu!

Odds are good that you'll need to show different actions at different times. So, the contents of the action panel may depend on the state of the application (e.g., are there any open documents yet?), on the items selected in some list somewhere, or other factors. Let the Action Panel be dynamic. The changes will attract the user's attention, which is good.

Structuring the actions

Next, you need to decide how to structure the actions you need to present. Here are some ways you could do it:

- Simple lists
- Multicolumn lists
- Categorized lists, such as the PowerPoint example earlier
- Tables or grids
- Trees
- Any combination of these in one panel

If you categorize the actions, consider using a task-centered approach. Group them according to what people intend to do. However, try to present linearly. Imagine reading the actions aloud to someone who can't see the screen—can you proceed through them in a logical fashion, with obvious start and end points? That, of course, is how a blind user would "hear" the interface.

Labeling the actions

For each action's label, you could use text, icons, or both, depending on what conveys the nature of the actions best. In fact, if you use mostly icons, you end up with…a traditional toolbar! (Or a palette, if your UI is a visual builder-style application.)

Text labels on an Action Panel can be longer than those on a menu or a button. You can use multiline labels, for instance—no need to be overly parsimonious with words here. Just remember that longer, more descriptive labels are better for first-time or infrequent users who need to learn (or be reminded) what these actions do. The extra space spent on long labels may not be appreciated in high-performance interfaces used mostly by experienced users. If there are too many words, even first-time users' eyes will glaze over.

The example in Figure 6-10 is from iPhoto. Other Picture Managers, such as Picasa (Figure 6-11), use similar panels to contain per-image actions. Compare the complexity of the Picasa Action Panel with the relatively simple one in iPhoto; both work for their particular audiences and needs (iPhoto for novice users, Picasa for more experienced users).

Figure 6-11. *Picasa*

The screenshot of Windows Finder in Windows XP (see Figure 6-12) shows a directory of pictures with an Action Panel attached to it. Microsoft calls this feature a Task Pane. The panel is composed of closable subpanels (see the Collapsible Panels pattern in Chapter 4), each of which contains a manageable handful of related actions.

Note that the first two sections, Picture Tasks and File and Folder Tasks, are completely task-oriented: they're phrased as verbs (View, Order, Print, and Copy), and they anticipate actions that users will commonly want to perform. But the third section in this panel, Other Places, is a list of objects instead.

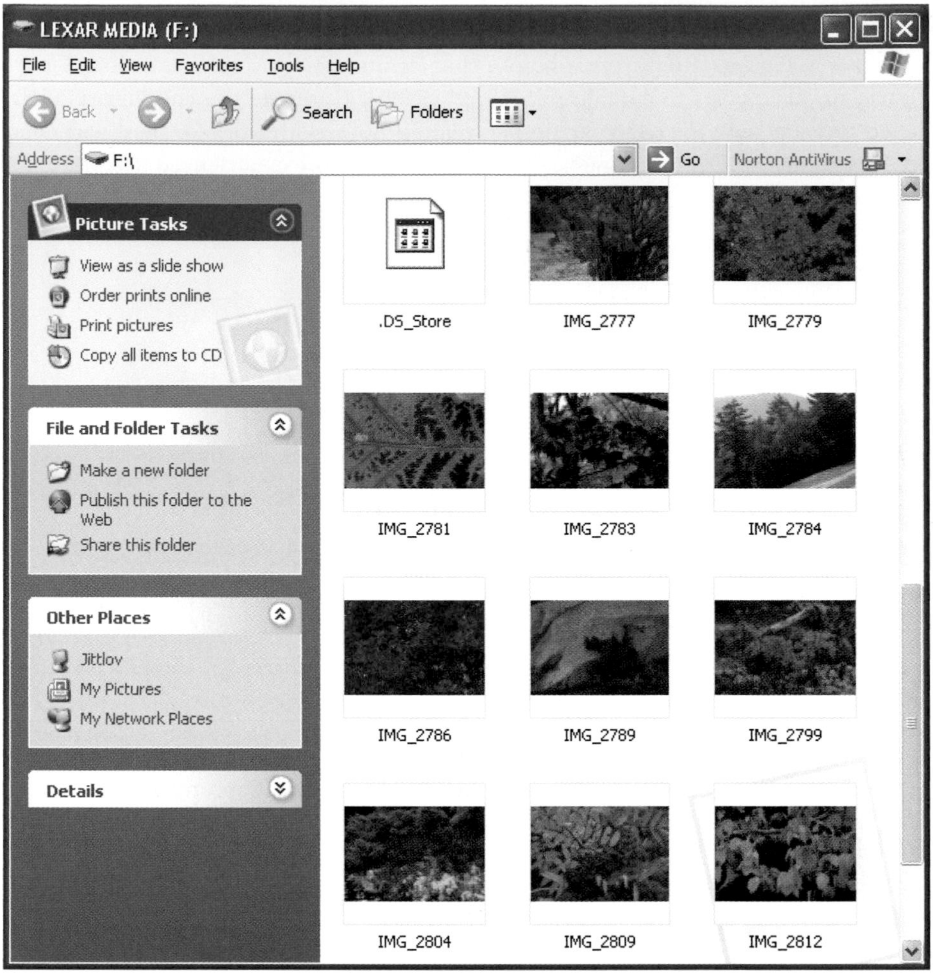

Figure 6-12. *Windows Finder*

In other libraries

Other web resources often call this pattern a Task Pane, including this pattern from Infragistics:

http://quince.infragistics.com/Patterns/Task%20Pane.aspx

Prominent "Done" Button

Welcome to the Songza Community!
Fill out the form to create your account and start making stations:

Email Address: _____

Username: _____

Password: _____

Confirm Pass: _____

[Create My Account]

Figure 6-13. *Songza*

What

Place the button that finishes a transaction at the end of the visual flow; make it big and well labeled.

Use when

Whenever you need to put a button such as Done, Submit, OK, or Continue on your interface, you should use this pattern. More generally, use a visually prominent button for the final step of any transaction—such as an online purchase—or to commit a group of settings.

Why

A well-understood, obvious last step gives your users a sense of closure. There's no doubt that the transaction will be done when that button is clicked; don't leave them hanging, wondering whether their work took effect.

Making that last step obvious is what this pattern is really about. Doing it well draws on the layout concepts in Chapter 4—visual hierarchy, visual flow, grouping, and alignment.

How

Create a button that actually looks like a button, not a link; either use platform standards for pushbuttons, or use a large or medium-size button graphic with bold colors and well-defined borders. This will help the button stand out on the page, and not get lost among other things.

When labeling the button, prefer text labels to icons. They're easier to understand for actions such as this, especially since most users will look for a button labeled "Done" or "Submit." The text in that label can be a verb or a short verb phrase that describes what will happen in the user's terms—"Send," "Buy," or "Change Record" (for example) are more specific than "Done," and can sometimes communicate more effectively.

Place the button where the user is most likely to find it. Trace the task flow down through the page or form or dialog box, and put the button just beyond the last step. Usually that will be on the bottom and/or right of the page. Your page layouts may have a standard place for them (see the Visual Framework pattern in Chapter 4), or the platform standard may prescribe it; if so, use the standard place.

In any case, make sure the button is near the last text field or control. If it's too far away, the user may not find it immediately upon finishing her work, and she may go looking for other affordances in her quest for "what to do next." On the Web, users may end up abandoning the page (and possibly a purchase) without realizing it.

Examples

Figure 6-14 shows a typical web form. You can see the action buttons without even reading the labels, due to visual design alone:

- The blue color stands out. It's a saturated color, it contrasts with the white background, and it echoes the blue of the headlines. (A white or light gray button with a black border would blend into the form.)

- The graphic used for each button looks like a button. It's a rounded or "pill" shape, with a very slight drop shadow, which makes it pop out from the background. The buttons are large, too.

- Both buttons are positioned directly under the body of the form itself. Both the task flow (the user will work from top to bottom) and the visual flow bring the user's eye to rest at that button.

- Each button is set off by whitespace on its left, right, and bottom.

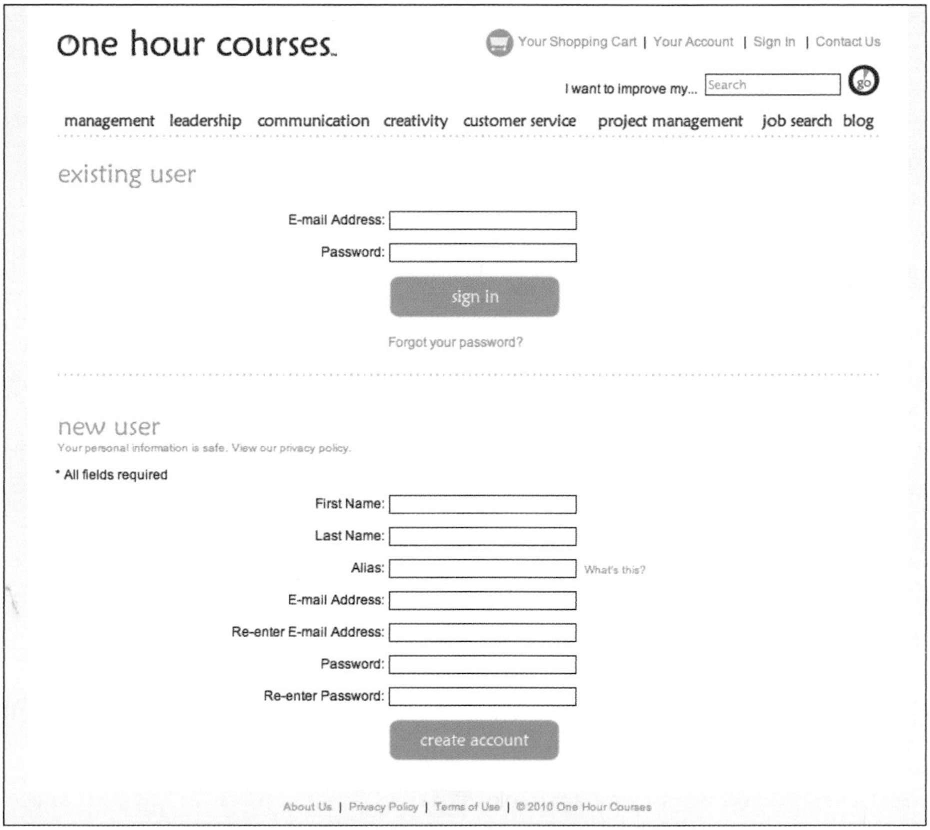

Figure 6-14. *OneHourCourses.com*

JetBlue, Kayak, and Southwest (see Figure 6-15) use strong buttons on their home page flight-search interfaces. These follow all the guidelines for Prominent "Done" Buttons, and again, you can see them immediately. The corresponding American Airlines button, on the other hand, gets lost in its form—it's too small, too far removed from the end of the form, too close to the form border, and too similar to other elements in the form to stand out well (see Figure 6-16). Furthermore, the label "GO" isn't as on-task as "Search" or "Find flights."

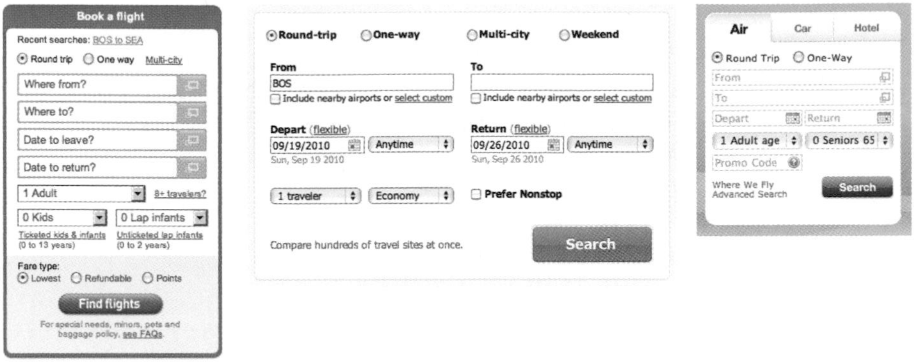

Figure 6-15. *JetBlue, Kayak, and Southwest*

Figure 6-16. *American Airlines*

Some other pattern libraries define patterns that are very closely related, such as Primary Action and Action Button. Luke Wroblewski, in his book *Web Form Design* (Rosenfeld Media), discusses primary versus secondary actions in forms such as those described in this pattern.

http://www.welie.com/patterns/showPattern.php?patternID=action-button

http://patternry.com/p=primary-secondary-actions/

http://quince.infragistics.com/Patterns/Primary%20Action.html

Smart Menu Items

Figure 6-17. *Mac Mail*

What

Change menu labels dynamically to show precisely what they will do when invoked.

Use when

Your UI has menu items that operate on specific documents or items, such as Close, or that behave slightly differently in different contexts, such as Undo.

Why

Menu items that say exactly what they're going to do make the UI self-explanatory. The user doesn't have to stop and figure out what object will be affected. She's also less likely to accidentally do something she didn't intend, such as deleting "Chapter 8" instead of "Footnote 3." It thus encourages safe exploration.

Every time the user changes the selected object (or current document, last undoable operation, etc.), change the menu items that operate on it to include the specifics of the action. Obviously, if there is no selected object at all, you should disable the menu item, thus reinforcing the connection between the item and its object.

Incidentally, this pattern could also work for button labels, or links, or anything else that is a "verb" in the context of the UI.

What if there are multiple selected objects? There's not a whole lot of guidance out there—in existing software, this pattern mostly applies to documents and undo operations—but you could write in a plural, as in "Delete Selected Objects."

Figure 6-18 shows a menu from Illustrator's menu bar. The last filter the user applied in this case was the "Drop Shadow" filter. The menu remembers that, so it changes its first two items to (1) reapply the same filter again, and (2) modify the filter before reapplying. ("Drop Shadow…" brings up the dialog box to modify it.) There are so many filters the user *might* have applied that it's quite useful to be reminded of the last one. And the accelerator keystrokes are handy for repeated application of the same filter!

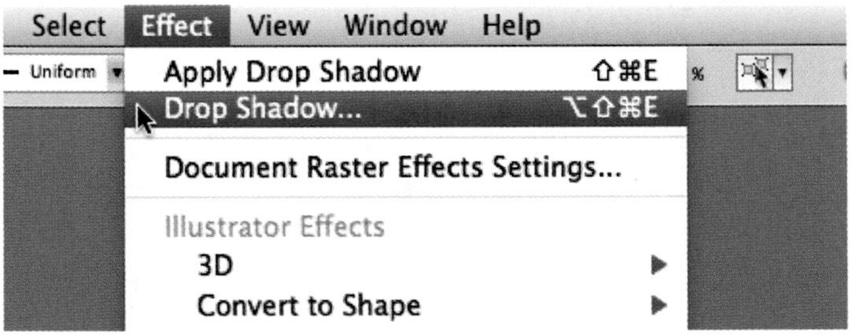

Figure 6-18. *Illustrator*

The previous two examples are from application menu bars, but this pattern can also be used effectively in per-item tools, such as the drop-down menu in Gmail (see Figure 6-19). The menu item "Add [person] to Contacts list" is much clearer and more self-explanatory than a generic alternative, such as "Add sender to Contacts list."

Figure 6-19. *Gmail menu*

Preview

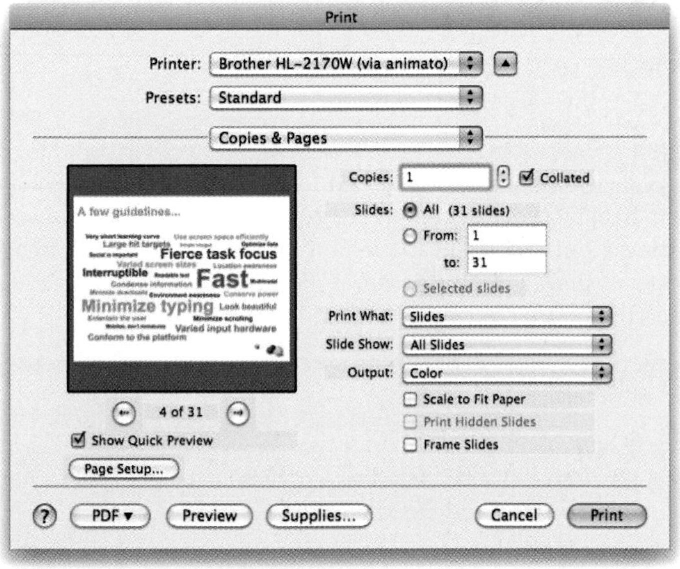

Figure 6-20. *PowerPoint print dialog*

What

Show users a preview or summary of what will happen when they perform an action.

The user is just about to perform a "heavyweight" action, such as opening a large file, printing a 10-page document, submitting a form that took time to fill out, or committing a purchase over the Web. The user wants some assurance that he's doing it correctly. Doing it incorrectly would be time-consuming or otherwise costly.

Alternatively, the user might be about to perform some visual change with a hard-to-predict result, such as applying a filter to a photo. He wants to know in advance whether the effect will be desirable.

Previews help prevent errors. A user may have made a typo, or he may have misunderstood something that led to the action in question (such as purchasing the wrong item online). By showing him a summary or visual description of what's about to happen, you give him a chance to back out or correct any mistakes.

Previews can also help an application become more self-describing. If someone's never used a certain action before, or doesn't know what it will do under certain circumstances, a preview explains it better than documentation—the user learns about the action exactly when and where he needs to.

Just before the user commits an action, display whatever information gives him the clearest picture of what's about to happen. If it's a print preview, show what the page will look like on the chosen paper size; if it's an image operation, show a close-up of what the image will look like; if it's a transaction, show a summary of everything the system knows about that transaction. Show what's important—no more, no less.

Give the user a way to commit the action straight from the preview page. There's no need to make the user close the preview or navigate elsewhere.

Likewise, give the user a way to back out. If he can salvage the transaction by correcting information previously entered, give him a chance to do that too, with "Change" buttons next to changeable information. In some wizards and other linear processes, this might just be a matter of navigating a few steps backward.

Picasa permits users to apply one of several filters to a photo (see Figure 6-21). Each filter has a preview thumbnail associated with it—what you see really is what you get! A user might need to experiment with many similar filters before finding one that has the desired effect, and he wants quick turnaround. This is a classic preview situation. (Photoshop and other image processing applications use similar previews.)

Figure 6-21. *Picasa*

Online product builders and customizers often use Previews to show what the user has created so far. The customizable Starbucks card in Figure 6-22 is a good example: in this review step, the user has a chance to go back and change things, or move ahead with card creation, or ask for help, or abandon the whole transaction.

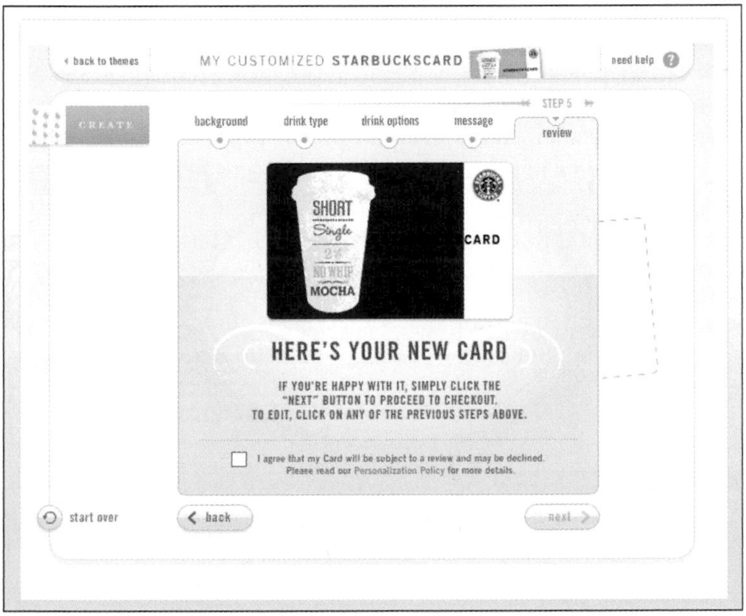

Figure 6-22. *Starbucks card customizer*

In other libraries

http://quince.infragistics.com/Patterns/Preview.aspx

http://ui-patterns.com/patterns/LivePreview

The book *Designing Web Interfaces* by Bill Scott and Theresa Neil (O'Reilly, *http://oreilly. com/catalog/9780596516253/*) also describes a \\. (Live Preview differs from Preview in that it shows changes immediately as they are made.)

Progress Indicator

Figure 6-23. *Mac OS Copy dialog*

What

Show the user how much progress has been made so far on a time-consuming operation.

Use when

A time-consuming operation interrupts the UI, or runs in the background, for longer than two seconds or so.

Why

Users get impatient when the UI just sits there. Even if you change the mouse pointer to a clock or hourglass (which you should in any case, if the rest of the UI is locked out), you don't want to make a user wait for an unspecified length of time.

Experiments show that if users see an indication that something is going on, they're much more patient, even if they have to wait longer than they would without a Progress Indicator. Maybe it's because they know that "the system is thinking," and it isn't just hung or waiting for them to do something.

How

Show an animated indicator of how much progress has been made. Either verbally or graphically (or both), tell the user:

- What's currently going on
- What proportion of the operation is complete

- How much time remains

- How to stop it

As far as time estimates are concerned, it's OK to be wrong sometimes, as long as your estimates converge on something accurate quickly. But sometimes the UI can't tell how far along it is. In that case, show something animated that is noncommittal about percentages. Think about the browsers' image loops that keep rolling while a page loads.

Most GUI toolboxes provide a widget or dialog box that implements this pattern. Beware of potentially tricky threading issues, however—the Progress Indicator must be updated consistently while the operation itself proceeds uninhibited. If you can, keep the rest of the UI alive, too. Don't lock up the UI while the Progress Indicator is visible.

If it's possible to cancel the operation whose progress is being monitored, offer a cancel button or similar affordance on or near the Progress Indicator; that's where a user is likely to look for it. See the Cancelability pattern (next) for more information.

Examples

When a Flickr user uploads multiple image files (which can take awhile), Flickr displays a rich and informative Progress Indicator (see Figure 6-24). It shows each file's size, progress, and status, along with an overall progress bar at the bottom. When the whole upload is done, it tells you so boldly and directs you to the next logical activity. (Another nice touch is that the page title itself gives you a percentage done.)

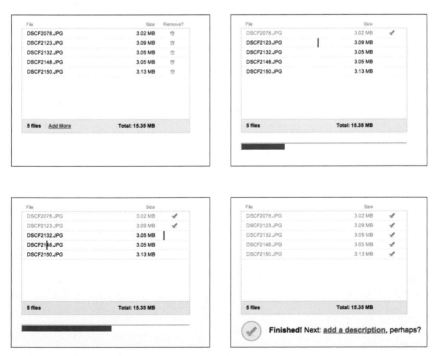

Figure 6-24. *Flickr multiple upload progress indicator*

Grooveshark's interface takes a little while to load. Its Progress Indicator is a whimsical and well-branded outline of a hammerhead shark, gradually filling left to right as the page code loads (see Figure 6-25).

Figure 6-25. *Grooveshark*

In other libraries

http://quince.infragistics.com/Patterns/Progress%20Indicator.aspx

http://www.welie.com/patterns/showPattern.php?patternID=processing-page

The book *Designing Web Interfaces* also describes a Progress Indicator pattern.

Cancelability

Figure 6-26. *Firefox*

What

Provide a way to instantly cancel a time-consuming operation, with no side effects.

Use when

A time-consuming operation interrupts the UI, or runs in the background, for longer than two seconds or so—such as when you print a file, query a database, or load a large file. Alternatively, the user is engaged in an activity that literally or apparently shuts out most other interactions with the system, such as when working with a modal dialog box.

Why

Users change their minds. Once a time-consuming operation starts, a user may want to stop it, especially if a Progress Indicator tells her that it'll take awhile. Or the user may have started it by accident in the first place. Cancelability certainly helps with error prevention and recovery—a user can cancel out of something she knows will fail, such as loading a page from a web server she realizes is down.

In any case, a user will feel better about exploring the interface and trying things out if she knows that anything is cancelable. It encourages Safe Exploration (see Chapter 1), which in turn makes the interface easier and more fun to learn.

How

First, find out if there's a way to speed up the time-consuming operation so that it appears to be instantaneous. It doesn't even have to be genuinely fast; if a user perceives it as immediate, that's good enough. On the Web or a networked application, this may mean preloading data or code—sending it to the client before it's asked for—or sending data in increments, showing it to the user as it comes in. Remember, people can only read so fast. You might as well use the loading time to let the user read the first page of data, then another page, and so on.

But if you really do need Cancelability, here's how to do it. Put a Cancel button directly on the interface, next to the Progress Indicator (which you are using, right?) or wherever the results of the operation will appear. Label it with the word *Stop* or *Cancel*, and/or put an internationally recognizable stop icon on it: a red octagon, or a red circle with a horizontal bar, or an "X".

When the user clicks or presses the Cancel button, cancel the operation immediately. If you wait too long—for more than a second or two—the user may doubt that the cancel actually worked (or you may just dissuade him from using it, since he might as well wait for the operation to finish). Tell the user that the cancel worked—halt the Progress Indicator, and show a status message on the interface, for instance.

Multiple parallel operations present a challenge. How does the user cancel a particular one and not others? The Cancel button's label or tool tip can state exactly what gets canceled when it's clicked (see the Smart Menu Items pattern for a similar concept). If the actions are presented as a list or a set of panels, you might consider providing a separate Cancel button for each action to avoid ambiguity.

Examples

The Adobe AIR install dialog, shown in Figure 6-27, is a simple, stripped-down example of Cancelability.

Figure 6-27. *Adobe AIR installation dialog*

When long file-copy operations stack up in Mac OS, each can be separately canceled, though they're all shown in the same dialog (see Figure 6-28). This makes sense—none of the copy operations depend on any of the others, and so any can be canceled without affecting the others.

Figure 6-28. *Mac OS Copy dialog, with four copy operations*

Multi-Level Undo

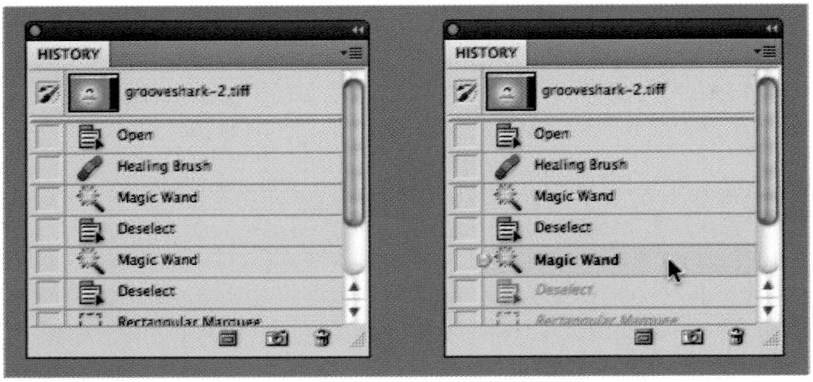

Figure 6-29. *Photoshop*

What

Provide a way to easily reverse a series of actions performed by the user.

You're building a highly interactive UI that is more complex than simple navigation or form fill-in. This includes mail readers, database software, authoring tools, graphics software, and programming environments.

The ability to undo a long sequence of operations lets users feel that the interface is safe to explore. While they learn the interface, they can experiment with it, confident that they aren't making irrevocable changes—even if they accidentally do something "bad." This is true for users of all levels of skill, not just beginners.[*]

Once the user knows the interface well, she can move through it with the confidence that mistakes aren't permanent. If her finger slips and she hits the wrong menu item, no complicated and stressful recovery is necessary; she doesn't have to revert to saved files, shut down and start afresh, or go ask a system administrator to restore a backup file. This spares users wasted time and occasional mental anguish.

Multi-Level Undo also lets expert users explore work paths quickly and easily. For instance, a Photoshop user might perform a series of filtering operations on an image, study the result to see if she likes it, and then undo back to her starting point. Then she might try out another series of filters, maybe save it, and undo again. She could do this without Multi-Level Undo, but it would take a lot more time (for closing and reloading the image). When a user works creatively, speed and ease of use are important for maintaining the experience of flow. See Chapter 1 for more information, especially the Safe Exploration and Incremental Construction patterns.

Undoable operations

The software your UI is built on first needs a strong model of what an action is—what it's called, what object it was associated with, and how to reverse it. Then you can build an interface on it.

Decide which operations need to be undoable. Any action that might change a file or database—anything that could be permanent—should be undoable, while transient or view-related states often are not. Specifically, these kinds of changes are expected to be undoable in most applications:

- Text entry for documents or spreadsheets
- Database transactions

---

[*] Alan Cooper and Robert Reimann devote an entire chapter to the undo concept in their book *About Face 2.0: The Essentials of Interaction Design* (Wiley).

- Modifications to images or painting canvases
- Layout changes—position, size, stacking order, or grouping—in graphics applications
- File operations, such as deleting or modifying files
- Creation, deletion, or rearrangement of objects such as email messages or spreadsheet columns
- Any cut, copy, or paste operation

The following kinds of changes are generally not undoable. Even if you think you want to go above and beyond the call of duty and make them undoable, consider that you might thoroughly irritate users by cluttering up the "undo stack" with useless undos.

- Text or object selection
- Navigation between windows or pages
- Mouse cursor and text cursor locations
- Scrollbar position
- Window or panel positions and sizes
- Changes made in an uncommitted or modal dialog box

Some operations are on the borderline. Form fill-in, for instance, is sometimes undoable and sometimes not. However, if tabbing out of a changed field automatically commits that change, it's probably a good idea to make it undoable.

(Certain kinds of operations are impossible to undo, but usually the nature of the application makes that obvious to users with any experience at all. Impossible undos include the purchase step of an e-commerce transaction, posting a message to a forum or chat room, or sending an email—as much as we'd sometimes like that to be undoable!)

In any case, make sure the undoable operations make sense to the user. Be sure to define and name them in terms of how the user thinks about the operations, not how the computer thinks about them. You should be able to undo a block of typed text, for instance, in chunks of words, not letter by letter.

Design an undo stack

Each operation goes on the top of the stack as it is performed. Each undo reverses the operation at the top first, then the one below it, then the next, and so on. Redo works its way back up the stack likewise.

The stack should be at least 10 to 12 items long to be the most useful, and longer if you can manage it. Long-term observation or usability testing may tell you what your usable limit is. (Constantine and Lockwood assert that having more than a dozen items is usually unnecessary, since "users are seldom able to make effective use of more levels."* Expert users of high-powered software might tell you differently. As always, know your users.)

Presentation

Finally, decide how to present the undo stack to the user. Most desktop applications put Undo/Redo items on the Edit menu. Also, Undo is usually hooked up to Ctrl-Z or its equivalent. The best-behaved applications use Smart Menu Items to tell the user exactly which operation is next up on the undo stack.

But see the screenshot at the top of this pattern (Figure 6-29) for a different, more visual presentation. Photoshop shows a scrolling list of the undoable operations—including ones that were already undone (two are shown, in gray). It lets the user pick the point in the stack that she wants to revert to. A visual command history like this can be quite useful, even just as a reminder of what you've recently done. See the Command History pattern for more information.

Examples

Figure 6-30 shows a more typical presentation of Multi-Level Undo. In this case, the user typed some text and then inserted a table. The first undo removes the table. Once that's done, the following undo—the next action in the undo stack—represents the typed text, and invoking Undo again will remove that text. Meanwhile, the user has the opportunity to "undo the undo" with the Redo menu item. If we're at the top of the stack (as in the first screenshot), there is no Redo, and that menu item is overloaded with a Repeat action.

Confusing? You bet. Most users will never develop a clear mental picture of the algorithms being used here; most people don't know what a "stack" is, let alone how it is used in conjunction with Repeat and Redo. That's why the Smart Menu Items are absolutely critical to usability here. They explain exactly what's going to happen, which reduces the cognitive burden on the user.

---

* Larry Constantine and Lucy Lockwood, "Instructive Interaction: Making Innovative Interfaces Self-Teaching," *http://foruse.com/articles/instructive.htm.*

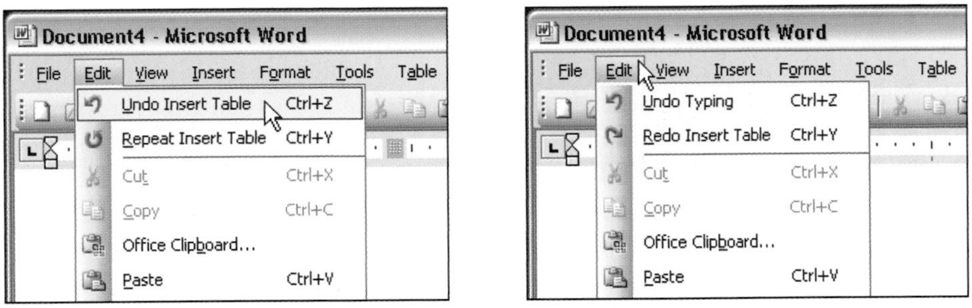

Figure 6-30. *Microsoft Word*

In other libraries

http://patternry.com/p=undo/

http://quince.infragistics.com/Patterns/Undo.aspx

Command History

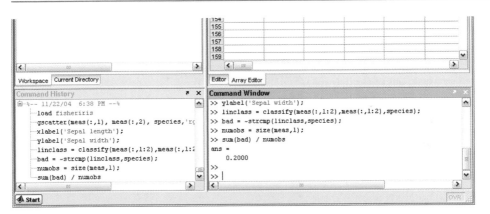

Figure 6-31. *MATLAB's command history, show in the lower left*

What

As the user performs actions, keep a visible record of those actions—what was done to what, and when.

Use when

Users perform long and complex sequences of actions, with either a GUI or a command line. Most users are fairly experienced, or if not, they at least want an efficient interface that's supportive of long-term and recurring work. Graphical editors and programming environments are usually good candidates.

Why

Sometimes a user needs to remember or review what he did in the course of working with the software. For instance, he may want to do any of these things:

- Repeat an action or command done earlier, which he doesn't remember well
- Recall the order in which some actions were done
- Repeat a sequence of operations, originally done to one object, on a different object
- Keep a log of his actions, for legal or security reasons
- Convert an interactive series of commands into a script or macro (see the Macros pattern in this chapter)

Computers are good at keeping an accurate record of steps taken; people aren't. Take advantage of that.

How

Keep a running list of the actions taken by the user. If the interface is driven from a command line, you have it easy—just record everything typed there. If you can, keep track of the history across sessions, so the user can see what was done even a week ago or longer.

If it's a graphic interface, or a combination of graphic and command-line interfaces, things get a little more complicated. Find a way to express each action in one consistent, concise way, usually with words (though there's no reason why it can't be done visually). Make sure you define these with the right granularity—if one action is done en masse to 17 objects, record it as one action, not 17.

What commands should be recorded, and what shouldn't? See the Multi-Level Undo pattern for a thorough discussion of what commands should "count." If a command is undoable, it should be recorded in the history, too.

Finally, display the history to the user. That display should be optional in most software, since it will almost certainly play a supporting role in the user's work, not a starring role. Lists of commands—oldest to newest—tend to work well. If you'd like, you could time-stamp the history display somehow. MATLAB, shown earlier in Figure 6-31, puts a date and time into the history whenever the program restarts.

Unix and its many variants use shell programs, such as tcsh and bash, that keep track of their own command histories in files. The user can call it up with the "history" command, as shown in Figure 6-32. The history is also accessible through various command-line constructs, such as !! (reuse the last command), !3 (reuse the command issued three commands ago), and Ctrl-P, which you can issue repeatedly to show the previous commands one at a time.

```
swing-shift:/var/log/httpd> history
    1  23:55   pwd
    2  23:55   pushd /var/log/httpd/
    3  23:55   ls -l access_log
    4  23:56   tail -1000 access_log | grep "index"
    5  23:56   tail -1000 access_log | grep "index" | wc
    6  23:57   tail -1000 access_log | grep "Diagonal" | wc
    7  23:57   ls -l
    8  23:57   cd jtidwellnet/
    9  23:57   tail -1000 access_log | grep "index" | wc
   10  23:58   tail -200 access_log | more
   11  23:58   tail -200 access_log | grep "google"
   12  23:58   cd ..
   13  23:58   tail -1000 access_log | grep "google"
   14  23:59   tail -1000 access_log | grep "googlebot"
   15  23:59   history
swing-shift:/var/log/httpd> []
```

Figure 6-32. *Unix shell*

Photoshop's undo stack, also seen in the Multi-Level Undo pattern, is effectively a command history. You can use it to undo the actions you performed, but you don't have to; you can also just look at it and scroll through it, reviewing what you did. It uses icons to identify different classes of actions, which is unusual, but nice to use (see Figure 6-33).

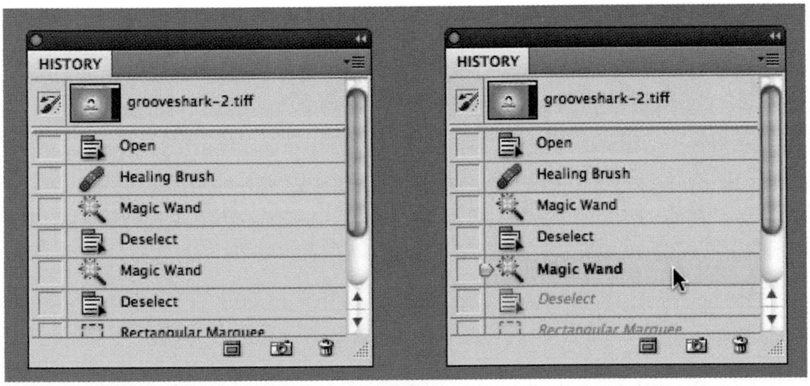

Figure 6-33. *Photoshop, again*

Macros

Figure 6-34. *Photoshop*

Macros are single actions composed of other, smaller actions. Users can create them by putting together sequences of actionsUse when:

Users may want to repeat long sequences of actions or commands. They might want to loop over lists of files, images, database records, or other objects, for instance, doing the same things to each object. You might already have implemented Multi-Level Undo or Command History.

No one wants to perform the same set of repetitive interactive tasks over, and over, and over again! This is exactly what computers are supposed to be good at. Chapter 1 described a user-behavior pattern called Streamlined Repetition; macros are precisely the kind of mechanism that can support that well.

Macros obviously help users work faster. But by reducing the number of commands or gestures needed to get something done, they also reduce the possibility of finger slips, oversights, and similar mistakes.

You might also recall the concept of "flow," also discussed in Chapter 1. When a long sequence of actions can be compressed down into a single command or keyboard shortcut, the experience of flow is enhanced—the user can accomplish more with less effort and time, and she can keep her larger goals in sight without getting bogged down in details.

Provide a way for the user to "record" a sequence of actions and easily "play them back" at any time. The playback should be as easy as giving a single command, pressing a single button, or dragging and dropping an object.

Defining the macro

The user should be able to give the macro a name of her choice. Let her review the action sequence somehow, so she can check her work or revisit a forgotten sequence to see what it did (as in the Command History pattern). Make it possible for one macro to refer to another, so they can build on each other.

Users will certainly want to save macros from one day to the next, so make sure they're persistent—save them to files or a database. Present them in a searchable, sortable, and even categorizable list, depending on the needs of your users.

Running the macro

The macro itself could be played back literally, to keep things simple; or, if it acts upon an object that can change from one invocation to another, you could allow the sequence to be parameterized (e.g., use a placeholder or variable instead of a literal object). Macros should also be able to act on many things at once.

How the names of the macros (or the controls that launch them) are presented depends heavily upon the nature of the application, but consider putting them with built-in actions rather than making them second-class citizens.

The ability to record these sequences—plus the facility for macros to build on one other— create the potential for the user to invent an entirely new linguistic or visual grammar, a grammar that is finely tuned to her own environment and work habits. This is a very powerful capability. In reality, it's programming; but if your users don't think of themselves as programmers, don't call it that or you'll scare them off. ("I don't know how to program anything; I must not be able to do this.")

Microsoft Excel allows macros to be recorded, named, stored along with the document, and even assigned to a keyboard shortcut. The user can also choose to run a macro from a button on the toolbar, or an ActiveX control in the document itself (which means macros can be used as callbacks for buttons, text fields, etc.).

The Excel macros shown in Figures 6-35 and 6-36 are written in Visual Basic, and the user can hand-edit them if desired. This is when it becomes programming. Because Visual Basic provides access to so much general-purpose functionality—most of it not directly related to, say, spreadsheet operations—macros can be a serious security risk for Office applications. By sharply constraining the functionality available to macros and by limiting the number of ways users can run macros (e.g., only by clicking on toolbar buttons), you can trade power for safety.

(Note that not all versions of Excel allow Visual Basic macros as of this writing.)

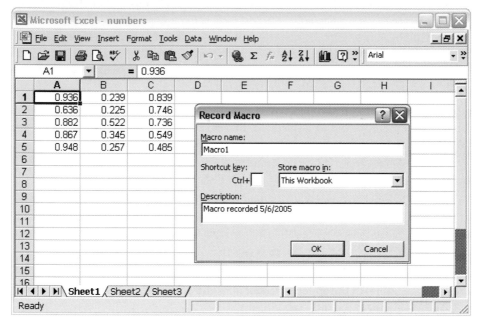

Figure 6-35. *Excel macro recording*

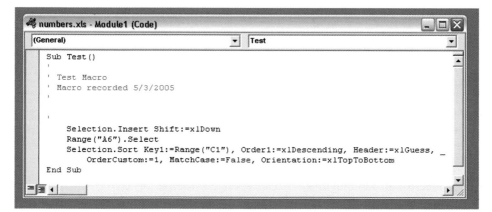

Figure 6-36. *Excel macros, written in Visual Basic*

Chapter 7

Showing Complex Data: Trees, Charts, and Other Information Graphics

Information graphics—including maps, tables, and graphs—communicate knowledge visually rather than verbally. When done well, they let people use their eyes and minds to draw their own conclusions; they show, rather than tell.

These are my favorite kinds of interfaces. However, poor tools or inadequate design can sharply limit what you can do with them, and many information-rich interfaces just don't quite work as well as they could.

The patterns in this chapter will help you make the best of the tools you have, and introduce you to some useful and interesting innovations in interactive information graphics. The ideas described in this introduction can help you sort out which design aspects are most important to you in a given interface.

The Basics of Information Graphics

Information graphics simply means data presented visually, with the goal of imparting knowledge to the user. I'm including tables and tree views in that description because they are inherently visual, even though they're constructed primarily from text instead of lines and polygons. Other familiar static information graphics include maps, flowcharts, bar plots, and diagrams of real-world objects.

But we're dealing with computers, not paper. You can make almost any good static design better with interactivity. Interactive tools let the user hide and show information as she needs it, and they put the user in the "driver's seat" as she chooses how to view and explore that information.

Even the mere act of manipulating and rearranging the data in an interactive graphic has value—the user becomes a participant in the discovery process, not just a passive observer. This can be invaluable. The user may not end up producing the world's best-designed plot or table, but the process of manipulating that plot or table puts her face to face with aspects of the data that she may never have noticed on paper.

Ultimately, the user's goal in using information graphics is to learn something. But the designer needs to understand *what* the user needs to learn. The user might be looking for something very specific, such as a particular street on a map, in which case she needs to be able to find it—say, by searching directly, or by filtering out extraneous information. She needs to get a "big picture" only to the extent necessary to reach that specific data point. The ability to search, filter, and zero in on details is critical.

On the other hand, she might be trying to learn something less concrete. She might look at a map to grasp the layout of a city rather than to find a specific address. Or she may be a scientist visualizing a biochemical process, trying to understand how it works. Now overviews are important; she needs to see how the parts interconnect with the whole. She may want to zoom in, zoom back out again, look at the details occasionally, and compare one view of the data to another.

Good interactive information graphics offer users answers to these questions:

- How is this data organized?
- What's related to what?
- How can I explore this data?
- Can I rearrange this data to see it differently?
- How can I see only the data that I need?
- What are the specific data values?

In these sections, keep in mind that the term *information graphics* is a very big umbrella. It covers plots, graphs, maps, tables, trees, timelines, and diagrams of all sorts; the data can be huge and multilayered, or small and focused. Many of these techniques apply surprisingly well to graphic types that you wouldn't expect.

Before describing the patterns themselves, let's set the stage by talking about some of the questions posed in the previous list.

Organizational Models: How Is This Data Organized?

The first thing a user sees in any information visualization is the shape you've chosen for the data. Ideally, the data itself has an inherent structure that suggests this shape to you. Table 7-1 shows a variety of organizational models. Which of these fits your data best?

Table 7-1. *Organizational models*

Model	Diagram	Common graphics
Linear		List, single-variable plot
Tabular		Spreadsheet, multicolumn list, Sortable Table, Radial Table, Multi-Y Graph, other multivariable plots
Hierarchical		Tree, Cascading Lists, Tree Table, Treemap, Radial Table, directed graph
Network of interconnections		Directed graph, flowchart, Radial Table
Geographic (or spatial)		Map, schematic, scatter plot
Textual		Word cloud, directed graph
Other		Plots of various sorts, such as parallel coordinate plots, Treemaps, etc.

Try these out against the data you're trying to show. If two or more might fit, consider which ones play up which aspects of your data. If your data could be both geographic and tabular, for instance, showing it as only a table may obscure its geographic nature—a viewer may miss interesting features or relationships in the data if it's not shown as a map, too.

Preattentive Variables: What's Related to What?

The organizational model you choose tells the user a lot about the shape of the data. Part of this message operates at a subconscious level; people recognize trees, tables, and maps, and they immediately make some assumptions about the underlying data before they even start to think consciously about it. But it's not just the shape that does this. The look of the individual data elements also works at a subconscious level in the user's mind: things that look alike must be associated with each other.

If you've read Chapter 4, that should sound familiar—you already know about the Gestalt principles. (If you jumped ahead in the book, this might be a good time to go back and read the introduction to Chapter 4.) Most of those principles, especially *similarity* and *continuity*, will come into play here, too. I'll tell you a little more about how they work.

Certain visual features operate *preattentively*: they convey information before the viewer pays conscious attention. Take a look at Figure 7-1 and find the blue objects.

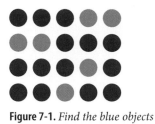

Figure 7-1. *Find the blue objects*

I'm guessing that you can do that pretty quickly. Now look at Figure 7-2 and do the same.

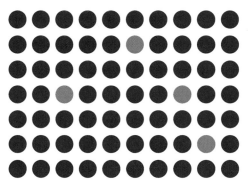

Figure 7-2. *Find the blue objects again*

You did that pretty quickly too, right? In fact, it doesn't matter how many red objects there are; the amount of time it takes you to find the blue ones is constant! You might think it should be linear with the total number of objects—order-N time, in algorithmic terms—but it's not. Color operates at a primitive cognitive level. Your visual system does the hard work for you, and it seems to work in a "massively parallel" fashion.

On the other hand, visually monotonous text forces you to read the values and think about them. Figure 7-3 shows exactly the same problem with numbers instead of colors. How fast can you find the numbers that are greater than one?

0.103	0.176	0.387	0.300	0.379	0.276	0.179	0.321	0.192	0.250
0.333	0.384	0.564	0.587	0.857	1.064	0.698	0.621	0.232	0.316
0.421	0.309	0.654	0.729	0.228	0.529	0.832	0.935	0.452	0.426
0.266	0.750	1.056	0.936	0.911	0.820	0.723	1.201	0.935	0.819
0.225	0.326	0.643	0.337	0.721	0.837	0.682	0.987	0.984	0.849
0.187	0.586	0.529	0.340	0.829	0.835	0.873	0.945	1.103	0.710
0.153	0.485	0.560	0.428	0.628	0.335	0.956	0.879	0.699	0.424

Figure 7-3. *Find the values greater than one*

When dealing with text such as this, your "search time" really is linear with the number of items. But what if we still used text, but made the target numbers physically larger than the others, as in Figure 7-4?

0.103	0.176	0.387	0.300	0.379	0.276	0.179	0.321	0.192	0.250
0.333	0.384	0.564	0.587	0.857	1.064	0.698	0.621	0.232	0.316
0.421	0.309	0.654	0.729	0.228	0.529	0.832	0.935	0.452	0.426
0.266	0.750	1.056	0.936	0.911	0.820	0.723	1.201	0.935	0.819
0.225	0.326	0.643	0.337	0.721	0.837	0.682	0.987	0.984	0.849
0.187	0.586	0.529	0.340	0.829	0.835	0.873	0.945	1.103	0.710
0.153	0.485	0.560	0.428	0.628	0.335	0.956	0.879	0.699	0.424

Figure 7-4. *Find the values greater than one again*

Now we're back to constant time again. Size is, in fact, another preattentive variable. The fact that the larger numbers protrude into their right margins also helps you find them—alignment is yet another preattentive variable.

Figure 7-5 shows many known preattentive variables.

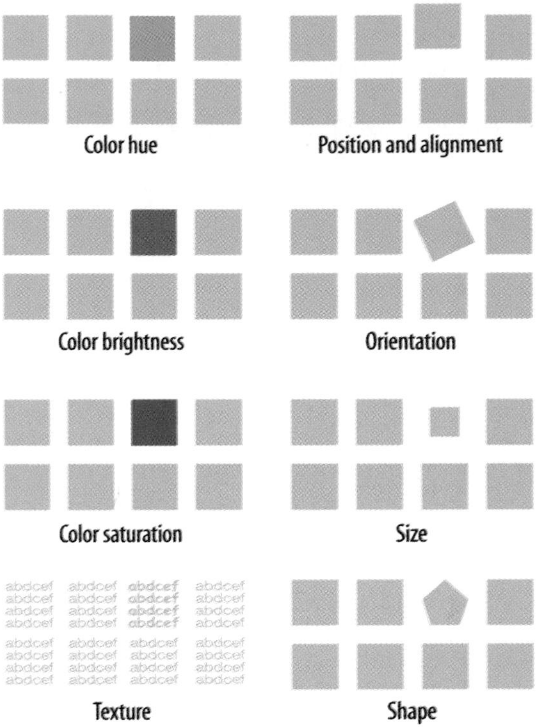

Figure 7-5. *Eight preattentive variables*

This concept has profound implications for text-based information graphics, like the table of numbers shown earlier in Figure 7-3. If you want some data points to stand out from the others, you have to make them look different by varying their color, size, or some other preattentive variable. More generally, you can use these variables to differentiate classes or dimensions of data on any kind of information graphic. This is sometimes called *encoding*.

When you have to plot a multidimensional data set, you can use several different visual variables to encode all those dimensions in a single static display. Consider the scatter plot shown in Figure 7-6. Position is used along the x- and y-axes; color hue encodes a third variable. The shape of the scatter markers could encode yet a fourth variable, but in this case, shape is redundant with color hue. The redundant encoding helps a user visually separate the three data groups.

All of this is related to a general graphic design concept called *layering*. When you look at well-designed graphics of any sort, you perceive different classes of information on the page. Preattentive factors such as color cause some of them to "pop" out of the page, and similarity causes you to see those as connected to each other, as though each was on a transparent layer over the base graphic. It's an extremely effective way of segmenting data—each layer is simpler than the whole graphic, and the viewer can study each in turn, but relationships among the whole are preserved and emphasized.

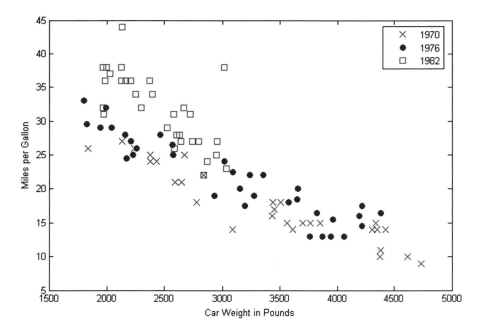

Figure 7-6. *Encoding three variables in a scatter plot*

Navigation and Browsing: How Can I Explore This Data?

A user's first investigation of an interactive data graphic may be browsing—just looking around to see what's there. He may also navigate through it to find some specific thing he's seeking. Filtering and searching can serve that purpose too, but navigation through the "virtual space" of a data set is often better. Spatial Memory (Chapter 1) kicks in, and the user can see points of interest in context with the rest of the data.

There's a famous mantra in the information visualization field: "Focus plus context." A good visualization should permit a user to focus on a point of interest, while simultaneously showing enough stuff around that point of interest to give the user a sense of where it is in the big picture.

Here are some common techniques for navigation and browsing:

Scroll and pan

If the whole data display won't fit on-screen at once, you could put it in a scrolled window, giving the user easy and familiar access to the off-screen portions. Scrollbars are familiar to almost everyone and are easy to use. However, some displays are too big, or their size is indeterminate (thus making scrollbars inaccurate), or they have data beyond the visible window that needs to be retrieved or recalculated (thus making scrollbars too slow to respond). Instead of using scrollbars in those cases, try setting up buttons that the user has to click to retrieve the next screenful of data. Other applications do panning instead, in which the information graphic is "grabbed" with the cursor and dragged until the point of interest is found, like in Google Maps.

These are appropriate for different situations, but the basic idea is the same: to interactively move the visible part of the graphic. Sometimes Overview Plus Detail can help the user stay oriented. A small view of the whole graphic can be shown with an indicator rectangle showing the visible "viewport"; the user might pan by dragging that rectangle, in addition to using scrollbars or however else it's done.

Zoom

Zooming changes the *scale* of the section being viewed, whereas scrolling changes the location. When you present a data-dense map or graph, consider offering the user the ability to zoom in on points of interest. It means you don't have to pack every single data detail into the full view—if you have lots of labels, or very tiny features (especially on maps), that may be impossible anyway. As the user zooms in, those features can emerge when they have enough space.

Most zooms are triggered with a mouse click or button press, and the whole viewing area changes scale at once. But that's not the only way to zoom. Some applications create nonlinear distortions of the information graphic as the user moves the mouse pointer over the graphic: whatever is under the pointer is zoomed, but the stuff far away from the pointer stays the same scale. See the Local Zooming pattern for more information.

Open and close points of interest

Tree views typically let users open and close parent items at will, so they can inspect the contents of those items. Some hierarchically structured diagrams and graphs also give users the chance to open and close parts of the diagram "in place," without having to open a new window or go to a new screen. With these mechanisms, the user can explore containment or parent/child relationships easily, without leaving that window. The Cascading Lists pattern (Chapter 5) describes another effective way to explore a hierarchy; it works entirely on single-click opening and closing of items.

Drill down into points of interest

Some information graphics just present a "top level" of information. A user might click or double-click on a map to see information about the city she just clicked on, or she might click on key points in a diagram to see subdiagrams. This "drilling down" might reuse the same window, use a separate panel on the same window, or bring up a new window. This technique is similar to opening and closing points of interest, except that the viewing occurs separately from the graphic and is not integrated into it.

If you also provide a search facility for an interactive information graphic, consider linking the search results to whichever of the aforementioned techniques is in use. In other words, when a user searches for the city of Sydney on a map, show the map zooming and/ or panning to that point. The search user thus gets some of the benefits of context and spatial memory.

Sorting and Rearranging: Can I Rearrange This Data to See It Differently?

Sometimes just rearranging an information graphic can reveal unexpected relationships. Look at Figure 7-7, taken from the National Cancer Institute's online mortality charts. It shows the number of deaths from lung cancer in the state of Texas. The major metropolitan regions in Texas are arranged alphabetically—not an unreasonable default order if you're going to look up specific cities, but as presented, the data doesn't lead you to ask very many interesting questions. It's not clear why Abilene, Alice, Amarillo, and Austin all seem to have similar numbers, for instance; it may just be chance.

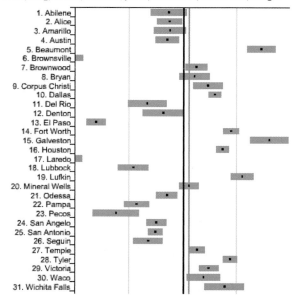

Figure 7-7. *Cancer data by city, sorted alphabetically*

But this chart lets you reorder the data into numerically descending order, as in Figure 7-8. Suddenly the graph becomes much more interesting. Galveston is ranked first—why is that, when its neighbor, Houston, is further down the scale? What's special about Galveston? (OK, you need to know something about Texas geography to ask these questions, but you get my point.) Likewise, why the difference between neighbors Dallas and Fort Worth? And apparently the Mexico-bordering southern cities of El Paso, Brownsville, and Laredo have less lung cancer than the rest of Texas; why might that be? You can't answer these questions with this data set, but at least you can ask them.

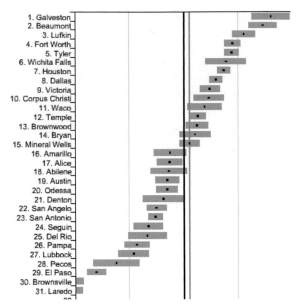

Figure 7-8. *The same chart, sorted numerically*

People who can interact with data graphics this way have more opportunities to learn from the graphic. Sorting and rearranging puts different data points next to each other, thus letting users make different kinds of comparisons—it's far easier to compare neighbors than widely scattered points. And users tend to zero in on the extreme ends of scales, as I did in the preceding example.

How else can you apply this concept? The Sortable Table pattern talks about one obvious way: when you have a many-columned table, users might want to sort the rows according to their choice of column. This pattern is pretty common. (Many table implementations also permit rearrangement of the columns themselves, by dragging.) Trees might allow reordering of their child nodes. Diagrams and connected graphs might allow spatial repositioning of their elements, while retaining their connectivity. Use your imagination!

Consider these methods of sorting and rearranging:

- Alphabetically
- Numerically
- By date or time
- By physical location
- By category or tag
- By popularity—heavily used versus lightly used

- User-designed arrangement
- Completely random (you never know what you might see)

For a subtle example, take a look at Figure 7-9. Bar charts that show multiple data values on each bar (known as *stacked* bar charts) might also be amenable to rearranging—the bar segments nearest the baseline are the easiest to evaluate and compare, so you might want to let users determine which variable is next to the baseline.

The light blue variable in this example might be the same height from bar to bar. Does it vary, and how? Which light blue bars are the tallest? You really can't tell until you move that data series to the baseline—that transformation lines up the bases of all those blue rectangles. Now a visual comparison is easy: light-blue bars 6 and 12 are the tallest, and the variation seems loosely correlated to the overall bar heights.

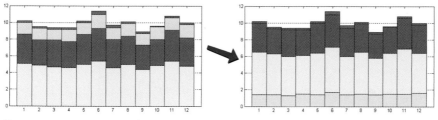

Figure 7-9. *Rearrangement of a stacked bar chart*

Searching and Filtering: How Can I See Only the Data That I Need?

Sometimes you don't want to see an entire data set at once. You might start with the whole thing and narrow it down to what you need—filtering—or you might build up a subset of the data via searching or querying. Most users won't even distinguish between filtering and querying (though there's a big difference from, say, a database's point of view). The user's intent is the same: to zero in on whatever part of the data is of interest, and get rid of the rest.

The simplest filtering and querying techniques offer users a choice of which aspects of the data to view. Checkboxes and other one-click controls turn parts of the interactive graphic on and off. A table might show some columns and not others, per the user's choice; a map might show only the points of interest (e.g., restaurants) selected by the user. The Dynamic Queries pattern, which can offer very rich interaction, is a logical extension of simple filter controls such as these.

Sometimes simply highlighting a subset of the data, rather than hiding or removing the rest, is sufficient. That way a user can see that subset in context with the rest of the data. Interactively, you can do this with simple controls, as described earlier. The Data Brushing pattern describes a variation of data highlighting; it highlights the same data in several data graphics at once.

Look at Figure 7-10. This interactive ski-trail map can show four categories of trails, coded by symbol, plus other features such as ski lifts and base lodges. When everything is "turned on" at once, it's so crowded that it's hard to read anything! But users can click on the trail symbols, as shown, to turn the data "layers" on and off. The screenshot on the left shows no highlighted trails; the one on the right switches on the trails rated black diamond with a single click.

Figure 7-10. *Interactive ski map*

Searching mechanisms vary heavily from one type of graphic to another. A table or tree should permit textual searches, of course; a map should offer searches on addresses and other physical locations; numeric charts and plots might let users search for specific data values or ranges of values. What are your users interested in searching on?

When the search is done and results obtained, you might set up the interface to show the results in context, on the graphic—you could scroll the table or map so that the searched-for item is in the middle of the viewport, for instance. Seeing the results in context with the rest of the data helps the user understand the results better. The Jump to Item pattern in Chapter 5 is a common way to search and scroll in one step.

The best filtering and querying interfaces are:

Highly interactive
> They respond as quickly as possible to the user's searching and filtering. (Don't react to individual keystrokes if it significantly slows down the user's typing, however.)

Iterative

They let a user refine the search, query, or filter until she gets the desired results. They might also combine these operations: a user might do a search, get a screenful of results, and then filter those results down to what she wants.

Contextual

They show results in context with surrounding data, to make it easier for a user to understand where they are in a data space. This is also true for other kinds of searches, as it happens; the best text search facilities show the search terms embedded in sentences, for instance.

Complex

They go beyond simply switching entire data sets on and off, and allow the user to specify nuanced combinations of conditions for showing data. For instance, can this information graphic show me all the items for which conditions X, Y, and Z are true, but A and B are false, within the time range M–N? Such complexity lets users test hypotheses about the data, and explore the data set in creative ways.

The Actual Data: What Are the Specific Data Values?

Several common techniques help a viewer get specific values out of an information graphic. Know your audience—if they're only interested in getting a qualitative sense of the data, there's no need for you to spend large amounts of time or pixels labeling every little thing. But some actual numbers or text is usually necessary.

Since these techniques all involve text, don't forget the graphic design principles that will make text look good: readable fonts, appropriate font size (not too big, not too small), proper visual separation between unrelated text items, alignment of related items, no heavy-bordered boxes, and no unnecessary obscuring of data.

Labels

Many information graphics put labels directly on the graphic, such as town names on a map. Labels can also identify the values of symbols on a scatter plot, bars on a bar graph, and other things that might normally force the user to depend on axes or legends. Labels are easier to use. They communicate data values precisely and unambiguously (when placed correctly), and they're located in or beside the data point of interest—no going back and forth between the data point and a legend. The downside is that they clutter up a graphic when overused, so be careful.

Legends

When you use color, texture, line style, symbols, or size on an information graphic to represent values (or categories or value ranges), the legend shows the user what represents what. You should place the legend on the same page as the graphic itself so the user's eyes don't need to travel far between the data and the legend.

Axes, rulers, scales, and timelines

Whenever position represents data, as it does on plots and maps (but not on most diagrams), these tell the user what values those positions represent. They are reference lines or curves on which reference values are marked. The user has to draw an imaginary line from the point of interest to the axis, and maybe interpolate to find the right number. This is more of a burden on the user than direct labeling. But labeling clutters things when the data is dense, and many users don't need to derive precise values from graphics; they just want a more general sense of the values involved. For those situations, axes are appropriate.

Datatips

This chapter describes the Datatips pattern. Datatips, which are tool tips that show data values when the user hovers over a point of interest, have the physical proximity advantages of labels without the clutter. They only work in interactive graphics, though.

Data Spotlight

Like Datatips, a data spotlight highlights data when the user hovers over a point of interest. But instead of showing the specific point's value, it displays a "slice" of the data in context with the rest of the information graphic, often by dimming the rest of the data. See the Data Spotlight pattern.

Data brushing

A technique called *data brushing* lets users select a subset of the data in the information graphic and see how that data fits into other contexts. You use this with two or more information graphics; for instance, selecting some outliers in a scatter plot causes those same data points to be highlighted in a table showing the same data. For more information, see the Data Brushing pattern in this chapter.

The Patterns

Because this book is about interactive software, most of these patterns describe ways to interact with the data: moving through it; sorting, selecting, inserting, or changing items; and probing for specific values or sets of values. A few of them deal only with static graphics: information designers have known about Multi-Y Graph and Small Multiples for a while now, but they translate well to the world of software.

And don't forget the patterns elsewhere in this book. From Chapter 2, recall Alternative Views, which can help you structure an interactive graphic. Chapter 3 offers Annotated Scrollbar and Animated Transition, which help users to stay oriented within large and complex data spaces. If your graphic is a table, you might also use some of the patterns in Chapter 5, such as Row Striping, Alphabet Scroller, and Jump to Item.

The first group of patterns can be applied to most varieties of interactive graphics, regardless of the data's underlying structure. (Some are harder to learn and use than others, so don't throw them at every data graphic you create—Data Brushing and Local Zooming in particular, are "power tools," best for sophisticated computer users.) These six interactive tools permit users to *focus* on certain parts of the data set while maintaining the *context* of the entire graphic.

1. Overview Plus Detail

2. Datatips

3. Data Spotlight

4. Dynamic Queries

5. Data Brushing

6. Local Zooming

The remaining patterns are ways to construct complex data graphics for multidimensional data—data that has many attributes or variables. They encourage users to ask different kinds of questions about the data, and to make different types of comparisons among data elements.

7. Sortable Table

8. Radial Table

9. Multi-Y Graph

10. Small Multiples

11. Treemap

Overview Plus Detail

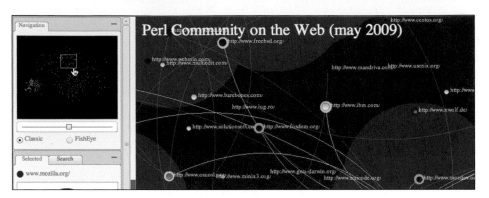

Figure 7-11. *Perl community diagram (http://labs.linkfluence.net/fpw09/map/)*

What

Place an overview of the graphic next to a zoomed "detail view." As the user drags a viewport around the overview, show that part of the graphic in the detail view.

Use when

You're showing a large data set in a large information graphic—especially an image or a map. You want users to stay oriented with respect to the "big picture," but you also want them to zoom down into the fine details. Users will browse through the data, inspect small areas, or search for points of interest. High-level overviews are necessary for finding those points of interest, but users don't need to see all available detail for all data points at once—zooming in on a small piece is sufficient for getting fine detail.

Why

It's an age-old way of dealing with complexity: present a high-level view of what's going on and let the users zoom from that view into the details as they need to, keeping both levels visible on the same page for quick iteration.

Edward Tufte uses the terms *micro reading* and *macro reading* to describe a similar concept for printed maps, diagrams, and other static information graphics. The user has the large structure in front of her at all times, while being able to peer into the small details at will: "The pace of visualization is condensed, slowed, and personalized." Similarly, users of Overview Plus Detail can scroll methodically through the content, jump around, compare, contrast, move quickly, or move slowly.

Finally, the overview can serve as a "You are here" sign. A user can tell at a glance where she is in the context of the whole data set by looking for the viewport on the overview.

Show an overview of the data set at all times. It can be an inset panel, as in the example at the top of the pattern (see Figure 7-11 at the top of the pattern). It could also be a panel beside the detail view, or even another window, in the case of a multiwindow application such as Photoshop.

On that overview, place a viewport. They're usually red boxes by convention, but they don't have to be—they just need to be visible at a glance, so consider the other colors used in the overview panel. If the graphic is typically dark, make it light; if the graphic is light, make it dark. Make the viewport draggable with the pointer, so users can grab it and slide it around the overview.

The detail view shows a magnified "projection" of what's inside the viewport. The two should be synchronized. If the viewport moves, the detail view changes accordingly; if the viewport is made smaller, the magnification should increase. Likewise, if the detail view has scrollbars or some other panning capability, the viewport should move along with it. The response of one to the other should be immediate, within one-tenth of a second (the standard response time for direct manipulation).

Examples

Photoshop places the image canvas (the "detail view") on the left and the overview on the right. The Navigator window shows the whole image, with a red box showing the size and scroll position of the image's canvas window (see Figure 7-12).

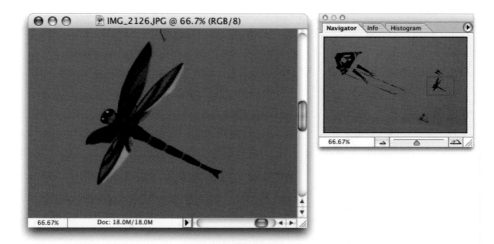

Figure 7-12. *Photoshop*

Google Finance uses an interactive overview panel to let the user adjust the time period shown on the graph. Note the grab handles on the viewport sides and the year labels that tell the user what timescale the overview uses (see Figure 7-13).

Figure 7-13. *Google Finance*

The *New York Times* also uses a timeline to drive its infographic about environmental change (see Figure 7-14). Users select events on the timeline to see details about them. A Pyramid navigation pattern is also at work here: the user can jump to the next item by clicking the Next button in the upper right.

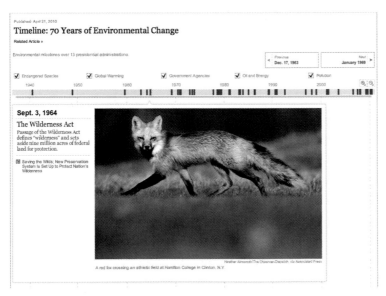

Figure 7-14. *The New York Times interactive feature (http://www.nytimes.com/interactive/2010/04/22/science/earth/20100422_environment_timeline.html)*

In other libraries

http://patternbrowser.org/code/pattern/pattern_anzeigen.php?4,226,17,0,0,247

http://quince.infragistics.com/Patterns/Overview%20Plus%20Detail.aspx

The broad concept of "overview and detail" can be found in numerous books on information visualization, including those by Edward Tufte, mentioned earlier.

Datatips

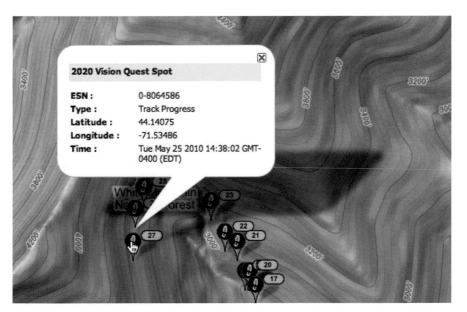

Figure 7-15. *SPOT Adventures live map*

What

As the mouse rolls over a point of interest on the graphic, put the data values for that point into a tool tip or some other floating window.

Use when

You're showing an overview of a data set, in almost any form. More data is "hidden behind" specific points on that graphic, such as the names of streets on a map or the values of bars in a bar chart. The user is able to "point at" places of interest with a mouse cursor or a touch screen.

Why

Looking at specific data values is a common task in data-rich graphics. Users will want the overview, but they might also look for particular facts that aren't present in the overview. Datatips let you present small, targeted chunks of context-dependent data, and they put that data right where the user's attention is focused: the mouse pointer. If the overview is reasonably well organized, users will find it easy to look up what they need, and you won't need to put it all on the graphic. Datatips can substitute for labels.

Also, some people might just be curious. What else is here? What can I find out? Datatips offer an easy, rewarding form of interactivity. They're quick (no page loading!), they're lightweight, and they offer intriguing little glimpses into an otherwise invisible data set.

If you find yourself trying to use a Datatip to show an enlargement of the data that it's hovering over, rather than data values, consider using the Local Zooming pattern instead.

How

Use a tool tip–like window to show the data associated with that point. It doesn't have to be technically a "tool tip"—all that matters is that it appears where the pointer is, it's layered atop the graphic, and it's temporary. Users will get the idea pretty quickly.

Inside that window, format the data appropriately. Denser is usually better, since a tool tip window is expected to be small; don't let the window get so large that it obscures too much of the graphic while it's visible. And place it well. If there's a way to programmatically position it so that it covers as little content as possible, try that.

You might even want to format the Datatip differently depending on the situation. An interactive map might let the user toggle between seeing place names and seeing latitude/longitude coordinates, for example. If you have a few data sets plotted as separate lines on one graph, the Datatips might be labeled differently for each line, or have different kinds of data in them.

Many Datatips offer links that the user can click on. This lets the user "drill down" into parts of the data that may not be visible at all on the main information graphic. The Datatip is beautifully self-describing—it offers not only information, but also a link and instructions for drilling down.

An alternative way of dynamically showing hidden data is to reserve some panel on or next to the graphic as a static data window. As the user rolls over various points on the graphic, data associated with those points appears in the data window. It's the same idea, but using a reserved space rather than a temporary Datatip. The user has to shift her attention from the pointer to that panel, but you never have a problem with the rest of the graphic being hidden. Furthermore, if that data window can retain its data, the user can view it while doing something else with the mouse.

In contemporary interactive infographics, Datatips often work in conjunction with a Data Spotlight mechanism. The spotlight shows a slice through the data—for example, a line or set of scattered points—while the Datatips shows the specific data point that's under the mouse pointer.

The San Francisco Crimespotting feature uses both Datatips (see Figure 7-16) and a Data Spotlight. All incidents of theft are highlighted on the map (via the spotlight), but a Datatip describes the particular incident at which the user is pointing. Note also the link to the raw data about this crime.

Figure 7-16. *San Francisco Crimespotting (http://sanfrancisco.crimespotting.org/)*

Some data sets are so dense or text-rich that they can't easily be labeled at all. The graph from IBM's Many Eyes project, shown in Figure 7-17, depends upon Datatips to communicate critical labels to the user. The Datatip offers plenty of space to express the text and numbers of interest—far more than labels can. It also tells the user that clicking on this part of the graph will highlight the relevant data—again, a Data Spotlight in action.

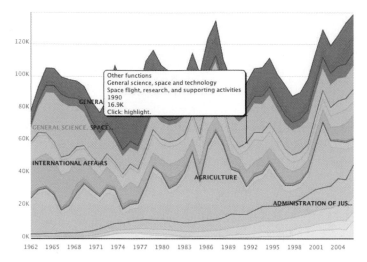

Figure 7-17. *Many Eyes graph (http://manyeyes.alphaworks.ibm.com/manyeyes/visualizations/us-government-expenses-1962-2004)*

So many geographic information graphics are built upon Google Maps that it deserves a particular mention. Its API makes it fairly easy to create Datatips specialized to the application's needs, such as the SPOT Adventures example at the top of the pattern (Figure 7-15) and in the example in Figure 7-18.

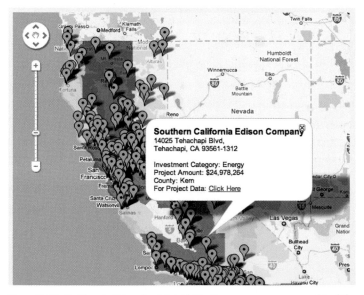

Figure 7-18. *California Stimulus Map (http://www.recovery.ca.gov/html/funding/stimulus%20map/districtsmap.jsp)*

http://patternbrowser.org/code/pattern/pattern_anzeigen.php?4,237,17,0,0,258

http://quince.infragistics.com/Patterns/Data%20Tips.aspx

Data Spotlight

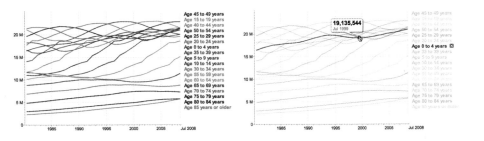

Figure 7-19. *Google Public Data Explorer*

What

As the mouse rolls over an area of interest on the graphic, highlight that slice of data and dim the rest.

Use when

The graphic contains so much information that it tends to obscure its own structure. It might be difficult for a viewer to pick out relationships and trace connections among the data because of its sheer richness.

The data itself is structurally complex—it might have several independent variables and complicated "slices" of dependent data such as lines, areas, scattered sets of points, or systems of connections. (If the rolled-over data is merely a point or a simple shape, a Datatip is a better solution than a Data Spotlight. They're often used in conjunction with each other, though.)

Why

A Data Spotlight untangles the threads of data from each other. It's one way that you can offer "focus plus context" on a complex infographic: a user eliminates some of the visual clutter on the graphic by quieting most of it, focusing only on the data slice of interest. However, the rest of the data is still there to provide context.

It also permits dynamic exploration by letting a user flick quickly from one data slice to another. She can see both large differences and very small differences that way—as long as the Data Spotlight transitions quickly and smoothly (without flicker) from one data slice to another as the mouse moves, even very tiny differences will be visible.

Finally, Data Spotlights can be fun and engaging to use.

How

First, design the information graphic so that it doesn't initially depend on a Data Spotlights. Try to keep the data slices visible and coherent so that a user can follow what's going on without interacting with the graphic. (Someone may print it, after all.)

To create a spotlight effect, make the spotlighted data either a light color or a saturated color, while the other data fades to a darker or grayer color. Make the reaction very quick on rollover to give the user a sense of immediacy and smoothness.

Besides triggering a spotlight when the mouse rolls over data elements, you might also put "hot spots" onto legends and other references to the data.

Consider a "spotlight mode." In this, the Data Spotlight waits for a longer initial mouse hover before turning itself on. Once in that mode, the user's mouse motions cause immediate changes to the spotlight. This means the spotlight effect won't be triggered accidentally, when a user just happens to roll the mouse over the graphic. The Crimespotting example (shown in Figure 7-20) does this.

An alternative to the mouse rollover gesture is a simple mouse click or finger tap. This lacks the immediacy of rollovers, but it works on touchpads and it isn't as subject to accidental triggering. However, you may want to reserve the mouse click for a different action, such as drilling down into the data.

Use Datatips to describe specific data points, describe the data slice being highlighted, and offer instructions where necessary.

Examples

The San Francisco Crimespotting project puts a Data Spotlight on the different types of crimes found in this geographic area. When the user hovers the mouse over a single data element—a crime report—or over the legend that describes the crime types (shown in Figure 7-20), all reports of that type are highlighted with light circles. The rest of the graphic is darkened, in the style of a lightbox.

Figure 7-20. *San Francisco Crimespotting*

The *Washington Post*'s interactive "Top Secret" graphic looks fine by itself, but the chart is complicated and may be hard for a passive viewer to follow (see Figure 7-21). The Data Spotlight lets the user easily see the information associated with a particular agency.

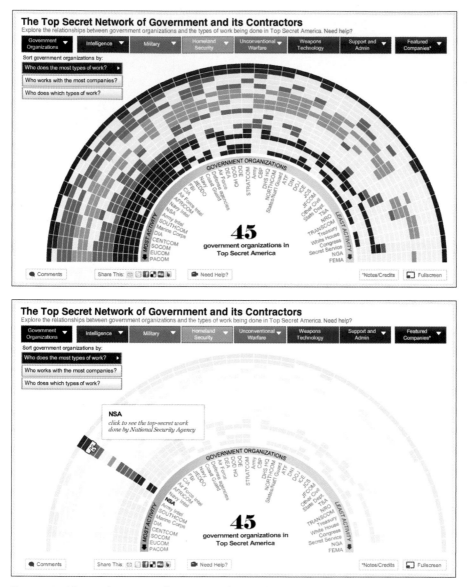

Figure 7-21. *The Washington Post's interactive feature (http://projects.washingtonpost.com/top-secret-america/)*

Sometimes a graphic can't easily show all the available data. The Radial Table graphic from the *Wall Street Journal*, shown in Figure 7-22, uses a variety of interactive tools to let the user explore the tracking-data connections among websites. Clicking on a cell shows specific relationships; rolling over nonclicked cells shows a "ghost" of the relationship lines. The "Show all" command makes a graphic that looks interesting, but doesn't give the user much actionable information—the limited interactive views are far more interesting!

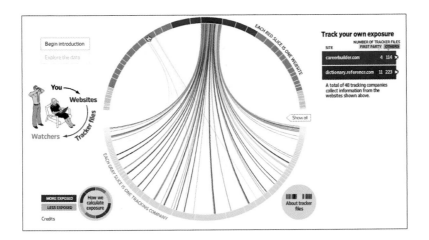

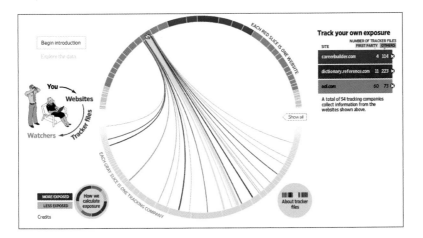

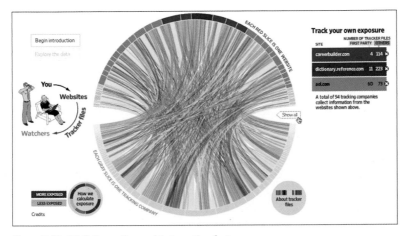

Figure 7-22. *Wall Street Journal interactive feature*

Dynamic Queries

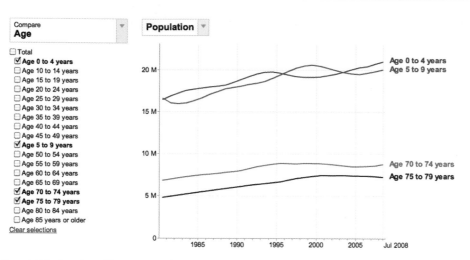

Figure 7-23. *Google Public Data Explorer*

What

Provide ways to filter the data set immediately and interactively. Employ easy-to-use standard controls, such as sliders and checkboxes, to define which slices or layers of the data set get shown. As the user adjusts those controls, show the results immediately on the data display.

Use when

You're showing the user a large, multivariate data set, of any shape, with any presentation. Users need to filter out some of the data in order to accomplish any of several objectives—to get rid of irrelevant parts of the data set, to see which data points meet certain criteria, to understand relationships among the various data attributes, or simply to explore the data set and see what's there.

The data set itself has a fixed and predictable set of attributes (or parameters, variables, dimensions, whatever term you prefer) that are of interest to users. They are usually numeric and range-bounded; they might also be sortable strings, dates, categories, or enumerations (sets of numbers representing non-numeric values). Or they might be visible areas of data on the information display itself that can be interactively selected.

Dynamic Queries can also apply to search results. Faceted searches might use a dynamic query interface to let users explore a rich database of items, such as products, images, or text.

First, Dynamic Queries are easy to learn. No complicated query language is necessary at the user's end; well-understood controls are used to express common-sense Boolean expressions such as "price > $70 AND price < $100". They lack the full expressive power of a query language—only simple queries are possible without making the UI too complicated—but in most cases, that's enough. It's a judgment call you have to make.

Second, the immediate feedback encourages open-ended exploration of the data set. As the user moves a slider thumb, for instance, she sees the visible data contract or expand. As she adds or removes different subsets of the data, she sees where they go and how they change the display. She can concoct long and complex query expressions incrementally, by tweaking this control, then that, then another. Thus, a continuous and interactive "question and answer session" is carried on between the user and the data. The immediate feedback shortens the iteration loop so that exploration is fun and a state of flow is possible. (See Chapter 1, Incremental Construction.)

Third—and this is a little subtler—the presence of labeled dynamic-query controls clarifies what the queryable attributes are in the first place. If one of the data attributes is a number that ranges from 0 to 100, for instance, the user can learn that just by seeing a slider that has 0 at one end and 100 at the other end.

The best way to design a dynamic query depends on your data display, the kinds of queries you think should be made, and your toolkit's capabilities. As mentioned, most programs map data attributes to ordinary controls that live next to the data display. This allows querying on many variables at once, not just those encoded by spatial features on the display. Plus, most people know how to use sliders and buttons.

Other programs afford interactive selection directly on the information display. Usually the user draws a box around a region of interest and the data in that region is removed (or retained while the rest of the data is removed). This is manipulation at its most direct, but it has the disadvantage of being tied to the spatial rendering of the data. If you can't draw a box around it—or otherwise select points of interest—you can't query on it! See the Data Brushing pattern for the pros and cons of a very similar technique.

Back to controls, then: picking controls for dynamic queries is similar to the act of picking controls for any kind of form—the choices arise from the data type, the kind of query to be made, and the available controls. Some common choices include:

- Sliders to specify a single number within a range.
- Double sliders or slider pairs to specify a subset of a range: "Show data points that are greater than this number, but less than this other number."

- Radio buttons or drop-down (combo) boxes to pick one value out of several possible values. You might also use these to pick entire variables or data sets. In either case, "All" is frequently used as an additional metavalue.

- Checkboxes or toggles to pick an arbitrary subset of values, variables, or data layers.

- Text fields to type in single values, perhaps to be used in a Fill-in-the-Blanks context (see Chapter 8). Remember that text fields leave more room for errors and typos than do sliders and buttons, but are better for precise values.

Examples

The example in Figure 7-24 shows a set of six filters for a treemap (see the Treemap pattern in this chapter). The checkboxes, filters 1 and 2, screen out entire swaths of data with two very simple canned queries: is this item available, and does it have a picture?

The remaining filters use double sliders. Each has two independently movable slider "thumbs" that let a user define a range. The Price slider sets a range of about $80 to about $1,000 (admittedly not very realistic), and as the user moves either end of the range, the whole treemap shifts and changes to reflect the new price range. The same is true for the other sliders.

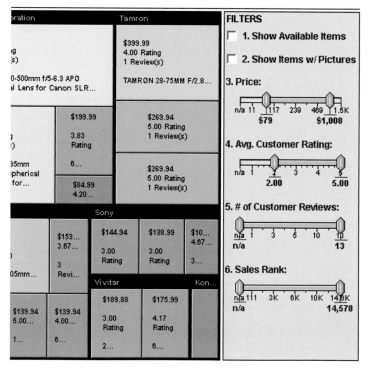

Figure 7-24. *Hive Group treemap adjustment panel*

The San Francisco Crimespotting project (see Figure 7-25) offers a set of simple, comprehensible toggles to show crime data for different times of day—dark, light, commute, swing shift, and so on. The user can also choose specific times of day with the clock-like control. To narrow down the calendar dates, a long bar chart (itself a data display) permits a range selection via a double slider, in addition to standard calendar drop downs.

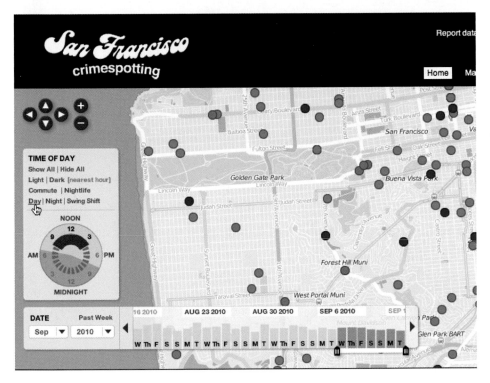

Figure 7-25. *San Francisco Crimespotting*

In other libraries

http://patternbrowser.org/code/pattern/pattern_anzeigen.php?4,231,17,0,0,252

http://www.infovis-wiki.net/index.php?title=Dynamic_query

Both the name and the concept for Dynamic Queries originated in the early 1990s with several seminal papers by Christopher Ahlberg, Christopher Williamson, and Ben Shneiderman. You can find some of these papers online, including the following:

http://hcil.cs.umd.edu/trs/91-11/91-11.html

http://hcil.cs.umd.edu/trs/93-01/93-01.html

Data Brushing

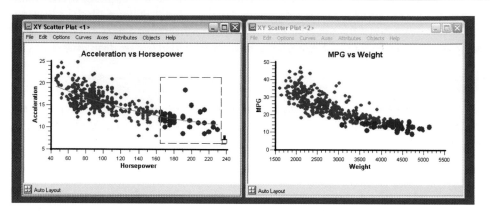

Figure 7-26. *BBN Cornerstone*

What

Let the user select data items in one view; show the same data selected simultaneously in another view.

Use when

You can show two or more information graphics at a time. You might have two line plots and a scatter plot, or a scatter plot and a table, or a diagram and a tree, or a map and a timeline, whatever—as long as each graphic is showing the same data set.

Why

Data Brushing offers a very rich form of interactive data exploration. First, the user can select data points using an information graphic itself as a "selector." Sometimes it's easier to find points of interest visually than by less direct means, such as Dynamic Queries—outliers on a plot can be seen and manipulated immediately, for instance, while figuring out how to define them numerically might take a few seconds (or longer). "Do I want all points where X > 200 and Y > 5.6? I can't tell; just let me draw a box around that group of points."

Second, by seeing the selected or "brushed" data points simultaneously in the other graphic(s), the user can observe those points in at least one other graphical context. That can be invaluable. To use the outlier example again, the user might want to know where those outliers are in a different data space, indexed by different variables—and by learning that, she might gain immediate insight into the phenomenon that produced the data.

A larger principle here is *coordinated* or *linked views*. Multiple views on the same data can be linked or synchronized so that certain manipulations—zooming, panning, selection, and so forth—done to one view are simultaneously shown in the others. Coordination reinforces the idea that the views are simply different perspectives on the same data. Again, the user focuses on the same data in different contexts, which can lead to insight.

How

First, how will users select or "brush" the data? It's the same problem you'd have with any selectable collection of objects: users might want one object or several, contiguous or separate, selected all at once or incrementally. Consider these ideas:

- Drawing a rubber-band box around the data points (this is very common)
- Single selection by clicking with the mouse
- Selecting a range (if that makes sense) by Shift-clicking, as one can often do with lists
- Adding and subtracting points by Ctrl-clicking, also like lists
- Drawing an arbitrary "lasso" shape around the data points
- Inverting the selection via a menu item, button, or key

If you go exclusively with a rubber-band box, consider leaving the box on-screen after the selection gesture. Some systems, such as Cornerstone, permit interactive resizing of the brushing box. Actually, the user can benefit from any method of interactively expanding or reducing the brushed set of points, because she can see the newly brushed points "light up" immediately in the other views, which creates more possibility for insight.

As you can see, it's important that the other views react immediately to Data Brushing. Make sure the system can handle a fast turnaround.

If the brushed data points appear with the same visual characteristics in all the data views, including the graphic where the brushing occurs, the user can more easily find them and recognize them as being brushed. They also form a single perceptual layer (see the section "Preattentive Variables: What's Related to What?" on page 283). Color hue is the preattentive variable most frequently used for brushing, probably because you can see a bright color so easily even when your attention is focused elsewhere.

Examples

The screenshots shown in both Figures 7-26 and 7-27 are taken from Cornerstone, a statistics and graphing package. The three windows in Figure 7-27 represent a scatter plot, a histogram of the residuals of one of the plotted variables, and a table of the raw data. All views afford brushing; you can see the brushing box around two of the histogram's columns. Both plots show the brushed data in red, while the table shows it in gray. If you "brushed" a car model in the table, you would see the dot representing that model appear in red in the top plot, plus a red strip in the histogram.

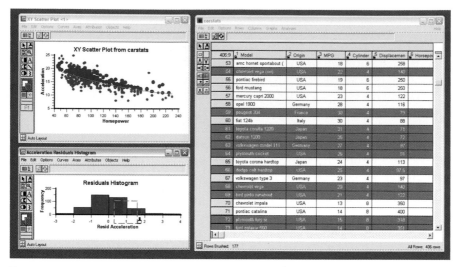

Figure 7-27. *BBN Cornerstone, again*

Maps lend themselves well to Data Brushing, because data shown in a geographic context can often be organized and rendered in other ways as well. The following three examples show map-based Data Brushing: images in a filmstrip-like line (from Flickr, Figure 7-28), GPS tracker locations in chronological order (from SPOT Adventures, Figure 7-29), and Foursquare checkins by a person going from one social event to another, also in chronological order (from Weeplaces, Figure 7-30). In all three examples, selection of items in the linear view causes the items to "light up" in the map view. Flickr and SPOT also do the reverse—they let the user select items on the map itself, so they light up in the linear view.

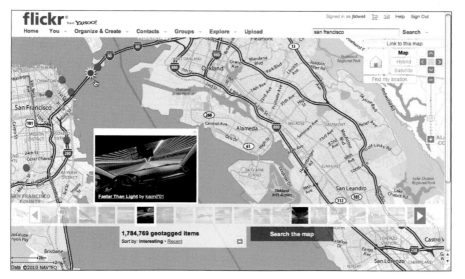

Figure 7-28. *Flickr map (http://www.flickr.com/map/)*

Figure 7-29. *SPOT Adventures live map*

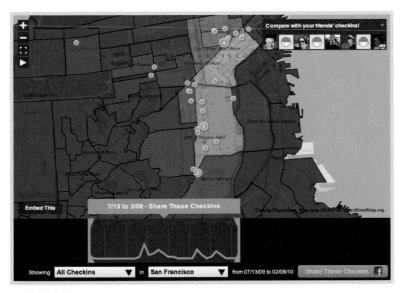

Figure 7-30. *Weeplaces (http://weeplaces.com)*

In other libraries

http://quince.infragistics.com/Patterns/Data%20Brushing.aspx

This pattern, called Linked Multiples, is a generalization of Data Brushing:

http://patternbrowser.org/code/pattern/pattern_anzeigen.php?4,225,17,0,0,246

Local Zooming

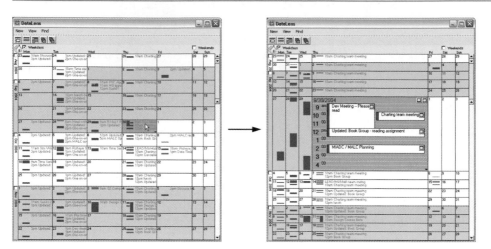

Figure 7-31. *The DateLens calendar*

Show all the data in a single dense page, with small-scale data items. Wherever the mouse goes, distort the page to make those data items large and readable.

You're showing a large data set using any organizational form—plots, maps, networks, or even tables—on either a large or a small screen. The user is able to "point at" places of interest with a mouse cursor or a touch screen.

Users will browse through the data or search for points of interest within that organizational structure (e.g., finding a date in a calendar). High-level overviews are necessary for finding those points of interest, but users don't need to see all available detail for all data points at once—zooming in is sufficient for getting fine detail.

Some forms of Local Zooming, especially fisheye lenses, are appropriate only if your users are willing to learn a new interaction technique to gain proficiency with a particular application. Using Local Zooming can require patience.

Ordinary zooming works well for most high-density information graphics, but it takes away context: a fully zoomed view no longer shows an overview of the whole data set. Local Zooming focuses on local detail while retaining context. The user remains in the same conceptual space.

One possible cost of Local Zooming, however, is distortion of that conceptual space. Notice how the introduction of a fisheye—a type of local zoom that maintains topological continuity between the zoomed area and the rest of the view—changes the landscape in Figure 7-31. Suddenly the overview doesn't look the same as it did before: landmarks have moved, and spatial relationships have changed ("It used to be halfway down the right side of the screen, but it's not there anymore").

Other kinds of Local Zooming don't introduce distortion, but instead hide parts of the overview. With a virtual magnifying glass, for instance, the user can see the zoomed area and part of the larger context, but not what's hidden by the magnifying glass "frame."

The Overview Plus Detail pattern is a viable alternative to Local Zooming. It too offers both detail (focus) and a full overview (context) in the same page, but it separates the two levels of scale into two side-by-side views, rather than integrating them into one distorted view. If Local Zooming is too difficult to implement or too hard for users to interact with, fall back to Overview Plus Detail.

The Datatips pattern is another viable alternative. Again, you get both overview and detail, but the information shown isn't really a "zoom" as much as a description of the data at that point. And a Datatip is an ephemeral item layered over the top of the graphic, whereas Local Zooming can be an integral part of the graphic and can therefore be printed and screen-captured.

How

Fill all the available space with the whole data set, drawn very small. Stretch it to fill the window dynamically (see the Liquid Layout pattern in Chapter 4). Remove detail as necessary. If text is an important element, use tiny fonts where you can; if the text still won't fit, use abstract visual representations such as solid rectangles or lines that approximate text.

Offer a local zoom mode. When the user turns it on and moves the pointer around, enlarge the small area directly under the pointer.

What the enlargement actually looks like depends on the kind of information graphic you use—it doesn't have to be literal, like a magnifying glass on a page. The DateLens, in Figure 7-31, uses both horizontal and vertical enlargement and compression. But the TableLens, in Figure 7-32, uses only a vertical enlargement and compression because the data points of interest are whole rows, not a single cell in a row. A map or image, however, needs to control both directions tightly in order to preserve its scale. In other words, don't stretch or squish a map. It's harder to read that way.

Local zoom lenses can be finicky to drive, because the user might be aiming at very tiny hit targets. They don't look tiny—they're magnified under the lens!—but the user actually moves the pointer through the overview space, not the zoomed space. A small motion becomes a big jump. So when the data points are discrete, like table cells or network nodes, you might consider jumping directly from one focal point to another.

It should be noted that fisheye views are an "advanced maneuver" in data visualization. Fisheye views distort the area immediately around the zoom to achieve topological continuity with the rest of the graphic. (The DateLens is a fisheye, but the other examples in this pattern are not.) This distortion can cause discomfort for the user who moves it around a lot, for instance.

Examples

The DateLens, shown in Figure 7-31 at the top of the pattern, was a calendar application that worked on both the desktop and a mobile device. (It was experimental, and support for it ceased back around 2004.) It shows an overview of your calendar—each row is a week—with blue blocks where your appointments are. For details, click on a cell. That cell then expands, using an Animated Transition (Chapter 3), to show the day's schedule. In this design, the entire graphic compresses to allow room for the focused day, except for the row and the column containing that cell. (That actually provides useful information about the week's schedule and about other weeks' Thursday appointments.)

The Inxight TableLens permitted the user to open arbitrary numbers of rows and move that "window" up and down the table. Figure 7-32 shows four magnified rows. Note that the only enlargement here is in the vertical direction.

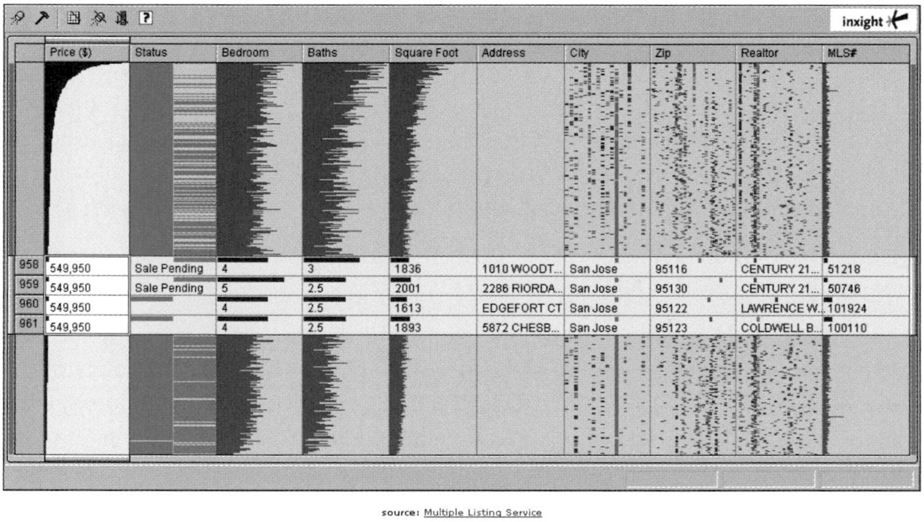

source: Multiple Listing Service

Figure 7-32. *Inxight TableLens*

The Mac OS dock does a simple version of Local Zooming (Figure 7-33), as does Google Images (Figure 7-34).

Figure 7-33. *Mac OS dock*

Figure 7-34. *Google Images*

Cartifact's map lenses—literal ones, yet remarkably beautiful—allow the user to set both the magnification level and the drawing style inside the lens (see Figure 7-35). These remove much of the user's need to keep zooming into the map for detail, then back out again for context, then back in again for more detail. The alternate drawing styles (aerial, Cartifact, historic, and 3D oblique) let the user see one area in several complementary ways, without affecting the entire map.

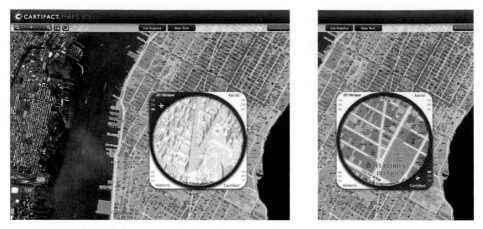

Figure 7-35. *Cartifact map lenses (http://cartifact.com/webmaps/)*

In other libraries

http://patternbrowser.org/code/pattern/pattern_anzeigen.php?4,222,17,0,0,243

http://quince.infragistics.com/Patterns/Local%20Zooming.aspx

Sortable Table

	Name	Time	Artist	Album	Genre	Play Count	Last Played	Rating
	If You Were To Wake Up	4:11	Lyle Lovett	Lyle Lovett and his Large ...	Big Band			
	Once Is Enough	4:25	Lyle Lovett	Lyle Lovett and his Large ...	Big Band			
	Every Time You Say Goodbye	3:18	Alison Krauss	Hand-Picked – 25 Years o...	Bluegrass	1	1/6/06 12:59 PM	
	When Someone Wants to Leave	2:24	The Allen Brothers	Hand-Picked – 25 Years o...	Bluegrass			
	Sourwood Mountain	0:35	Allen Shelton	Hand-Picked – 25 Years o...	Bluegrass	1	7/30/05 5:35 PM	
	Down To The River To Pray	2:56	Allison Krauss	O Brother, Where Art Thou?	Bluegrass	10	2/8/10 2:49 PM	
	I'll Fly Away	3:58	Allison Krauss & Gillian Welch	O Brother, Where Art Thou?	Bluegrass	6	9/17/10 11:14 AM	

Figure 7-36. *iTunes sortable table header*

What

Show the data in a table, and let the user sort the table rows according to the cell values in a selected column.

Use when

The interface shows multivariate information that the user may want to explore, reorder, customize, search through for a single item, or simply understand on the basis of those different variables.

Giving the user the ability to change the sorting order of a table has powerful effects. First, it facilitates exploration. A user can now learn things from the data that she may never have been able to otherwise. How many of this kind? What proportion of this to that? Is there only one of these? What's first or last? Suddenly it becomes easier to find specific items, too; a user need only remember one attribute of the item in question (e.g., its last-edited date), sort on that attribute, and look up the value she remembers.

Furthermore, if the sort order is retained from one invocation of the software to another, this is a way for the user to effectively customize the UI for her preferred usage patterns. Some users want the table sorted first to last, some last to first, and some by a variable no one else thinks is interesting. It's good to give a user that kind of control.

Finally, the clickable-header concept is familiar to many users now, and they may expect it even if you don't provide it.

How

Choose the columns (i.e., the variables) carefully. What would a user want to sort by or search for? Conversely, what *doesn't* need to be shown in this table? What can be hidden until the user asks for more detail about a specific item?

The table headers should have some visual affordance that can be clicked on. Many have beveled, button-like borders, or blue underlined text. You should use up or down arrows to show whether the sort is in ascending or descending order. (And the presence of an arrow shows which column was last sorted on—a fortuitous side effect!) Consider using rollover effects, such as highlighting or cursor changes, on the headers to reinforce the impression of clickability.

Use a stable sort algorithm. This means that if a user sorts first by name and then by date, the resultant list will show ordered groups of same-date items that are each sorted by name within the group. In other words, the current sort order will be retained in the next sort to the extent possible—subtle, but very useful.

If your UI technology permits, you might let users reorder columns by dragging and dropping.

Examples

Inxight's TableLens is a table whose rows compress down into tiny bars, the lengths of which represent the values of the table cells. (Users can click on specific rows to see ordinary-looking table rows, but that's not what I want to talk about here.) One of the wonderful things about this visualization is the ability to sort on any column—when the data is highly correlated, as in this example, the user can see that correlation before her eyes.

The data set shown in Figure 7-37 comprises houses for sale in Santa Clara County, California. In this screenshot, the user has clicked on the Bedroom column header, thus sorting on that variable: the more bedrooms, the longer the blue bar. Previously, the stable-sorted table had been sorted on Square Foot (representing the size of the house), so you see a secondary "saw-tooth" pattern there; all houses with four bedrooms, for instance, are sorted by size. The Baths variable almost mirrors the Square Foot attribute, and so does Price, which indicates a rough correlation. And it makes intuitive sense—the more bedrooms a house has, the more bathrooms it's likely to have, and the bigger it's likely to be.

You can imagine other questions that can be answered by this kind of interactive graphic. Does zip code correlate to price? How strong is the correlation between price and square footage? Do certain realtors work only in certain cities? How many realtors are there? And so on.

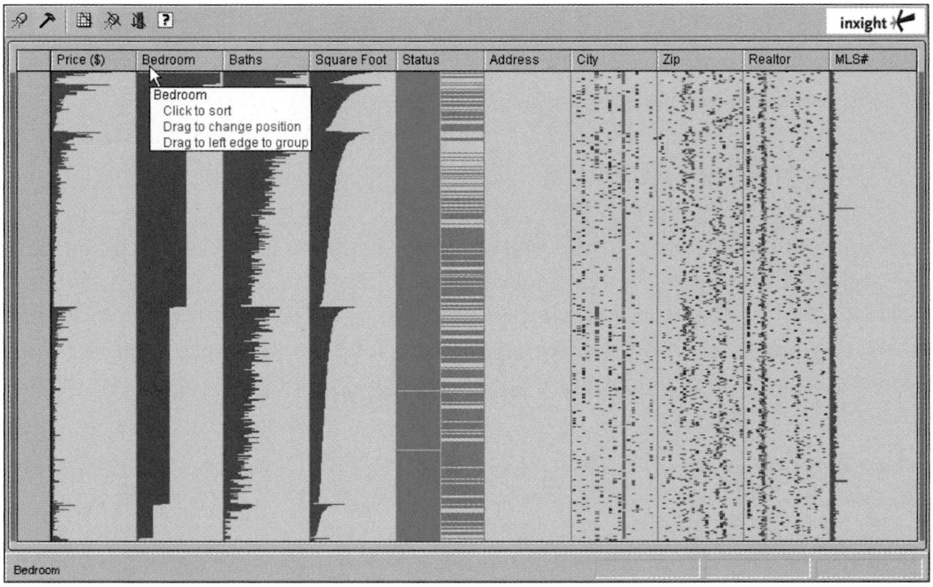

Figure 7-37. *Inxight TableLens*

In other libraries

http://ui-patterns.com/patterns/SortByColumn

http://www.welie.com/patterns/showPattern.php?patternID=table-sorter

http://quince.infragistics.com/Patterns/Sortable%20Table.aspx

http://patternbrowser.org/code/pattern/pattern_anzeigen.php?4,233,17,0,0,254

Radial Table

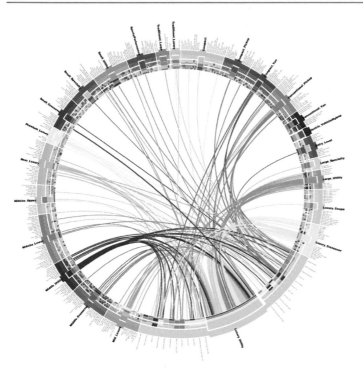

Figure 7-38. *Analysis of car purchases (http://mkweb.bcgsc.ca/circos/intro/general_data/)*

Show a table or list of items as a circle instead of a column. Draw connections among items through the interior of the circle.

You have a long list or table of items and you need to show arbitrary relationships among them: flows, connections, affinities, similarities, and even numerical values (encoded by the thickness of the connection).

A circular presentation enables free-form connection lines to be visualized far more easily than a line or column of elements would permit. Such connections have a shorter, straighter distance to travel when drawn between points on an arc than points on a line, and viewers can usually see patterns in the data more easily. (This is not always the case. If you can, try out different types of connection visualizations to see if it's true for your particular data sets.)

Even when there are no connections to draw, some kinds of tabular data might be easier to see when drawn as a circle—very long data sets with both large-scale and small-scale features, for instance. Large-scale features might include groups and clusters, upper levels of a hierarchy, or labels for large numbers of items. See the examples for illustrations.

From the website of Circos, a creator of radial table designs, comes this explanation:

> *Within the circle, the resolution varies linearly, increasing with radial position. This makes the center of the circle ideal for compactly displaying summary statistics or indicating points of interest (i.e. low resolution data) which the reader can then follow outward to explore the data in greater detail (i.e. high resolution data).*[*]

Finally, radial information graphics can be beautiful. When drawn skillfully, these kinds of visualizations are fresh, attractive, and engaging.

How

Bend the linear table or list into a circle and put the text labels around the outside of the circle (if you need them). Some Radial Tables place the x-axis on one half of the circle and the y-axis on the other half; this is useful if your data table is trying to show connections between two one-dimensional sets of items.

If the original table shows multiple columns of dependent data—numbers, bars, pictograms, scatter plots, and so on—arrange those either inside or outside the circle, depending on the visual scale and interrelatedness of these features. Large-scale, convergent features should go inside; small-scale, detailed, divergent features should go outside, where they have more space.

If the items in the table are categorized, you could encode those categories as groups separated by gaps, or in different colors, or as arcs parallel to the circle (either inside or outside the data axis).

Inside the circle, draw relationships among the items. Those relationships might take the shape of free-form lines or arcs between table cells. The line color and thickness can encode additional variables about the relationships, such as source or destination (color), and volume or strength (thickness). Sometimes these relationships need to be drawn so thickly that they're hard to distinguish from each other. Here are some ways to deal with that problem:

---

[*] *http://mkweb.bcgsc.ca/circos/intro/circular_approach/*

- Eliminate superfluous lines; draw only what you want viewers to focus on.

- Use drawing algorithms that can cluster lines together and keep them visually organized.

- If the graphic is interactive, use techniques such as Data Spotlight and Dynamic Queries to let the user see chosen subsets of the lines.

You may need to explain how to interpret a Radial Table. These graphics can be very useful to the patient and informed viewer, but their meaning may not be immediately apparent to a viewer who is naive or not motivated to spend time studying the graphic carefully. If your users are likely to move on without understanding the Radial Table, consider simplifying it or using an easier alternative rendering.

Examples

SolidSX Software Explorer is an application that draws Radial Tables of software packages. Figure 7-39 shows dependencies, calls, and hierarchical relationships among code elements in a library. Note the containing arcs around the outside of the circle (showing the static hierarchy), and the call-graph lines within the circle, which are carefully drawn for clarity.

Figure 7-39. *SolidSX Software Explorer (http://www.solidsourceit.com/products/SolidSX-source-code-dependency-analysis.html)*

From the Eigenfactor Project and Moritz Stefaner comes an elegant diagram of citation patterns among branches of science, shown in Figure 7-40. There are many connections, but they are drawn so well that the viewer can follow them with some degree of success. The diagram shows which fields of science are more insular than others (e.g., economics) and which are better connected.

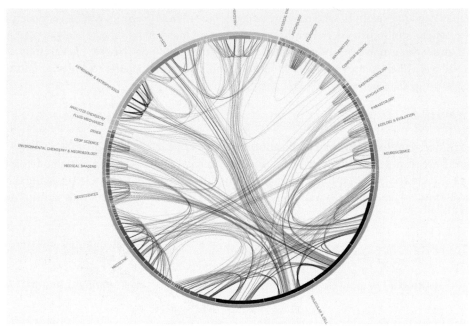

Figure 7-40. *Eigenfactor science citation patterns (http://well-formed.eigenfactor.org/radial.html)*

The genetics diagram in Figure 7-41 demonstrates that the curved format can be effective in illustrating data patterns other than connections. The diagram could have been "unrolled" into a horizontal strip-chart format, but this version is more compact and arguably more readable than a long, thin linear chart. Note that the line charts on the inside of the table are a larger-scale feature than the tiny multicolored slivers around the outside of the circle, so they are appropriately shown inside the circle.

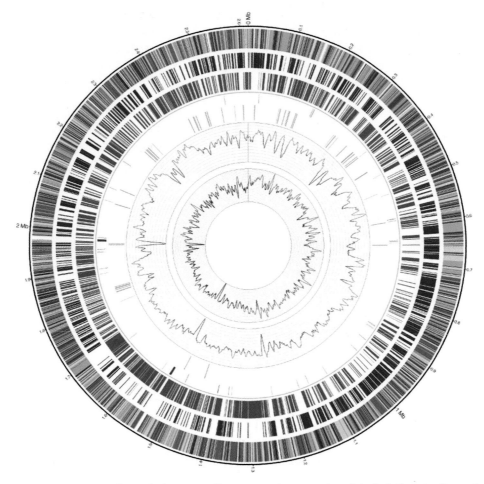

Figure 7-41. *Genomic chart of a bacterium (http://www.plosone.org/article/info:doi/10.1371/journal. pone.0011748)*

http://patternbrowser.org/code/pattern/pattern_anzeigen.php?4,217,17,0,0,238

For many more examples, visit the Circos and Visual Complexity websites:

http://mkweb.bcgsc.ca/circos/

http:/visualcomplexity.com/

Multi-Y Graph

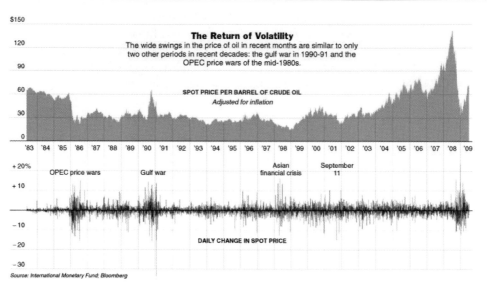

Figure 7-42. *New York Times graphic*

Stack multiple graph lines in one panel; let them all share the same x-axis.

You present two or more graphs, usually simple line plots, bar charts, or area charts (or any combination thereof). The data in those graphs all share the same x-axis, often a time-line, but otherwise they describe different things, perhaps with different units or scale on the y-axis. You want to encourage the viewer to find "vertical" relationships among the data sets being shown—correlations, similarities, unexpected differences, and so on.

Aligning the graphs along the x-axis first tells the viewer that these data sets are related, and then it lets her make side-by-side comparisons of the data. In Figure 7-42, the proximity of the two graphs makes visible the correlations in the curves' shapes; you can see that spikes in the bottom graph generally line up with interesting features in the top graph, and the grid lines enable precise observation. For instance, the vertical grid line between 1990 and 1991 lines up peaks in both curves.

You could have done this by superimposing one graph upon the other. But by showing each graph individually, with its own y-axis, you enable each graph to be viewed on its own merits without visual interference from the other.

Also, these data sets have very different Y values: one ranges from zero to nearly 150, while the other ranges from −30 to +20! You couldn't put them on the same y-axis anyhow without the first one looking like a flat line. You'd need to draw another y-axis along the left side, and then you'd need to choose a scaling that doesn't make the graph look too odd. Even so, direct superimposition encourages the viewer to think that the data sets use the same Y scale, and to compare them on that basis—"apples to apples," instead of "apples to oranges." If that's not the case, superimposing them can be misleading.

How

Stack one graph on top of the other. Use one x-axis for both, but separate the y-axes into different vertical spaces. If the y-axes need to overlap somewhat, they can, but try to keep the graphs from visually interfering with each other.

Sometimes you don't need y-axes at all; maybe it's not important to let the user find exact values (or maybe the graph itself contains exact values, such as labeled bar charts). In that case, simply move the graph curves up and down until they don't interfere with each other.

Label each graph so that its identity is unambiguous. Use vertical grid lines if possible; they let viewers follow an X value from one data set to another, for easier comparison. They also make it possible to discover an exact value for a data point of interest (or one close to it) without making the user take out a straightedge and pencil.

Examples

Google Trends allows a user to compare the use frequency of different search terms. The example in Figure 7-43 shows two sports-related terms that are comparable in volume, so they're easy to compare in one simple chart. But Google Trends goes beyond that. Relative search volume is illustrated on the top chart, while the bottom chart shows news reference volume. The metrics and their scales are different, so Trends uses two separate y-axes.

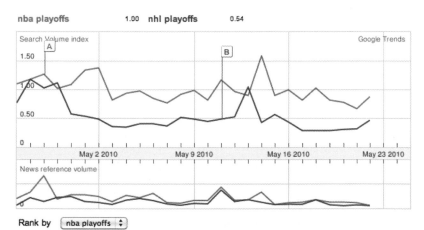

Figure 7-43. *Google Trends*

The example in Figure 7-44 shows an interactive multi-Y graph constructed in MATLAB. You can manipulate the three data traces' y-axes, color-coded on the left, with the mouse— you can drag the traces up and down the graph, "stretch" them vertically by sliding the colored axis end caps, and even change the displayed axis range by editing the y-axis limits in place. Here's why that's interesting: you might notice that the traces look similar, as though they were correlated somehow—all three drop in value just after the vertical line labeled 1180, for instance. But just how similar are they? Move them and see.

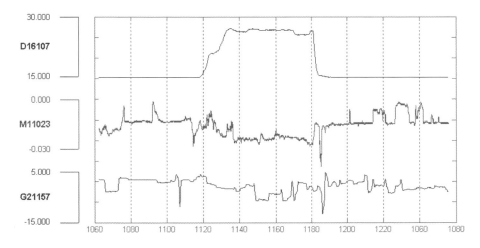

Figure 7-44. *MATLAB plot*

Your eyes are very, very good at discerning relationships among data graphics. By stacking and superimposing the differently scaled plot traces shown in Figure 7-45, a user might gain valuable insight into whatever phenomenon produced this data.

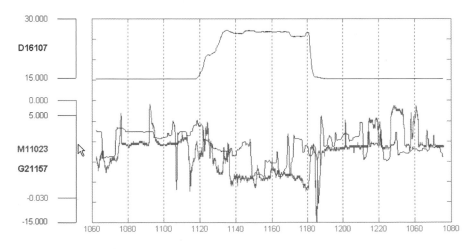

Figure 7-45. *MATLAB plot, again*

The information graphics in a multi-Y display don't need to be traditional graphs. The weather chart shown in Figure 7-46 uses a series of pictograms to illustrate expected weather conditions; these are aligned with the same time-based x-axis that the graph uses. (This chart hints at the next pattern, Small Multiples.)

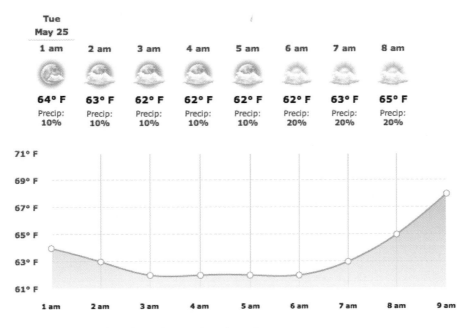

Figure 7-46. *Weather chart from The Weather Channel*

In other libraries

http://quince.infragistics.com/Patterns/Multi-Y%20Graph.aspx

Small Multiples

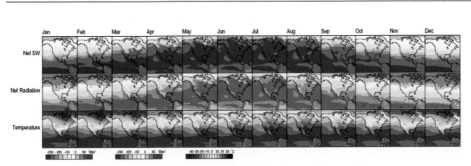

Figure 7-47. *Climate heat map, from a University of Oregon publication*

What

Create many small pictures of the data using two or three data dimensions. Tile them on the page according to one or two additional data dimensions, either in a single comic-strip sequence or in a 2D matrix.

Use when

You need to display a large data set with more than two dimensions or independent variables. It's easy to show a single "slice" of the data as a picture—as a plot, table, map, or image, for instance—but you find it hard to show more dimensions than that. Users might be forced to look at one plot at a time, flipping back and forth among them to see differences.

When using Small Multiples, you need to have a fairly large display area available. Mobile devices rarely do this well, unless each individual picture is very tiny. Use this pattern when most users will be seeing these on a large screen or on printed paper.

That being said, *sparklines* are a particular type of Small Multiples that can be very effective at tiny scales, such as in running text or in a column of table cells. They are essentially miniature graphs, stripped of all labels and axes, created to show the shape or envelope of a simple data set.

Why

Small Multiples are data-rich—they show a lot of information at one time, but in a comprehensible way. Every individual picture tells a story. But when you put them all together, and demonstrate how each picture *varies* from one to the next, an even bigger story is told.

As Edward Tufte put it in his classic book, *Envisioning Information* (Graphics Press), "Small multiple designs, multivariate and data bountiful, answer directly by visually enforcing comparisons of changes, of the differences among objects, of the scope of alternatives." (Tufte named and popularized Small Multiples in his famous books about visualization.)

Think about it this way. If you can encode some dimensions in each individual picture, but you need to encode an extra dimension that just won't fit in the pictures, how could you do it?

Sequential presentation
Express that dimension varying across time. You can play them like a movie, use Back/Next buttons to page one at a time, and so on.

3D presentation
Place the pictures along a third spatial axis, the z-axis.

Small multiples
Reuse the x- and y-axes at a larger scale.

Side-by-side placement of pictures lets a user glance from one to the other freely and rapidly. She doesn't have to remember what was shown in a previous screen, as would be required by a sequential presentation (although a movie can be *very* effective at showing tiny differences between frames). She also doesn't have to decode or rotate a complicated 3D plot, as would be required if you place 2D pictures along a third axis. Sequential and 3D presentations sometimes work very well, but not always, and they often don't work in a noninteractive setting at all.

How

Choose whether to represent one extra data dimension or two. With only one, you can lay out the images vertically, horizontally, or even line-wrapped, like a comic strip—from the starting point, the user can read through to the end. With two data dimensions, you should use a 2D table or matrix—express one data dimension as columns, and the other as rows.

Whether you use one dimension or two, label the Small Multiples with clear captions—individually if necessary, or otherwise along the sides of the display. Make sure the users understand which data dimension is varying across the multiples, and whether you're encoding one or two data dimensions.

Each image should be similar to the others: the same size and/or shape, the same axis scaling (if you're using plots), and the same kind of content. When you use Small Multiples, you're trying to bring out the meaningful differences between the things being shown. Try to eliminate the visual differences that don't mean anything.

Of course, you shouldn't use too many Small Multiples on one page. If one of the data dimensions has a range of 1 to 100, you probably don't want 100 rows or columns of small multiples, so what do you do? You could *bin* those 100 values into, say, five bins containing 20 values each. Or you could use a technique called *shingling*, which is similar to binning but allows substantial overlap between the bins. (That means some data points will appear more than once, but that may be a good thing for users trying to discern patterns in the data; just make sure it's labeled well so that they know what's going on.)

Some small-multiple plots with two extra encoded dimensions are called *trellis plots* or *trellis graphs*. William Cleveland, a noted authority on statistical graphing, uses this term, and so do the software packages S-PLUS and R.

Examples

The North American climate graph, at the top of the pattern in Figure 7-47, shows many encoded variables. Underlying each small-multiple picture is a 2D geographic map, of course, and overlaid on that is a color-coded "graph" of some climate metric, such as temperature. With any one picture, you can see interesting shapes in the color data; they might prompt a viewer to ask questions about why blobs of color appear over certain parts of the continent.

The Small Multiples display as a whole encodes two additional variables: each column is a month of the year, and each row represents a climate metric. Your eyes have probably followed the changes across the rows, noting changes through the year, and comparisons up and down the columns are easy, too.

The example shown in Figure 7-48 uses the grid to encode two independent variables—ethnicity/religion and income—into the state-by-state geographic data. The dependent variable, encoded by color, is the estimated level of public support for school vouchers (orange representing support, green opposition). The resultant graphic is very rich and nuanced, telling countless stories about Americans' attitudes toward the topic.

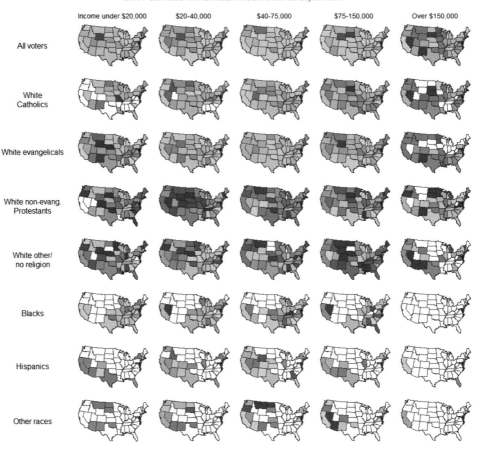

Figure 7-48. *Geographic and demographic small-multiples chart (http://www.stat.columbia.edu/~cook/movabletype/archives/2009/07/hard_sell_for_b.html)*

A more abstract two-dimensional trellis plot, also called a *coplot* in William Cleveland's *Visualizing Data*, is shown in Figure 7-49. Created with the R software package, this example shows a quantity measured along four dimensions: latitude, longitude, depth, and magnitude. The values along the depth and magnitude dimensions overlap—this is the shingling technique mentioned earlier.

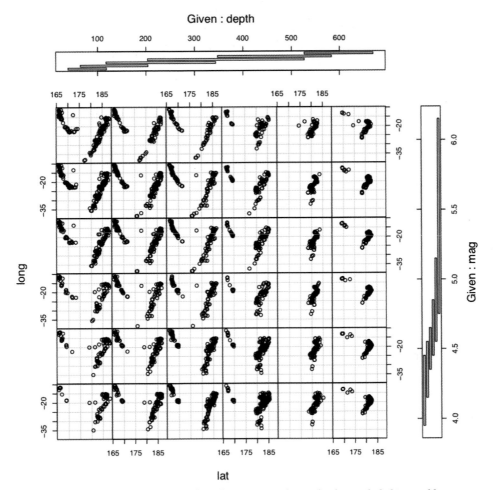

Figure 7-49. *Trellis plot of earthquake data (http://www.sph.umich.edu/~nichols/biostat_bbag-march2001.pdf)*

http://patternbrowser.org/code/pattern/pattern_anzeigen.php?4,298,17,0,0,319

http://quince.infragistics.com/Patterns/Small%20Multiples.aspx

See also the works by Edward Tufte and William Cleveland listed earlier.

Treemap

Figure 7-50. *SmartMoney Map of the Market (http://www.smartmoney.com/map-of-the-market/)*

What

Express multidimensional and/or hierarchical data as rectangles of various sizes. You can nest those rectangles to show the hierarchy, and color or label them to show additional variables.

Use when

Your data is tree-shaped (hierarchical). Alternatively, it may be multivariate—each item has several attributes, such as size and category, which permit items to be grouped according to those attributes. Users want to see an overview of many data points—maybe hundreds or thousands—and they're using screens large enough to accommodate a large display.

Your users should be patient and motivated enough to learn to use an unusual interface. Treemaps are not always easy to read, especially for people who haven't seen them before. Furthermore, they work better on-screen than they do on paper, because Datatips, Dynamic Queries, and other interactive mechanisms can help users understand the data.

Why

Treemaps encode many data attributes into a single dense diagram. By taking advantage of position, size, containment, color hue and/or value, and labeling, a treemap packs a lot of information into a space that encourages the human visual system to seek out trends, relationships among variables, and specific points of interest.

Look at the SmartMoney treemap in Figure 7-50, which shows the past 52 weeks' performance of more than 500 publicly traded stocks. Section size illustrates the relative sizes of different market sectors and of companies within those sectors—the blocks of solid color are individual companies. You can instantly see that in the past year, the big gainers in bright green were from the Technology and Consumer Cyclicals categories, and the losers in red have been in the Financial and Energy categories.

This treemap makes it very easy to get an instant overview and to spot outliers. It encourages you to see relationships between size and color, size and position, and position and color—all of which give you different kinds of insight into the market. It would take you forever to get that insight from a long table of stock prices.

How

The critical step in designing a treemap is deciding which data attributes are encoded by which visual variables:

Rectangle size

Usually this encodes a numeric value, such as size, price, or percentage. Make each rectangle's area proportional to that number. If the number has too great a range, you'll end up with some enormous rectangles and some microscopic rectangles, in which case you could either let the user zoom in on them for a closer look, or filter out the large ones to let the small ones scale up. Dynamic Queries (earlier in this chapter) are often used for that. Refer back to Figure 7-24 for an example of Dynamic Queries used in conjunction with a treemap.

Grouping and nesting

If your data is already inherently hierarchical, like a taxonomic tree or a filesystem, you should group and nest the rectangles accordingly. If not, see whether the data items have a natural grouping or categorization that is meaningful to the user. Do they have several possible categorizations? You might consider giving the user a choice on how to group them. Do they have no obvious categorization at all? Then you could take a numeric attribute, such as price, and bin it into categories ($0 to $5, $5 to $10, etc.). Or you could not group the data items at all. But consider whether some other type of information graphic may be more appropriate; grouping is one of the treemap's strengths.

Color

> You can use color to represent a numeric or otherwise ordered value, as in the SmartMoney example in Figure 7-50, or another categorization. For a numeric value, choose two colors for the "endpoints" of the range of possible values, such as red and green, white and blue, yellow and red, and so on; shades of color between those endpoints represent values in between. For a categorization, use a different hue to represent each category. (If the shades are too similar, though, viewers may assume an ordering where there isn't one.)

Position

> A rectangle's position within the treemap is partially dictated by where it belongs in the hierarchy or categorization. But within a category, you might still have freedom to decide where a given rectangle goes. Some treemaps place the largest rectangles in the upper left of a category, and then space-fill the rest of the category so that the smallest rectangles are in the lower right. This establishes a nice rhythm on the page, and it helps the user to visually compare the number of small or large rectangles in each main category. In this case, position doesn't encode yet another variable; instead, it's redundant with size and grouping. But other treemap implementations do encode an order—by age, or alphabetical by name, for example. It depends on how many variables you want to encode at once.

Most treemaps allow users to drill down to the actual data items. Mouse rollovers, for instance, usually produce largish tool tips that describe the item in full (see the Datatips pattern in this chapter). You'll usually have to elide some text anyway to fit the descriptions into the treemap blocks, so this is a good thing to do. Furthermore, a single or double click often brings the user to some other page or window about that item.

As for implementation, it is not trivial to write code to lay out a treemap in a pleasing way. Fortunately, many algorithms exist for drawing a treemap. Some are in academic papers; some are in open source software or freeware; and others are in products. The different algorithms vary according to how they choose the rectangles' aspect ratios (i.e., the proportion between width and height; the squarer, the better), how they fill the space for a given category, and their stability with respect to data changes.

You may need to explain how to interpret a Treemap. These graphics can be very useful to the patient and informed viewer, but their meaning isn't immediately apparent to a viewer who is naive or not motivated to spend time studying the graphic carefully. If your users are likely to move on without understanding the Treemap, consider simplifying it or using an easier alternative rendering.

The now-defunct Newsmap illustrated the "news landscape" as described by Google News (see Figure 7-51). At any given moment, the Newsmap could collect Google's top headlines and draw a treemap in which the largest blocks represented the most reported-on stories. The encodings here are:

- Block size: "popularity" of news item; how many news outlets reported this story
- Color hue: topic
- Top-level grouping: also topic
- Color value (darkness/lightness): age

Because the headline's text size is proportional to block size, which in turn is proportional to popularity, your eyes are immediately drawn to the biggest news items. (What did you read first? Perhaps the "False warnings" headline, then "Please Work for Free!"?) The treemap is thus an automatically constructed visual hierarchy.

Figure 7-51. *Newsmap*

From the Hive Group comes a small collection of similar treemap visualizations: items available for purchase from Amazon, world population data, and so on. Figure 7-52 shows a list of articles recently promoted via Digg.

Some encodings—block size, color hue, grouping—are settable by the user via the bar on the top ("Group by," "Size represents," "Color represents"). That kind of customizability is really handy in this type of application. After all, there are many data attributes associated with each article—too many to be encoded by the available three or four visual variables. The treemap designers didn't know which attributes each user would be most interested in. They made a good default guess, and put in a simple, learnable UI to allow users to do their own thing.

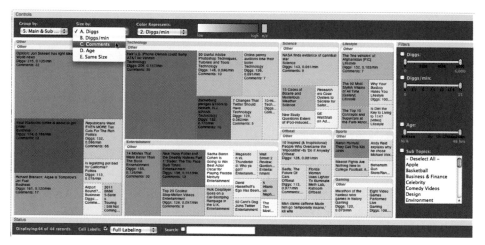

Figure 7-52. *Hive Group visualization of Digg articles (http://www.hivegroup.com/gallery/)*

In other libraries

http://patternbrowser.org/code/pattern/pattern_anzeigen.php?4,215,17,0,0,236

http://quince.infragistics.com/Patterns/Treemap.aspx

Ben Shneiderman invented the treemap in 1990, and he and his colleagues at the University of Maryland have been refining the technique for some time now. A history of the treemap, along with many links to papers and implementations, can be found at *http://www.cs.umd.edu/hcil/treemap-history/*.

Chapter 8

Getting Input from Users: Forms and Controls

Sooner or later, the software you design will probably ask the user to answer some kind of question. It might even happen in the first few minutes of interaction. Where should this software be installed? What's your login name? What words do you want to search for?

These kinds of interactions are among the easiest to design. Everyone knows how to use text fields, checkboxes, and combo boxes. These input controls are often the first interface elements that novice designers use as they build their first GUIs and websites.

Still, it doesn't take much to set up a potentially awkward interaction. Here's another sample question: for what location do you want a weather report? The user might wonder, do I specify a location by city, country, postal code, or what? Are abbreviations OK? What if I misspell it? What if I ask for a city it doesn't know about? Isn't there a map to choose from? And why can't it remember the location I gave it yesterday, anyhow?

This chapter discusses ways to smooth out these problems. The patterns, techniques, and controls described here apply mostly to form design—a *form* being simply a series of question/answer pairs. However, they will also be useful in other contexts, such as for single controls on web pages or on application toolbars. Input design and form design are core skills for interaction designers, as you can use them in every genre and on every platform.

The Basics of Form Design

First, a few principles to remember when doing input and form design:

Make sure the user understands what's asked for, and why
> This is entirely context-dependent, and any generalizations here risk sounding vapid, but let's try anyway. You should write labels with words that your target users understand—plain language for novice or occasional users, and carefully chosen jargon or specialized vocabulary for domain experts. If you design a long or tedious form, explain why you need all the information you're asking for, break it up into descriptive Titled Sections, and give some reassurance that sensitive information will

be handled with care. If you're putting a button on a toolbar (or somewhere else that's too crowded for a label) and the button's function isn't immediately obvious, use a descriptive tool tip or other type of context-sensitive help to tell the user what it does.

If you can, avoid asking the question at all

Asking the user to answer a question, especially if it comes in the middle of some other task, is a bit of an imposition. You might be asking him to break his train of thought and deal with something he hadn't expected to think about. Even in the best of cases, typing into text fields isn't most people's idea of a fun time. Can you "prefill" an input control with already-known or guessable information, as the Autocompletion pattern recommends? Can you offer Good Defaults that remove the burdens of choice from most of your users? Can you avoid asking for the information altogether?

There's one glaring exception to this principle: security. Sometimes we use input controls in a challenge/response context, such as asking for passwords or credit card numbers. You obviously don't want to circumvent these security mechanisms by casually prefilling sensitive information.

Knowledge "in the world" is often more accurate than knowledge "in the head"

You can't expect human beings to recall lists of things perfectly. If you ask users to make a choice from a prescribed set of items, try to make that list available to them so that they can read over it. Drop downs, combo boxes, lists, and other such controls put all the choices out there for the user to review.

(Obviously, a user can remember his name, birthday, address, state or country, phone number, and other common personal information—and he can type such information very easily and accurately. There's no need for "knowledge in the world" in these cases; text fields work just fine, and are easier to use than drop downs.)

Similarly, if you ask for input that needs to be formatted in a specific way, you might want to offer the user clues about how to format it. Even if the user has used your UI before, he may not remember what's required—a gentle reminder may be welcome. Good Defaults, Structured Format, and Input Hints all serve this purpose. Autocompletion goes a step further by telling the user what input is valid, or by reminding the user what he entered some previous time.

Respond sensitively to errors, and be forgiving when possible

Accept multiple formats for dates, addresses, phone numbers, credit card numbers, and so on, per the Forgiving Format pattern. If a user does enter information that the form rejects, show an error message as soon as it becomes clear that the user made a mistake (you may need to wait until more form fields are filled out before deciding that for sure). On the form, politely indicate which input field is problematic, why, and how the user might fix it. See the patterns called Password Strength Meter and Same-Page Error Messages.

Beware a literal translation from the underlying programming model

Many forms are built to edit database records, or to edit objects in an object-oriented programming language. Given a data structure like these to fill out, it's really easy to design a form to do it. Each structure element gets (1) a label, and (2) a control (or a bundle of controls acting together). Put them in some rational order, lay them out top to bottom, and you're done, right?

Not entirely. This kind of implementation-driven form design does work, but it can give you a utilitarian and dull interface—or a difficult one. What if the structure elements don't match up with the input the user expects to give, for instance? And what if the structure is, say, 30 elements long? For some contexts, such as property sheets in a programming environment, it's appropriate to show everything the way it's implemented—that's part of the point. But for everything else, a more elegant and user-centered presentation is better.

So, here's the challenge: can you exploit dependencies among the structure elements, familiar graphic constructs (such as address labels), unstated assumptions, or knowledge of the user gained from previous interactions to make the form less onerous? Can you turn the problem into one handled by direct manipulation, such as dragging and dropping things around? Be creative!

Usability-test it

For some reason, when input forms are involved, it's particularly easy for designers and users to make radically different assumptions about terminology, possible answers, intrusiveness, and other context-of-use issues. This book has said it before, and will say it again: do some usability testing, even if you're reasonably sure your design is good. This will give you empirical evidence of what works and what doesn't for your particular situation.

Your choice of controls will affect the user's expectation of what is asked for, so choose wisely

A radio box suggests a one-of-many choice, while a one-line text field suggests a short, open-ended answer. Consciously or not, people will use the physical form of a control—its type, its size, and so forth—to figure out what's being asked for, and they'll set their expectations accordingly. If you use a text field to ask for a number, users may believe that any number is OK; if they enter "12" and you then surprise them with an error dialog box saying "The number you enter must be between 1 and 10," you've yanked the rug out from under them. A slider or spin box would have been better.

The following section gives you a table of possible controls for different input types. You or the engineers you work with will need to decide the semantics of each question. Is it binary? A date or time? One-of-many? Many-of-many? Open-ended but requiring validation? Look it up here, and then choose a control based on your particular design constraints.

Control Choice

The next sections describe controls and patterns for the kinds of information you might require from the user, such as numbers or choices from lists. It's not a complete set by any means; in fact, you can probably come up with plenty of others. But the types shown here are common, and the listed controls are among your best choices for clarity and usability.

Consider these factors when choosing among the possible controls for a given information type:

Available space

Some controls take up lots of screen real estate; others are smaller, but may be harder to use than larger ones. Short forms on web pages might be able to spend that screen space on radio buttons or illustrated lists, whereas complex applications may need to pack as much content as possible into small spaces. Toolbars and table-style property sheets are especially constraining, since they generally allow for only one text line of height and often not much width, either.

User sophistication with respect to general computer usage

Text fields should be familiar to almost all users of anything you'd design, but not everyone would be comfortable using a double-thumbed slider. For that matter, many occasional computer users don't know how to handle a multiple-selection listbox, either.

User sophistication with respect to domain knowledge

A text field might be fine if your users know that, say, only the numbers 1–10 and 20–30 are valid. Beginners will stumble, but if they're a very small part of your user base (and if the context is readily learned), maybe that's OK—a tiny text field might be better than using a big set of interlinked controls.

Expectations from other applications

For instance, Bold/Italic/Underline controls are known as iconic buttons; it would just be weird to see them as radio buttons instead.

Available technology

As of this writing, HTML provides only a very small subset of the controls in common usage on the desktop: text fields, radio boxes and checkboxes, scrolled lists, and simple drop downs. Commercial and open source GUI toolkits provide richer sets of controls. Their offerings vary, but many of them are extensible via programming, allowing you to create custom controls for specific situations.

The following sections summarize the various control options for four common input scenarios: lists of items, text, numbers, and dates or times. Each choice is illustrated with a typical example, taken from the Windows 2000 look-and-feel. (Keep in mind that these examples are not necessarily the best possible rendering of these controls! You do have some freedom when you decide how to draw them, especially on the Web. See Chapter 9's introduction for further discussion.)

Lists of Items

A wide variety of familiar controls allow users to select items or options from lists. Your choice of control depends on the number of items or options to be selected (one or many) and the number of potentially selectable items (two, a handful, or many).

Here are controls for selecting one of two options (a binary choice).

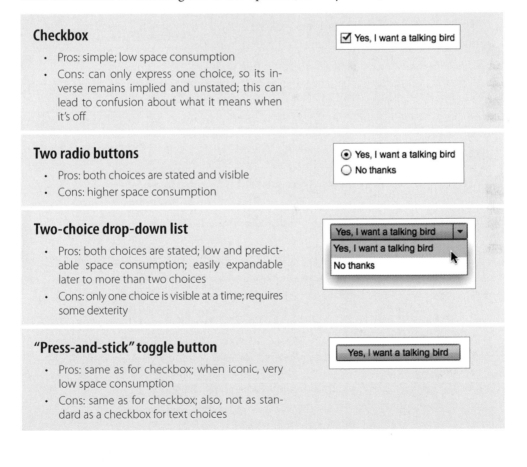

Checkbox

- Pros: simple; low space consumption
- Cons: can only express one choice, so its inverse remains implied and unstated; this can lead to confusion about what it means when it's off

☑ Yes, I want a talking bird

Two radio buttons

- Pros: both choices are stated and visible
- Cons: higher space consumption

⦿ Yes, I want a talking bird
○ No thanks

Two-choice drop-down list

- Pros: both choices are stated; low and predictable space consumption; easily expandable later to more than two choices
- Cons: only one choice is visible at a time; requires some dexterity

Yes, I want a talking bird ▼
Yes, I want a talking bird
No thanks

"Press-and-stick" toggle button

- Pros: same as for checkbox; when iconic, very low space consumption
- Cons: same as for checkbox; also, not as standard as a checkbox for text choices

Yes, I want a talking bird

The following controls are for selecting one of *N* items, where *N* is small.

N radio buttons

- Pros: all choices are always visible
- Cons: high space consumption

N-item drop-down list

- Pros: low space consumption
- Cons: only one choice is visible at a time, except when the menu is open; requires some dexterity

N-item set of mutually exclusive iconic toggle buttons

- Pros: low space consumption; all choices are visible
- Cons: icons might be cryptic, requiring tool tips for understanding; user might not know they're mutually exclusive

Single-selection list or table

- Pros: many choices are visible; can be kept as small as three items
- Cons: higher space consumption than drop-down list or spinner

Spinner

- Pros: low space consumption
- Cons: only one choice is ever visible at a time; requires a lot of dexterity; unfamiliar to naive computer users; drop-down list is usually a better choice

These controls are for selecting one of *N* items, where *N* is large.

N-item drop-down list, scrolled if necessary

- Pros: low space consumption
- Cons: only one choice is visible at a time, except when menu is open; requires a lot of dexterity to scroll through items on the drop-down menu

Single-selection list or table

- Pros: many choices are visible; can be kept small if needed
- Cons: higher space consumption than drop-down list

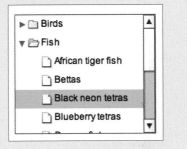

Single-selection tree or Cascading List, with items arranged into categories

- Pros: many choices are visible; organization helps findability in some cases
- Cons: may be unfamiliar to naive computer users; high space consumption; requires high dexterity

Custom browser, such as for files, colors, or fonts

- Pros: suited for browsing available choices
- Cons: may be unfamiliar to some users; difficult to design; usually a separate window, so it's less immediate than controls placed directly on the page

Here are controls for selecting many of *N* items, in any order.

Array of *N* checkboxes

- Pros: all choices are stated and visible
- Cons: high space consumption

Array of *N* toggle buttons

- Pros: low space consumption; all choices are visible
- Cons: icons might be cryptic, requiring tool tips for understanding; might look mutually exclusive

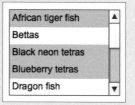

Multiple-selection list or table

- Pros: many choices are visible; can be kept small if needed
- Cons: not all choices are visible without scrolling; high (but bounded) space consumption; user might not realize it's multiple-selection

List with checkbox items

- Pros: many choices are visible; can be kept small if needed; affordance for selection is obvious
- Cons: not all choices are visible without scrolling; high (but bounded) space consumption

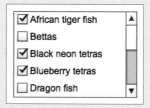

Multiple-selection tree or Cascading List, with items arranged into categories

- Pros: many choices are visible; organization helps findability in some cases
- Cons: may be unfamiliar to naive computer users; requires high dexterity; looks the same as single-selection tree

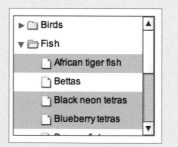

Custom browser, such as for files, colors, or fonts

- Pros: suited for browsing available choices
- Cons: may be unfamiliar to some users; difficult to design; usually a separate window, so it's less immediate than controls placed directly on the page

List Builder pattern

- Pros: selected set is easy to view; selection can be an ordered list if desired; easily handles a large source list
- Cons: very high space consumption due to two lists; does not easily handle a large set of selected objects

Use these controls for constructing an unordered list of user-entered items.

List or table with Add or New button

- Pros: "add" action is visible and obvious
- Cons: higher space consumption; visual clutter

List or table with New-Item Row pattern

- Pros: lower space consumption; editing is done in place
- Cons: "add" action is not quite as obvious as a button

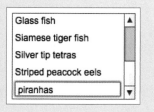

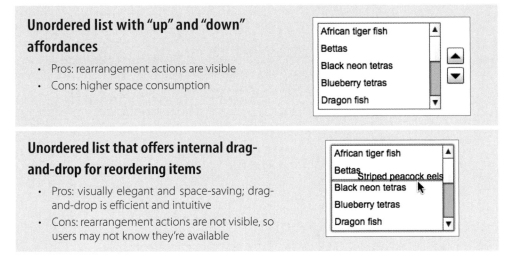

List or table that can receive dragged-and-dropped items

- Pros: visually elegant and space-saving; drag-and-drop is efficient and intuitive
- Cons: "add" action is not visible, so users may not know the list is a drop target

These controls are useful for constructing an ordered list of items.

Unordered list with "up" and "down" affordances

- Pros: rearrangement actions are visible
- Cons: higher space consumption

Unordered list that offers internal drag-and-drop for reordering items

- Pros: visually elegant and space-saving; drag-and-drop is efficient and intuitive
- Cons: rearrangement actions are not visible, so users may not know they're available

Text

Collecting text input from a user is one of the most basic form tasks. The controls typically are chosen according to the number of lines to be entered, whether or not the lines are predetermined choices, and whether or not the text will include formatting.

The following control is for entering one line of text.

Single-line text field

These controls are useful for entering either one line of text or a one-of-*N* choice.

Combo box

- Pros: quicker to use than a separate dialog box; familiar
- Cons: limited number of items can reasonably fit in drop down

Text field with More button or Dropdown Chooser

- Pros: permits the launch of a specialized chooser dialog box, e.g., a file finder or drop down
- Cons: not as familiar as a combo box to some users; dialogs are not as immediate

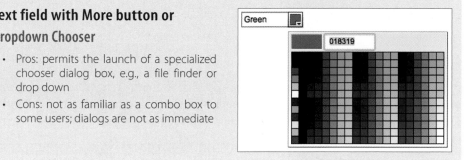

This control is for entering multiple lines of unformatted text.

Multiline text area

> Does anyone here have a border collie? I would really like one, and I have some questions. |

These controls are for entering multiple lines of formatted text.

Text area with inline tags

- Pros: skilled users can avoid the toolbar by typing tags directly
- Cons: not truly WYSIWYG

> Does anyone here have a border collie? I would [b]really[/b] like one, and I have some questions.

Arial   12   B   I   U

http://

Rich-text editor

- Pros: immediacy, since the edited text serves as a preview
- Cons: use of toolbar is required, so it cannot always be keyboard-only

Numbers

Because numbers often must follow more complex formatting rules, entering numbers on a form is slightly more complex than entering basic text. The choice of input options depends on the type of number you enter and its allowable range.

The following are controls for entering numbers of any type or format.

Text field using Forgiving Format

- Pros: visually elegant; permits wide variety of formats or data types
- Cons: expected format is not evident from the control's form, so it may cause temporary confusion; requires careful backend validation

Text field using Structured Format

- Pros: desired format evident from control's form
- Cons: possibly higher space consumption; more visual complexity; does not permit any deviation from the specified format, even if user needs to do so; may be more difficult for assistive technologies than a single field

Spin box (best for integers or discrete steps)

- Pros: user can arrive at a value via mouse clicks, without touching the keyboard; can also type directly if desired
- Cons: not familiar to all users; you may need to hold down the button long enough to reach the desired value; requires dexterity to use tiny buttons

Use these controls for entering numbers from a bounded range.

Slider

- Pros: obvious metaphor; position of value in range is shown visually; the user cannot enter a number outside the range
- Cons: high space consumption; unobvious keyboard access; tick labels can make it very crowded

Spinner

- Pros: values are constrained to be in range when buttons are used; low space consumption; supports both keyboard-only and mouse-only access
- Cons: not familiar to all users; requires dexterity to use tiny buttons; needs validation; cannot visually see value within range

Text field with after-the-fact error checking (can have Input Hints, Input Prompt, etc.)

- Pros: familiar to everyone; low space consumption; keyboard access
- Cons: requires validation; no constraints on what can be entered, so you have to communicate the range by some other means

Slider with text field (can take the form of a Dropdown Chooser with a slider on the drop down)

- Pros: allows both visual and numeric forms of input
- Cons: complex; high space consumption when both elements are on the page; requires validation of text field when the user types the value

These controls are for entering a subrange from a larger range.

Double slider (can be used with two text fields)

- Pros: lower space consumption than two sliders
- Cons: unfamiliar to most users; no keyboard access unless you also use text fields

Two sliders (also can be used with text fields)

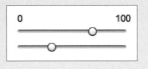

- Pros: less intimidating than a double slider
- Cons: very high space consumption; no keyboard access unless text fields are used, too

Two spinners (can be linked via Fill-in-the-Blanks)

- Pros: values are constrained to be in range when buttons are used; low space consumption; supports both keyboard-only and mouse-only access
- Cons: not familiar to all users; requires dexterity to use tiny buttons; needs validation; cannot visually see value within range

Two text fields with error checking (can use Input Hints, Input Prompt, or Fill-in-the-Blanks)

- Pros: familiar to everyone; much lower space consumption than sliders
- Cons: requires validation; no constraints on what can be entered, so you need to communicate the range by some other means

Dates or Times

Because of the potential formats and internationalization issues, dates and times can be a tricky item to accept from users. Input options for dates or times include the following.

Forgiving Format **text field**

- Pros: visually simple; permits wide variety of formats or data types; keyboard access
- Cons: expected format not evident from control's form, so it may cause brief confusion; requires careful backend validation

Oct 17, 2010

Structured Format **text field**

- Pros: desired format evident from control's form
- Cons: possibly higher space consumption; more visual clutter; does not permit deviation from specified format, even if user wants to do so; may be more difficult for screen readers than a single field

Oct   17 , 2010

Calendar or clock control

- Pros: obvious metaphor; input is constrained to allowable values
- Cons: high space consumption; may not provide keyboard-only access

Dropdown Chooser **with calendar or clock control**

- Pros: combines the advantages of text field and calendar control; low space consumption
- Cons: complex interaction; requires dexterity to pick values from a drop down

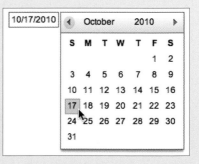

The Patterns

As you might have guessed if you read through the control tables in the preceding section, most of these patterns describe controls—specifically, how you can combine controls with other controls and text in ways that make them easier to use. Some patterns define structural relationships between elements, such as Dropdown Chooser and Fill-in-the-Blanks. Others, such as Good Defaults and Autocompletion, discuss the values of controls and how those values change.

A large number of these patterns deal primarily with text fields: Forgiving Format, Structured Format, Fill-in-the-Blanks, Input Hints, Input Prompt, Password Strength Meter, and Autocompletion. That shouldn't be surprising. Text fields are as common as dirt, but they don't make it easy for users to figure out what should go in them. They're easiest to use when presented in a context that makes their usage clear. The patterns give you many ways to create that context.

1. Forgiving Format

2. Structured Format

3. Fill-in-the-Blanks

4. Input Hints

5. Input Prompt

6. Password Strength Meter

7. Autocompletion

The next two patterns deal with controls other than text fields. Dropdown Chooser describes a way to create a custom control, and List Builder, referenced in the control table shown earlier, describes a commonly reinvented combination of controls that lets users construct a list of items.

8. Dropdown Chooser

9. List Builder

You should design the remaining patterns into the whole form. They apply equally well to text fields, drop downs, radio buttons, lists, and other stateful controls, but you should use them consistently within a form (or within a dialog box, or even an entire application).

10. Good Defaults

11. Same-Page Error Messages

Patterns from other chapters apply to form design as well. From Chapter 4, Right/Left Alignment discusses one way to arrange labels alongside controls. Labels can also be placed above the form fields (at the cost of vertical space, but with plenty of horizontal room for long labels), or left-aligned along the left edge of the form. The choice can affect the speed of form completion.

Chapters 3 and 4 also give you some larger-scale design possibilities. A *gatekeeper form*—any form that stands between the user and his immediate goal, such as sign-up or purchase forms—should be in Center Stage, with very few distractions on the page. Alternatively, you might make it a Modal Panel, layered over the page.

If you have a long form that covers different topics, you might consider breaking it up into Titled Sections or even separate pages. (Tabs tend to work poorly as grouping mechanisms for forms.) If you break up a form into a sequence of pages, use the Wizard and Sequence Map patterns to show users where they are and where they're going.

Finally, forms should use a Prominent "Done" Button (Chapter 6) for the completion or submission action. If you have secondary actions, such as a form reset or a help link, make those less prominent.

Forgiving Format

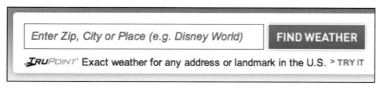

Figure 8-1. *Weather.com*

What

Permit users to enter text in a variety of formats and syntax, and make the application interpret it intelligently.

Use when

Your UI asks for data that users might type with an unpredictable mix of whitespace, hyphens, abbreviations, or capitalizations. More generally, the UI can accept input of various kinds from the user—different meanings, formats, or syntax. But you want to keep the interface visually simple.

Why

The user just wants to get something done, not think about "correct" formats and complex UIs. Computers are good at figuring out how to handle input of different types (up to a point, anyway). It's a perfect match: let the user type whatever he needs, and if it's reasonable, make the software do the right thing with it.

This can help simplify the UI tremendously, making it much easier to figure out. It may even remove the requirement for an Input Hint or Input Prompt, though they're often seen together, as in the example in Figure 8-1.

You might consider Structured Format as an alternative, but that pattern works best when the input format is entirely predictable (and usually numeric, like telephone numbers).

How

The catch (you knew there would be one): it turns a UI design problem into a programming problem. You have to think about what kinds of text a user is likely to type in. Maybe you ask for a date or time, and only the format varies—that's an easy case. Or maybe you ask for search terms, and the variation is what the software *does* with the data. That's harder. Can the software disambiguate one case from another? How?

Each application uses this pattern differently. Just make sure the software's response to various input formats matches what users expect it to do. Test, test, and test again with real users.

Examples

The *New York Times* uses Forgiving Format in several features that need information from users. Figure 8-2 shows examples from its real estate search and from its financial quotes feature.

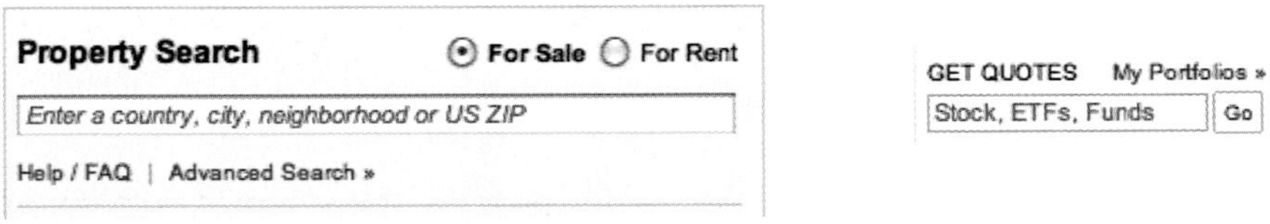

Property Search   ⦿ **For Sale** ◯ For Rent

Enter a country, city, neighborhood or US ZIP

Help / FAQ | Advanced Search »

GET QUOTES   My Portfolios »

Stock, ETFs, Funds   Go

Figure 8-2. *Two text fields in the New York Times website*

One place where this pattern should be used, but usually isn't, is when credit card numbers are requested from the user. As long as 16 digits are typed, why should the form care whether the user separates them by spaces, or by hyphens, or by nothing at all? It's not difficult to strip out separating characters. PayPal, for example, doesn't accept spaces in credit card numbers (see Figure 8-3).

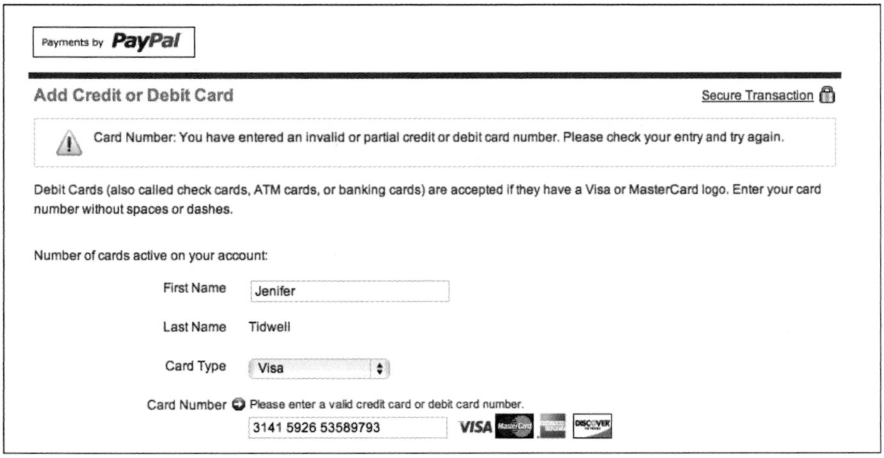

Figure 8-3. *PayPal*

Figure 8-4 comes from Outlook's tool for setting up a meeting. Look at the "Start time:" and "End time:" fields at the bottom of the screenshot—you don't need to give it a fully defined date, like what's in the text fields now. If today is April 24 and you want to set up a meeting for April 29, you can type any of the following terms:

- next Thu
- nxt thu
- thu

- 29/4/2004
- 4/29/2004
- 29/4

- 4/29
- five days
- 5 days

And so on—there are probably other accepted formats, too. The specified date then is "echoed back" to the user in the appropriate format for the user's language and location.

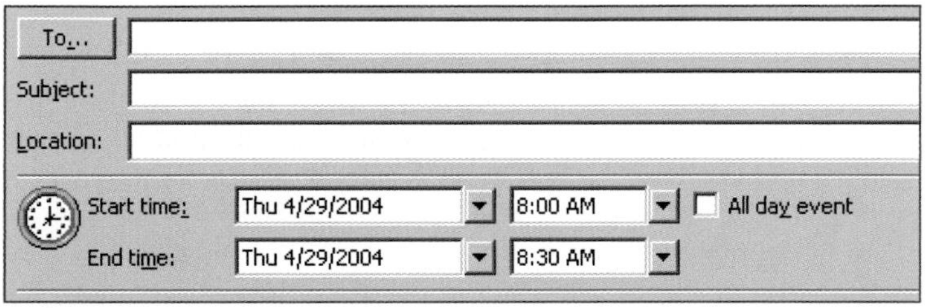

Figure 8-4. *Microsoft Outlook*

In other libraries

http://ui-patterns.com/patterns/ForgivingFormat

http://quince.infragistics.com/Patterns/Forgiving%20Format.aspx

Structured Format

Figure 8-5. *Photoshop installation screen*

What

Instead of using one text field, use a set of text fields that reflect the structure of the requested data.

Use when

Your interface requests a specific kind of text input from the user, formatted in a certain way. That format is familiar and well defined, and you don't expect any users to need to deviate from the format you expect. Examples include credit card information, local telephone numbers, and license strings or numbers.

It's generally a bad idea to use this pattern for any data in which the preferred format may vary from user to user. Consider especially what might happen if your interface is used in other countries. Names, addresses, postal codes, and telephone numbers all have different standard formats in different places. Consider using Forgiving Format in those cases.

Why

The structure of the text fields gives the user a clue about what kind of input is being requested. For example, she can mentally map the six text fields in Figure 8-5 to the six-chunk number written on her Photoshop CD case, and conclude that that's the license number she now needs to type in. Expectations are clear. She probably also realizes that she doesn't need to type in any spaces or hyphens to separate the six chunks.

This pattern usually gets implemented as a set of small text fields instead of one big one. That alone can reduce data entry errors. It's easier for someone to double-check several short strings (two to five characters or so) than one long one, especially when numbers are involved. Likewise, it's easier to transcribe or memorize a long number when it's broken up into chunks. That's how the human brain works.

Contrast this pattern to Forgiving Format, which takes the opposite tack: it allows you to type in data in any format, without providing structural evidence of what's being asked for. (You can use other clues instead, like Input Hints.) Structured Format is better for very predictable formats, Forgiving Format for open-ended input.

Design a set of text fields that reflect the format being asked for. Keep the text fields short, as clues to the length of the input.

Once the user has typed all the digits or characters in the first text field, confirm it for her by automatically moving the input focus to the next field. She can still go back and re-edit the first one, of course, but now she knows how many digits are required there.

You can also use Input Prompts to give the user yet more clues about what's expected. In fact, structured format fields for dates often do use Input Prompts, such as "dd/mm/yyyy".

Examples

At its simplest, Structured Format literally can take the shape of the data, complete with spaces, hyphens, and parentheses, as illustrated in the following table.

Telephone number	(504) 555-1212	(504) 555 - 1212
Credit card number	1021 1234 5678 0000	1021 1234 5678 0000
Date	12/25/2004	12 / 25 / 2004
ISBN number	0-1950-1919-9	0 - 1950 - 1919 - 9

For date input, LiveJournal uses Structured Format in combination with a drop down to choose a month (see Figure 8-6). It defaults to the current day and time.

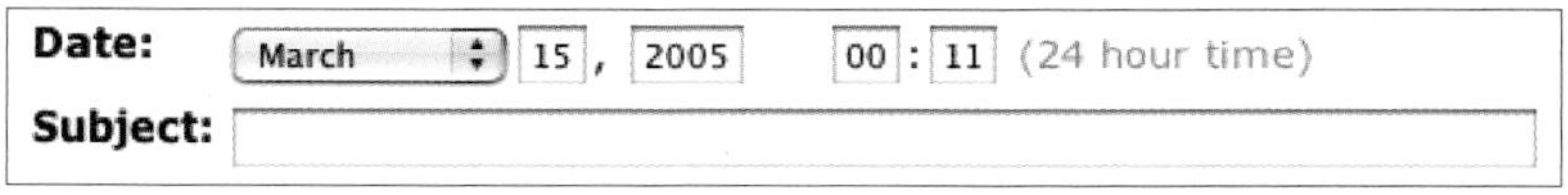

Date: [March ‡] 15 , 2005 00 : 11 (24 hour time)
Subject: [   ]

Figure 8-6. *LiveJournal*

In other libraries

http://ui-patterns.com/patterns/StructuredFormat

http://quince.infragistics.com/Patterns/Structured%20Format.aspx

Fill-in-the-Blanks

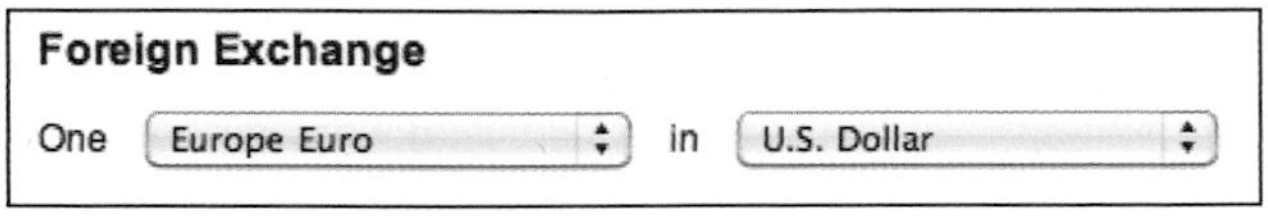

Foreign Exchange

One [Europe Euro   ▲▼]   in   [U.S. Dollar   ▲▼]

Figure 8-7. *The New York Times*

What

Arrange one or more fields in the form of a prose sentence or phrase, with the fields as "blanks" to be filled in by the user.

Use when

You need to ask the user for input, usually one-line text, a number, or a choice from a drop-down list. You tried to write it out as a set of label/control pairs, but the labels' typical declarative style (such as "Name:" and "Address:") isn't clear enough for users to understand what's going on. You can, however, verbally describe the action to be taken once everything's filled out, in an active-voice sentence or phrase.

Why

Fill-in-the-Blanks helps to make the interface self-explanatory. After all, we all know how to finish a sentence. (A verb phrase or noun phrase will do the trick, too.) Seeing the input, or "blanks," in the context of a verbal description helps the user understand what's going on and what's being asked of him.

How

Write the sentence or phrase using all your word-crafting skills. Use controls in place of words.

If you're going to embed the controls in the middle of the phrase instead of at the end, this pattern works best with text fields, drop-down lists, and combo boxes—in other words, controls with the same form factor (width and height) as words in the sentence. Also, make sure the baseline of the sentence text lines up with the text baselines in the controls, or it'll look sloppy. Size the controls so that they are just long enough to contain the user's choices, and maintain proper word spacing between them and the surrounding words.

This is particularly useful for defining conditions, as one might do when searching for items or filtering them out of a display. The Excel and eBay examples in Figures 8-8 and 8-9 illustrate the point. Robert Reimann and Alan Cooper describe this pattern as an ideal way to handle queries; their term for it is *natural language output.*

There's a big "gotcha" in this pattern, however: it becomes very hard to properly *localize* the interface (convert it to a different language), since comprehension now depends upon word order in a natural language. For some international products or websites, that's a nonstarter. You may have to rearrange the UI to make it work in a different language; at the very least, work with a competent translator to make sure the UI can be localized.

Examples

The Excel cell-formatting dialog box shown in Figure 8-8 lets you choose the phrases in this "sentence" from drop-down boxes. As the phrases change, the subsequent text fields—showing 0.7 and 0.9 in this example—might be replaced by other controls, such as a single text field for "greater than."

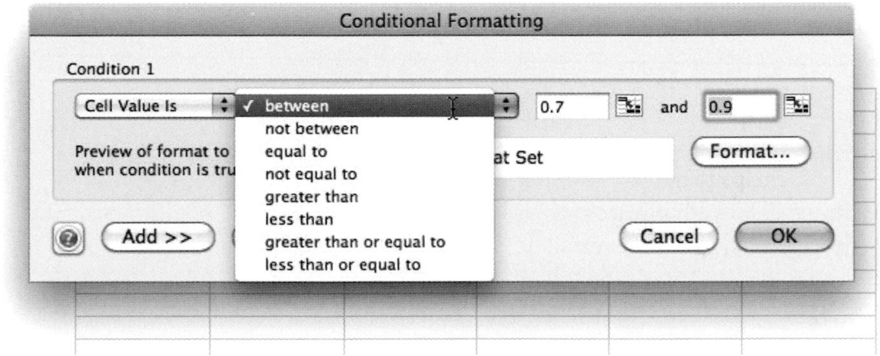

Figure 8-8. *Excel*

When users search for items on eBay, they can use a long form to filter search results according to various criteria. The form shown in Figure 8-9 has several examples of Fill-in-the-Blanks.

---

* See their book *About Face 2.0: The Essentials of Interaction Design* (Wiley), page 205.

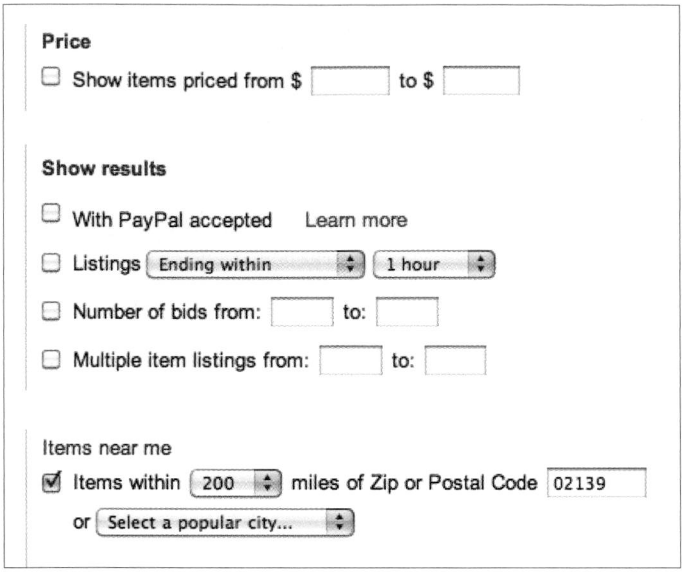

Figure 8-9. *eBay search filter form*

In other libraries

http://ui-patterns.com/patterns/FillInTheBlanks

Input Hints

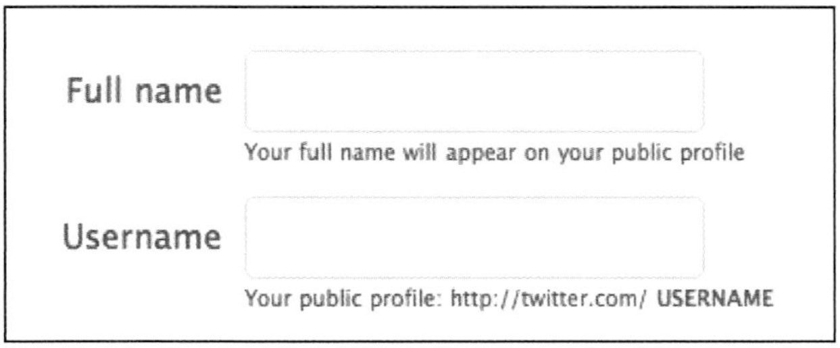

Figure 8-10. *Twitter registration page*

What

Beside or below an empty text field, place a phrase or example that explains what is required.

The interface presents a text field, but the kind of input it requires isn't obvious to all users. You don't want to put more than a few words into the text field's label.

A text field that explains what goes into it frees users from having to guess. The hint provides context that the label itself may not provide. If you visually separate the hint from the main label, users who know what to do can more or less ignore the hint, and stay focused on the label and control.

Write a short example or explanatory sentence, and put it below or beside the text field. The hint may be visible all the time, or it may appear when the text field receives input focus.

Keep the text in the hint small and inconspicuous, though readable; consider using a font two points smaller than the label font. (A one-point difference will look more like a mistake than an intended font-size change.) Also, keep the hint short. Beyond a sentence or two, many users' eyes will glaze over, and they'll ignore the text altogether.

This pattern is often used in conjunction with Forgiving Format, as illustrated by the Word example in Figure 8-11, or Structured Format. Alternative solutions include Input Prompt (in which a short hint goes into the control itself), tool tips that show a description on hover, and Good Defaults (which put an actual valid value into the control). The advantage of Input Hints is that it leaves the control blank—the user is forced to consider the question and give an answer, which is sometimes better than letting the user not think about it at all.

The printing dialog boxes used by several Microsoft Office applications supply an Input Hint below a Forgiving Format text field—it takes page numbers, page ranges, or both (Figure 8-11). The hint is very useful to anyone who's never had to use the "Pages" option, but users who already understand it don't need to focus on the written text; they can just go straight for the input field.

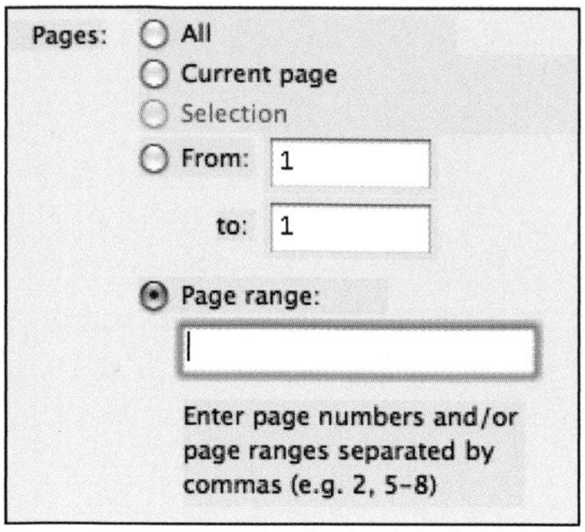

Figure 8-11. *Microsoft Word print dialog*

Longer descriptions can be used in Input Hints when necessary. The examples from Gmail's registration page, shown in Figure 8-12, are about as long as you'd want to put next to a text field—a user can click the links for further information. But most users will never follow a link when they're filling out a form, especially if they're trying to get through it quickly and don't have major privacy concerns, so don't depend on linked pages to convey critical information.

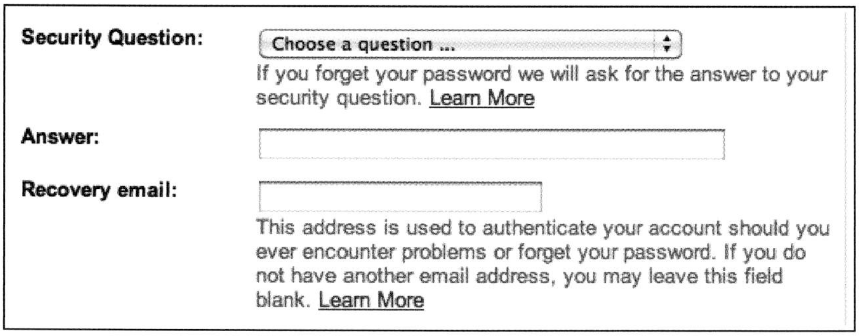

Figure 8-12. *Gmail registration page*

Blogger places Input Hints on the far right of the form, with horizontal rules that align the controls with their hints (see Figure 8-13). This is a graceful way to structure a page full of Input Hints.

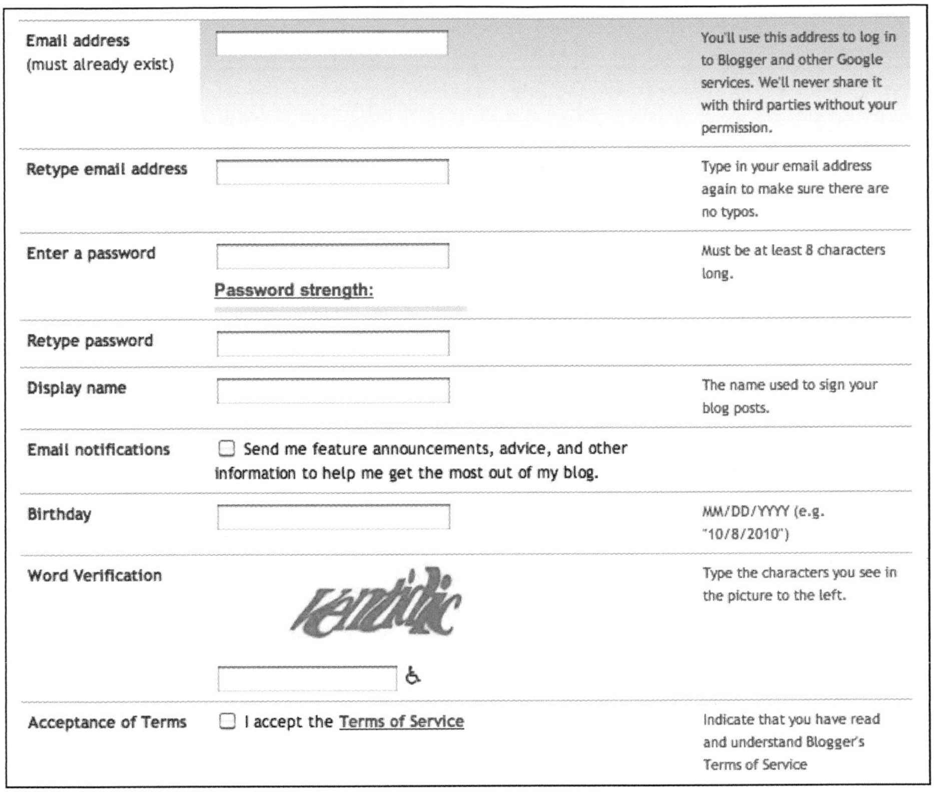

Email address (must already exist)		You'll use this address to log in to Blogger and other Google services. We'll never share it with third parties without your permission.
Retype email address		Type in your email address again to make sure there are no typos.
Enter a password		Must be at least 8 characters long.
	Password strength:	
Retype password		
Display name		The name used to sign your blog posts.
Email notifications	☐ Send me feature announcements, advice, and other information to help me get the most out of my blog.	
Birthday		MM/DD/YYYY (e.g. "10/8/2010")
Word Verification	*kentidic*	Type the characters you see in the picture to the left.
	☐ ♿	
Acceptance of Terms	☐ I accept the <u>Terms of Service</u>	Indicate that you have read and understand Blogger's Terms of Service

Figure 8-13. *Blogger registration page*

Some forms show an Input Hint when the user puts input focus into the text field itself (see Figure 8-14). This is nice because the hidden hints don't clutter the interface or add visual noise; however, the user doesn't see them at all until he clicks on (or tabs into) the text field. If you use these, note that you must leave space for them in the interface, just as you would for Hover Tools (Chapter 6). Twitter, shown first in this example, uses both kinds.

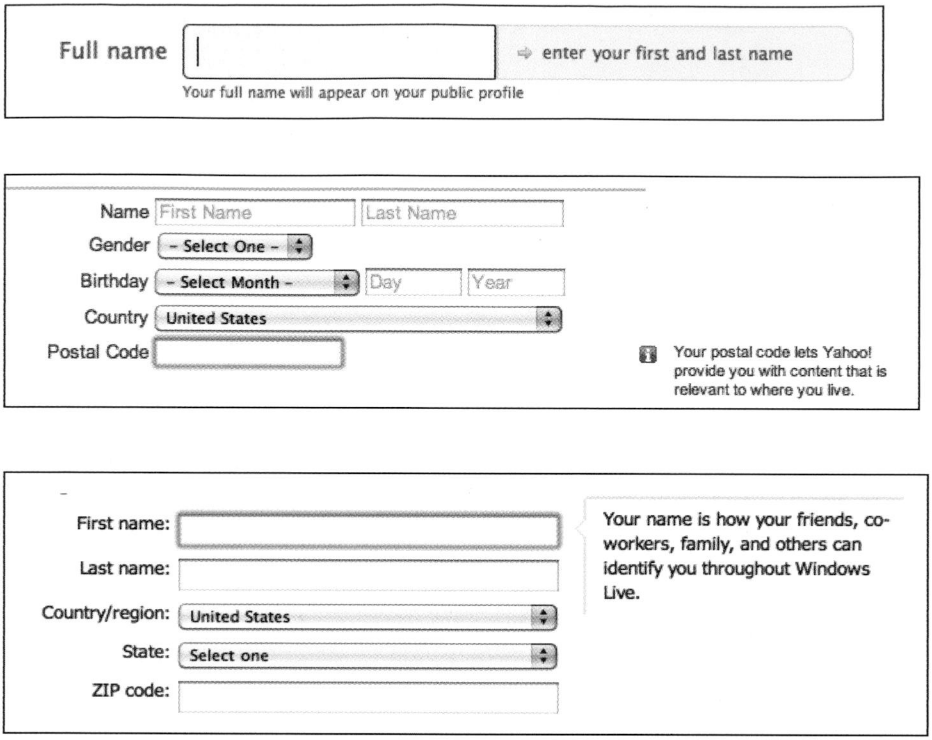

Figure 8-14. *Twitter, Yahoo!, and Hotmail registration pages, all with dynamic Input Hints*

In other libraries

http://quince.infragistics.com/Patterns/Input%20Hints.aspx

Input Prompt

Figure 8-15. *Yahoo! registration page*

What

Prefill a text field or drop down with a prompt that tells the user what to do or type.

Use when

The UI presents a text field, drop down, or combo box for input. Normally you would use a good default value, but you can't in this case—perhaps there is no reasonable default, as in the Yahoo! form in Figure 8-15.

Why

It helps make the UI self-explanatory. Like Input Hints, an Input Prompt is a sneaky way of supplying help information for controls whose purpose or format may not be immediately clear.

With an Input Hint, someone quickly scanning the UI can easily ignore the hint (or miss it entirely). Sometimes this is your desired outcome. But an Input Prompt sits right where the user will type, so it can't be ignored. The advantage here is that the user doesn't have to guess whether she has to deal with this control or not—the control itself tells her she does. (Remember that users don't fill out forms for fun—they'll do as little as needed to finish up and get out of there.) A question or an imperative "Fill me in!" is likely to be noticed.

An interesting side effect of this pattern is that users may not even bother to read the label that prefixes the text field. Look again at Figure 8-15. The label "Name" is now completely superfluous, in terms of the form's meaning. Because the user's eye will be drawn first to the text fields, the "First Name" and "Last Name" prompts probably will be read before the "Name" label anyway! That being said, don't remove the labels—that prompt is gone once the user types over it, and on subsequent readings of this form, she may not remember what the control asks for.

If you're very careful to implement this pattern correctly, you may be able to do away with the label altogether. The prompt must be put back when the user erases the value, and the requested information must be very familiar to the user (such as name or email).

Choose an appropriate prompt string, perhaps beginning with one of these words:

- For a drop-down list, use *Select*, *Choose*, or *Pick*.

- For a text field, use *Type* or *Enter*.

End it with a noun describing what the input is, such as "Choose a state," "Type your message here," or "Enter the patient's name." Put this phrase into the control where the value would normally be. (The prompt itself shouldn't be a selectable value in a drop down; if the user selects it, it's not clear what the software should do with it.)

Since the point of the exercise was to tell the users what they were required to do before proceeding, don't let the operation proceed until they've done it! As long as the prompt is still sitting untouched in the control, disable the button (or other device) that lets the user finish this part of the operation. That way, you won't have to throw an error message at the user.

For text fields, put the prompt back into the field as soon as the user erases the typed response.

Use Good Defaults instead of an Input Prompt when you can make a very accurate guess about what value the user will put in. The user's email address may already have been typed somewhere else, for instance, and the originating country can often be detected by websites.

Figures 8-16 and 8-17 are two examples of forms that depend on the Input Prompt, in the absence of actual labels. Both are asking for very simple, well-understood answers that users should be able to type or select without thinking very hard about them. Both put the Input Prompt back into the field if there is no user-typed value, as shown by the second screenshot in each example. (Apple then turns the field yellow to reinforce that the value is required to complete the form; this is a gentle variant of Same-Page Error Messages.)

The Culinary Culture example demonstrates the striking visual look that can be achieved with a skillful combination of typography, icon design, and Input Prompt.

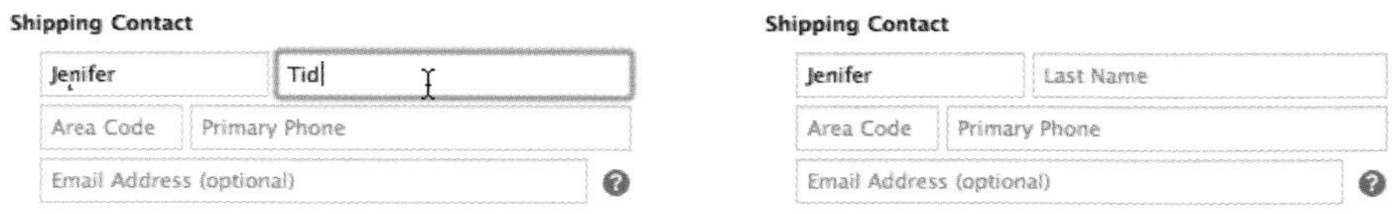

Figure 8-16. *Apple's purchase form*

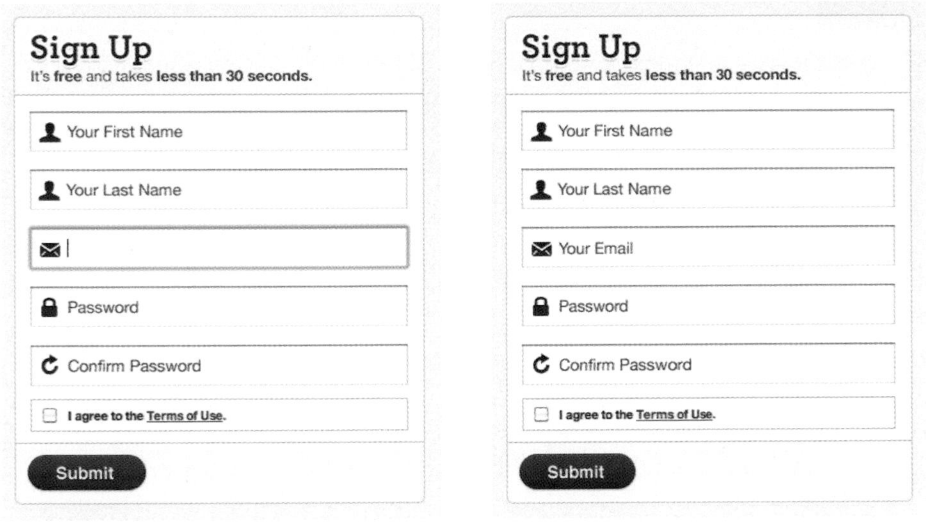

Figure 8-17. *CulinaryCulture.com*

In other libraries

http://quince.infragistics.com/Patterns/Input%20Prompt.aspx

http://ui-patterns.com/patterns/InputPrompt

Password Strength Meter

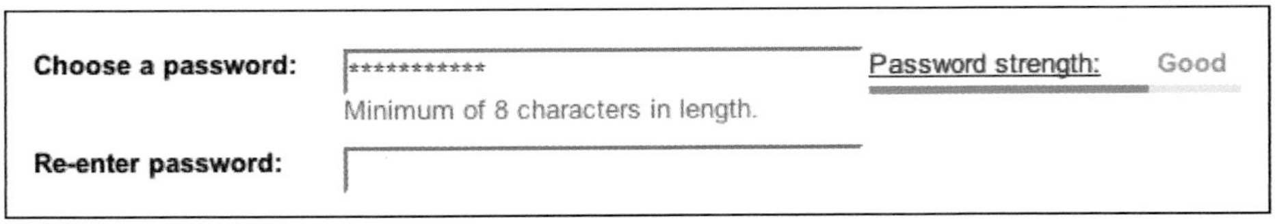

Figure 8-18. *Gmail registration page*

What

Give the user immediate feedback on the validity and strength of a new password while it is being typed.

Use when

The UI asks the user to choose a new password. This is quite common for site registrations. Your site or system cares about having strong passwords, and you want to actively help users choose good ones.

Why

Strong passwords protect both the individual user and the entire site, especially when the site handles sensitive information and/or social interactions. Weak passwords ought to be disallowed because they permit break-ins.

A Password Strength Meter gives immediate feedback to the user about his new password—is it strong enough or not? Does he need to make up a new one, and if so, with what characteristics (numbers, capital letters, etc.)? If your system is going to reject weak passwords, it's usually best to do it instantly, not after the user has submitted the registration form.

How

While the user types his new password, or after keyboard focus leaves the text field, show an estimate of the password strength beside the text field. At minimum, display a text and/or graphic label indicating a weak, medium, or strong password, and special wording to describe a too-short or invalid password. Colors help: red for unacceptable, green or blue for good, and some other color (often yellow) in between.

If you can, show additional text with specific advice on how to make a weak password better—a minimum length of eight characters (for instance), or the inclusion of numbers or capital letters. A user might get frustrated if he repeatedly fails to produce a valid password, so help him be successful.

Also, the form containing the password field should use Input Hints or other text to explain this beforehand. A short reminder of good password heuristics can be useful to users who need reminders, and if your system will actually reject weak passwords, you should warn the user about it before he finishes the form! Many systems require a minimum number of characters for a valid password, such as six or eight.

(Remember, never actually show a password, and don't make suggestions of alternative passwords. General hints are all you can really give.)

An explanation of password security is beyond the scope of a UI pattern. There are excellent online and print references for this topic, however, should you need to understand it more deeply.

Blogger's Password Strength Meter, shown in Figure 8-19, displays five states, one of which ("Too short") tells the user specifically how to fix the password—eight characters are required. The blue link puts up a window describing how to create a strong password, and there is an Input Hint (not shown) on the right side that tells the user about the eight-character minimum.

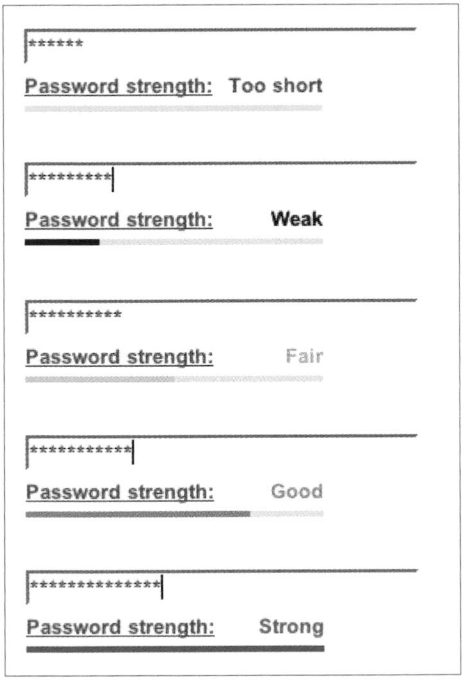

Figure 8-19. *Blogger's five states*

MSN shows only three states (see Figure 8-20). It also uses an Input Hint to describe the minimum—"Six-character minimum with no spaces"—and offers a link to a more detailed explanation. This meter is visually more heavyweight than Blogger's.

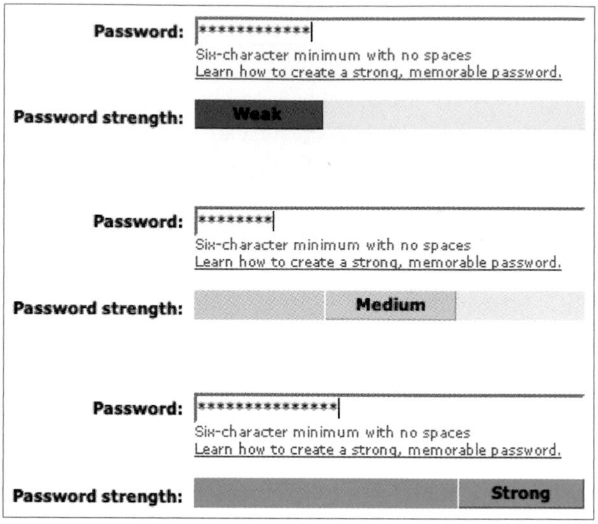

Figure 8-20. *MSN's three states*

Yahoo! offers specific, detailed password advice in two different Input Hints that appear when the password field received input focus (see Figure 8-21).

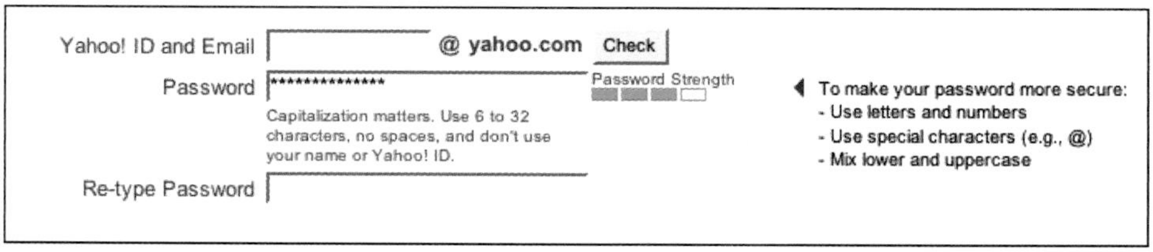

Figure 8-21. *Yahoo!*

In other libraries

http://ui-patterns.com/patterns/PasswordStrengthMeter

Code to do password checking is available for JavaScript and other languages. Look online not just for the term *password strength meter* but also *password meter*, *password checker*, and other variations.

Autocompletion

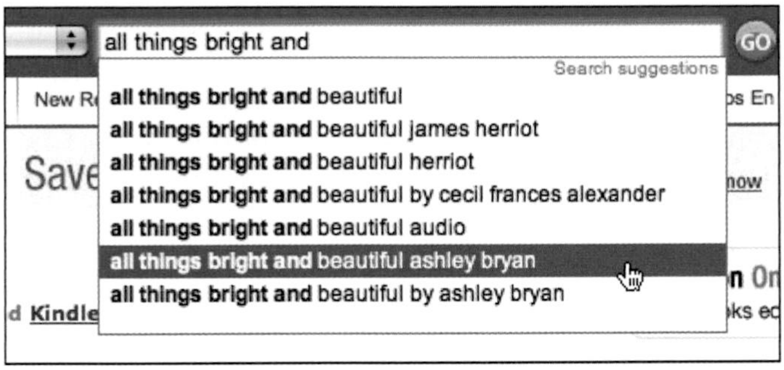

Figure 8-22. *Amazon*

What

As the user types into a text field, anticipate the possible answers, show a selectable list of them, and automatically complete the entry when appropriate.

Use when

The user types something predictable, such as a URL, the user's own name or address, today's date, or a filename. You can make a reasonable guess as to what she's attempting to type—perhaps there's a saved history of things this user has previously typed, for instance, or perhaps she is picking from a set of preexisting values, such as a list of filenames in a directory.

Search boxes, browser URL fields, email fields, common web forms (such as site registration or purchase), text editors, and command lines all seem to be much easier to use when supported by Autocompletion.

Why

Autocompletion saves time, energy, cognitive burden, and wrist strain for the user. It turns a laborious typing effort into a simple pick list (or less, if a single completion can be reliably supplied). You can thus save your users countless seconds of work, and contribute to the good health of thousands of wrists.

When the typed entries are long and hard to type (or remember), like URLs or email addresses, Autocompletion is quite valuable. It reduces a user's memory burden by supplying "knowledge in the world" in the form of a drop-down list. An additional benefit can be error prevention: the longer or stranger the string that must be typed, the greater the odds of the user making a typographical error. Autocompleted entries have no such problems.

For mobile devices, it's even more valuable. Typing text on a tiny device is no fun; if a user needs to enter a long string of letters, appropriate Autocompletion can save her a great deal of time and frustration. Again, email addresses and URLs are excellent candidates, to support mobile email and web usage.

Autocompletion is also common in text editors and command-line UIs. As users type commands or phrases, the application or shell might offer suggestions for completion. Code editors and OS shells are well suited for this, because the language used is limited and predictable (as opposed to a human language, such as English); it's therefore easier to guess what the user tries to type.

Finally, lists of possible autocompletions can serve as a map or guide to a large world of content. Search engines and site-wide search boxes do this well—when the user types the beginning of a phrase, an Autocompletion drop down shows likely completions that other people have typed (or that refer to available content). Thus, small corrections and gentle guidance are provided to a curious or uncertain user, and they offer a way to navigate a small corner of the public mental landscape.

How

With each additional character that the user types, the software quietly forms a list of the possible completions to that partially entered string. If the user enters one of a limited number of possible valid values, use that set of valid values. If the possible values are wide open, one of these might supply completions:

- Previous entries typed by this user, stored in a preferences or history mechanism
- Common phrases that many users have used in the past, supplied as a built-in "dictionary" for the application
- Possible matches drawn from the content being searched or perused, as for a site-wide search box
- Other artifacts appropriate to the context, such as company-wide contact lists for internal email

From here, you can approach the interaction design of Autocompletion in two ways. One is to show the user a list of possible completions on demand—for example, by pressing the Tab key—and let him choose one explicitly by picking from that list. Many code editors do this (see Figure 8-26 in the Examples section). It's probably better used when the user would recognize what he wants when he sees it, but may not remember how to type it without help. "Knowledge in the world is better than knowledge in the head."

The other way is to wait until there's only one reasonable completion, and then put it in front of the user, unprompted. Word does this with a tool tip; many forms do it by filling in the remainder of the entry but with selection turned on, so another keystroke would wipe out the autocompleted part. Either way, the user gets a choice about whether to retain the Autocompletion or not—and the default is to not keep it.

You can use both approaches together, as in Figure 8-26.

Make sure that Autocompletion doesn't irritate users. If you guess wrong, the user won't like it—he then has to erase the Autocompletion and retype what he meant in the first place, avoiding having Autocompletion pick the wrong completion yet again. These interaction details can help prevent irritation:

- Always give the user a choice to take the completion or not take it; default to "no."

- Don't interfere with ordinary typing. If the user intends to type a certain string and just keeps typing in spite of the attempts at Autocompletion, make sure the result is what the user intended to type.

- If the user keeps rejecting a certain Autocompletion in one place, don't keep offering it. Let it go at some point.

- Guess correctly.

Here's one possible way to implement Autocompletion cheaply. You can turn a text field into a combo box (which is a combination of a typable text field and a drop down). Each time the user enters a unique value into the text field, make a new drop-down item for it. Now, if your GUI toolkit allows type-ahead in combo boxes (as many do), the drop-down items are automatically used to complete whatever the user types. Refer back to Figure 8-22 at the top of the pattern for a typical example; most web browsers now keep the most recently visited sites in a combo box where the user types URLs.

Examples

Many email clients, of course, use Autocompletion to help users fill in To: and CC: fields. They generally draw on an address book, contacts list, or list of addresses you've exchanged email with. The example from Mac Mail, shown in Figure 8-23, shows a single completion suggested upon typing the letter *c*; the completed text is automatically highlighted, so a single keystroke can get rid of it. You can thus type straight "through" the completion if it's wrong.

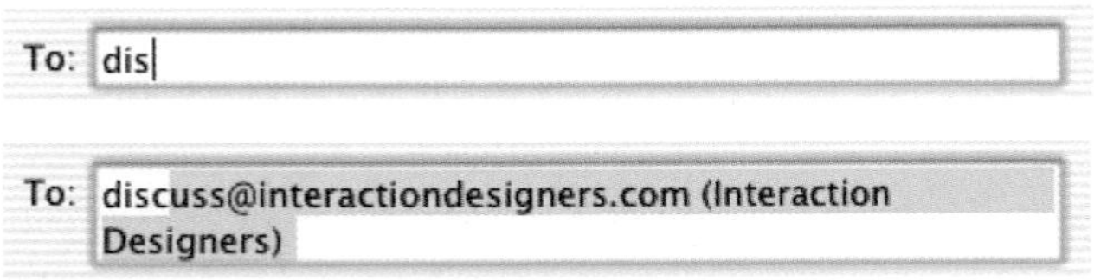

To: dis|

To: discuss@interactiondesigners.com (Interaction Designers)

Figure 8-23. *Mac Mail*

Drop-down lists of Autocompletion possibilities can take many forms. Figure 8-24 shows several examples of drop-down list formatting.

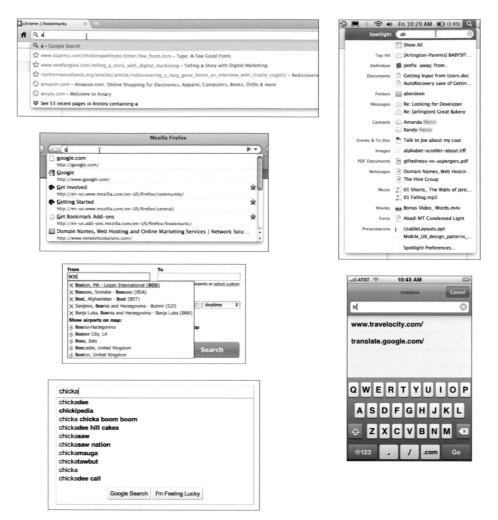

Figure 8-24. *Counterclockwise from top left: Chrome, Firefox, Kayak, Google, Safari for iPhone, and Mac OS Spotlight*

Dopplr, shown in Figure 8-25, doesn't show the whole long list of completions. Instead, it simply tells the user that there are 40 possible completions (for instance), and puts them behind a link.

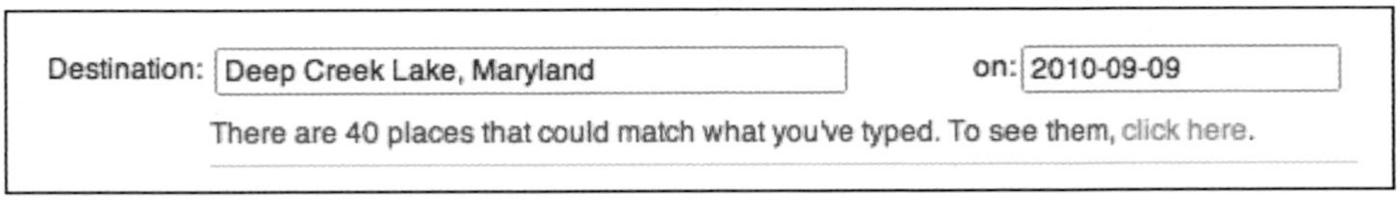

Destination: | Deep Creek Lake, Maryland | on: | 2010-09-09

There are 40 places that could match what you've typed. To see them, click here.

Figure 8-25. *Dopplr*

Finally, code editors such as Visual Studio invest in very complex Autocompletion mechanisms (see Figure 8-26). Visual Studio's IntelliSense completes the built-in keywords of a programming language, of course, but it also draws on the functions, classes, and variable names defined by the user. It even can show the arguments to functions that you invoke (in the righthand screenshot). Furthermore, both "select from a list" and "take the one completion that matches" approaches are supported, and you can call up Autocompletion on demand by pressing Ctrl-space bar.

Autocompletion in Visual Studio thus serves as a typing aid, a memory aid, and a browser of context-appropriate functions and classes. It's very useful.

Figure 8-26. *Visual Studio*

In other libraries

http://developer.yahoo.com/ypatterns/selection/autocomplete.html

http://ui-patterns.com/patterns/Autocomplete

http://patternry.com/p=autocomplete/

http://www.welie.com/patterns/showPattern.php?patternID=autocomplete

(Note that most other libraries call this pattern "Autocomplete.")

Dropdown Chooser

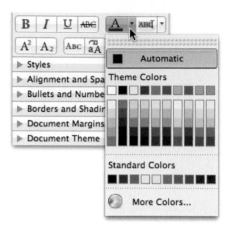

Figure 8-27. *Microsoft Word*

What

Extend the concept of a menu by using a drop-down or pop-up panel to contain a more complex value-selection UI.

Use when

The user needs to supply input that is a choice from a set (such as in the color example in Figure 8-27), a date or time, a number, or anything other than free text typed at a keyboard. You want to provide a UI that supports that choice—a nice visual rendering of the choices, for instance, or interactive tools—but you don't want to use space on the main page for that; a tiny space showing the current value is all you want.

Why

Most users are very familiar with the drop-down list control (called a "combo box" when used with a free-typing text field). Many applications successfully extend this concept to drop downs that aren't simple lists, such as trees, 2D grids, and arbitrary layouts. Users seem to understand them with no problem, as long as the controls have down-arrow buttons to indicate that they open when clicked.

Dropdown Choosers encapsulate complex UIs in a small space, so they are a fine solution for many situations. Toolbars, forms, dialog boxes, and web pages of all sorts use them now. The page the user sees remains simple and elegant, and the chooser UI only shows itself when the user requests it—an appropriate way to hide complexity until it is needed.

For the Dropdown Chooser control's "closed" state, show the current value of the control in either a button or a text field. To its right, put a down arrow. This may be in its own button or not, as you see fit; experiment and see what looks good and makes sense to your users. A click on the arrow (or the whole control) brings up the chooser panel, and a second click closes it again.

Design a chooser panel for the choice the user needs to make. Make it relatively small and compact; its visual organization should be a familiar format, such as a list, a table, an outline-type tree, or a specialized format like a calendar or calculator (see the examples in the next section). See Chapter 5 for a discussion of list presentation.

Scrolling the panel is OK if the user understands that it's a choice from a large set, such as a file from a filesystem, but keep in mind that scrolling one of these pop-up panels is not easy for people without perfect dexterity!

Links or buttons on the panel can in turn bring up secondary UIs—for example, color-chooser dialog boxes, file-finder dialog boxes, or help pages—that help the user choose a value. These devices usually are modal dialog boxes. In fact, if you intend to use one of these modal dialogs as the primary way the user picks a value (say, by launching it from a button), you could use a Dropdown Chooser instead of going straight to the modal dialog. The pop-up panel could contain the most common or recently chosen items. By making frequently chosen items so easy to pick, you reduce the total time (or number of clicks) it takes for an average user to pick values.

Photoshop's compact, interaction-rich toolbars use Dropdown Choosers heavily. Two examples, Brush and Opacity, are shown in Figure 8-28. The Brush chooser is a selectable list with a twist—it has extra controls such as a slider, a text field, and a pull-right button (the circular one) for yet more choices. The Opacity chooser is a simple slider, and the text field above it echoes its value.

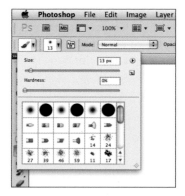

Figure 8-28. *Photoshop drop downs*

The Thumbnail Grid pattern (Chapter 5) is often used in Dropdown Choosers in place of a text-based menu. The examples from PowerPoint (Figure 8-29) and iWeb (Figure 8-30) demonstrate two styles of Thumbnail Grid.

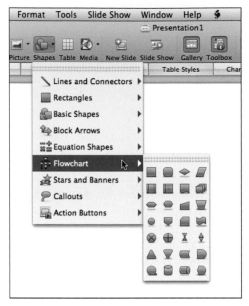

Figure 8-29. *Microsoft PowerPoint*

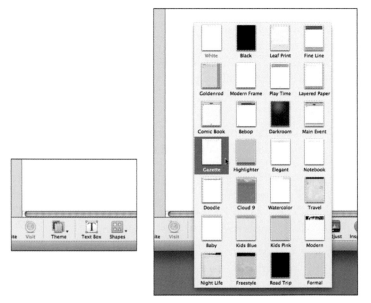

Figure 8-30. *iWeb "Theme" Dropdown Chooser*

In other libraries

http://quince.infragistics.com/Patterns/Drop%20Down%20Chooser.aspx

You could also look online for specific types of Dropdown Choosers, such as color pickers, date pickers or calendars, font pickers, or numeric sliders.

List Builder

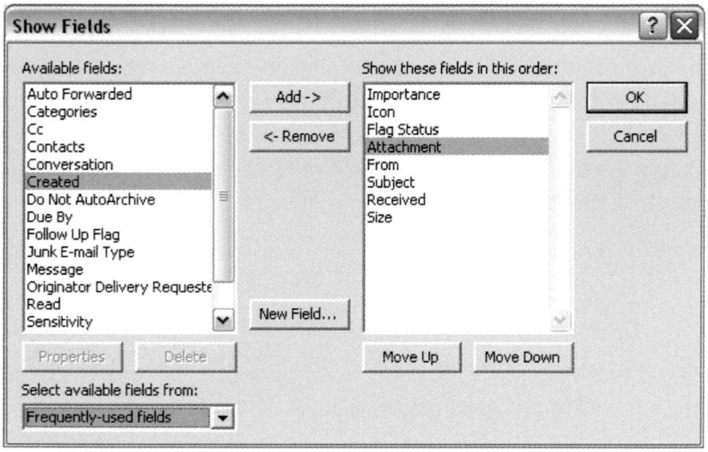

Figure 8-31. *A dialog box from Microsoft Outlook*

What

Show both the "source" and the "destination" lists on the same page; let the user move items between them, via buttons or drag-and-drop.

Use when

You're asking the user to create a list of items by choosing them from another list. The source list may be long—too long to easily show as a set of checkboxes, for instance.

Why

The key to this pattern is to show both lists on the same page. The user can see what's what—she doesn't have to jump to and from a modal chooser dialog box, for instance.

A simpler alternative to List Builder might be a single list of checkbox items. Both solve the "select a subset" problem. But if you have a very large source list (such as an entire filesystem), a list of checkboxes doesn't scale—the user can't easily see what's been checked off, and thus may not get a clear picture of what she selected. She has to keep scrolling up and down to see it all.

How

Put the source list and the destination list next to each other, either left to right or top to bottom. Between the two lists, put Add and Remove buttons (unless your users find drag-and-drop to be obvious, not requiring explanation). You could label the buttons with words, arrows, or both.

This pattern provides room for other buttons, too. If the destination list is ordered, use Move Up and Move Down buttons, as shown in Figure 8-31. (They could have arrow icons too, instead of or in addition to the words.)

Depending on what kind of items you deal with, you could either move the items literally from the source to the destination—so the source list "loses" the item—or maintain a source list that doesn't change. A listing of files in a filesystem shouldn't change; users would find it bizarre if it did, since they see such a list as a model of the underlying filesystem, and the files aren't actually deleted. But the list of "Available fields" in the Outlook example in Figure 8-31 does lose the items. That's a judgment call.

Give the lists multiple-selection semantics instead of single-selection, so users can move large numbers of items from list to list.

Examples

Most modern implementations of this pattern depend upon drag-and-drop to move items between areas; if those items are visual, all the better. Flickr, shown in Figure 8-32, demonstrates a more contemporary approach to a List Builder: you can drag items from a potentially long list of source images into a "batch" group in order to perform operations on all batched images at once. Large text tells the user what to do at critical moments in the interaction, such as starting a new batch or removing an image from the batch.

Figure 8-32. *Flickr*

In other libraries

http://www.welie.com/patterns/showPattern.php?patternID=parts-selector

Good Defaults

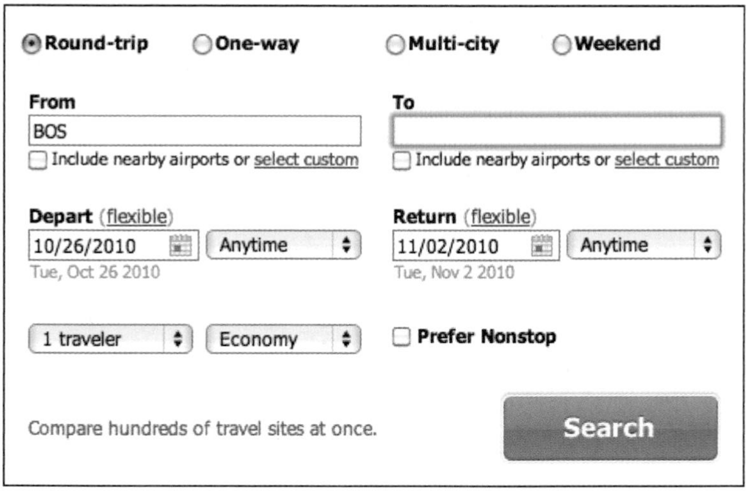

Figure 8-33. *Kayak*

Wherever appropriate, prefill form fields with your best guesses at the values the user wants.

Your UI asks the user any questions requiring form-like input (such as text fields or radio buttons), and you want to reduce the amount of work that users have to do. Perhaps most users will answer in a certain way, or the user has already provided enough contextual information for the UI to make an accurate guess. For technical or semirelevant questions, maybe he can't be expected to know or care about the answer, and "whatever the system decides" is OK.

But supplying defaults is not always wise when answers might be sensitive or politically charged, such as passwords, gender, or citizenship. Making assumptions like that, or prefilling fields with data you should be careful with, can make users uncomfortable or angry. (And for the love of all that is good in the world, don't leave "Please send me advertising email" checkboxes checked by default!)

Why

By providing reasonable default answers to questions, you save the users work. It's really that simple. You spare the user the effort of thinking about, or typing, the answer. Filling in forms is never fun, but if having default answers provided halves the time it takes the user to work through the form, he'll be grateful.

Even if the default isn't what the user wants, at least you offered an example of what kind of answer is asked for. That alone can save him a few seconds of thought—or, worse, an error message.

Sometimes you may run into an unintended consequence of Good Defaults. If a user can skip over a field, that question may not "register" mentally with him. He may forget that it was asked; he may not understand the implications of the question, or of the default value. The act of typing an answer, selecting a value, or clicking a button forces the user to address the issue consciously, and that can be important if you want the user to learn the application effectively.

How

Prefill the text fields, combo boxes, and other controls with a reasonable default value. You could do this when you show the page to the user for the first time, or you could use the information the user supplies early in the application to dynamically set later default values. (For instance, if someone supplies a U.S. zip code, you can infer the state, country, and municipality from just that number.)

Don't choose a default value just because you think you shouldn't leave any blank controls. Do so only when you're reasonably sure that most users, most of the time, won't change it—otherwise, you will create extra work for everybody. Know your users!

Occasional-use interfaces such as software installers deserve a special note. You should ask users for some technical information, such as the location of the install, in case they want to customize it. But 90% of users probably won't. And they won't care where you install it, either—it's just not important to them. So it's perfectly reasonable to supply a default location.

Examples

Kayak (Figure 8-33) supplies default values when a user begins a search for flights. Most are quite reasonable: a round-trip economy flight with one traveler is common, and the "From" city can be derived from either the user's geographic location or the user's previous searches. (The departure and arrival dates seem arbitrary, however.) The effect of having all these defaults is that the user spends less time thinking about those parts of the form, and she gets a quicker path to her immediate goal—the search results.

When an image canvas is resized in Photoshop, the dialog box shown in Figure 8-34 appears. The original image was 476 × 306, as shown. These dimensions become the default Width and Height, which is very convenient for several use cases. If I want to put a thin frame around the image, I can start with the existing dimensions and increase them by just two pixels each; if I want to make the image canvas wider but not taller, I only need to change the Width field; or I could just click OK now and nothing changes.

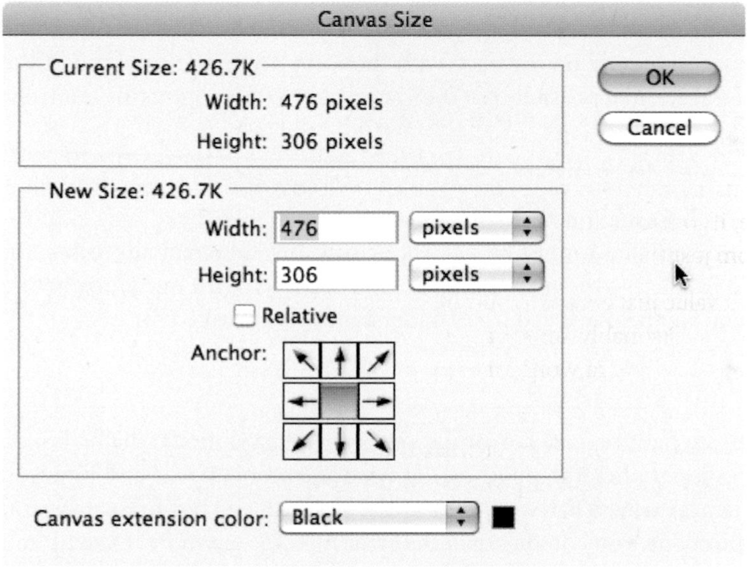

Figure 8-34. *A dialog from Photoshop*

In other libraries

http://patternry.com/p=good-defaults/

http://ui-patterns.com/patterns/GoodDefaults

Same-Page Error Messages

Figure 8-35. *Netflix registration box*

> **What**

Place form error messages directly on the page with the form itself; mark the top of the page with an error message, and if possible, put indicators next to the originating controls.

> **Use when**

Users might enter form information that somehow isn't acceptable. They may skip required fields, enter numbers that cannot be parsed, or type invalid email addresses, for instance. You want to encourage them to try again. You want to point out typos before they become a problem, and help puzzled users understand what is asked for.

> **Why**

Traditionally, applications have reported error messages to users via modal dialog boxes. Those messages could be very helpful, pointing out what the problem was and how you could fix it. The problem is that you had to click away the modal dialog box to fix the error. And with the dialog box gone, you couldn't read the error message anymore! (Maybe you were supposed to memorize the message.)

Then, when web forms came along, error messages often were reported on a separately loaded page, shown after you clicked the Submit button. Again, you can read the message, but you have to click the Back button to fix the problem; once you do that, the message is gone. Then you need to scan the form to find the field with the error, which takes effort and is error-prone.

Most web forms now place the error message on the form itself. By keeping both messages and controls together on the same page, you allow the user to read the message and make the form corrections easily, with no jumping around or error-prone memorization.

Even better, some web forms put error messages physically next to the controls where the errors were made. Now the user can see at a glance where the problems were—no need to hunt down the offending field based just on its name—and the instructions for fixing it are right there, easily visible.

First, design the form to prevent certain kinds of errors. Use drop downs instead of open text fields, if the choices are limited and not easy to type. For text fields, offer Input Hints, Input Prompts, Forgiving Format, Autocompletion, and Good Defaults to support text entry. Clearly mark all the required fields as required (with asterisks), and don't ask for too many required fields in the first place.

When errors do happen, you should show some kind of error message on top of the form, even if you put the detailed messages next to the controls. The top is the first thing people see. (It's also good for visually impaired users—the top of the form is read to them first, so they know immediately that the form has an error.) Put an attention-getting graphic there, and use text that's stronger than the body text: make it red and bold, for instance.

Now mark the form fields that caused the errors. Put specific messages next to them, if you can—this will require extra space beside, above, or below the fields—but at the least, use color and/or a small graphic to mark the field, as shown in Figure 8-35.Users commonly associate red with errors in this context. Use it freely, but since so many people are colorblind with respect to red, use other cues, too: language, bold text (not huge), and graphics.

If you're designing for the Web or some other client/server system, try to do as much validation as you can on the client side. It's much quicker. Put the error messages on the page that's already loaded, if possible, to avoid a page-load wait.

A tutorial on error-message writing is beyond the scope of this pattern, but here are some quick guidelines:

- Make them short, but detailed enough to explain both which field it is and what went wrong: "You haven't given us your address" versus "Not enough information."

- Use ordinary language, not computerese: "Is that a letter in your zip code?" versus "Numeric validation error."

- Be polite: "Sorry, but something went wrong! Please click 'Go' again" versus "JavaScript Error 693" or "This form contains no data."

Twitter's and Mint's registration pages (Figures 8-36 and 8-37, respectively) show either an error message or an "OK" message. This can help for short forms.

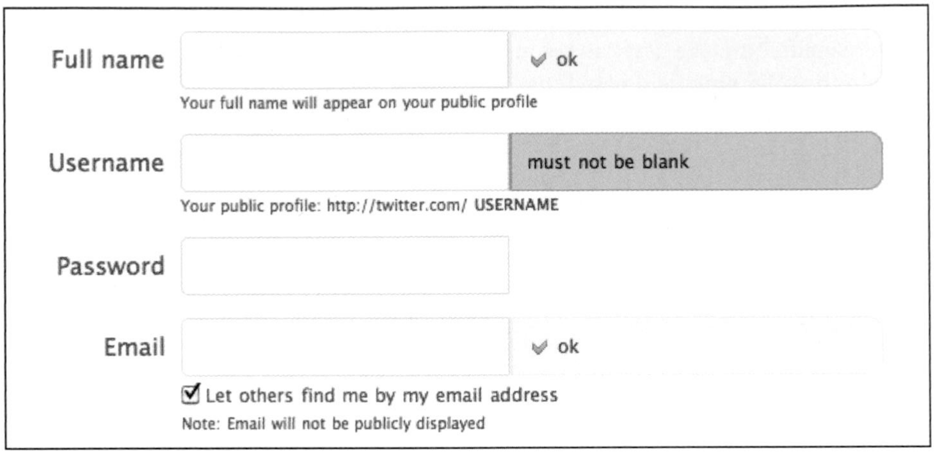

Figure 8-36. *Twitter registration page*

Figure 8-37. *Mint registration page*

Yahoo! uses humor in some of its error messages, while others are straight (see Figure 8-38).

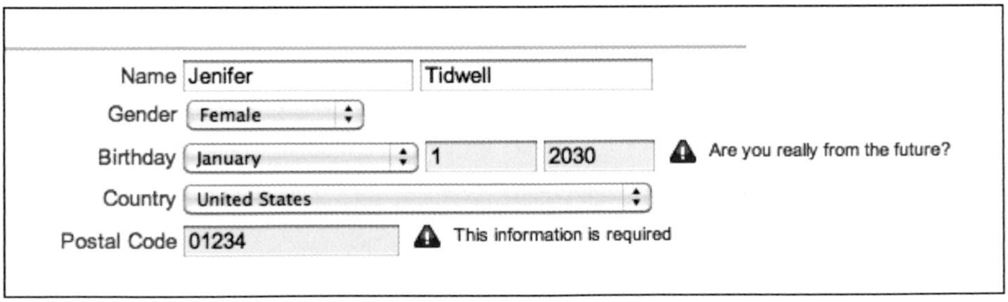

Figure 8-38. *Yahoo! registration page*

When you add a not fully specified item to your cart at Hanna Andersson's site, it uses a gentle message to remind you to fill in missing information, as shown in Figure 8-39. (The Input Prompt makes it too easy to overlook this field on the form, actually.) Once you do add it, the same space might be used for an additional message of interest. Note also that once the form detects that enough information is present, it puts the Begin Checkout button on the form.

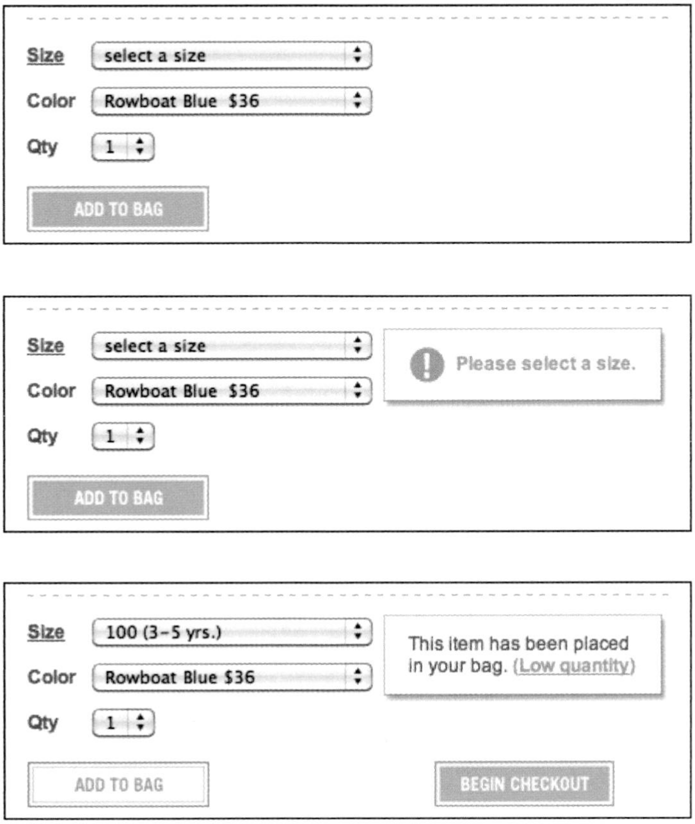

Figure 8-39. *Hanna Andersson's purchase form*

In other libraries

http://ui-patterns.com/patterns/InputFeedback

http://www.welie.com/patterns/showPattern.php?patternID=input-error

These two patterns are named "Input Feedback" and "Input Error Message." You can search for similar variations on the pattern name.

Chapter 9

Using Social Media

In 2009 and 2010, social media went mainstream. Companies, products, and nonprofits rushed to establish presences on Facebook, Twitter, and media repositories such as Flickr and YouTube. If they already had blogs, the streams of bite-size messages on Twitter and Facebook gave those blogs new audiences. Organizations discovered that if they published a steady stream of appealing content, customers and influencers would pay attention to them—and if a piece of content "went viral," that organization's brand would spread far and wide. For free!

Well, not really for free.

Organizations put in a lot of effort to establish successful social media presences. Someone has to spend a lot of time writing and disseminating content; someone else needs to spend time reading relevant conversations across the Web and responding sensitively to them. Valuable home page real estate may support these social media efforts, and pages on other sites (such as Facebook or YouTube) must be designed and tended. And someone needs to devise an overall strategy: where is effort spent, when, and on what topics?

A few best practices are emerging that can inform those efforts. Social media is still a young field, and specific recommendations will change rapidly over the months and years. Like the rest of this book, this chapter's principles and patterns aren't hard-and-fast rules, though ideally they will outlast 2010's most popular sites and technologies.

This chapter will focus on one aspect of online social interaction: how to use the various forms of social media to promote a brand, share an idea, disseminate a video or other artistic expression, and otherwise support your particular enterprise. The key is to acquire *followers*—people who voluntarily listen to what you have to say. Brands that create excellent experiences for their followers gain huge audiences from their social media efforts. (Here, we will keep the scope of this chapter broad enough to include "brands" that are personal, nonprofit, arts-based, cause-driven, or just for fun.)

What This Chapter Does Not Cover

Personal use of social media varies dramatically from person to person. There may be best practices for personal consumption of social media—in fact, that might be a very fun conversation to have among practitioners. But this book was written for designers of sites and software, and so the focus will be on what those designers need.

Another topic this chapter will not cover is the design of online communities. That's an art unto itself, and its patterns and best practices are somewhat different from the ones that are described in this chapter. As of this writing, a few organizations and brands have successfully built online communities around their brand, but there's not much evidence that they actually help the brand. (If the brand *is* an online community, such as Stack Overflow or Ravelry, that's a different story; they can be quite successful. In any case, this chapter doesn't address them.)

Finally, many sites have sprung up that use social interaction in innovative ways. Delicious, Yelp, Foursquare, and others have all created products out of collective intelligence, mediated online. I expect that more of these kinds of sites will arise over the years. Erin Malone and Christian Crumlish have skillfully written about some of these ways of gathering and concentrating opinions in their book *Designing Social Interfaces* (O'Reilly, *http://oreilly.com/catalog/9780596154936/*). This chapter complements that book.

The Basics of Social Media

What principles and patterns should you consider as you help develop a strategy for using social media?

The first topic is so obvious and so basic that I gave it the number zero. It's something you need to do before you create any social media presence at all:

0. Listen.
> Find out where people are talking about your brand, product, organization—or competitors. Go beyond that, too: which broad topics touch on your brand's purpose or mission, and what are people saying about those topics? If your organization has something positive to contribute, take part in those conversations.

> - Find the online conversations and read them. Use tools to help you monitor them if necessary, especially if you're working for a well-known brand with a strong online presence.

> - Make sure the organization knows what is being said about it, even if the comments are negative.

> - In reputable places with a large readership, such as certain well-known blogs, have someone from your organization sign up and participate in the conversations. Make it clear that that person formally represents the organization.

- When you participate, answer questions, offer information, gently correct misperceptions, and acknowledge gripes.

- Be a responsive, dignified presence; don't be too chatty, and don't be too defensive. And hold back on the sales pitches.

Now we'll talk about the active, creative aspects of using social media. How do you build a fruitful social media presence that people enjoy following?

The following six principles come more or less in order of importance. If you don't write content that people like to read (principle 1), there's no point in spending effort to disseminate it or make it findable, for instance. Some of these recommendations will be relevant to your situation, and some will not. Principles 5 and 6, especially, are uncommon because of the effort they require.

1. *Produce good stuff.*
   Write, design, record, or otherwise create items that people enjoy consuming. Produce them regularly and frequently enough to keep people interested. Set up conversations around those items to make them even more intriguing—invite Facebook comments, for instance—and participate in those conversations yourself.

   - Create an Editorial Mix that represents your organization well. Generate original content that appeals to different people, using a mixture of length, style, and media type (text, images, video, podcast).

   - Link to other people's content. Use Repost and Comment to augment your original material and to give credit to other worthy sites on the Web.

   - Having Personal Voices in your mix can be more appealing than a single, generic corporate voice.

   - Use Conversation Starters to prompt followers to respond. Once someone engages in a conversation with you, she's more likely to come back.

2. *Push that good stuff out to readers.*
   Go to wherever they spend their time: email, Facebook, Twitter, RSS feeds, Digg, or wherever you discover your readers are hanging out online. With your readers' permission, get your content into their personal News Streams (Chapter 2)—the daily flow of news and updates they get via those services. (In other words, make them followers.)

   - Use more than one social media channel or service to reach as many readers as you reasonably can. Meet them where they are; don't expect them to join a new service just to get your updates.

   - Don't overwhelm your followers with too much content. Use the different services wisely, according to the conventions developed for each one. Develop a Timing Strategy for releasing content.

   - Put Social Links on your home page to direct readers to your social media channels; make it easy for them to become followers.

- If your organization produces a lot of content and has many different audiences for different products or topics, consider using Specialized Streams instead of one very busy stream of content.

- Use the Inverted Nano-pyramid to write status updates, summaries, and headlines. These attract more readers when they are written skillfully and "hook" people into reading more of your content.

3. Let readers decide which stuff is good.

Give readers a way to share your content with their own followers, and let readers send items privately to close ties. Gather feedback via voting systems, thumbs-up/down gadgets, and other systems. Note which items have active conversations about them, as this is another signal of "good"-ness.

- Provide mechanisms for people to comment on the items you post, but be selective. Low-interest news items or blog posts don't draw many comments, and empty comment areas don't draw attention. Lively ones, however, can pull in more readers.

- Put a Sharing Widget beside your posts, so people can easily share them with their own social followers. This is a very powerful mechanism; it disseminates your content to more people, engages the people who do the sharing, and gives you data about which items are most popular.

- "Email this" buttons let readers send items privately to their closer social ties. Emailed articles are likely to be read by the recipients, since someone they know has specifically recommended it to them; this kind of Personal Recommendation (Chapter 1) is powerful.

- When you post items such as product descriptions or recipes—things for which negative reviews won't reflect badly on your organization—consider letting people review or rate these items. Their collective intelligence can identify the bad and good for other readers. (You may invite trouble, however, if you ask people to rate items that your organization directly produces and is invested in.)

- Let viewers "vote up" their favorite pieces of content. You might do this with a "Like" control, a star, a thumbs-up, or some other mechanism. For more details, see the "Vote to Promote" pattern in the Yahoo! pattern library or in *Designing Social Interfaces*.

4. Make the good stuff findable.

Organize your home page well; put fresh content there regularly, and use sidebars to show most-viewed items, best-of lists, and other views into your library of content items. Show related items to users who click through, and make archived items and conversations available. Put your content where search engines can find it, because in the long run, that's how most people will arrive at it anyway.

- Put a News Box on your home page to showcase your most recent articles, news items, blog posts, videos, and so on. These are usually "social objects," disseminated via social media and commented upon by the public.

- If you collect data on how many times an item is shared, emailed, rated, or commented upon, you can create a Content Leaderboard to showcase the most popular items.

- Consider creating a "best-of" list for your blog, video library, or other large collection of content. This gives newcomers a convenient place to start. Make sure someone curates it competently so that it remains both accurate and fresh.

- When a reader clicks through to the blog post, news item, and so forth, show him a set of links to related content. Presumably the reader is interested in this topic; would he like to read more material on the same topic? Keep him reading and clicking through to pages on your site.

- Check that your material shows up on search engines. Make sure the titles and other metadata identify the content items well. Also check that your site's search box finds content correctly.

- Maintain stable, well-named social media identities. Can a random Facebook user find the right Facebook page via a search for your organization's name? Or does she have to go to your actual website and follow the Social Links to get there? (That should also be possible, of course, but searching within a social media site is less effort for the user.)

5. *Mingle readers' good stuff with your good stuff.*

Publish guest-written articles, blog posts, reviews, and amateur videos. Hold photo contests and show off the winning images—with attribution, of course. Most organizations never quite reach this point, which is fine; it's not appropriate for every company or nonprofit. But when your followers are both enthusiastic and talented, work with them!

6. *Foster community.*

Again, this is not appropriate for every organization, but some have built entire online communities around a well-loved idea or activity—gardening, gaming, music, technology, and so on. There's not much evidence that communities actually help build a brand or increase market share, so don't count on that. What these *can* do is give people an online place to go, where they can ask questions, form friendships, share ideas, help each other out, vent, be silly, and share things that they (not you) judge to be interesting.

The Patterns

Consider using the following patterns for social content production:

1. Editorial Mix

2. Personal Voices

3. Repost and Comment

4. Conversation Starters

5. Inverted Nano-pyramid

When you design the mechanisms for when, where, and how to disseminate content, use these:

6. Timing Strategy

7. Specialized Streams

8. Social Links

9. Sharing Widget

10. News Box

11. Content Leaderboard

12. Recent Chatter

Editorial Mix

Figure 9-1. *Topics covered by Epicurious on Facebook*

What

Publish a regular series of articles or links that include a mix of news, human-interest pieces, photos, videos, public service announcements, and other types of content. Refrain from direct self-promotion most of the time.

Use when

You want to increase name recognition, goodwill toward your organization, connections with customers, and possibly sales. You want readers to follow and enjoy the content you publish, and you have the resources to find or produce that content.

Why

A variety of topics and media types will appeal to a broader group of people than a narrower set of interests. Some of those people may learn about topics they wouldn't otherwise have known about, simply because you put it in their stream.

A more fundamental point is that each piece needs to be interesting by itself. You want followers to read the pieces you write, follow the links you post, view your videos, and look forward to your future posts. Better yet, you want your followers to repost those items to their own followers and close ties—this gets your name out there to more people in a viral fashion. Some of them may then choose to follow you.

How

Choose a set of topics that are both related to your mission and interesting to lots of people. Of the organizations studied for this chapter, those topics have included food, sports, nature, travel, green technologies, politics, parenting, disaster relief, high tech, and science. People get passionate about these subjects. What topics can you cover that evoke passion and high interest?

Develop a mix that's appropriate for your organization. Everyone who uses social media successfully has a unique blend of content types and topics, though variety and "interestingness" are common to all.

Long written content can be posted to your blog. That blog post can then be linked from shorter-form or microblogging sites, such as Twitter. (Most organizations don't propagate all their blog posts to these other channels.) Short, ephemeral items might be posted directly to the microblogs.

Encourage followers to comment on the things you post. This is more likely to happen on social networks such as Facebook, or microblogging sites such as Twitter. Sometimes people leave comments on blog posts, but as of this writing, conversations don't take place on blogs when there are better alternatives.

Don't overload the social media channels with too much content! See the Timing Strategy pattern for more information about quantity and timing.

Avoid overt marketing most of the time. In a larger sense, of course, it's all marketing; but readers know when they're being subjected to a sales pitch, and they don't like it. They probably didn't subscribe to your updates to be deluged by commercials. So post informative or entertaining content most of the time, and limit the advertisements to very specific and useful items—discount codes, new products, or reminders about popular sales events. Ask yourself before posting: if your followers didn't see this, would some of them be sad to have missed it?

Here are some types of content that you may consider:

- News articles
- Interviews with subject experts
- Short, pithy quotes and one-liners
- Product reviews
- Essays or videos about what happens "behind the scenes" at your organization
- Recipes and how-to instructions
- Public service announcements
- Ways that people can help out with charities or other altruistic efforts
- Humor
- Opinion pieces
- Letters from readers
- Short stories, real or fictional
- Musical or artistic performances, usually on video
- Slideshows
- Podcasts
- Questions intended to evoke reader responses; see the Conversation Starters pattern
- Regular commentary from high-profile employees; see the Personal Voices pattern
- Other people's blog posts; see the Repost and Comment pattern

Remember that the material you provide in your social stream will be used by your followers for their own purposes: forming or supporting an online identity ("I'm interested in this topic"), passing information to their close ties, entertaining their larger circle of friends, indirectly stating an opinion, or just connecting. Will your followers be willing to do that with the content you produce? Is it funny, controversial, beautiful, truthful, or authentic?

Starbucks publishes content that its customers would be interested in: subjects include coffee, tea, store specials, music, altruistic efforts, and other topics. Some are text-based articles, some are video clips, and some are reposted from other sources. Figure 9-2 shows Starbucks' Facebook page.

Corporate blogs need to achieve a delicate balance between focus and diversity of topics. As shown in Figure 9-3, Whole Foods' blog deals with many topics related to natural food, whereas the Google blog, reflecting Google's variety of products and services, covers a much broader range of topics.

Figure 9-2. *The Facebook page for Starbucks*

Figure 9-3. *Headlines from the Whole Foods and Google blogs*

Personal Voices

Figure 9-4. *Tony Hsieh's Twitter feed*

Encourage individuals to use their own voices, separate from the social media streams published by the organization itself. Let them publish blogs and write guest blog posts; encourage them to use Twitter and other social channels.

You have social media champions within your organization—people who are willing to put themselves out there, as both individuals and representatives. These may be domain experts, engineers, marketing people, or even CEOs. You don't object to having multiple social media voices, other than the one official voice of the organization.

A personal voice humanizes your brand. Readers often connect better with an individual human being, with a name and a face, than with a brand or organization.

Let your employees write social content as themselves, with their names on their posts. Use personal anecdotes, experiences, memories, reviews of products in actual use, and other topics that humanize the author.

Consider whether to publish guidelines for employees' social media participation, beyond the obvious "don't publish anything that will get us sued." Some companies, such as SAP and Oracle, put their guidelines on the Web to serve as examples.

The CEO of Zappos tweets frequently, and as of this writing has 1.7 million followers (see Figure 9-4 at the top of the pattern). Tony Hsieh's quirky, humorous, very personal tweets draw lots of attention, without ever being overt advertising for the brand. Zappos also encourages its other employees to use Twitter, and the company's website devotes a page to the tweets sent out by its employees (see Figure 9-5).

Figure 9-5. *Zappos employee tweets*

Several of CNN's well-known anchors and reporters use Twitter, including Wolf Blitzer, Anderson Cooper, and Ed Henry (see Figure 9-6). These posts tend to have much more personality and intimacy than the "official" CNN tweets. For a complete list, see the CNN Twitter list called *@CNN/anchors-and-reporters.*

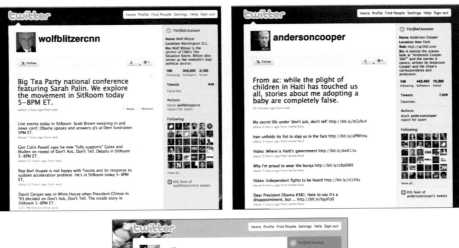

Figure 9-6. *Personal Twitter feeds for CNN's anchors*

Large technology companies Google and IBM encourage their employees to create public blogs, which are then listed prominently in corporate web pages; see Figure 9-7. (In fact, employees are the only social media presence that IBM has.)

Figure 9-7. *Some of IBM's and Google's employee blogs*

Repost and Comment

Figure 9-8. *Mashable repost of a viral YouTube video*

What

Instead of always generating your own content, find works on other sites that you can link to, quote, or repost. Add your own commentary, or invite your readers to comment.

Use when

You see the role of your social media presence to partially be that of an aggregator: you find good stuff out there that you know your audience will enjoy, and you post it for them. You serve as an editor and thought leader whose taste is trusted by your readers.

Not all organizations will find this pattern appropriate. Some may prefer to publish only the content they create themselves.

Why

If your presence is seen as a go-to site for good stuff, you'll acquire more followers. These followers then see your logo or name whenever your reposted content appears in their streams.

You don't have to generate content every time you want to push something out to followers. Writing fresh, original content is hard, and more so when you have to do it weekly or more (as you should, to maintain freshness). In exchange for the time you spend looking for repostable items, you can put together a steady stream of posts that interest your readers.

If the content you produce tends to be of only one type, such as essays or photos, including links to other people's content gets you closer to a desired Editorial Mix.

Reposts and links direct deserved attention toward other sites and people. On the Web, no organization is isolated; there are always other bloggers, reviewers, forums, and organizations that deal with similar topics. By reposting their work and giving credit where it's due, you give them attention, validate them, and help them increase their readership. And social reciprocity may kick in—they might do the same for you!

You become part of a larger conversation around events and topics of interest. By finding an obscure news story or video and showing it to your readers, for instance, you invite your readers to carry on a conversation around it, either in your repost or in the original poster's context. (Your readers, in turn, may repost it themselves to their own followers.)

How

Find content that appeals to your followers. Use your judgment carefully: does it meet the same high standards that you use for your own content? Is it something that your followers will appreciate enough to repost to their own followers? Has it already been widely reposted on the Web so that you would look outdated if you reposted it? (And is it a scam or urban legend? Check first!)

Make sure followers can tell what the reposted article is about. Does its title or summary describe it well enough to attract interested readers? If not, the onus is on you to create a headline or summary for it.

Give your followers a reason why you thought this was worth reposting. If you're working in a blog, you have enough space to both quote portions of the source text and write a commentary. You should give the full URL to the original material, too. (In Twitter, use a URL shortening mechanism instead.)

Facebook has a built-in link posting mechanism that captures the destination's title, summary, and thumbnail picture—all the factual stuff. Use the message to summarize just enough to get the reader's attention, and perhaps to write a commentary only a sentence or two long.

If you use Twitter, you know about retweeting. Before Twitter provided an actual mechanism for it, Twitter users developed their own customs for retweeting and attributions. If tweets were significantly shorter than the maximum length, that would leave room for retweeters to add their own super-short commentary to a retweet ("Inspiring story." "Will this work?" "What do you think?" "Ironic."). But the built-in retweet doesn't permit that, which is unfortunate. That being said, plenty of retweets stand on their own, since they're just informational; someone might propagate a tweet about an upcoming event, for instance, and no commentary is expected.

Finally, offer your followers a chance to comment on the works that you repost. Facebook comments are one obvious place; blog comments are another. When users do comment, engage with them and help carry the conversation forward. There might be a conversation already underway wherever the content was originally posted. However, your followers constitute a unique group of people! Their conversations might have an entirely different quality.

Examples

Many companies use their Facebook pages to repost other people's content so that their followers can see things they wouldn't have found on their own. In the examples in Figure 9-9, REI reposts items that further its mission to promote the outdoors and sell outdoor gear. (Note also the use of questions as Conversation Starters.)

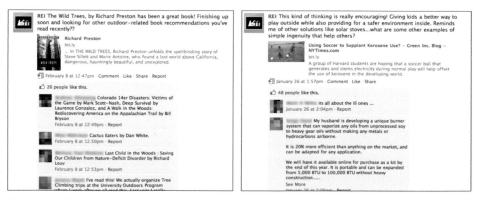

Figure 9-9. *REI's use of Repost and Comment*

Figure 9-10 shows two ways that the American Red Cross's blog reposts and comments upon other sites' content. Politely, the blogger makes a point of thanking the person who called her attention to the earthquake graphic.

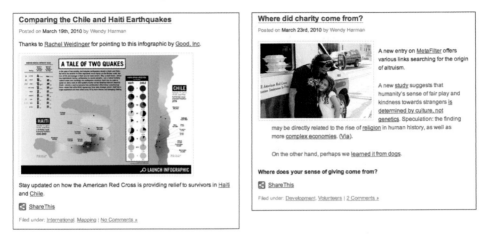

Figure 9-10. *The American Red Cross's use of Repost and Comment*

Retweeting on Twitter can be done either with Twitter's built-in mechanism or "by hand." In Figure 9-11, Tim O'Reilly uses both.

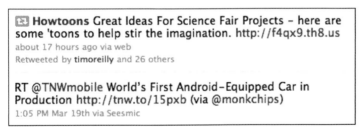

Figure 9-11. *Two ways to retweet*

Conversation Starters

Figure 9-12. *Tim Gunn posing a question to fans*

What

Pose questions, riddles, or topics for discussion. Let your followers post answers and carry on conversations, with you and among themselves.

Use when

You want people to respond to you and other readers so that you can engage them. Your social media audience is capable of carrying on thoughtful discussions within the channel you're using, and you are willing to moderate those conversations if necessary.

Why

If you invite readers to participate, especially on a topic that interests them, they often will!

Once someone posts an answer to your conversation starter, he may come back and see the additional responses (or have the responses emailed to him, in some systems).

You may also get more readers or followers simply because your conversation starters are entertaining. You thus get more exposure for your social media channel.

In the best of cases, the readers' comments become interesting content in their own right. People talk to each other, debate each other, agree with each other, go off on tangents, and thus construct a conversational thread worth reading.

Conceptually, this pattern has some overlap with the idea of "crowdsourcing" problem solutions. For instance, a blogger may ask her readers for answers to a factual question or for stories on how they solved a problem that she is facing.

How

Understand which topics might get your audience fired up. Ask them to share their opinions, guesses, and stories by posing questions. Some questions might have simple answers that are easy for users to type quickly; others might evoke long and thoughtful responses. Choose topics that will get your readers talking to each other—but consider whether a controversial topic might turn into an unwanted flame war, or reflect badly on your site or brand.

As of this writing, Facebook seems to be the place where conversation starters work best. Short questions, sometimes with an accompanying link or photo, evoke answers from followers who read your updates in their news feeds, and Facebook is especially good at encouraging quick answers. (So is Twitter.)

Some blogs seem conducive to long conversations in the comments; others don't, perhaps because their readers haven't established a tradition of extensive commenting. But those blogs that do have an active readership may pose a question to those readers at the end of a post—and readers respond.

Examples

Whole Foods and REI are two brands that use Facebook to initiate conversations with the public. Food and the outdoors are topics that many people find inspirational; the participants in the conversations shown in Figures 9-13 and 9-14 are probably responding to that more than to the brand itself. In the Whole Foods example, people happily share information that other readers find valuable.

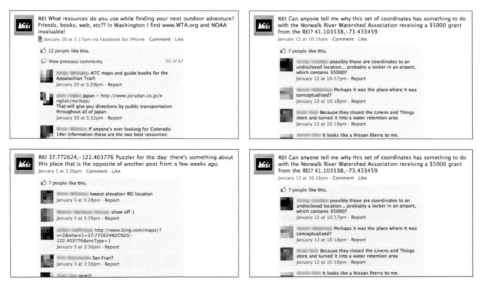

Whole Foods Market Alana Sugar shares her thoughts on how to lighten up with dairy alternatives. There is so much more than soy milk out there nowadays! What are your favorites?

> **blog.wholefoodsmarket.com**
> blog.wholefoodsmarket.com
> Any chance you've noticed the number of non–dairy milk, cheese and ice cream replacements available these days? The choices are soaring – even in conventional grocery stores! Plenty of people ...

January 25 at 10:39am · Comment · Like · Share · Report

👍 91 people like this.

💬 View previous comments   50 of 113

Almond milk! YUMMY and easy to make your own if you want! (almonds and water, thats it)
January 25 at 11:50am · Report

Just tried some coconut milk–based "ice cream" yesterday. Passionate mango. Great creamy texture and amazing taste! I wouldn't worry about fat content too much. Everyone needs saturated fats, and many vegans/vegetarians may not be getting enough as is. I wouldn't recommend eating large quantities of coconut milk every day, but it's a nice little treat every now and then.
January 25 at 11:55am · Report

Hemp milk has been my new try... creamy and good! :)
January 25 at 11:59am · Report

WF carries the Purely Decadent ice cream made with coconut milk – it's awesome!
January 25 at 12:00pm · Report

I love Soy Milk because I'm lactose intolerance. Almond milk is out for me, because I'm allergic to all tree nuts. I would like to taste Hemp milk. I understand

Figure 9-13. *One of Whole Foods' conversation starters*

Figure 9-14. *REI's conversation starters*

Blogs such as Boing Boing have very talkative readers. In Figure 9-15, one of the bloggers poses an open-ended question to the readership.

Figure 9-15. *Boing Boing's conversation starter*

Inverted Nano-pyramid

Figure 9-16. *Short but informative tweet*

What

Write short, dense status updates and headlines. The first few words are most important; they should catch the interest of the right readers, and transmit the most information.

Use when

You post updates to Twitter, Facebook, or other microblogging channels, or you write headlines for blog posts and articles.

Why

People skim updates and headlines quickly, to determine what's worth their attention. Take full advantage of the small amount of space and time you have.

Long tweets, status updates, and so on can't be quoted or retweeted as effectively as short ones. You want followers to repost your updates and get your name out there in front of more people.

How

Traditionally, print journalists have used the "inverted pyramid" for news reporting. The most important information is front-loaded into the first sentence and paragraph of a story. Secondary information comes next, and so on until the least important information ends up at the bottom. Since many readers won't go any farther than the first few sentences, you should give them the essence of the story right at the beginning.

Twitter's ruthlessly low character limit forced us to learn how to write in a very short format. Every word counts; every character counts. So use the pyramid form—the most important points in front—but shrink your messages down to the size of a tweet or status update! Here are some ways to write them well:

- Choose words that accurately represent the topic and scope of what you're talking about. Use words that are specific, not general; make each word carry its weight. To help focus your thinking, consider whether people will understand you if your tweet or headline is taken completely out of context (as though it were a search result, for instance).

- Strip out words that don't carry their weight, especially linking words such as *the* and *have*, but don't be so cryptic that you can't be understood.

- Use abbreviations sparingly; don't sound like a text message written by a 10-year-old.

- Make one single point. If you need to make two points or describe two links, use two tweets or status messages.

- If you use a long word, try to find a shorter substitute. But if the longer word has character and specificity, you might choose to keep it to draw attention.

- For phrasing, consider using one of the eight types of headlines described in Robert Bly's *The Copywriter's Handbook* (Holt Paperbacks). These are: direct, indirect, news, how-to, question, command, reason why, and testimonial. For a good online summary of these types, with examples, see Copyblogger's summary at *http://www.copyblogger.com/how-to-write-headlines-that-work/*.

- Be patient as you write. Short content requires more thought and iteration than you might expect.

Examples

The tweets shown in Figure 9-17 tell ultra-short stories. You can't help but read them.

Figure 9-17. *Ultra-short stories*

The news headlines shown in Figure 9-18 were designed to tempt readers to click through the link.

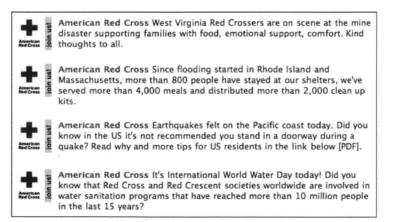

Figure 9-18. *News headlines designed to tempt readers to click through the link*

As shown in Figure 9-19, the American Red Cross uses Facebook status messages and links to both convey information and persuade the reader to learn more (links not shown).

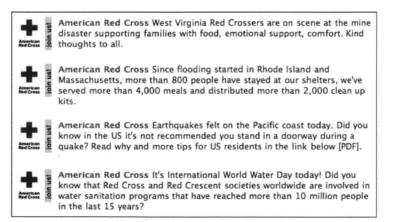

Figure 9-19. *The American Red Cross's Facebook status messages and links*

Timing Strategy

Figure 9-20. *Possible social media timing for an organization*

What

Pace your social media posts according to the expectations of the channels you use; some channels require more frequent posts, some less. Cross-post the best pieces, and consider when in the day or week you make your posts.

Use when

Anyone who uses social media should develop and follow a Timing Strategy.

Why

Overusing a social media channel can overwhelm your followers with too much chatter. Followers may drop you, or form a negative impression of your organization. Don't irritate people.

On the other hand, underusing a channel is an opportunity cost: you won't have your name in front of followers as often as you could.

Users of Twitter and Facebook in particular have expectations about how often they hear from nonfriend entities (such as company pages) in their personal news stream. The mechanisms of the channels themselves dictate some of this; tweets are shorter and more rapidly consumed than Facebook updates, for instance. These expectations may change as the technologies mature and shift.

The most important thing is to understand users' expectations about these channels. If you post too frequently, your updates clutter followers' personal news streams to the point of being annoying, and they may unsubscribe from you.

However, the advice here is only a starting point. You should watch the numbers of followers change as you use social media, listen to followers' feedback, and be willing to adjust your timing strategy on the fly if followers leave.

As of this writing, here are some of the posting frequencies that I have observed.

Facebook pages tend to be updated only once per day, or less. Most of the successful and active pages I studied had a post rate of roughly once every two days, though some had two per day (such as Wired) and others had much fewer. Exceptions are sometimes made for time-sensitive events, concentrated outreach efforts, and crises such as major earthquakes—followers will tolerate short bursts of frequent posting if the cause is worthy. Your mileage may vary.

Twitter posts can be much more frequent than Facebook updates. The organizations I studied posted between three and 15 tweets per day, on average. Also, these posts were usually made between noon and 8:00 p.m. Eastern Standard Time, with a lower rate on weekends. This is important because tweets should go out when the most people are online and listening—Twitter users (unlike Facebook users) tend not to scroll back through time to find interesting material. Note that many tweets from some organizations are direct replies to individuals; those can run up the count quickly.

For organizations that use multiple social media channels, *blog posts* range between 0.5 and 2.5 posts per day. This is where long-form writing takes place: essays, stories, interviews, and other content longer than one or two sentences. Sometimes these blogs "feed" the Facebook and Twitter efforts—selected blog entries (usually not all of them) are reposted as links in these other media, along with a one-sentence description. Lively conversations about the blog posts are more likely to take place on Facebook or Twitter than on the blog itself.

Email should be infrequent. If you send email more than once every few days, you may get labeled as spam by some of your followers.

I found no evidence of timing strategies for media repositories such as Flickr and YouTube. This is probably because they don't normally "push" content out into followers' personal news streams, as others do.

The chart in Figure 9-21 shows the timing strategies for several companies and organizations that have strong social media presences. The data was collected over two months at the very beginning of 2010, in January and February. The numbers represent the average number of posts per day on each of three social media channels: Twitter, Facebook, and the organization's main blog. (Not all of these sites had a main blog.) Clearly, the Twitter numbers are higher than the others, reflecting its more ephemeral nature.

The last two companies, the American Red Cross and Partners in Health, are charities. Over the time period that I collected data, these two organizations were conducting intensive news and fundraising efforts related to the Haiti earthquake. Their usage of Facebook skyrocketed in January, and then faded back to something more normal in February; this shows up in the averages as slightly elevated Facebook numbers.

	Twitter	Facebook	Blog
Dell	3	0.3	0.6
Whole Foods	14	1	1.4
Coca-Cola	10.5	0.5	0.6
Red Bull	5.3	0.5	
Starbucks	10	0.2	0.6
REI	3	1	
Volkswagen	2	0.5	
American Red Cross	3	1.3	1
Partners in Health	2.7	2.5	2.4

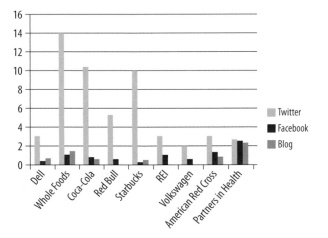

Figure 9-21. *Actual post rates for nine sites*

Specialized Streams

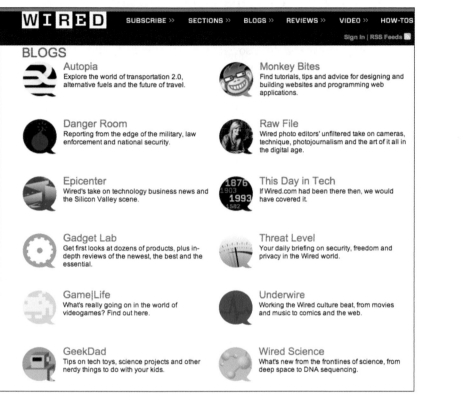

Figure 9-22. *Wired blogs, specialized by topic*

What

Divide your content stream into many different channels, each with a different readership and different "feel." Use multiple Twitter identities, Facebook pages, blogs, and so on to steer these items to the right audiences.

Use when

Your organization generates a large number of status updates, news articles, blog posts, or other items that are socially distributed. You can categorize them easily by subject or some other factor (such as frequency or author). You have a large readership, but many readers are only interested in one or two of these categories, not all of them.

Why

If you dump all of your organization's updates into one huge stream, that stream might overwhelm its followers. For instance, a Facebook page shouldn't be updated many times per day, lest its readers unsubscribe because of too many updates.

With several discrete streams or pages to follow, people can easily pick and choose among the topics you offer, thus tailoring their own experience.

How

Categorize your updates according to your followers' needs. Consider the following ways to segment a readership, and see if any of them can work for you. (Not all will be suitable for your organization, of course.)

By product
> Do you sell different products to different types of customers, for instance? What are the common needs and perspectives of a product's users? For example, users of smartphones will have one set of needs; users of desktop systems, quite another.

By topic
> If you publish a lot of news articles or opinion pieces, how do you segment your market according to subject?

By professional role
> See the Google example in Figure 9-25; some of its blogs are aimed at a general audience, some at managers, and some at developers.

By social media usage style
> How often do your followers read their news stream? Some people practically live on Twitter; they may have a high tolerance for chatter. Other people will only want occasional updates, and those updates had better be worth reading. CNN has several news feeds that operate with different Timing Strategies to serve these different markets; see the example in Figure 9-23.

Within the social media services that you've chosen to use, create different channels or streams. Each should be labeled clearly with your organization's name and logo, and visually branded appropriately—there should be no question that this stream is an official part of the organization's social media strategy.

Direct people to those streams at the right points. Put links to them on your front page, or from your main presence on the social media services. For instance, if your organization has a main Facebook page, link to the Specialized Streams from that page. If you spend effort to build them, you might as well tell people about them.

Consider using selected content from the Specialized Streams—not all of it, of course—in your main blog, Facebook page, or Twitter feed. Reference the Specialized Stream from that content so that interested readers can find it and subscribe.

Updates are CNN's business, and it generates a lot of them. CNN has a main Twitter feed that it updates every few hours with general-interest news stories, but as of this writing, "cnnbrk" (for breaking news) has almost three times as many followers. "cnnireport" is CNN's third main Twitter stream, and the CNN site directs readers toward all three. However, for the skilled and motivated Twitter user, there are even more streams to be found! Entertainment, weather, technology, money, international news, and other topics all have their own specialized CNN Twitter feeds, though they're not easy to find. Figure 9-23 shows some of CNN's Twitter feeds.

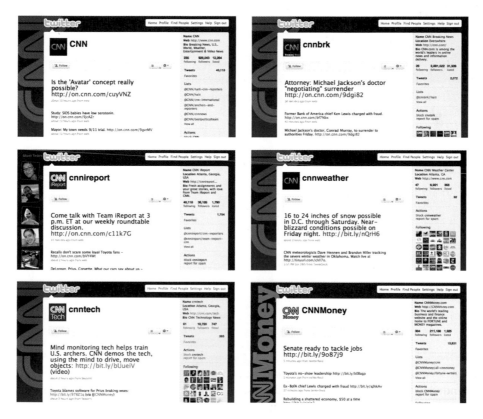

Figure 9-23. *Some of CNN's Twitter feeds*

Likewise, Wired divides its numerous updates into Twitter feeds that are specialized by topic. Many of these primarily tweet links to posts in Wired's corresponding blogs—see Figure 9-22, which shows some of those blogs. One nice thing Wired does is post a long list of specialized Twitter feeds in its background image, as shown in Figure 9-24. (Even though they're not clickable links, they still convey information.)

Figure 9-24. *Wired's main Twitter feed, with Specialized Streams listed in the lefthand margin*

Google has built many products, each of which has its own constituency (casual readers, developers, domain experts, etc.). It also serves many regions of the world, and evokes interest worldwide in many aspects of its operation. Google therefore sends out its updates via a diverse set of corporate blogs (see Figure 9-25). Its main blog publishes general-interest stories, but it sometimes runs entries that are cross-posted from a more specific blog.

Figure 9-25. *Some of Google's blogs*

Microsoft has a vast number of social content streams on Facebook, Twitter, YouTube, Flickr, MySpace, Delicious, forums, and blogs. Some are listed in Figure 9-26. They are aimed at customers for particular products, in particular roles; some are very specialized, and some are general with very large audiences. (Credit for this table goes to EngagementDB, at *http://www.engagementdb.com/Company/77*.)

Social Networking		Image/Video/Audio Sharing	
MySpace	Microsoft Windows on MySpace	**YouTube**	Windows YouTube
MySpace	Windows on MySpace	**YouTube**	Office Live YouTube
Facebook	Microsoft Research	**YouTube**	Bing YouTube
Facebook	Office Live on Facebook	**YouTube**	Internet Explorer YouTube
Facebook	Microsoft MVP Award Program	**YouTube**	Microsoft Surface on YouTube
Facebook	Internet Explorer on Facebook	**YouTube**	The Office Channel at YouTube
Facebook Microsoft Windows on Facebook		**YouTube**	Windows Mobile
Facebook	Microsoft Surface on Facebook	**YouTube** UK Developer and Platform Evangelism Group	
Facebook	Microsoft PDC		
Facebook	Bing	**YouTube**	Bright Side of Government
Facebook Microsoft Certified Partners with a Learning Solutions competency		**YouTube** Internet Explorer Videos on YouTube	
		YouTube	Microsoft Windows on YouTube
Facebook Microsoft Federal Partner Group		**YouTube**	Microsoft Bing on YouTube
Facebook	Windows Mobile	**YouTube**	Microsoft Office on YouTube
Facebook	BizSpark	**YouTube**	Internet Explorer on YouTube
Facebook	Internet Explorer	**YouTube** Microsoft Dynamics Partner Community	
Facebook	Windows on Facebook		
Facebook Microsoft Windows on Facebook		**YouTube** The 60 Second Business Insider	
Facebook	Windows on Facebook	**Flickr**	Microsoft Surface on Flickr
Facebook	Windows Home Server	**Flickr**	Microsoft Research
Facebook	Windows Home Server		Edit »
Facebook Windows Essential Business Server			
Facebook Windows Small Business Server			
Facebook	Windows Home Server		
Facebook Windows Essential Business Server			
Facebook Windows Small Business Server			

Figure 9-26. *A partial profile of Microsoft's social presence*

Social Links

Figure 9-27. *Ten ways to follow Huffington Post*

What

On your site's home page, put a group of links to your social media presences.

Use when

You are putting effort into supporting one or more social media channels—blogs, Facebook, Twitter, Delicious, and so on—and you want to drive people toward those channels. If they're self-contained services, like Facebook, you don't mind visitors going to those sites instead of remaining on your own site.

Why

If you're already investing in various social media channels, you might as well tell people about them. Visitors to your home page may find those links quite useful, especially if they're specifically looking for your social media presence.

Widgets that let visitors follow you give them a convenient way to put your updates into their personal news stream. That's valuable to you and to them, and it shows visitors that you are wise to the latest social technologies.

How

Create a small area containing well-labeled links to social media sites and public repositories: Facebook, Twitter, YouTube, Flickr, Delicious, your blog, and so on. RSS feeds often are found here, too. Some sites put their email sign-ups into this section.

Brand icons will stand out more than ordinary links—you may want this for ease of findability. They are out of place in some designs, however, and simple text links in a "written invitation" may be refreshing. See the upcoming Slate, Whole Foods, and Copyblogger examples.

A disadvantage of a Social Links section is that it may send your visitors to a different site, and they might stay there instead of continuing to peruse your own site. Social network sites, especially, have a long "dwell time"—once someone goes there, she tends to stay for a while and not come back. (Many news-based sites with strong social presences, such as CNN and Wired, do not have Social Links on their home page.) One way to avoid this problem is to change the links in the Social Links section into buttons. A Facebook button may bring up a widget to make the user a fan, for instance, rather than taking him to Facebook itself.

Some sites have more than one Twitter stream or Facebook page to reflect different aspects of their organization; see the Specialized Streams pattern for more discussion. Those streams may show up here. The Vancouver Olympics example in Figure 9-28 shows one way to handle this.

Consider adding "hooks" to pique the viewer's interest. For instance, Copyblogger uses its Social Link widget to tell the viewer that 48,206 people follow them on Twitter. That's brilliant—it's appealingly specific, it uses gentle peer pressure to convince you to follow them, and it puts a smile on your face. Similarly, Mashable shows how many people all together are following them, aggregated over several services (Twitter, Facebook, RSS, etc.).

Examples

Figure 9-28 shows the Social Links widgets on various home pages.

Figure 9-28. *The Social Links widgets on the home pages of (counterclockwise from upper left) Mashable, the American Red Cross, the Vancouver Olympics, Levi's, Whole Foods, Copyblogger, and Slate*

In the examples shown in Figure 9-29, Microsoft and Ford use the greater space available on their sites' inner pages. They show clickable samples of the latest social activity at each service they list. These live examples may make the social presences more alluring for people who are interested in the topic. (The disadvantage of such a treatment, of course, is the amount of space it consumes.)

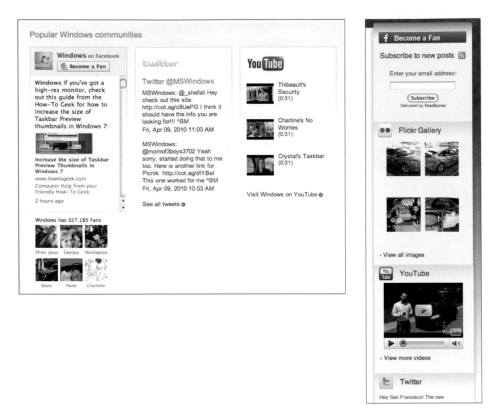

Figure 9-29. *A Microsoft Windows–related product page and one of Ford's press release pages*

Sharing Widget

Figure 9-30. *Slate's end-of-article sharing widget*

What

Beside your articles, videos, and other pieces of content, place a set of controls that let viewers easily share that content with their own close ties and social followers. These often link to social media sites such as Facebook and Twitter.

Sharing Widgets are used almost everywhere now. If you post original content of any kind, you would do well to have one of these, even if it's rudimentary.

It's convenient for viewers who may really want to share this cool piece you wrote. It helps them do Repost and Comment, which supports their own social reputation.

Your viewers will then disseminate your content for you through their own social contacts. An article recommended by a personal contact—especially a close tie, such as a family member or close friend—is more likely to be read than an article found randomly on the Web. See the Personal Recommendations pattern in Chapter 1.

Some sharing tools let you track what gets shared, thus giving you data about which of your posts get disseminated broadly. You can then use that data for your own analysis and to display Content Leaderboards for the most-shared items.

You can build your own Sharing Widget, or you can use a third-party site such as ShareThis to construct one. Populate it with the sharing channels that you think will be most used by your followers, but don't clutter it up with too many items. (At least find numbers on the relative popularity of social networking sites and bookmarking sites; you should always include the biggest ones. Facebook and email had the highest usage as of this writing, while Twitter was lower but rising rapidly.)

You might consider putting the following services on your Sharing Widget:

- Social networking sites such as Facebook and MySpace
- Microblogging mechanisms such as Twitter
- Public bookmarking sites such as Digg or Delicious
- Email, which is still preferred by many Internet users
- Sharing via an SMS message
- Other, nonsharing tools, such as printing, commenting, or thumbs-up/down

If you have space, you may also show counters for each sharing service: how many people have shared a particular piece of content via this channel? This gives readers an immediate sense of how "hot" this content is. (If the numbers are consistently low, you may not want to show them.)

Place the Sharing Widget very close to the content to be shared. The top and bottom of an article are traditional places to put this, and some articles place it as an inset within the article (with the text flowing around it). You're trying to keep the widget within the gaze of someone reading the content. Also, before you put the Sharing Widget into a drop-down or anchored toolbar, think about accessibility—how will someone using a screen reader use this? And what about people who don't have good mouse control? They may have an easier time with an area directly on the page.

If you offer a Facebook sharing control, make sure your HTML page is structured correctly for Facebook's linking tools to present it well. Verify that Facebook picks up the title, summary, and thumbnail correctly. (Check other social sharing mechanisms as well.)

Examples

Many sites create multiple Sharing Widgets for different contexts, as shown in Figure 9-31. A widget containing the top three services might appear near the top of the content, for instance, while a more complete widget might appear at the end. This complicates the design, but it might work well if you have a lot of services to show and not much space at the top.

Figure 9-31. *Sharing widgets from Wired, Boing Boing, Technorati, and Pandora*

Pop ups and drop downs to show the "long tail" of social services are a common way to implement progressive disclosure—the user doesn't see the numerous other sharing services until she clicks on a button—but again, these hide functionality and are not as accessible as items shown directly on the page.

Mashable, shown in Figure 9-32, uses three different strategies: a small Sharing Widget beside a news snippet on the front page, a slightly expanded widget on the page containing the article (it now has an Email feature and a Share button), and a pop up shown when the reader clicks the Share button.

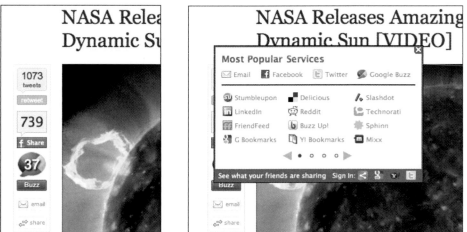

Figure 9-32. *Mashable's Sharing Widgets*

In other libraries

http://www.designingsocialinterfaces.com/patterns/Share_This

News Box

Red Cross News

Posted in _News_, 02/24/10

Children Pitch In to Support Red Cross Relief Efforts in Haiti

Elementary, middle school students raise funds to help people of Haiti. » _More_

Posted in _News_, 02/24/10

Red Cross Volunteer Brings Medical Aid to Haitian Boy

Abrupt change in plans as volunteer recognizes medical emergency. » _More_

Posted in _The Blog_, 2/25/10

Weekly Worldwide Wrap-Up

Welcome to the Weekly Worldwide Wrap-Up, in which we consolidate the international Red Cross and Red Crescent news into one list of bite-sized links for you. It's a non-comprehensive sampling of the larger and/or more intriguing aspects of our global work… [The place names link to maps so that you can get a quick idea of [...] » More

» _More Red Cross News_

Figure 9-33. _American Red Cross News Box_

What

On your site's front page, show your latest news items, blog posts, videos, and other time-sensitive content. Each item should attract the viewer with readable headlines, summaries, links to read more, and possibly thumbnail images.

Use when

Your organization regularly produces news items, original content about topics that are interesting to your site's visitors, or "social objects" that gather comments and discussions. You want to encourage visitors to read those items.

Why

A News Box gives your visitors content that can hold their attention. Without it, a visitor may come to your site, glance briefly at it, see nothing interesting, and leave without lingering. With it, they may stay for a while and learn about your organization.

It's also informative. Visitors to your site may come with the intent of finding out about recent news or events, so give it to them.

Your website will get updated with new content on a regular basis. It's considered a best practice to regularly refresh the content on a front page. Visitors can see that things are happening here—your site is not a ghost town, and they may even want to come back later to see what else happens.

Once a visitor clicks on a news link, the "jump page" can have all kinds of other features: links to related stories, other blog posts, a Sharing Widget, reader comments, and other things you don't have room for on the front page. All of these draw visitors in and keep them on your site, learning more and engaging more.

The topics, words, and images you choose to display in a News Box all contribute to a first impression of your organization. A visitor will indirectly learn about your organization from the scope of the topics covered, the tone of voice used in the text, and other signals.

How

Place the News Box on your home page; it doesn't have to be above the fold (though many sites put it there when they don't need the whole home page to explain the site's value proposition). Make the News Box large enough to contain a handful of news items, each of which has a generous amount of space—at least several lines of text. You may wish to divide the News Box into subsections for different sources or media types (such as photos or videos). Some sites create a subsection to show additional, smaller items—usually just linked headlines—in addition to the larger links to featured articles.

Each item should have:

- A headline, which is also a link to the main article.

- A short description that "sells" the article to the reader.

- A "more" link to the main article. This should look like a link, with underlining, chevrons, color, or other obvious visual cues.

They may optionally have:

- A thumbnail image. The most attractive News Boxes generally have these.

- The date on which the content was released.

- The source of the item—blog, news page, press release, YouTube, and so on. If your link sends viewers to a different site, it's polite to tell them so.

- A Sharing Widget and a link to reader comments. These are more commonly found on the destination page, where the whole article can be read.

Every word counts in these headlines and summaries. Use the Inverted Nano-pyramid pattern to write the headlines, and eliminate all extraneous information (such as bylines or locations) in the summaries. If you can, have someone custom-write the summaries; don't use the first line of the article. The tone and voice you use in these pieces of text help define your organization, so make sure they reflect its values accurately: informal, authoritative, humorous, youthful, silly, ironic, and so on.

If you're pulling content from media repositories such as Flickr, they might have widgets you can install directly on your page. Make sure they don't cause your home page to slow down or break.

Examples

Red Bull sponsors athletes in many different sports. Though its product is a drink, its News Box is full of news items about the athletes and events, as shown in Figure 9-34. The overall impression of the pictures and words is one of action and speed. Notice the rhythm of the layout, the brief but effective writing, and the clarity of links to articles and videos.

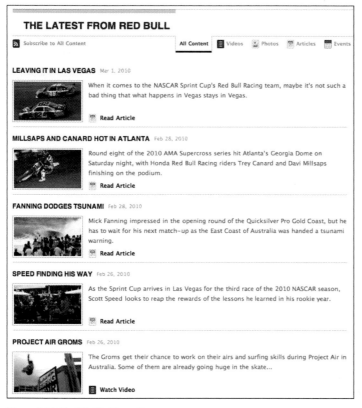

Figure 9-34. *Red Bull's News Box*

Whole Foods seeks a very different audience and emotional "feel," but its News Box is similar to Red Bull's in its clarity and rhythm (see Figure 9-35).

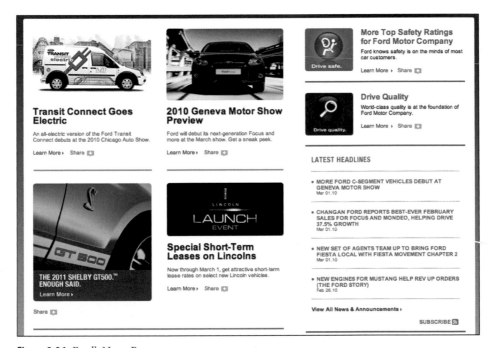

Figure 9-35. *Whole Foods' News Box*

Ford's News Box contains items of varied size and emphasis (see Figure 9-36). The visual hierarchy clearly shows which articles Ford wants you to see first; the large images and text attract your eyes upward and left first, but the smaller size of the "Latest Headlines" heading allows more of them to be packed into the available space.

Figure 9-36. *Ford's News Box*

But make sure you don't make your headlines and summaries too short or cryptic. The news items in the Sierra Club's News Box don't explain themselves well enough to entice someone to click through (see Figure 9-37).

Our Latest Blogs [See More]

Climate Crossroads
Sierra Club India Environment Post:
India, Ramesh Push Climate of
Opportunity
[comment here]

On Track
Astronomy: In Like a Lion
[comment here]

The Green Life
Daily Roundup: February 26, 2010
[2 comments]

Figure 9-37. *The Sierra Club's News Box*

Content Leaderboard

Most Popular ›

Read	Emailed	Video	Commented

1. iPhone U.S. Monopoly May End

2. Obama Gets Aggressive

3. Opinion: Rude for Reid

4. Manure Raises a New Stink

5. Opinion: Norman Podhoretz: In Defense of Sarah Palin

Most Read Articles Feed

Figure 9-38. *From the Wall Street Journal*

What

Show a list of the most popular articles, blog posts, videos, or other content pieces. Use social media-based metrics such as most shared, most emailed, and most blogged.

Your site generates a large amount of content, authored either by your organization or by other participants. You may already have an organizing principle for all that content (e.g., News Stream; see Chapter 2), but you also want readers to see what other readers found interesting. You have enough readers and sharers so that clear leaders can emerge among the content you publish.

Why

This is a way of crowdsourcing a "top 10 list" for your site. Metrics for sharing and emailing show what a readership likes—or at least what those readers think their own followers will like. If the readers have excellent taste, they'll pull the best-quality pieces from your content; if not, they'll at least find the wackiest or most dramatic ones. (You may not agree with their taste!) Either way, your other readers are likely to be interested in the same kinds of things.

How

Gather data about which items have been shared, emailed, and so forth. If you haven't already, make sure a Sharing Widget of some kind is shown beside each piece of content so that readers can easily share things in the first place.

Show a list of the most popular items for that day (or week, if the pace of your site is slower). The items in the list should be links to the original posts. Sites that track multiple such lists—emailed, blogged, and so on—often put them together into Module Tabs (see Chapter 4).

Content Leaderboards are usually displayed as small sidebars on the home page and internal pages. Most sites primarily present content according to some other priority, such as freshness or editorial choice; leaderboards don't usually belong in Center Stage (see Chapter 4).

Examples

The *New York Times* has an archetypical Content Leaderboard that you've probably seen (see Figure 9-39). It contains four leaderboards tabbed together, one of which shows search terms and not articles. When you read an article in a particular section such as Business the leaderboard changes to show the most popular articles in that section.

Engadget uses an eye-catching leaderboard, shown in Figure 9-40, to display the most heavily commented posts. Compare this very bright display to the more neutral content leaderboards in Figure 9-41. Note also the different tab names, which reflect the different criteria these sites use to determine the "hottest" articles—though we can't tell what criterion Mashable (at the top right) uses.

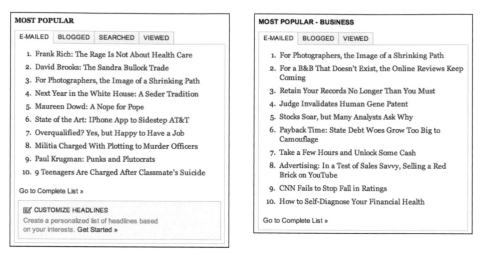

Figure 9-39. *Content leaderboards on the New York Times' website*

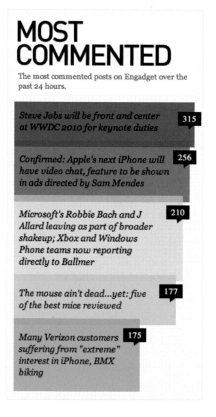

Figure 9-40. *Engadget*

Most Commented / Shared

1. Gravity Emerges from Quantum Information, Say Physicists
2. Ultra-Efficient Gas Engine Passes Test
3. Revealing the Source of Ritalin's Brain Boosting Benefits
4. HTML 5 Could Challenge Flash
5. Toyota Applies the Brakes
6. New Charging Method Could Slash Battery Recharge Times
7. Loan to Kick-start U.S. Solar Thermal Industry
8. Smarter Chargers for Electric Vehicles
9. China Spends More on Clean Energy than the U.S.
10. Using Peer Pressure to Cut Energy Use

TOP 6 TODAY

1. Apple to Launch Two New iPhones, One for Verizo...
2. 5 Essential Apps for Your Business's Facebook F...
3. 10 Must-See Google Street View Sightings
4. Lady Gaga + Sesame Street = Out of this World M...
5. Top 10 Funny Videos on YouTube
6. Top 10 Funny Dog Videos on YouTube

LATEST BLOG POSTS   MOST POPULAR ARTICLES   HOTTEST WEB LINKS

1. **Reader Photo Gallery: Your Desk Celebrates Hubble's 20th Anniversary**
   04.23.10

2. **High-Tech Underwear for Adventurous Geeks**
   04.21.10

3. **Air Force Launches Secretive Space Plane; 'We Don't Know When It's Coming Back'**
   04.23.10

4. **Wow! Celebrate Hubble's 20th With Best Space Image Ever**
   04.23.10

5. **Hands-On: Left 4 Dead 2 Mutates With The Passing**
   04.23.10

6. **Video: Ride Along With Ferrari's New King of the 'Ring**
   04.23.10

7. **Chevrolet Volt Gets a Bigger Brother**
   04.23.10

Figure 9-41. *Content leaderboards from Technology Review, Mashable (top right), and Wired (bottom)*

Recent Chatter

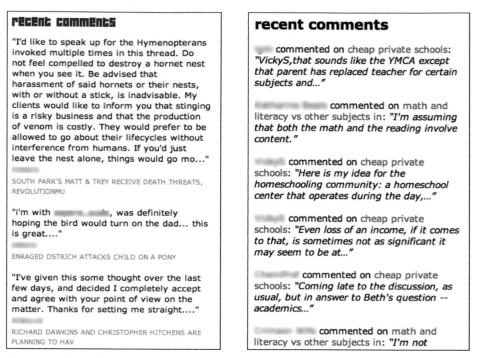

Figure 9-42. *Recent Chatter on two blogs: Boing Boing and Kitchen Table Math*

What

Show the latest reader comments, tweets, contributions, or other community activity in a sidebar.

Use when

You want to explicitly encourage participation—it's fine if people read your pieces or follow you, but you want them to actually take that next step and contribute.

You have a lot of social activity going on around the content you publish, and the comments are of a high enough quality that you're comfortable showing snippets of them on your home page.

Why

Readers know that your site is not a "ghost town." They can see that there are other people here, actively taking part in conversations. This appeals to people, and may encourage them to contribute their own thoughts.

Readers can be drawn into conversations if they're shown snippets of dialog—they may want to respond to a particular comment, for instance.

How

Create a widget that shows a list of the latest activities in reverse chronological order. It doesn't need to be placed above the fold; often these are in an inconspicuous place on the home page (or internal page).

Decide which social activities you want to show. Comments are probably the most common thing to show, and they're interesting to other readers; so are tweets on a certain topic. You could also display favoriting or voting activities (such as Vote to Promote in the Yahoo! pattern library), or sharing, but make sure these don't swamp the comments, which are more appealing.

In the list of recent chatter, show these pieces of information:

- What the activity was, and a snippet of it if appropriate
- The name of the reader who initiated this activity
- The title of the affected content, and a link to it
- Possibly a timestamp or relative time (e.g., "10 minutes ago")

Some blog software, including Blogger and WordPress, makes this very easy to do. There's almost no cost to it, other than the screen space that a Recent Chatter area takes up.

Examples

As you can see in Figure 9-43, some sites feature different types of public contributions. Yelp shows reviews ("Fresh Lists") and over-the-fence chatter in two different sections. MyStarbucksIdea shows the latest ideas posted by readers, but with titles only. Technology Review is a more traditional news site, and its Recent Chatter section is more understated than the blogs shown in Figure 9-42. Note that without direct quotes, MyStarbucksIdea and Technology Review have a less personal, more formal feel than Yelp or the blog examples shown in Figure 9-42. (This may be exactly what you want, of course.)

Yahoo! News, shown in Figure 9-44, updates its Recent Chatter widget whenever someone "buzzes up" an article, which happens very, very frequently. It certainly shows activity, but because you don't see people's actual words, it isn't nearly as engaging.

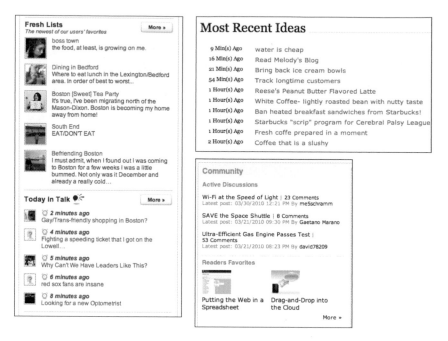

Figure 9-43. *Recent Chatter at Yelp, MyStarbucksIdea, and Technology Review*

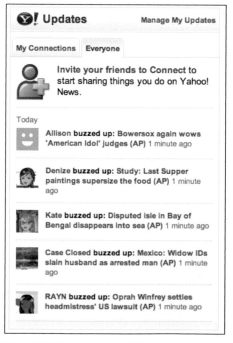

Figure 9-44. *Buzzing up at Yahoo! News*

Chapter 10
Going Mobile

If you have ever designed anything for the Web, you are already a mobile designer. Congratulations!

That's the reality of a world full of iPhones, other kinds of smartphones, ebook readers, tablet computers, and entire countries where people reach the Internet primarily through their phones. All these users will see your sites through browsers that are small, slow, quirky, and hard to interact with. They will use your sites in environmental conditions—and mindsets—that are entirely different from what they would experience if they were sitting quietly at a comfortable desk, in front of a large screen.

Even if you don't choose to become an expert at mobile design, you can still treat mobile design consciously and thoughtfully. A relatively small investment of knowledge, design work, and time can go a long way toward improving the mobile experience of the sites you design.

For many sites, it will make sense for you to create a separate version of the site aimed at mobile users (or, at least, users of small screens). You would present a scaled-down, focused version of your site that answers the needs of users who are out moving around. In this chapter, we won't go into the technical details of platform detection and how to present the correct design for the user's situation (e.g., different CSS stylesheets)—but the knowledge is out there and fairly easy to find.

Other sites will want to supply all of their functionality via the mobile site, but all of it would be tailored to the small screen and other mobile constraints. Again, many people view the Internet exclusively through their mobile device, and they'll want all your site's features. You may choose to do two separate and parallel designs, one for mobile and one for the desktop.

If you create tools and applications for large screens, instead of websites, this chapter may not apply to you at all. You and your organization may wish to evaluate whether your tools (or some subset thereof) could be re-created as apps on mobile devices and still be useful. Know your users—understand their needs, tasks, and contexts of use. Creating mobile apps is a nontrivial investment, but it may be worth it for you.

The Challenges of Mobile Design

When you design for a mobile platform, you face challenges that you don't encounter when your user can be presumed to be sitting quietly in front of a large screen and keyboard.

Tiny screen sizes

Mobile devices just don't offer much space to present information or choices. Sadly, you don't have the luxury of sidebars, long header menus, big images that don't do anything, or long lists of links. You need to strip your design down to its essence—take away all the extra stuff you can. Leave the most important functions on the front page and either discard the rest or bury them deeper in the site.

Variable screen widths

It's hard to make a design that works well on three different screens that are 128 pixels wide, 320 pixels wide, and 600+ pixels wide—and there might be some in between, too. Scrolling down a mobile page isn't terribly onerous (which is why width gets special mention, not height), but a design needs to use the available screen width intelligently. Some sites end up creating different versions—with different logo graphics, different navigation options, and so on—for the smallest keypad devices, and another for the iPhone-size class of touch devices (around 320 pixels wide).

For an excellent discussion of design and technical issues related to screen width, see the following mobiForge article. A search for more recent articles may help you as well.

http://mobiforge.com/designing/story/effective-design-multiple-screen-sizes

Touch screens

As of this writing, most mobile web access comes from devices with touch screens. Keypad devices obviously should be served too, since they constitute the majority of existing mobile devices, but you may want to bias the design toward the touch screen experience. Links on keypad devices can be navigated with keys fairly easily, as long as you follow good overall design principles (restricted content, linearized layout, etc.).

It's hard to touch small targets accurately with fingers. Make your links and buttons large enough to hit easily; at a minimum, make important hit targets at least 1 cm on each side, and put some space between them. This reduces the available space for other content, of course.

Difficulty of typing text

No one likes typing text on a touch screen or keypad. You should design interaction paths through your site or tool in such a way that typing is unnecessary or very limited. Use Autocompletion (Chapter 8) in text fields whenever possible, for instance, and prefill form fields whenever you can do so reliably. Remember that numbers are much easier than text in some contexts, however.

Challenging physical environments

People use their phones and other devices in all kinds of places: outside in the bright sun, in dark theaters, in conference rooms, cars, buses, trains, planes, stores, bathrooms, and in bed. Think about the ambient light differences, to begin with—tasteful gray text on a gray background may not work so well in direct sun. Think also about ambient noise differences: assume that some users won't hear the device at all, and that others might find sudden noises jarring and inappropriate.

Finally, think about motion. Tiny text is hard to read when the device (or the user) is moving around. And a tiny hit target on a touch screen device will be hard to use under the best of circumstances, but it can be nearly impossible on a rocking and jolting bus! Again, design for "fat fingers," and design so that mistakes are easily corrected.

Social influences and limited attention

Most of the time, mobile users won't spend lots of time and attention on your site or app. They'll be looking at your design while doing other things—walking, riding in a vehicle, talking with other people, sitting in a meeting, or (God forbid) driving. Occasionally a mobile user will focus his full attention on the device, such as when playing a game, but he won't do it as often as someone sitting at a keyboard will. Therefore, design for distracted users: make the task sequences easy, quick, and reentrant. And make everything self-explanatory.

Another assumption you can make is that lots of mobile users will be engaging in conversations or other social situations. They may pass around the device to show people something on-screen. They may have people looking over their shoulder. They may need to suddenly turn off the sound if it's not socially acceptable to have a noisy device—or they may turn it up to let others hear something. Does your design behave well in these situations? Can it support graceful social interaction?

How to Approach a Mobile Design

In his book *Mobile Design and Development* (O'Reilly, *http://oreilly.com/catalog/9780596155452/*), Brian Fling tells a difficult truth: "Great mobile products are created, never ported. Start by understanding your users and the benefits the medium has to offer."

If you're simply trying to take a site's usual content and cram it into a 320 × 480 window, stop. Take a big step back and look at the whole picture.

1. What do users in a mobile context actually need?

A person who is out and about with a mobile device may only want to use your site (or app) in particular ways; she won't have the same range of needs that a user of the full site will have. Design for use contexts such as these:

- "I need to know this fact right now, quickly."
- "I have a few minutes to spare, so entertain me." (See the Microbreaks pattern in Chapter 1.)
- "Connect me socially."
- "If there's something I need to know right now, tell me."
- "What's relevant to the place I'm in right now?"

2. Strip the site or app down to its essence

Don't be afraid to take away all that other stuff—the extra content, eye-catching features, sidebars, pull quotes, ads, images, site maps, social links, and so on. Focus tightly on the few tasks that mobile users will need from your site, use minimal branding, and chuck the rest.

In fact, make sure that even on the home page (for a website) or the first working page of an app, relevant content appears high on the screen. That means getting rid of the "layer cake effect" of logos, ads, tabs, and headers that stack up on the screen. See Figure 10-1 for a poor example; the only piece of content that a user really cares about is the score at the bottom of the screen! (If the user rotated the phone sideways, the score wouldn't even be visible above the fold.)

Figure 10-1. *NBA.com, where the only information the user cares about is at the bottom*

Having reduced the site to its minimal form, you should then make sure that a user who really needs the full nonmobile site can get it. Put a link to the full site in an obvious place. Remember that many of the world's people can get web access only through their phones, so you can't count on them just going to the full site on their large screen—they may not have one.

Alternatively, you might create the two "separate and parallel" designs mentioned earlier, in which all the site's functions and information are presented in the mobile site (meaning the user never has to go to the full nonmobile site). You may still need to strip down the home page or main screen. Instead of having a flat and broad navigational hierarchy in which the home page has a zillion links directly to other pages, you may need to reorganize the site so that the hierarchy is somewhat narrower and deeper. This lets you put fewer options on the home page, which means less clutter on a small screen. (Of course, you'll have to balance that against the time it takes for a user to jump from page to page!)

3. If you can, use the device's hardware

Mobile devices offer wonderful features that you don't get on the desktop. Location, camera, voice integration, gestural input, haptic feedback such as bumps and vibrations, and other features may be available to you. Some devices multitask so that your app can be running in the background while the user is doing other things; can you use that?

4. Linearize your content

This goes back to the width problem. Many devices simply don't give you enough pixels in the width dimension to do any interesting side-by-side layouts. Instead of forcing the issue, just accept that one way or another, your content will end up being laid out vertically. Order the mobile site's content so that it "reads well" when laid out this way. See the Vertical Stack pattern in this chapter.

(Several writers have pointed out that this linearization of content also makes the mobile site's content more accessible to screen readers and other types of devices. This is a nontrivial point. Can your main site, in fact, be linearized this way? Does it make sense if you read the content in its HTML order, with no CSS styling or layout?)

5. Optimize the most common interaction sequences

Once you've decided which tasks your typical mobile users will want to perform, and you've narrowed down the site to only the most relevant content, try to make those tasks as easy as possible by following these heuristics:

- *Eliminate typing*, or reduce it to as few characters as possible.

- Use as *few page loads* as possible, and don't inflate pages with unnecessary bytes. Download times can be very slow; most parts of the world are still outside the reach of high-bandwidth wireless Internet facilities.

- *Reduce scrolling* and sideways dragging, except where it eliminates page loads and typing. In other words, prefer one long vertical page to many small pages if you have to present a lot of content.

- Reduce the *number of taps* it takes a user to reach the desired information or accomplish a task. Tapping large hit targets—or using hardware buttons—is better than typing by a long shot, but try to reduce them anyway.

For more information on mobile design guidelines and an analysis of mobile usability tests done on various websites, see the Nielsen Norman Group's study "Usability of Mobile Websites," at *http://www.nngroup.com/reports/mobile*.

Dan Saffer's book *Designing Gestural Interfaces* (O'Reilly, *http://oreilly.com/catalog/9780596518394/*) discusses the common gestures used in touch screens, among other topics relevant to mobile devices.

Finally, the Design For Mobile pattern library, at *http://patterns.design4mobile.com*, contains many good patterns in addition to those found in this book.

Some Worthy Examples

Here are some mobile versions of home pages that manage to meet most of the design constraints listed in the preceding section, while retaining the branding and personality of each site. Figure 10-2 shows examples of each.

JetBlue.com

If someone is accessing JetBlue's website from a mobile device, it's a really good bet that he's actually traveling on JetBlue that day! He may be trying to get information about his flight, for instance. That's exactly what the JetBlue mobile site offers. The first items are the most useful to a traveler: flight information, check-in, and alerts, with further options for booking flights and in-flight entertainment. The page is simple and linear, and the items are easy to read and tap.

RuthsChris.com

Mobile users who go to restaurant sites probably want to see locations, peruse menus, or make a reservation. This simple site does those tasks with style. (The site would be even better if the device's browser knew the current location so that the user could tell the site to "find the restaurants closest to me.")

Boston.com

This news site has a clean design and packs useful information into a small space: the weather, the baseball score, leading headlines, and the first 20 or so words of each article. The site satisfies mobile users' needs to fill up a minute here and a minute there of "found time." The entire area of each article summary can be tapped, making the summaries easy to navigate.

Fidelity.com

People who watch the financial markets compulsively will find current data on the three big U.S. market indexes at the top of the mobile page, plus a way to search for specific quotes and navigation links into other timely topics (such as news, watch lists, and personal portfolios). Useful information is surfaced right on the home page, and a much deeper data set is easily available from the choices given.

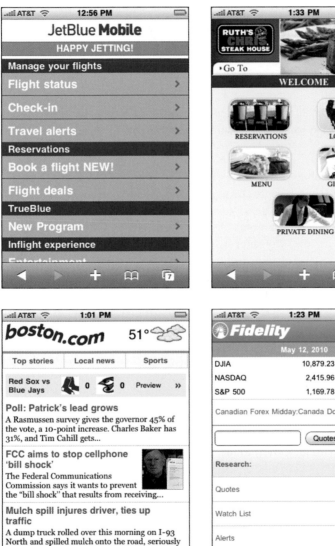

Figure 10-2. *Good examples of mobile sites: JetBlue, Ruth's Chris, Boston.com, and Fidelity*

The Patterns

In the introduction, we talked about the need to structure content in a vertical column for maximum flexibility. The Vertical Stack pattern goes into more detail.

1. Vertical Stack

A mobile application needs a way to show its top-level navigational structure. A persistent toolbar across the top or bottom of each app page is one standard way to organize a mobile interface; tabs and full-page menus are two other common ways. Less obvious, yet worth mentioning, are the Filmstrip and Touch Tools patterns.

2. Filmstrip

3. Touch Tools

Mobile web pages often use the Bottom Navigation pattern for their global menus, preferring to use valuable top-of-page space for more immediately relevant content.

4. Bottom Navigation

Lists are everywhere in the mobile world—lists of apps, pictures, messages, contacts, actions, settings, everything! Both web pages and applications should present well-designed lists that look good and are usable. Ordinary text lists are often adequate, and Carousels and Thumbnail Grids work beautifully in mobile designs. (See Chapter 5 for those patterns and more discussion of list design.) Consider using a Thumbnail-and-Text List as well, because they're usually simpler than Carousels and Thumbnail Grids. Sometimes an Infinite List suits the needs of mobile designs.

5. Thumbnail-and-Text List

6. Infinite List

The remaining patterns are a grab bag of topics related to mobile design.

7. Generous Borders

8. Text Clear Button

9. Loading Indicators

10. Richly Connected Apps

11. Streamlined Branding

Vertical Stack

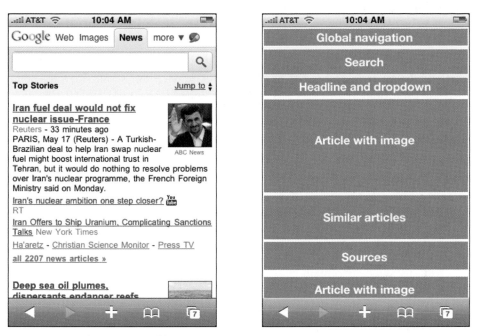

Figure 10-3. *Google News vertical layout*

What

Order the mobile page's content in a vertical column, with little or no use of side-by-side elements. Let text elements line-wrap, and let the page scroll down past the bottom of most device screens.

Use when

Most mobile web pages that must work on devices of different sizes should use this pattern, especially if they contain text-based content and forms. (Immersive content, such as a full-screen video or game, won't generally use this because it doesn't usually scroll like a text-based page does.)

When going from one page to another is expensive—as is the case with web pages, which take time to download—this pattern is applicable. On the other hand, an app that resides on the device can go from page to page almost instantly, since the content doesn't have to be downloaded. For these, it makes more sense to structure the content into single screenfuls so that the user never has to scroll vertically—she can just tap or swipe. But vertical scrolling of a long page is preferable to interminable waits for downloads.

Why

Devices come in different widths. You can't always anticipate what the actual width in pixels will be, unless you detect the screen width at runtime or build apps for particular devices. (You can create optimized designs for single devices or standard device-specific widths, but not everyone has the resources to do so.)

A fixed-width design that's too big for the physical device can scroll sideways or be zoomed, but these designs are never as usable as those that let the user simply scroll down.

Font sizes may also change unbeknownst to you, and as in the Liquid Layout pattern, a Vertical Stack with line-wrapped text elements will adjust gracefully when this happens.

How

Lay out the page's content in a scrolling vertical column. Put the most important items on top and less important items farther down so that most users can see the important stuff.

Useful content—from the user's perspective, that is—should show up in the first 100 pixels (or less) of this Vertical Stack. This top part of the screen is precious real estate. Don't waste it with too-tall logos, ads, or endless toolbars all stacked up into a "layer cake" that pushes all the useful content off the bottom of the page! That annoys users to no end.

Put form labels above their controls, not next to them, to save horizontal space. You will need all the space you can get to show text fields and choice controls with adequate width.

Put buttons side by side only if you're really sure their total width will never be wider than the visible screen. If the buttons contain long text that might be subject to localization or font enlargements, forget it.

Thumbnail images can fit beside text fairly easily, and it's common to do this in lists of articles, contacts, books, and so on—see the Thumbnail-and-Text List pattern. Make sure the design degrades well when the screen width is reduced to 128 pixels (or whatever the realistic minimum happens to be when you create your design).

Examples

The sites for ESPN, the *Washington Post*, and REI (Figure 10-4) demonstrate three styles of using a Vertical Stack. ESPN places only the most immediately relevant content on the home page, preferring to put the rest behind menu items on the bottom of the page. The *Washington Post* puts it all out there; the stack shown in the figure is just a small fragment of the entire page! REI simply shows a menu of all the available places and ways to shop, with no ads or teasers on its home page.

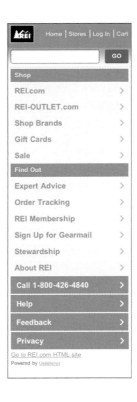

Figure 10-4. *Vertical Stacks on the mobile sites for ESPN, the Washington Post, and REI*

Filmstrip

Figure 10-5. *iPhone Weather app*

Arrange top-level pages side by side, and let the user swipe them back and forth to view them one at a time.

You have pages of content that are conceptually parallel, such as the weather in different cities or the scores in different sports. Users won't mind swiping through these pages, going through several before reaching the one they're looking for, because they are all potentially interesting.

This pattern can sometimes be a viable alternative to other navigation schemes for mobile apps, such as toolbars, tabs, or full-page menus.

Each item to be displayed can occupy the entire screen; no space needs to be used for tabs or other navigation.

Since the user can't jump straight to a desired screen—he has to swipe through others to get there—this pattern encourages browsing and serendipity.

Swiping seems to be a very satisfying gesture for some users.

A disadvantage of this pattern is that it doesn't scale very well; you can't use too many top-level pages, or users might get irritated at having to swipe too many times to get to a desired page. Another disadvantage is lack of transparency. A new user, just seeing your app for the first time, cannot easily see that swiping is how he gets from one page to another.

How

Essentially, a Filmstrip is like a Carousel (see Chapter 5) for a mobile application's main pages. One difference is that a Carousel usually shows metadata—information about the item or page—and context, such as fragments of the previous and next pages. Mobile apps that use Filmstrips as a top-level organizing device don't generally do that.

If you want to give the user a clue that multiple top-level pages exist, and that he can swipe between them, use a dot indicator like the Weather app uses at the bottom of its screen.

Examples

The iPhone's built-in Weather app (shown in Figure 10-5, at the top of the pattern) uses a Filmstrip to show the weather in the various geographic locations that the user chooses.

Likewise, ESPN's iPhone app structures its main pages as a Filmstrip. The user swipes back and forth between football, baseball, basketball, and other sports scores (see Figure 10-6).

Figure 10-6. *ESPN application*

Touch Tools

Figure 10-7. *Touch tools on the iPhone photo viewer*

What

Show tools only in response to a touch or key press, and put them in a small, dynamic overlay atop the content.

Use when

You are designing an immersive or full-screen experience, such as videos, photos, games, maps, or books. To manage that experience, the user will sometimes need controls—navigation tools, media player tools, information about the content, and so forth. The tools require significant space, but are only needed sometimes.

Why

The content is allowed to dominate the experience most of the time. The user isn't distracted by controls taking space and attention away from the content. Remember that in a mobile context, space and attention are even more precious resources than usual.

The user controls the experience by choosing when to show the tools.

Show the unadorned content using the full screen. When the user touches the device's screen or presses a particular key or softkey, show the tools.

Many apps only show Touch Tools when the user touches a certain region of the screen. This way, the user doesn't accidentally bring up the tools just by ordinary handling of the device. Also, you can bring up different tools when different regions of the screen are touched—the Stanza book reader does this, for instance. See the example in Figure 10-9.

Show the tools in a small, translucent area that appears to float above the content. The translucency makes the tools look ephemeral (which they are).

Remove the tools after a few seconds of nonuse, or immediately if the user taps the screen outside the bounds of the tools. It can be annoying to wait for the tools to go away by themselves.

Examples

The video player on the iPhone shows Touch Tools when the user taps the indicated area of the screen (see Figure 10-8). They go away again after about five seconds of nonuse.

Figure 10-8. *YouTube for iPhone Touch Tools*

Stanza, one of the many ebook readers on smartphones and other touch screen devices, also uses Touch Tools. Most of the time, the full screen is used to show book text. But when the user taps the center of the screen, extra information and controls appear—book title, author, chapter and page, settings, search, viewing mode, and a menu of yet more tools. To explain this and the page-turning gestures, a first-time reader is shown an explanatory dialog. See Figure 10-9.

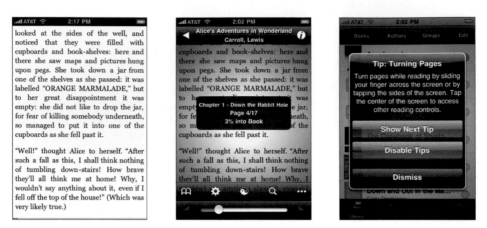

Figure 10-9. *The Stanza book reader: default page, with Touch Tools, and an explanatory dialog*

Bottom Navigation

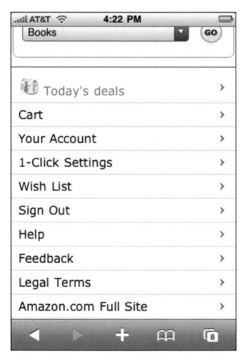

Figure 10-10. *Amazon's Bottom Navigation*

What

Place global navigation at the bottom of the page, below the fold.

Use when

A mobile website needs to show some global navigation links, but these links represent low-priority paths through the interface for many users.

Your highest priority on the site's front page is to show fresh, interesting content.

Why

The top of a mobile home page is precious real estate. You should generally put only the two or three most important navigation links there—if any at all—and devote the rest of the front page to content that will interest most users.

A user looking for navigational links can easily scroll to the bottom of a page, even when those links are far below the fold.

How

Create a set of vertically arranged menu items on the bottom of the page. Make them easy to tap with a finger on touch screens—stretch them across the full width of the mobile page, and make the text large and readable.

This pattern is closely related to the Sitemap Footer pattern in Chapter 3. In a mobile application, you probably aren't trying to fit an entire site map into the footer—you only have room for a few well-chosen links. But the idea is similar: instead of taking up too much top-of-page space for navigation, you can push it to the bottom of the page, where real estate is less valuable.

Examples

NPR puts an extensive footer across the bottom of each of its pages (see Figure 10-11). It includes standard navigational links, a search box, the full-size site, a link to download an app, and a font size control.

Amazon uses a simpler, shorter Bottom Navigation system. See the screenshot in Figure 10-10 at the top of the pattern.

In contrast, Google uses a more web-like footer on many of its mobile properties (see Figure 10-12). These links are smaller and look more like the brand, but they are far harder to hit with clumsy fingertips.

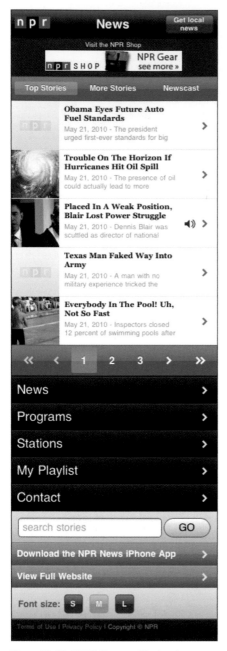

Figure 10-11. *NPR's Bottom Navigation*

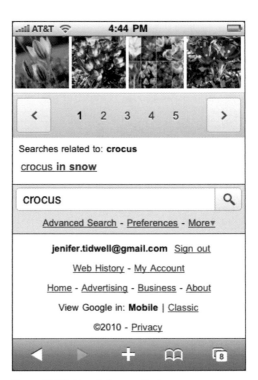

Figure 10-12. *Google Images footer*

Thumbnail-and-Text List

Figure 10-13. *iPhone App Store*

What

Present a selectable list of items, with each item containing a thumbnail image, some text, and possibly smaller text as well. If appropriate, use bold colors, icons, and other visual differentiators.

Use when

You need to show lists of articles, blog entries, videos, applications, or other complex content. Many or all of these have associated images. You want to invite the user to click on these items and view them.

Why

Thumbnail images improve text-only lists because they look appealing, help identify items, and establish a generous height for the list items.

Reading conditions on mobile devices are rarely ideal. By adding colorful images, you can improve the visual differentiation among items, which helps people scan and parse the list quickly.

Many news and blog websites have converged on this design pattern as a way to show links to their articles. They look more appealing, and more "finished," than similar sites that only list article titles or text fragments.

How

Place a thumbnail image next to the text of the item. Most sites and apps put the thumbnail on the left.

In addition to picture thumbnails, you can include other visual markers, such as five-star ratings or icons representing people's social presence.

Don't be afraid to use bright or saturated colors. You probably wouldn't design so much visual stimulation in a desktop context, but in a mobile context, it works. Even if the colors seem garish, don't worry—small screens can handle strong colors better than large screens can!

Examples

Many news sites use this pattern to show their articles. Yahoo! News and Boston.com offer good examples. Special-interest journalism sites such as Mashable also use Thumbnail-and-Text Lists effectively for their feature articles. See Figure 10-14.

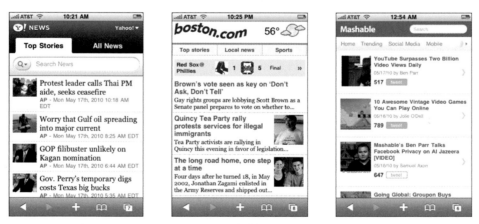

Figure 10-14. *Yahoo! News, Boston.com, and Mashable*

Videos and other media fit this pattern naturally. As shown in Figure 10-15, YouTube, IMDb, and Kobo show thumbnails representing their videos, movies, and books. Note the rating stars on the YouTube and Kobo listings (and on the iPhone app store, in Figure 10-13 at the top of the pattern). These help a user scan down a list and pick out items with more stars.

IMDb also shows user ratings, but it eschews stars in favor of plain text, and it doesn't draw the eye—it just blends in with the rest of the text. Note also that the subdued and tasteful colors of the Kobo book reader look beautiful, but don't help differentiate items as strongly as the bolder colors used by YouTube or the app store.

Figure 10-15. *YouTube, IMDb, and Kobo apps*

Finally, many apps show Thumbnail-and-Text Lists of other, diverse kinds of items: birds (from iBird Explorer), products (the Google iPhone app), and menu items in a complex information architecture (Buzz Aldrin's Portal to Science and Space Exploration); see Figure 10-16.

Figure 10-16. *iBird, Google, and Buzz Aldrin*

Infinite List

Figure 10-17. *iPhone Mail app*

What

At the bottom of a long list, put a button that loads and appends more items to the list.

Use when

You need to show long lists of email messages, search results, an archive of articles or blog posts, or anything else that is effectively "bottomless."

Users are likely to find desired items near the top, but they sometimes need to search further.

Why

The initial loading of a screenful or two of items is fast, and the user doesn't get stuck waiting for a very long initial page load before she sees anything useful.

Each subsequent loading of a new chunk of items is also fast, and it's under user control—the user decides when (and whether) she needs to load more items.

Since the new items are just appended to the current page, the user never has to context-shift by going to a new page to see new items, as she would with paginated search results.

How

When the page or list is initially sent to the mobile device, truncate the list at a reasonable length. That length will vary greatly with item size, download time, and the user's goal—is she reading everything (as with Facebook), or just scanning a large number of items to find the one she wants (as with search results)?

At the bottom of the scrolled page, put a button that lets the user load and show more items. Let the user know how many more will be loaded.

Alternatively, you could use no button at all. After the user has loaded and can view the first chunk of items, silently start loading the next chunk. Append them to the visible list when they're ready, and the user has scrolled down to the end of the original list. (This is your clue that the user may want to see more. If the user doesn't scroll down, don't bother getting more items.)

In software engineering, this well-known approach to managing lists of undefined length is often called *lazy loading*.

Examples

Several iPhone applications use Infinite Lists, including Mail (Figure 10-17), as well as iTunes and third-party apps such as Facebook (Figure 10-18). The iTunes button only loads 10 more items, which seems like too small a number for an eager music listener, but the Mail app loads many screenfuls of new messages; it seems to balance download time and quantity fairly well. The Facebook app, like the full-size Facebook page, loads up the first several pages of updates and then lets the user load more.

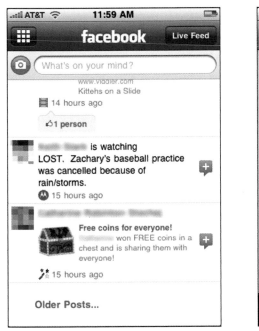

Figure 10-18. *Facebook and iTunes*

You can also do this with a web page. Gmail Buzz loads a few screenfuls of updates and then offers a "Load more" button; so does Mashable (see Figure 10-19).

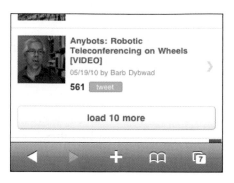

Figure 10-19. *Buzz and Mashable*

Generous Borders

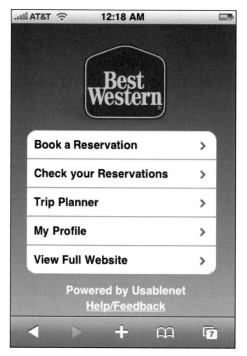

Figure 10-20. *Best Western's mobile site*

What

On devices with touch screens, put large margins and whitespace around buttons, links, and any other tappable control.

Use when

You need to use buttons with text labels, or a list of items, or ordinary text-based links—in short, any touch target that isn't already large on the screen.

Why

Touch targets must be large enough for clumsy fingers to hit successfully. In particular, they need to be tall enough, which is challenging for buttons and links that consist only of text.

How

Surround each touch target with enough inner margin, border, and surrounding whitespace to make a sufficiently large hit target for fingertips.

One trick is to make the whitespace immediately surrounding a target tappable. The button will look the same size, thus fitting into your visual design as expected, but you gain a few pixels of sensitivity in each direction around the button. Dan Saffer, in *Designing Gestural Interfaces*, uses the term *iceberg tips* for controls such as these—they are bigger than they appear.

Exactly how big to make these targets is a very good question. Ideally, you want a size that ends up large enough on the physical device to be manipulated by most people—many of whom will have large fingers. Some others will not have great control over their fingertips. Yet others will be using their mobile devices in challenging conditions: bad light, moving vehicles, little attention to spare.

So ultimately, how big should you make your targets? It depends on whom you ask. There's no consensus on minimum target size, but different references make these claims:

- 3/4 × 3/4 inches, separated by 1/8 inch (*http://www.sapdesignguild.org/resources/TSDesignGL/Index.htm*)
- 9.6 mm (*http://portal.acm.org/citation.cfm?id=1152260*)
- 1 × 1 cm square (Nokia's S60 5th Edition C++ Developer's Library v2.1, among others)
- 44 × 44 pixels on an iPhone (iPhone Human Interface Guidelines)

And there's more. See Luke Wroblewski's discussion at *http://www.lukew.com/ff/entry.asp?1085* for even more information.

Examples

The IMDb application for the iPhone reliably puts plenty of margin space around its touch targets. The whole application has a relaxed, uncramped feeling, as shown in Figure 10-21.

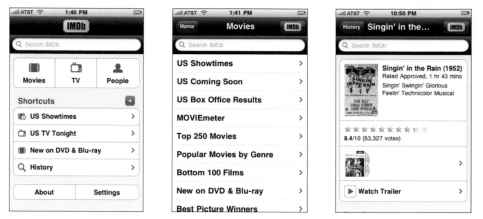

Figure 10-21. *Screens from the IMDb app*

The Epicurious app is similar, though its visual styling is quite different. The buttons for key actions—"find a recipe," "view recipe"—are quite large and distinctive, as shown in Figure 10-22.

Figure 10-22. *Screens from the Epicurious app*

Text Clear Button

Figure 10-23. *The URL box in Safari*

What

Clear a text field with one button press.

Use when

Whenever a text field is needed in the mobile interface, consider using a Text Clear Button. It is especially valuable for fields that hold long strings of text, such as search strings, URLs, and multiline text.

Why

Erasing long strings of text letter by letter is slow and error-prone. Don't force your users to do this.

Some mobile platforms have no facility for cut, copy, and paste. A cut operation may suffice for erasing text—so would the selection of all of a text field's contents—but even if those exist it's easier just to tap a single target to erase the field.

How

Put a simple "X" or "Clear" button into the text field. A button beside the text field can also work, though you'd want to usability-test it to find out whether users see it or not—they may see it as a "Go" or "Search" button instead.

If the platform offers a "Clear" button as a built-in feature for text fields, use it. I have watched users struggle to clear text fields when this feature was not provided, on early versions of Android—it's painful to watch people erase a long search field letter by letter. I've also watched people use iPhone apps that didn't use its standard clear button; these users had a strong expectation that the "X" button would appear in text fields, and were unhappy when it wasn't provided.

There aren't many varied examples of this pattern to show as of this writing. Figure 10-24 shows the websites of two large search engines that insert a Text Clear Button into their search fields.

Figure 10-24. *Clear buttons as used by Google and Bing*

Loading Indicators

Figure 10-25. *The iPhone Stocks app waiting for chart data*

While a page or page section is loading, show a progress indicator in the place where it will be (or where the user tapped or clicked).

Use when

The user has to wait for content to load, especially in a page that changes dynamically in response to user interaction.

Why

Loading new content can be slow and erratic over mobile connections.

You should always show as much of a partially loaded page as you can, so the user can actually see something useful.

In general, progress indicators make loading times appear faster to a user. She is reassured that something is actually happening in response to a gesture, especially when that indicator appears where the gesture occurred.

How

Show as much of the page as can be loaded quickly, but if part of it takes a long time, such as a graphic or video, show a lightweight animated progress indicator where the graphic will appear. (The mobile platform may supply a default indicator.)

When the user initiates an action that causes part of the page to be reloaded—or loads a whole new page—show a progress indicator *in situ* on the page.

Examples

Flickr's mobile website uses loading indicators very skillfully. When the user taps a picture thumbnail to see the whole picture, the thumbnail is overlaid by a Flickr logo that moves until the new image is ready to show (see Figure 10-26).

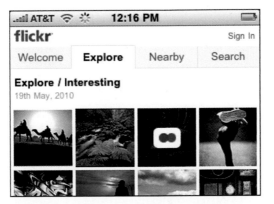

Figure 10-26. *Flickr's animated loading indicator*

When an iPhone installs a new app, the app's icon literally shows a miniature progress bar to show how far it's gotten with the download (see Figure 10-27). It's cute, and its meaning is unmistakable.

Figure 10-27. *iPhone's app installation progress bar*

Richly Connected Apps

Figure 10-28. *Freedom Trail app for iPhone*

What

Inside your mobile app put direct links to other apps, such as the phone dialer, map, or browser. "Prefill" them with data from the user's current context.

The mobile app shows data that is "connectable" in obvious ways, such as phone numbers and hyperlinks.

More subtly, your app may offer ways to capture images (via the device camera), sound, or video. It may even be aware of social networking conventions, such as Facebook or Twitter usernames. In all cases, your app might direct the user to another app to perform these device-based functions.

A user can only see one mobile app at a time, even when multiple apps are being used at once, and it's annoying to switch between them by hand.

Mobile devices often have enough context and available functionality to offer intelligent paths between apps.

As of this writing, mobile devices have no good way to arbitrarily shuffle small amounts of information from one application to another. On the desktop, you can type easily, or use copy and paste, or even use the filesystem. You don't have those options on a mobile platform. So, you need to support moving that data automatically.

In your app, keep track of data that might be closely associated with other apps or services. When the user taps or selects that data, or uses special affordances that you provide, open another app and handle the data there.

Here are some examples. Consider all the ways that data in your app can connect directly to other mobile functions.

- Phone numbers connect to the dialer.

- Addresses connect to the map, or to the contacts app.

- Dates connect to the calendar.

- Email addresses connect to the email app.

- Hyperlinks connect to the browser.

- Music and videos connect to media players.

In addition, you might be able to do such things as take a picture, or use a map, entirely within the context of your application.

You can do some of this on a desktop, but the walled-garden nature of many mobile devices makes it easier to launch the "right" app for certain kinds of data. You don't have to decide which email reader to use, or which address or contact management system, and so on. Plus, many mobile devices supply a phone dialer, a camera, and geographic location services.

The Freedom Trail application for the iPhone, shown in Figure 10-28, explicitly illustrates its links to other apps. The user chooses whether to follow them for more information, or just to stay within the app; this transparency is useful and refreshing.

The Facebook app for iPhone connects to the camera on the device (see Figure 10-29). The integration is close; users can take a picture and immediately post it to Facebook, without ever seeming to leave the Facebook app. Facebook can also reach the preexisting photos on the iPhone.

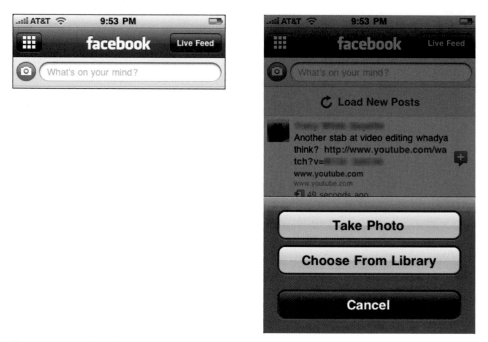

Figure 10-29. *Facebook's integration with the camera*

The iPhone's map application (Figure 10-30) connects to the contacts app to add a person's address to her contact info, and to email and MMS for sharing a location. (Of course, many other applications, both mobile and otherwise, also have "Email this" or "Share this" features. See the Sharing Widget pattern in Chapter 9, for example.)

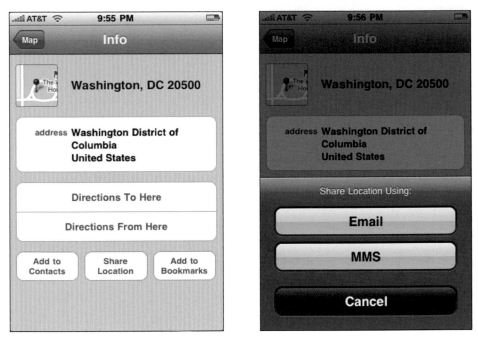

Figure 10-30. *The iPhone map application connecting to contacts, mail, and MMS*

Streamlined Branding

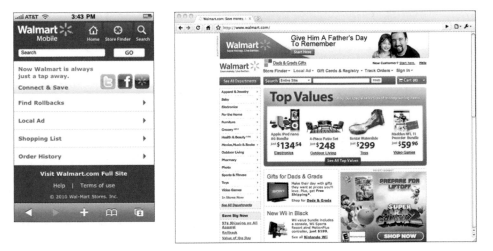

Figure 10-31. *Walmart's mobile site compared to its full site*

Use your organization's logo, colors, and other brand elements on the mobile site or app, but keep them small on the screen and fast to load.

All mobile apps or sites that are associated with a company or organization should use this.

Users need to be able to identify your app or site as yours. In usability testing, people respond well to reliable, familiar branding, especially when the brand is already known outside of the mobile context.

Mobile screens don't have much space to spare for elements that aren't actual content.

Mobile network connections can be slow, and heavyweight images don't download fast enough.

Create a small version of your logo, no taller than around 50 pixels, so that it takes up as little vertical space as you can get away with. If you're creating different designs for different screen sizes or platforms, consider making different versions of the logo for each.

Apply your brand's colors and font families in the mobile design. A basic text interface may function well enough, but it won't look professional or polished.

Avoid using very large and complex images as stylistic elements. Download time is as important in a mobile context as on the desktop (and often more so). If you're working in HTML, depend on stylesheets when you can, rather than handcrafted images.

Strong contrast and large, readable text will help people use your mobile site when the conditions are poor (bright light, motion, distraction). Even if your brand calls for visual subtlety and small, tasteful text, do what needs to be done for the sake of usability—adapt the brand look to the platform.

There are good examples of this pattern all over the mobile web. Going back to the first example given in this chapter, JetBlue pares down its branding to a look that is polished and recognizable, but works well on even a tiny mobile device (see Figure 10-32).

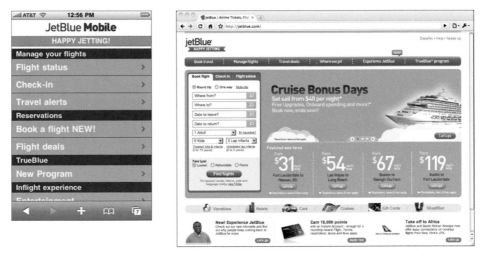

Figure 10-32. *JetBlue's mobile branding*

Fandango's mobile site also takes a minimalist approach (see Figure 10-33). Like JetBlue, Fandango uses a polished-looking logo and style, but the site loads fast and can be used on tiny screens. None of the bandwidth-hogging images, ads, or video is loaded onto the mobile device.

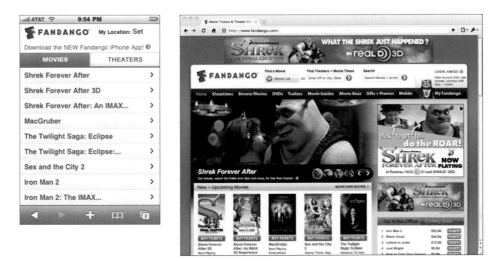

Figure 10-33. *Fandango's mobile branding*

Whole Foods maintains a very consistent brand look across its full-page and mobile sites. But its mobile site consumes more above-the-fold space than necessary with top navigation, and it downloads several large images, making it slower than it could be (see Figure 10-34).

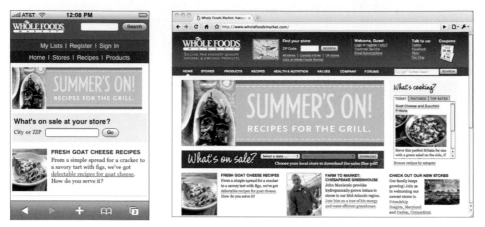

Figure 10-34. *Whole Foods' mobile branding*

Chipotle's mobile website shows how *not* to do mobile branding (see Figure 10-35). The brand is strong enough on the main site, but none of it shows up on the mobile site except for a too-small version of the logo! The site uses only a neutral font and colors. (To be fair, the site does supply an iPhone app that has stronger branding, but it's not likely that a very occasional customer will bother with the hassle of downloading it if the website fills her needs.)

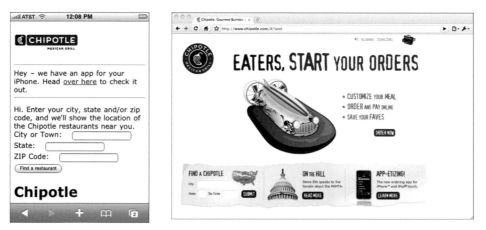

Figure 10-35. *Chipotle's mobile branding (or lack thereof)*

Chapter 11

Making It Look Good: Visual Style and Aesthetics

In 2002, a research group discovered something interesting. The Stanford Web Credibility Project[*] set out to learn what causes people to trust or distrust websites, and much of what they found made intuitive sense: company reputation, customer service, sponsorships, and ads all helped users decide whether or not a website was credible.

But the most important factor—number one on their list—was the appearance of the website. Users did not trust sites that looked amateurish. Sites that made the effort to craft a nice, professionally designed look made a lot more headway with users, even if those users had few other reasons to trust the site.

Here's another data point. Donald Norman, one of the best-known gurus of interaction design, concluded that "positive affect enhances creative, breadth-first thinking whereas negative affect focuses cognition, enhancing depth-first processing and minimizing distractions." He added: "Positive affect makes people more tolerant of minor difficulties and more flexible and creative in finding solutions."[†] Interfaces actually become more usable when people enjoy using them.

Looking good matters.

For many chapters now, we've talked about the structure, form, and behavior of an application; now we'll focus more on its "skin" or its "look-and-feel." Chapter 4 discussed some graphic design basics. That chapter covered visual hierarchy, visual flow, focal points, and the Gestalt principles of *proximity*, *similarity*, *continuity*, and *closure*. These topics form the foundation of page organization, and should not be shortchanged.

---

[*] See *http://credibility.stanford.edu*.

[†] See Donald Norman, "Emotion and Design: Attractive Things Work Better," at *http://jnd.org/dn.mss/emotion_design_attractive_things_work_better.html*. See also his book on the subject, *Emotional Design: Why We Love (or Hate) Everyday Things* (Basic Books).

But there's more to a nice house than just its room layout. When you pay for a well-designed new house, you also expect beautiful carpets, paint colors, wall textures, and other surface treatments. Without them, a house can be perfectly functional but uninspiring. Completing the job means paying attention to detail, fit, and finish.

Beautiful details don't necessarily affect the efficiency with which people accomplish tasks in the house or interface (although research indicates that it sometimes does). But they certainly affect whether or not people enjoy it. That, in turn, affects other behavior—such as how long users linger and explore, whether they choose to go there again, and whether they recommend it to other people.

You could even think about it as a moral issue. What kind of experience do you want your users to have? Do you want to give them an all-gray application that bores them, or a flashy ad-filled application that irritates them? Would you rather give them something they enjoy looking at, maybe for hours at a time?

Of course, far more than visual style influences a user's emotional response (affect). Chapter 1 began discussing other considerations, such as how well you anticipate users' usage habits. Software can pleasantly surprise people with considerate design. Tightly packed layouts evoke a different affective response than sparse, open layouts. Language and verbal tone play a huge part in this response, as does the quality of the software itself—does it "just work," and is it fast and responsive?

A well-designed interface takes all of these factors into account. When content, meaning, and interactive behavior all work in concert with your visual style, you can evoke a chosen emotional response very effectively.

With products and websites, stylistic elements are often designed to support *branding*. The design of any software product or site expresses something about the organization that produced it (even if it's a loosely knit group of open source developers). It might say something neutral, or it might send a focused message: "You can trust us," "We're cool," "We build exciting things." A brand identity encompasses more than just a logo and tag line. It runs throughout an organization's product designs, its website, and its advertising materials—in fact, the brand's chosen color schemes, fonts, iconography, and vocabulary show up everywhere. When planned well, a complete brand identity is coherent and intentional.

A brand identity is important because it establishes familiarity and sets expectations for someone's experience with an organization's products. Ultimately, a good brand should make people feel better about using those products. Look at what Apple was able to do with brand loyalty: many people love Apple products and seek them out.

In any case, whether or not they are intended to support a brand, stylistic elements make statements about your product. They communicate attributes such as reliability, excitement, playfulness, energy, calmness, strength, tension, and joy. What do you want to communicate?

This chapter discusses more visual design concepts, this time focusing less on formal structure and more on these emotionally based attributes. The chapter won't make an artist out of you—that takes serious practice and study. But the patterns capture some techniques commonly found on well-designed artifacts and explain why they work.

Same Content, Different Styles

To explore how styles evoke different visceral and emotional reactions, we can try applying different visual styles to identical content. The actual content isn't even that important—we're looking for immediate, prerational reactions here, not the impressions gained from reading and interacting with the content.

The CSS Zen Garden website (*http://csszengarden.com*) offers us exactly that situation. Invented as a showcase for CSS-based web design, this site provides a single HTML page to all participants—everyone gets the same body text, the same HTML tags, and the same lists of links. Participants then create unique CSS files to define new visual designs for the page, and contribute them to the site. Visitors can browse through all the contributed CSS designs. It's a delightful way to spend an hour or three, especially if you're teaching yourself about visual design and trying to understand what you do and do not like.

Figures 11-1 through 11-8 present a sample of these designs. In each case, the basic content is the same; only the design has changed. Take some time to examine each one. When you look at each design, what is your immediate, visceral reaction? What words come to mind that describe the page? Does it draw you in, repel you, make you nervous, or delight you?

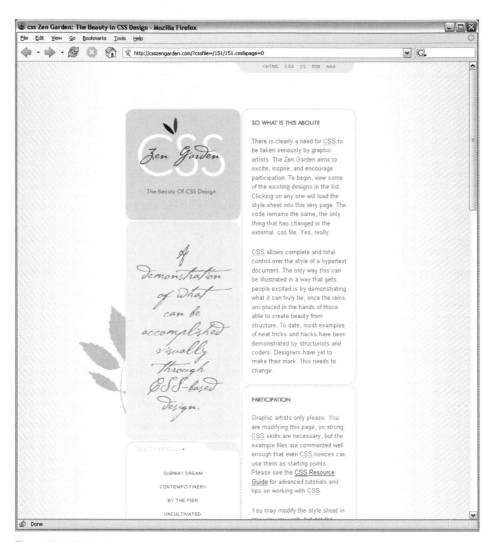

Figure 11-1. *Design 1*

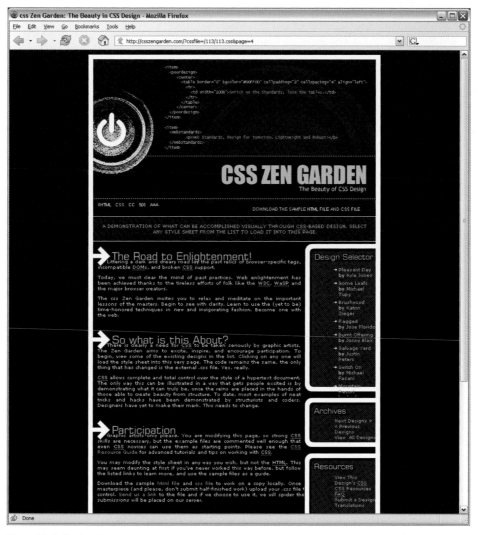

Figure 11-2. *Design 2*

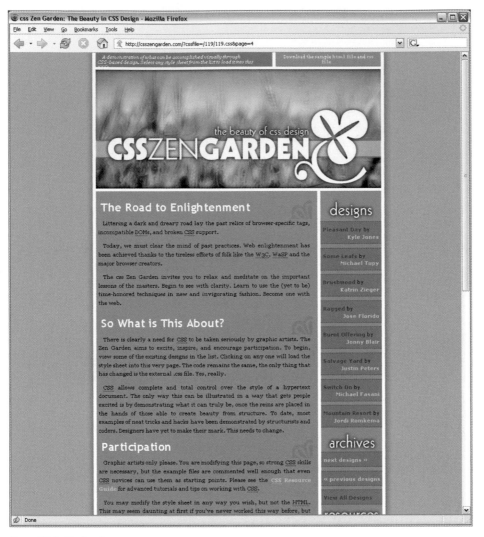

Figure 11-3. *Design 3*

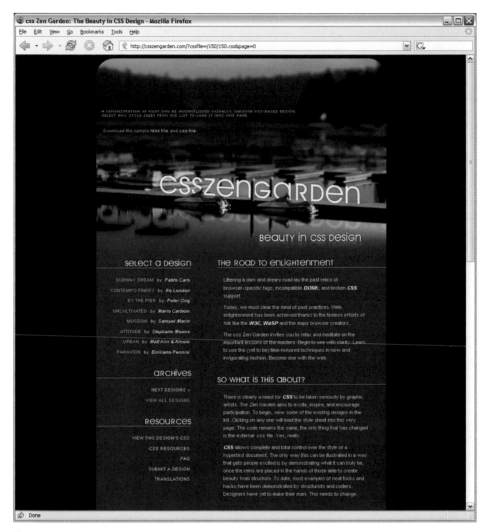

Figure 11-4. *Design 4*

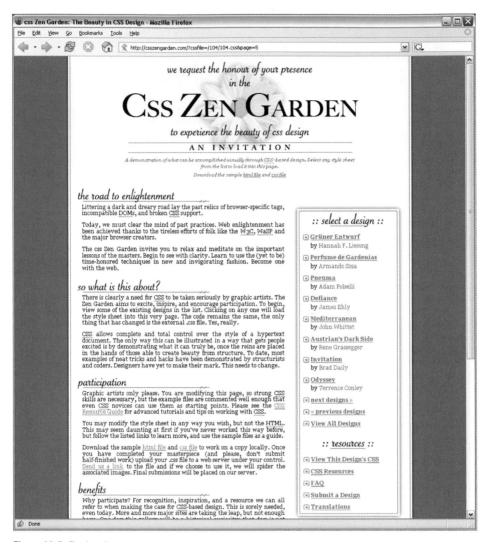

Figure 11-5. *Design 5*

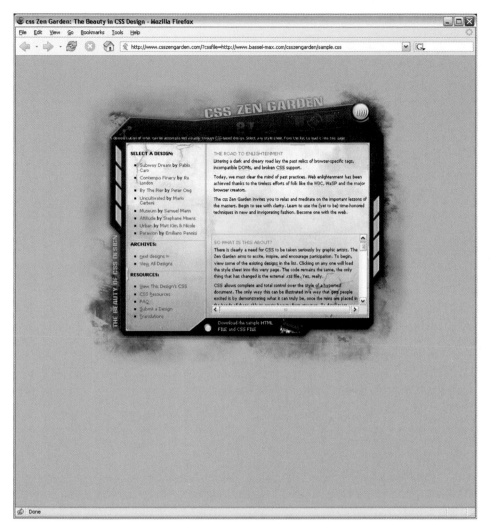

Figure 11-6. *Design 6*

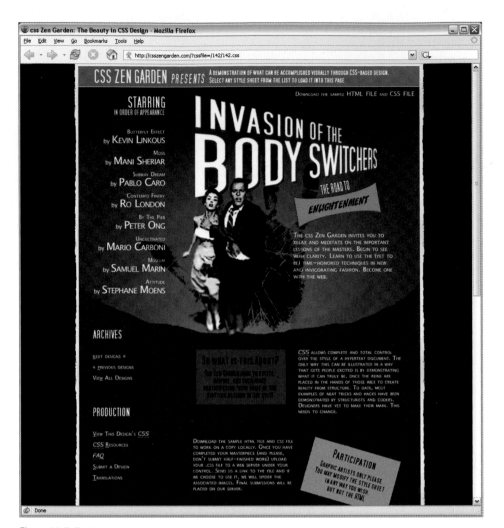

Figure 11-7. *Design 7*

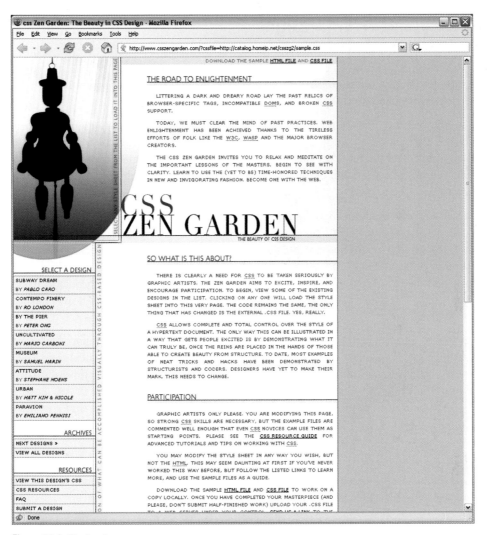

Figure 11-8. *Design 8*

The Basics of Visual Design

As you looked at the Zen Garden examples, you might have observed how they achieve such different impressions—a page's color scheme may cause you to either smile or cringe, for example. Using these examples as a touchstone, we can talk about some of the principles of good visual design.

You might recall that we already covered some visual design principles in Chapters 4 and 7. Those chapters explored how the human visual system responds *cognitively* to certain inputs. The time it takes for someone to click on an orange square out of a field of blue squares, for example, doesn't depend upon a user's aesthetic sense or cultural expectations.

But now we're talking about *emotional and visceral* reactions—does a single orange square add tension to a design, brightness, balance, or nothing at all? The answer depends on so many factors that it's genuinely hard to get it "right" without a lot of practice. The cognitive aspects of these design choices certainly play a part; for starters, you can make a page hard or easy to read (a cognitive effect). But each person is unique. Each person has a different history of experiences, associations, and preferences; and each person is part of a culture that imposes its own meanings on color, typography, and imagery.

Furthermore, the context of the design affects the user's response. Users see your design as part of a genre (such as office applications, games, or e-commerce sites), and they will have certain expectations about what's appropriate, trite or original, and dull or interesting. Branding also sets expectations. So here's the problem: as soon as you learn a "rule" for evoking an emotional reaction using a design principle, you can find a million exceptions.

That being said, if you know your audience well, visceral and emotional responses are surprisingly predictable. For example, most readers of this book probably thought that the first CSS example was a calm, soothing design, but that the second one was noisier and tenser. Why is that?

The answer lies in a combination of many factors working in concert: color, typography, spaciousness, angles and shapes, repeated visual motifs, texture, images, and cultural references.

Color

Color is immediate. It's one of the first things you perceive about a design, along with basic forms and shapes. Yet the application of color to art and design is infinitely subtle—master painters have studied it for centuries. We can only scratch the surface here.

When devising a color scheme for an interface, first rule out anything that makes the text difficult to read:

- Always put dark foregrounds against light backgrounds, and vice versa—to test, pull the design into an image tool such as Photoshop and desaturate it (make it grayscale).

- Never use red versus green as a critical color distinction, since many colorblind people won't be able to see the difference. Statistically, 10% of men have some form of colorblindness, as do about 1% of women.

- Never put bright blue, small text on a bright red or orange background or vice versa, because human eyes quickly get fatigued when reading text written in complementary colors (colors on opposite sides of the color wheel).

With that out of the way, here are some very approximate rules for color usage:

Warm versus cool

Red, orange, yellow, brown, and beige are considered "warm" colors. Blue, green, purple, gray (in large quantities), and white are considered "cool." The yellow CSS Zen Garden in Design 6 (Figure 11-6) feels vividly "hot," despite the cool gray metallic surface used behind the content itself. Sites and interfaces that need to connote respectability and conservativeness often use predominantly cool colors (especially blue). Still, warm and cool colors can combine very effectively to achieve a balanced look—and they frequently do, in classic paintings and poster designs.

Dark versus light background

The pages with light backgrounds—white, beige, and light gray—feel very different from the ones with very dark backgrounds. Light is more typical of computer interfaces (and printed pages); dark pages can feel edgier, more somber, or more energetic, depending on other design aspects.

High versus low contrast

Whether the background is dark or light, the elements on that background might have either high or low contrast against it. Strong contrast evokes tension, strength, and boldness; low contrast is more soothing and relaxing.

Saturated versus unsaturated

Highly saturated, or pure, colors—brilliant yellows, reds, and greens, for example—evoke energy, vividness, brightness, and warmth. They are daring; they have character. But when overused, they can tire the eyes, so most UI designs use them sparingly; they often choose only one or two. Muted colors, either dark or light (*tones* or *tints*, respectively), make up the bulk of most color palettes. The green and blue Zen Garden design gets away with two saturated colors by using white borders, white text, and dark halos to separate the green and blue. (Even so, you probably wouldn't want to stare at that green all day long in a desktop application.)

Combinations of hues

Once you start combining colors, interesting effects happen. Two saturated colors can evoke far more energy, motion, or richness than one alone. A page that combines one saturated color with a set of muted colors directs attention to the saturated color and sets up "layers" of color—the brighter and stronger ones appear closer to the viewer, while the grayer and paler colors recede. Strong dimensionality can make a design dramatic. Flatter designs, with more muted or lighter colors, are calmer. See the Few Hues, Many Values pattern for more discussion.

Typography

By choosing a font (properly called a *typeface*) for a piece of text, you decide what kind of voice that text is "spoken" in. The voice might be loud or soft, friendly or formal, colloquial or authoritative, hip or old-fashioned.

As with color, readability—the cognitive part—comes first when choosing type. Small text—or what's called "body text" in print and on websites—demands careful choice. The following considerations for body text also apply to "label fonts" in GUIs, used to caption text fields and other controls:

- On computer displays, sans-serif fonts often work better at very small point sizes, unlike print, in which the serifed fonts tend to be more readable as body text. Pixels aren't big enough to render tiny serifs well. (Some serifed fonts, such as Georgia, do look OK, though.)

- Avoid italicized, cursive, or otherwise ornamental fonts; they are unreadable at small sizes.

- Highly geometric fonts tend to be difficult to read at small point sizes, as the circular letters (*e*, *c*, *d*, *o*, etc.) are hard to differentiate. Futura, Univers, and some other mid-20th-century fonts are like this.

- All-caps is too hard to read for body text, though it works fine for headlines and short texts. Capital letters tend to look similar, and are hard for a reader to differentiate.

- Set large amounts of text in a medium-width column when possible—say, around 10 to 12 English words on average. Don't right-justify narrower columns of text; let it be "ragged right."

Now for the visceral and emotional aspects. Fonts have distinctive voices—they have different graphic characteristics, textures, and colors on the page. For instance, some fonts are dense and dark, while others are more open—look at the thickness of strokes and the relative sizes of letter openings for clues, and use the "squint test" if you need a fresh and objective look at the font. Some fonts have narrower letters than others, and some font families have "condensed" versions to make them even narrower. The separation between lines of text (the leading) might be distant or close, making the block of text look either more open or more solid.

Serifs and curves add another dimension to font color and texture. Serifs add a level of scale that's much smaller than the letterform itself, and that adds refinement to the font's texture—the thick sans-serif fonts look blunt, strong, or even coarse in comparison (especially Helvetica). The curves and angles used in each letterform, including those that form the serifs, combine to form an overall texture. Compare an old-fashioned typeface such as Goudy Old Style to another classic serifed font such as Didot; they look very different on the page. See Figure 11-9.

Lorem ipsum dolor sit amet, consectetuer adipiscing elit. Sed a sem. Nullam nonummy libero id libero. Donec libero erat, consequat in, tincidunt at, malesuada id, urna. Fusce tincidunt consectetuer ante. Nam sit amet lorem. Nulla nec ante ac risus tincidunt suscipit. Aliquam luctus. Vivamus lobortis odio at risus porttitor ultrices. Maecenas odio libero, rhoncus et, dignissim id, rhoncus at, quam. Vivamus dolor. Quisque feugiat fringilla enim.

Didot

Lorem ipsum dolor sit amet, consectetuer adipiscing elit. Sed a sem. Nullam nonummy libero id libero. Donec libero erat, consequat in, tincidunt at, malesuada id, urna. Fusce tincidunt consectetuer ante. Nam sit amet lorem. Nulla nec ante ac risus tincidunt suscipit. Aliquam luctus. Vivamus lobortis odio at risus porttitor ultrices. Maecenas odio libero, rhoncus et, dignissim id, rhoncus at, quam. Vivamus dolor. Quisque feugiat fringilla enim.

Georgia

Lorem ipsum dolor sit amet, consectetuer adipiscing elit. Sed a sem. Nullam nonummy libero id libero. Donec libero erat, consequat in, tincidunt at, malesuada id, urna. Fusce tincidunt consectetuer ante. Nam sit amet lorem. Nulla nec ante ac risus tincidunt suscipit. Aliquam luctus. Vivamus lobortis odio at risus porttitor ultrices. Maecenas odio libero, rhoncus et, dignissim id, rhoncus at, quam. Vivamus dolor. Quisque feugiat fringilla enim.

Goudy Old Style

Lorem ipsum dolor sit amet, consectetuer adipiscing elit. Sed a sem. Nullam nonummy libero id libero. Donec libero erat, consequat in, tincidunt at, malesuada id, urna. Fusce tincidunt consectetuer ante. Nam sit amet lorem. Nulla nec ante ac risus tincidunt suscipit. Aliquam luctus. Vivamus lobortis odio at risus porttitor ultrices. Maecenas odio libero, rhoncus et, dignissim id, rhoncus at, quam. Vivamus dolor. Quisque feugiat fringilla enim.

Palatino Italic

Lorem ipsum dolor sit amet, consectetuer adipiscing elit. Sed a sem. Nullam nonummy libero id libero. Donec libero erat, consequat in, tincidunt at, malesuada id, urna. Fusce tincidunt consectetuer ante. Nam sit amet lorem. Nulla nec ante ac risus tincidunt suscipit. Aliquam luctus. Vivamus lobortis odio at risus porttitor ultrices. Maecenas odio libero, rhoncus et, dignissim id, rhoncus at, quam. Vivamus dolor. Quisque feugiat fringilla enim.

Futura

Lorem ipsum dolor sit amet, consectetuer adipiscing elit. Sed a sem. Nullam nonummy libero id libero. Donec libero erat, consequat in, tincidunt at, malesuada id, urna. Fusce tincidunt consectetuer ante. Nam sit amet lorem. Nulla nec ante ac risus tincidunt suscipit. Aliquam luctus. Vivamus lobortis odio at risus porttitor ultrices. Maecenas odio libero, rhoncus et, dignissim id, rhoncus at, quam. Vivamus dolor. Quisque feugiat fringilla enim.

Verdana

Lorem ipsum dolor sit amet, consectetuer adipiscing elit. Sed a sem. Nullam nonummy libero id libero. Donec libero erat, consequat in, tincidunt at, malesuada id, urna. Fusce tincidunt consectetuer ante. Nam sit amet lorem. Nulla nec ante ac risus tincidunt suscipit. Aliquam luctus. Vivamus lobortis odio at risus porttitor ultrices. Maecenas odio libero, rhoncus et, dignissim id, rhoncus at, quam. Vivamus dolor. Quisque feugiat fringilla enim.

Arial Narrow

Lorem ipsum dolor sit amet, consectetuer adipiscing elit. Sed a sem. Nullam nonummy libero id libero. Donec libero erat, consequat in, tincidunt at, malesuada id, urna. Fusce tincidunt consectetuer ante. Nam sit amet lorem. Nulla nec ante ac risus tincidunt suscipit. Aliquam luctus. Vivamus lobortis odio at risus porttitor ultrices. Maecenas odio libero, rhoncus et, dignissim id, rhoncus at, quam. Vivamus dolor. Quisque feugiat fringilla enim.

Comic Sans MS

Figure 11-9. *Eight fonts, as rendered on Mac OS X; notice the different sizes, densities, textures, and formalities*

Though it's not always easy to explain why, some fonts speak with a formal voice, while others speak with an informal voice. Comic Sans and other playful fonts are certainly informal, but so is Georgia, when compared to Didot or Baskerville. All-caps and capitalized words speak more formally than lowercase; italics speak informally. In the CSS Zen Garden designs shown earlier, Design 8 (Figure 11-8) uses an all-caps, sans-serif font to speak in a cool and removed voice. Meanwhile, Design 5 (Figure 11-5), which uses Georgia, speaks in a warm and informal voice.

Cultural aspects come into play here, too. Old-fashioned fonts, usually with serifs, tend to look—wait for it—old-fashioned, although anything set in Futura (a sans-serif font) still looks like it came from a 1963 science textbook. Verdana has been used so much on the Web that it's now standard for that medium. And Chicago always will be the original Mac font, no matter what context it's used in.

Spaciousness and Crowding

Some of the CSS Zen Garden designs use plenty of whitespace, while others crowd the page elements together. Spaciousness on a page gives an impression of airiness, openness, quiet, calmness, freedom, or stateliness and dignity, depending on other design factors.

Crowded designs can evoke urgency or tension under some circumstances. Why? Because text and other graphic elements need to "breathe"—when they're colliding against each other or against the edges or borders of the page, they cause visual tension. Our eyes want to see margins around things. We get slightly disturbed by designs such as CSS Zen Garden Design 2 (Figure 11-2), which shoves the headlines right against the text. Likewise, the compact layout of Design 6 (Figure 11-6) somehow contributes to the busy, industrial feel of the page, though it doesn't have collisions like Design 2.

However, not all crowded designs evoke that kind of tension. Some connote friendliness and comfort. If you give the text and other elements just enough space and reduce the interline spacing (leading) to the smallest amount that is comfortably readable, you might achieve a friendlier and less rarified look. Design 5 (Figure 11-5) illustrates this well.

Angles and Curves

A page composed of straight up-and-down lines and right angles generally looks calmer and more still than a page containing diagonal lines and nonrectangular shapes. Likewise, a page with many different angles has more apparent motion than a page with a single repeated angle on it; see Design 7 (Figure 11-7) for a dramatic example. Design 6 uses angles to create uneasiness and visual interest.

Curves can also add motion and liveliness, but not always. A design made with a lot of circles and circular arcs can be calming and restful. But a curve swooping through a page sets the whole design in motion, and a few carefully chosen curves in an otherwise rectangular design add sophistication and interest. Design 8 (Figure 11-8) uses a single large elliptical curve for a dramatic effect—it contrasts strongly against the otherwise rectilinear design, so its impact is high.

Wherever two curves intersect, notice what the geometrical tangents to those curves are doing. Are the tangents at right angles? That results in a calmer, more still composition; if they cross at a more acute angle, the design has more tension and apparent motion. (Again, these aren't hard-and-fast rules, but they're generally true.)

When using angles, curves, and nonrectangular shapes, think about where the focal points are: at sharp angles, where lines cross, and where multiple lines converge, for instance. Use these focal points to draw the viewer's eye where you want it to go.

Texture and Rhythm

Texture adds richness to a visual design. As described in the "Typography" section, text forms its own texture,* and you can control the look of that texture by choosing good fonts. For many pages and interfaces, fonts are the most important texture element.

But other kinds of textures deserve attention, too. Blank regions, such as the strips of empty space down the sides of a web page, can look much better when filled with a texture. You also can use textures to surround strong visual elements and set them off, as done in Designs 6 and 7. Textures add visual interest, and depending on what they look like, they can add warmth, richness, excitement, or tension. The most effective textures in interface design are subtle, not vivid checkerboards of eye-hurting colors. They use gentle color gradations and very tiny details. When spread over large areas, their impact is greater than you might think. Figure 11-10 shows some of the margin textures in the CSS designs. Single-pixel dots, parallel lines, and finely drawn grids are nice geometric textures; they're easy to generate and render, and they add refinement to a design. See the Hairlines pattern.

Be careful when using textures behind words on a computer screen—it rarely works. All but the subtlest textures interfere with the readability of small text. You can put them behind large text, but watch the way the edges of the letterforms interact with the different colors in the texture, as that can visually distort the letters. Try fading a texture into a solid color as it approaches a block of text.

---

* On an interesting etymological note, the English words *text*, *texture*, and *textile* all derive from the same Latin root, *texere*, meaning "to weave." Isn't that evocative?

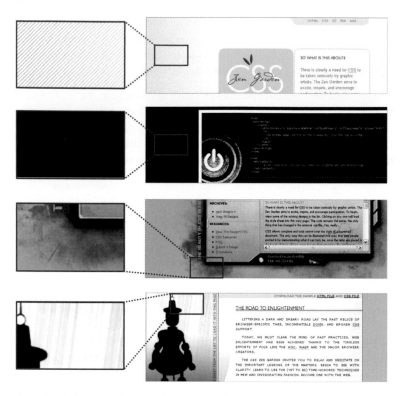

Figure 11-10. *Details of textures in four CSS designs*

Images

Each of the CSS Zen Garden designs reproduced here uses imagery. Some of the images are photographs; others are iconic semi-abstract pictures. In all cases, the images exist purely to set the mood of the design. These particular designs can go as far as they need to set that mood, since in the CSS Zen Garden, design is more important than content.

Your situation is probably different. In most web pages and applications, content and ease of use are more important than style. You should use purely decorative images sparingly and with great care on functional GUIs, since they tend to be distracting.

That being said, you should look at the functional icons and images in your design—such as toolbar icons and website image links—and see if they make the emotional statement you want the whole design to make. Use the same criteria listed here: color, texture, angles, curves, spacing, and so on. Specifically, color schemes, angles, and curves should be consistent across an icon set. Don't make them look too much alike, though, or users won't see the differences easily. Larger icons usually "feel" better than small ones, partly because you can draw them more generously and partly because of the crowding and space issues discussed earlier.

Back to decorative imagery. Photographs are extraordinary tools for evoking emotional responses. How many web pages have you seen showing happy, smiling faces? Kids flying kites? Competent-looking businesspeople in crisp suits? How about roads winding through beautiful mountain scenery? Sunsets or beaches? Rolling grassy hills under sunny blue skies?

These kinds of pictures appeal to our deepest human instincts, and they all predispose the viewer to respond positively—as long as the context is right. If you try to put powerful images like these on an unassuming little utility application, users might laugh or criticize it as marketing overkill. This is a delicate area, so if you're not sure something works, test it with users.

Cultural References

A design might remind you of something cultural—a brand, movie, art style, historical era, literary genre, or inside joke. A familiar reference may evoke memories or emotions strong enough to trump all these other design factors, though the best designs make cultural references work in concert with everything else.

Design 7 might remind you of 1970s pop art. That's almost certainly deliberate. The feel of the page is informal, lively, and playful—note the angles, color, typography, and denim texture. The emotional reaction from most American adults probably will be "silly," "nostalgic," "retro cool," or something like that. Everything in this design works together to produce a specific gut reaction. Some other CSS Zen Garden designs that are not shown here replicate the styles of Bauhaus, art nouveau, Dadaism, comic books, and even Soviet-era Communist propaganda posters.

Obviously, if you make overt cultural references, consider your audience. A 10-year-old will not get the 1970s pop-art reference. Chances are good that a young adult in India won't either. But if your audience is sufficiently well defined for you to know that a cultural reference will be familiar to them, it can be a good "hook" to engage a viewer emotionally with your design.

Cultural references rarely are used in functional application designs, but you can see them in Skins and Themes for platforms and individual applications. You also can find cultural references in applications like QuickBooks, in which some pages are designed to look like checks and bills. They actually move beyond a stylistic treatment and become an interaction metaphor, but the metaphor still is entirely cultural—someone who has never seen a checkbook wouldn't respond in the same way as someone who has.

Repeated Visual Motifs

A good design has unity: it hangs together as one entity, with each element supporting the others structurally and viscerally. That's a hard goal to achieve. I can't give you hard-and-fast rules on how to do it; it takes skill and practice.

But one thing that contributes greatly toward visual unity is the repetition of visual elements or motifs. We've already talked about angles and curves; you can use diagonal lines of the same angle, or lines with similar curvature, as repeated elements in a design. The Corner Treatments pattern talks about a common way to do this.

Also consider typography. Use only one main body-text font, though other fonts can work very effectively in small areas such as sidebars or navigation links. (Their contrast to the main font makes them stand out.) If you have several headlines or titled sections, use the same headline font for them. You also can pull smaller graphic elements—line width and color, for instance—out of your fonts into the rest of the design. See the Borders That Echo Fonts pattern.

When similar groupings of text or controls repeat along a line, a visual rhythm results. You can see this especially in the "Select a Design" sections of Designs 3, 4, and 8. They show each design name/author pair in a well-defined grouping, and then repeat that grouping along a column. You easily could accomplish the same effect with form fields, palette buttons, and other UI elements.

Rhythms like these can be powerful design tools. Use them with care, and apply them to groups of comparable things—users will assume that similarity in form means similarity in function. Chapter 4 discusses element repetition as part of a visual hierarchy; see the Grid of Equals pattern there. Repetition also lies at the heart of other layout patterns such as Thumbnail Grid (Chapter 5), Thumbnail-and-Text List (Chapter 10), and Small Multiples (Chapter 7).

What This Means for Desktop Applications

Those of you who work on websites might already be familiar with everything discussed so far. People expect websites—and by extension, web applications—to have strong graphic styling, and you rarely will find them looking completely plain and neutral.

But what if you work on desktop applications? If you try to apply these principles just to the controls' look-and-feel—how the controls are drawn—you may not have many choices. Java applications get to choose from a few look-and-feel options, most of which are native looking or fairly neutral. Linux applications have some nice choices too, such as GNOME's application themes. But native Windows or Mac applications generally use the standard platform look-and-feel, unless you're willing to work hard to develop a custom one.

Given the situation, you can be forgiven for just using the platform look-and-feel standards, and concentrating your graphic design attentions elsewhere.

But some applications now look more "web-ish" or "designer-y" than they used to, and they generally look better for it. Microsoft Money 2000 was one of the first mainstream applications to break the mold. Its designers chose to use background images in the top margins, gradient fills, anti-aliased headline fonts, and an unusual color scheme. Other applications have since done similar things.

Even if you do use a neutral look-and-feel for your actual widgetry, there still are ways to be creative.

Backgrounds

Unobtrusive images, gradient fills, and subtle textures or repeated patterns in large background areas can brighten up an interface to an amazing extent. Use them in dialog or page backgrounds; tree, table, or list backgrounds; or box backgrounds (in conjunction with a box border). See the Deep Background pattern for more.

Colors and fonts

You often can control overall color schemes and fonts in a native-looking UI, too. For instance, you might draw headlines in an unusual font at several point sizes larger than standard dialog text, and maybe even on a strip of contrasting background color. Consider using these if you design a page layout with Titled Sections (Chapter 4).

Borders

Borders offer another possibility for creative styling. Again, if you use Titled Sections or any other kind of physical grouping, you might be able to change how box borders are drawn. Solid-color boxes of narrow widths work best; beveled borders look very 1990s now. See Corner Treatments and Borders That Echo Fonts.

Images

In some UI toolkits, certain controls let you replace their standard look-and-feel with custom images on a per-item basis. Buttons often allow this, for instance, so your buttons, including their borders, can look like anything you want. Tables, trees, and lists sometimes permit you to define how their items are drawn (in Java Swing, you have complete control over item rendering, and several other toolkits at least let you use custom icons). You also can place static images on UI layouts, giving you the ability to put images of any dimension just about anywhere.

The biggest danger here is accessibility. Operating systems such as Windows let users change desktop color/font themes, and that's not just for fun—visually impaired users use desktop themes with high-contrast color schemes and giant fonts just so they can see what they're doing. Make sure your design works with those high-contrast themes. It's the right thing to do.*

---

* And, depending on who buys your software, it may also be the legal thing to do. The U.S. government, for example, requires that all software used by federal agencies be accessible to people with disabilities. See *http:// www.section508.gov* for more information.

Along the same lines, you might replace ordinary text labels with images containing unusual fonts, maybe with halos, drop-shadow effects, or complex backgrounds. This is common in web pages. If you insist on using an image for text, you need to provide enough information with that image to let a screen reader such as JAWS read it aloud. (How exactly you do that depends entirely upon the UI technology you're using.)

Another danger is fatiguing your users. If you design an application meant to be used at full size or for a long time, tone down the saturated colors, huge text, high contrast, and eye-catching textures—make the design quiet, not loud. More importantly, if your application is meant to be used in high-stress situations, such as a control panel for heavy machinery, strip out anything superfluous that might distract users from the task. Here, cognitive concerns are far more important than aesthetics.

The Patterns

All of these patterns (except Skins and Themes) draw on the concepts described in the introduction. They talk about specific ways to apply those concepts; Corner Treatments, for instance, captures one kind of repeated visual motif, and Borders That Echo Fonts captures another. Deep Background and Hairlines touch on texture choice, and fonts are discussed in Contrasting Font Weights.

1. Deep Background

2. Few Hues, Many Values

3. Corner Treatments

4. Borders That Echo Fonts

5. Hairlines

6. Contrasting Font Weights

The Skins and Themes pattern is different. It deals more with metadesign—it says nothing about how you design the specific look-and-feel of your application, but how you design your application to let others replace your look-and-feel with their own designs.

7. Skins and Themes

Deep Background

Figure 11-11. *Firefox download page*

What

Place an image or gradient into the page's background that visually recedes behind the foreground elements.

Use when

Your page layout has strong visual elements (such as text blocks, groups of controls, or windows), and it isn't very dense or busy. You want the page to look distinctive and attractive; you may have a visual branding strategy in mind. You'd like to use something more interesting than flat white or gray for the page background.

Why

Backgrounds that have soft focus, color gradients, and other distance cues appear to recede behind the more sharply defined content in front of them. The content thus seems to "float" in front of the background. This pseudo-3D look results in a strong figure/ground effect—it attracts the viewer's eye to the content.

Fancy explanations aside, it just looks good.

How

Use a background that has one or more of these characteristics:

Soft focus

Keep lines fuzzy and avoid too much small detail—sharp lines interfere with readability of the content atop it, especially if that content is text or small icons. (You can kind of get away with sharp lines if they are low-contrast, but even then, text doesn't work well over them unless the text contrasts strongly with the background.)

Color gradients

Bright, saturated colors are OK, but again, hard lines between them are not. Allow colors to blend into each other. In fact, if you don't have an image to use in the background, you can create a simple color gradient in your favorite drawing tool—it still looks better than a solid color. (You don't need to store or download pure gradients as images, either. On the Web, you can create them by repeating one-pixel-wide strips, either horizontally or vertically. In systems where you can use code to generate large areas of color, gradients generally are easy to program.)

Depth cues

Fuzzy detail and vertical color gradients are two features that tell our visual systems about distance. To understand why, imagine a photograph of a hilly landscape—the farther away something is, the softer and hazier the color is. Other depth cues include texture gradients (features that get smaller as they get farther away) and lines radiating from vanishing points.

No strong focal points

The background shouldn't compete with the main content for the user's attention. Diffuse (weak) focal points can work, but make sure they contribute to a balanced composition on the whole page, rather than distracting the viewer from seeing the parts of the page he should look at instead. See Figure 11-12.

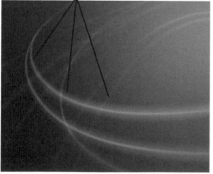

Figure 11-12. *Diffuse versus strong focal points*

As you design an interface with a Deep Background, consider what happens when the user changes the size of the page. How will the background accommodate a larger (or smaller) size? Will it rescale to fit, or will the window just clip an unscaled image? Clipping is probably less unsettling to the user; it's how most web pages behave, and it feels more stable. Besides, you don't have to worry about changing aspect ratios, which is problematic with many images.

Examples

In Figure 11-13, four Mac OS background images illustrate the relative difficulties of reading text and icons over complex backgrounds. The first two make it quite hard to distinguish the folders and application shortcuts; the third is easier, and the fourth is the easiest by far. Note the characteristics of these four backgrounds: high versus low contrast with the text, hard versus soft focus, and general "noisiness."

Figure 11-13. *Four Mac OS backgrounds of varying readability*

Some websites make heavy use of textures that lend the whole site a distinctive look. In the example from Ecoki, shown in Figure 11-14, the textures are everywhere; but because they are lightweight and low-contrast, they don't interfere with the readability of the text.

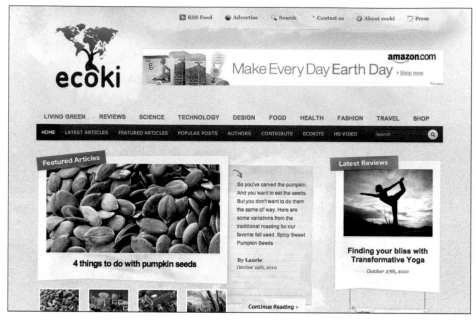

Figure 11-14. *Ecoki home page*

The version of the Mercedes-Benz website shown in Figure 11-15 uses an image as a background. This image has some very strong focal points—the cars, of course—and they are the central features of the page. But the outer parts of the image, which are much softer, are Deep Backgrounds for other content: the search box, the four small images at the bottom, and the "4MATIC All-Wheel Drive" tag line.

The most interesting aspect of this figure is the darker band running down the lefthand side. The site needed a navigation bar with small text, but layering those links directly over the background image wouldn't have worked—the words may have been unreadable over small detail, and would have gotten lost in the composition. A translucent smoked-glass background highlights those white links by increasing contrast; it balances the page (which otherwise is right-weighted); it doesn't obscure the nice background image; and it adds a sense of layered depth.

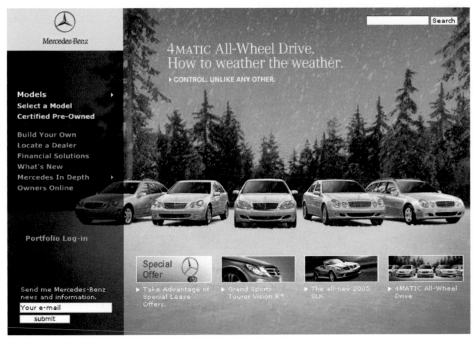

Figure 11-15. *Mercedes-Benz*

Few Hues, Many Values

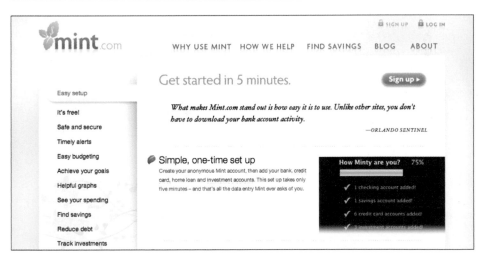

Figure 11-16. *Mint*

Choose one, two, or at most three major color hues to use in the interface. Create a color palette by selecting assorted values (levels of brightness) from within those few hues.

You want a relatively conservative color scheme for an application or site. You want to avoid a flashy, rainbow-colored, "angry fruit salad" look, but you still want the interface to have some character.

Where colors are concerned, sometimes less is better. Too many color hues scattered throughout the interface, especially when they're bright and saturated, can potentially make a design noisy and cluttered. The colors compete for the user's attention.

But when you use many subtle variations on a single color, you can create a design that has depth and dimension. Consider the blue-green, yellow-green, and orange colors used in the example in Figure 11-16 and reproduced in the color strips in Figure 11-17. Notice how the more saturated colors move forward, while the paler colors appear to recede. (Grayer tones will tend to recede as well, hence the drop-shadow effect seen in the Mint page.)

Figure 11-17. *Colors used in Mint's interface*

As mentioned earlier, pick one, two, or even three main hues. You get black and white for free, but gray counts. In fact, gray works very well in multiple values and brightness levels; it's very versatile, especially if you add a little color to make it more blue (cool) or more beige (warm).

Within those hues, vary the color value to get a range of bright and dark shades. You also can vary the saturation at the same time; this can produce subtler color combinations than you would get by varying just the value. Use as many of these colors as you want to compile a color palette for the application.

You can, of course, use other colors in the interface besides these hues; just use them sparingly. Icons, ads, and other features that take up relatively small spaces don't have to fit this restricted color scheme. You might want to choose only one or two accent colors too, such as using red or cyan to mark points of interest. In fact, using a single hue for the "background" of the UI actually emphasizes these minor colors because they don't get lost in a sea of color hues.

Examples

The graph in Figure 11-18 uses two hues, blue and pink, to show its data. Blue represents boys' names and pink represents girls' names. Within those colors, the color value represents the popularity of those names in 2003. A third color, dark gray, shows the frame around the data—the grid lines, the numbers, and the title—and a dark blue highlights the selected name ("Dale").

This color combination is very effective, both cognitively and aesthetically. The hues and values mean something with respect to the data, and the coding is very easy to follow—you hardly even need the legend after you've looked at it once. Aesthetically, the whole thing has a layered richness that isn't garish, as rainbow hues would have been. And in U.S. culture, people understand light blues and pinks as "baby" colors, so the emotional and cultural connection is there, too. See *http://babynamewizard.com.*

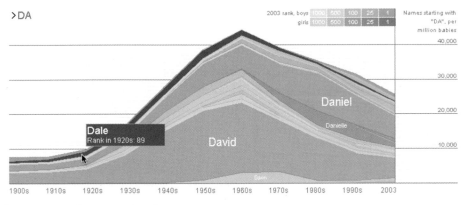

Figure 11-18. *Baby Name Wizard*

Figure 11-19 shows two websites that make very restrained use of color. The first balances hot and cool colors, while the second uses a single color for most of the design, reserving the hot orange color to accent the call-to-action buttons.

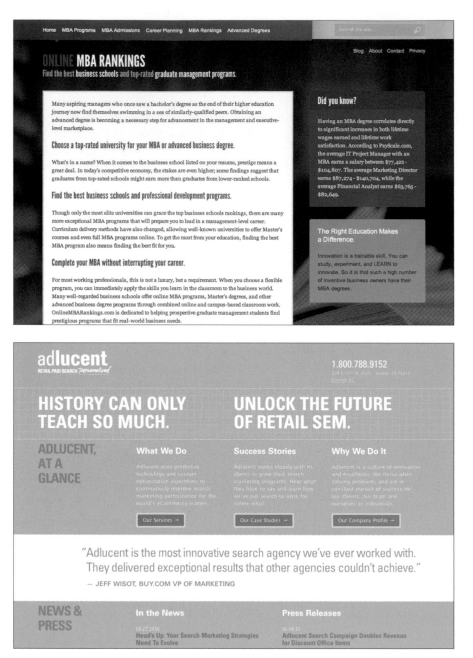

Figure 11-19. *OnlineMBARankings.com and AdLucent.com*

In other libraries

http://quince.infragistics.com/Patterns/Few%20Hues.aspx

Corner Treatments

Figure 11-20. *JetBlue*

Instead of using ordinary right angles, use curves or diagonals for some of the interface's box corners. Make these corner treatments consistent across the interface.

The interface uses rectangular elements such as boxes, buttons, menus, and tabs.

The repetition of visual motifs helps unify a design. When you devise a single "corner" motif and use it consistently in many places, it gives a distinctive look to the whole design. It's certainly less boring than ordinary right-angled corners.

Many websites use curved corners. Others use diagonal lines, and a few use cutouts. What you choose depends on the overall look of your site. Do you have a logo, an image, or a font that has eye-catching visual elements to it? Use one of those visual elements. Are you going for something soothing (as curves often are), edgy, or energetic? Try out several different ideas.

Not all of the rectangular elements in the interface need to use corner treatments—don't use too much of a good thing. But group boxes or panels usually do, and tabs commonly are done this way, too. If you use corner treatments on one element in a repeated group, do them all for consistency.

Furthermore, not every corner on a given box needs to use a corner treatment. Sometimes two opposing corners get it, such as the upper right and lower left. Sometimes it's just one corner, usually the upper left or upper right.

Everywhere the element is repeated, make sure it resembles the others. In other words, curved corners should use the same type of curve (though not necessarily the same radius). Angles should all be the same angle—don't mix a 45-degree angle motif with a 20-degree angle, for instance. Also, curved and right angles tend to mix badly on visually busy sites. Use Corner Treatments this with care.

Examples

The JetBlue website in Figure 11-20 at the top of the pattern repeats its curved corners all over the site: in menu bars, the main content box, tabs, and buttons. Pandora, shown in Figure 11-21, does the same, even for "callout" pop ups containing lyrics.

In other libraries

http://quince.infragistics.com/Patterns/Corner%20Treatments.aspx

Figure 11-21. *Pandora*

The Getty Museum's site in Figure 11-22 uses bars across the tops of its content boxes, and curves on the bottom corners. (The tabs also use curved corners, which is common.)

Figure 11-22. *Getty.org*

Borders That Echo Fonts

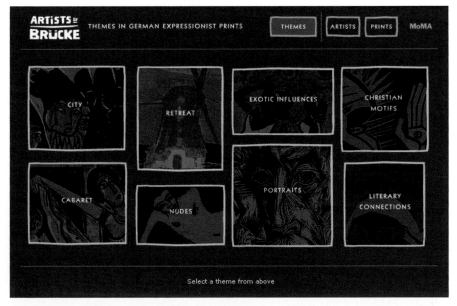

Figure 11-23. *A MoMA online exhibit from 2002*

When drawing borders and other lines, use the same color, thickness, and curves used by one of the design's major fonts.

Your design contains a font carefully chosen for its visual effect, such as the font used in headlines, a title, or a logotype.

The repetition of visual motifs helps unify a design. Fonts and borders work at similar scales in a design—only a few pixels wide—and when they reinforce each other visually, their effect is magnified. When they clash (especially if you use many different kinds of borders), their contributions are weakened.

First, pick a font from your design. Title and headline fonts often work well, as do fonts used in logotypes, but sometimes body text works, too. Observe its formal properties: color, primary line thickness, texture, curve radius, angles, and spacing.

Now try to draw borders and lines that use some of those same properties. The color should be the same as the font's, though you can cheat on thickness and make borders a bit thinner than the font's strokes. If the font has pronounced circular curves, as many modern sans-serif fonts do, try using that same curve radius on the border corners.

If it's a particularly interesting font, ask yourself what makes it interesting. See if you can pull those visual elements from the font into the rest of the design.

You don't need to do this with all the borders in your interface, of course; just a few will do, especially if the lines are thick. Be careful not to make borders too thick or coarse. Thick borders make a strong statement, and after a point, they overwhelm whatever's inside them. Images usually can handle a thicker border than lightweight body text, for instance. You can use single-pixel lines effectively in combination with heavier borders.

In Figure 11-24, Mochimedia uses its logotype's "fat curves" all over the design. The heavy black border strongly echoes the logotype; so do the icons, the headline, the top menu bar, and the cartoon character itself.

Figure 11-24. *Mochimedia*

Many sites use very thin borders and separator lines that reflect the visual qualities of a body font. In Good's website, shown in Figure 11-25, the one-pixel dotted lines echo the delicate serifed body font in the sidebar. (A sans-serif font might be better echoed by a solid line.)

Figure 11-25. *Detail of Good's site*

Dakine's website from several years ago mixes it up a bit. In Figure 11-26, it uses many varied design elements, but the jagged white lines do in fact echo the logo font. All together, they lend a feeling of motion, tension, and edginess to the page, which was undoubtedly what its designers were after—Dakine sells sports equipment to a young demographic.

Figure 11-26. *Dakine*

Hairlines

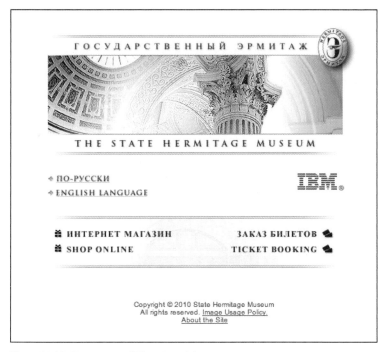

Figure 11-27. *Front page of HermitageMuseum.org*

What

Use one-pixel-wide lines in borders, horizontal rules, and textures.

Use when

You want a refined and sophisticated look to your interface.

How

Here are some of the many ways you can use hairlines in an interface:

- To demarcate Titled Sections by underlining the titles

- To separate different content areas, either with horizontal or vertical rules or with closed borders

- As guidelines to lead the eye through a composition

- Between areas of different background colors to clarify the boundary between them

- In textures, such as a grid or a block of horizontal lines

- In icons, images, and drawn graphics

- As borders around controls, such as buttons

Hairlines look particularly good when placed near very thin sans-serif fonts. Remember that a gray line looks thinner than a black line, even if both are a single pixel wide. The same is true for other lighter colors, such as the teal used in Figure 11-27 at the top of this pattern. The less contrast between the line and its background, the thinner and lighter it appears.

Another way you can lighten a hairline—and add another texture while you're at it—is to make it a dotted line instead of a solid line. As of this writing, finely drawn dotted lines are becoming common on the Web, even as underlines for links.

A trick to increase the tension and edginess in a design is to push a hairline flush up against the bottom of a line of text. Design 8 of the CSS Zen Garden designs does exactly that with its title and headlines (see Figure 11-8, back in the introduction).

Examples

The website in Figure 11-28 shows hairlines used in many places: as a faint grid in the background, as horizontal rules, and as very lightweight borders around the boxes. The hairlines work with the background texture and excellent typography to create a very rich look.

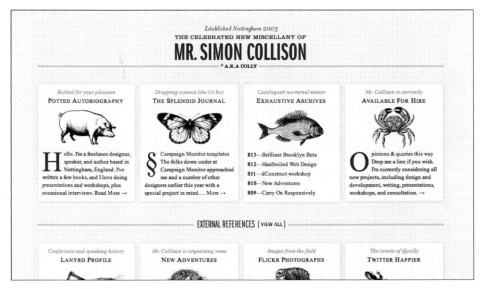

Figure 11-28. *Colly.com*

Likewise, hairlines are used in several ways in the design studio site shown in Figure 11-29. Note their usage in the logo, in the dotted separator lines, and in the diagonal texture used around the thumbnails and at the bottom of the page.

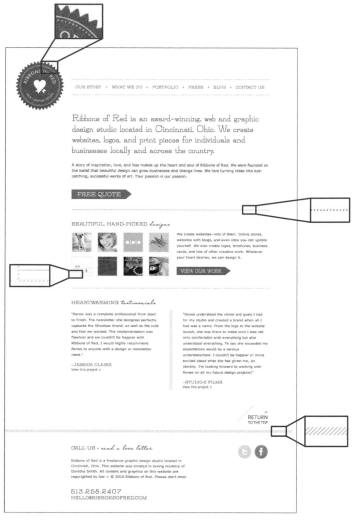

Figure 11-29. *RibbonsOfRed.com*

Contrasting Font Weights

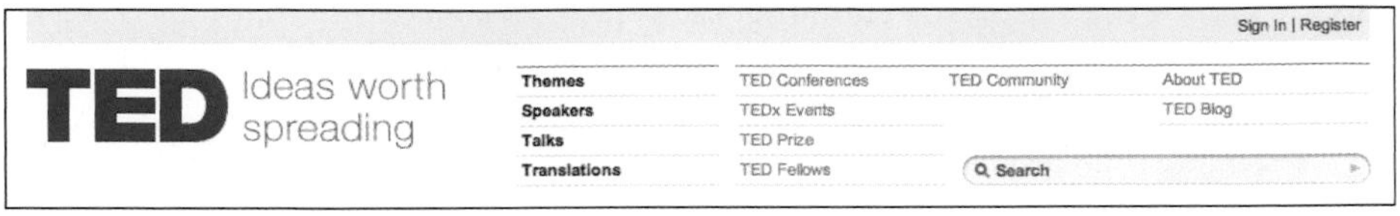

Figure 11-30. *TED*

What

Use at least two contrasting fonts—one thin and lightweight, another heavier and darker—to separate different levels of information and add visual interest.

Use when

Text makes up important elements on the page, and you want the page's organization to be very clear at first glance. You want the page to look dramatic.

Why

When two fonts differ in weight, they form a strong and vibrant visual contrast. Aesthetically, contrast contributes to a dramatic and eye-catching look. High typographic contrast, which includes size, texture, and color—but especially weight—guarantees that your page will not look dull.

You can use this contrast to structure the text on the page. For instance, heavier-looking letters can form titles and headlines, thus helping build a visual hierarchy. The bold text in Figure 11-30 pulls the eye toward it. Thus, contrasting font weights contribute to the cognitive perception of the page as much as the aesthetics. (See Chapter 4 for a discussion of visual hierarchy.)

How

This pattern has many possible applications. This book already mentioned the use of bold text for headlines, but applications might include:

- Creating very strong, magazine-like headlines and subheads
- Separating labels from data in a two-column listing
- Separating navigational links from information
- Indicating selection, such as selected links or list items
- Emphasizing words in a phrase
- Separating one word from another in a logotype

If you're using fonts that are larger than body text, make sure the contrast is strong enough to be noticed. When the font family offers several weights, as does Helvetica Neue, pick ones that are at least a couple of steps apart—if the contrast is weak, it looks accidental, not intentional. (The same goes for other font attributes. If you make two text elements different sizes, make them really different; if you want to mix font families, make sure they don't look too much alike!)

Examples

In Figure 11-31, a film site from the National Film Board of Canada uses three very different font sizes in a harmonious and compact composition. Its drama and starkness reflect the seriousness of the film's subject.

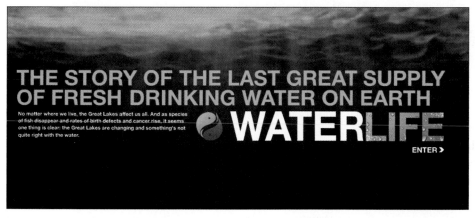

Figure 11-31. *Detail of Waterlife.nfb.ca*

The playful design in Figure 11-32 has a more complex visual hierarchy, rendered with many font styles and sizes. Contrasting Font Weights is used to emphasize the "WORKFLOW" headline, the arrows, the column titles, and particular phrases within the body text. The weighted phrases are not only a heavier font weight; they are also white, while the surrounding body text is gray. This gives the phrases even more contrast against the dark background, thus increasing their visual weight.

Figure 11-32. *A page from KaleidoscopeApp.com*

Finally, Figure 11-33 shows one of the most dramatic type size differences I have ever seen on the Web. Because they are dark, the enormous headline letters remain in balance (sort of) with the body text. Within the block of body text, Contrasting Font Weights is again used for emphasized words and phrases; likewise for the URL in the upper left, which places a heavier font next to a lighter one.

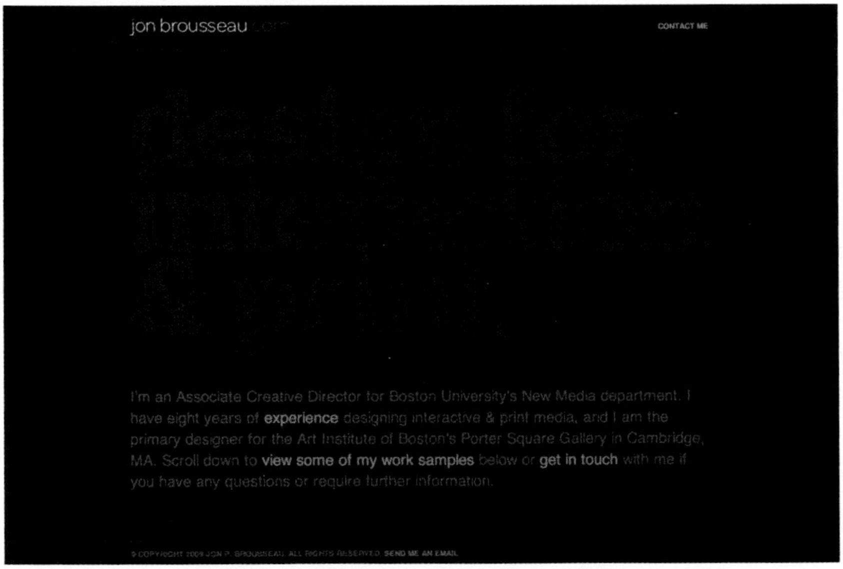

Figure 11-33. *JonBrousseau.com*

Skins and Themes

Figure 11-34. *Four sample Firefox themes*

What

Open up the look-and-feel architecture of your application so that users and third parties can design their own graphics and styles.

Use when

Your user base includes a large population of people who know your interface well. For those people, the interface has relatively low cognitive requirements—it's not used in high-stress situations, for instance—so it's not necessary to make all elements easily recognizable.

Furthermore, these users like to tinker. They value style, and they are inclined to set software preferences to suit their tastes.

Why

When people rearrange and customize their personal space, physical or virtual, they derive a sense of ownership of that space. This is a basic human need (though not all people act on it; many people are perfectly content with software's "factory settings"). Changing simple color and font preferences is one common way to customize someone's software environment, but Skins and Themes go far beyond color schemes and fonts.

There's evidence all over the Internet that users really like themes. Actually, we're talking about two groups of users here: those who download and use themes, and those who not only use them but also design them. Those who design them see themes as an opportunity to be creative, and to get their work out into the public eye. Many are graphic artists. These people may get to know your UI design very, very well.

In any case, there are numerous applications and web services out there that have skins or themes, and the sheer number of user-designed themes is enormous. The number of person-hours spent on these works is testimony to the power of the creative impulse. For the designers, skinnable applications fulfill another basic human need: creativity.

(The difference between a skin and a theme in this context is vague. Some applications or sites use one, and some use the other. As of this writing, *themes* seems to be the term of choice for the concept of user-designed interface styles, while the term *skins* appears to apply more to physical skins on laptops or mobile devices. That wasn't the case when the first edition of this book was written.)

How

Exactly how to design and implement a skinnable application depends entirely on the UI technologies you use, so it's very hard to generalize anything here.

First, remember that any native Windows application can already be changed by a skin or theme. Several popular browsers can be "themed" as well, as shown in Figure 11-34.

Second, themes for web services such as WordPress (see Figure 11-35) affect far more than just the graphic styling shown on the blog pages. Their themes also determine how blog posts are laid out, what content appears in the sidebars, and even what information gets shown or hidden for each entry. Designing a UI architecture to support this is hard, and beyond the scope of this book. I encourage you to look at existing examples of themed applications and websites.

One objection that is sometimes raised about skins is that they make interfaces harder to use. That's true about many badly designed skins. Ask yourself, though: how much does that matter? Does each application have to be cognitively perfect? (Look-and-feel defaults aren't perfect, though they're certainly more usability-tested than skins are.) For an application that someone already knows well and that doesn't require high cognitive demands, there's a point at which its basic usability is "good enough" and personal aesthetic preferences take over. When skins are available, people make that choice for themselves, whether or not they've educated themselves about usability.

To an extent, you can—and should, as part of a designer's responsibility—decide at which level to permit theming and skinning. You may only allow colors, fonts, and backgrounds to be changed. You may permit bitmap-level skinning that preserves layout while changing the look-and-feel of controls. Or you may allow full customizability; it's up to you to decide if that kind of freedom is likely to make the interface criminally hard to use.

I'm going to speculate that excellent application design—such as well-chosen functionality, easily understood organizational models, appropriate navigation, good page layout, and standard widgetry—can make an interface more resilient to bad themes. Design it as well as you can, and then put it out there for people to customize at a level you decide is appropriate. See what happens!

Figure 11-35 shows four of the many themes available for WordPress blogs. Vast numbers of themes are also available for other blogs and website systems, such as Blogger and Drupal. Most such themes are further customizable by the end users (especially those who know how to edit HTML and CSS).

Figure 11-35. *Four WordPress themes*

http://quince.infragistics.com/Patterns/Skins.aspx

References

Websites

These are the online pattern libraries or collections that served as references for this book. Some well-known patterns appear to be duplicated in several libraries, but each author writes and illustrates them differently. You may find insight into some of this book's patterns by reading their counterparts in these collections.

The Yahoo! Design Pattern Library:
http://developer.yahoo.com/ypatterns/

User Interface Design Patterns:
http://ui-patterns.com

Patternry:
http://patternry.com

Martijn van Welie's Patterns in Interaction Design:
http://welie.com/patterns

Quince:
http://quince.infragistics.com

The Design of Sites book site:
http://www.designofsites.com/design-patterns/

Designing Web Interfaces book site:
http://designingwebinterfaces.com/explore

Designing Social Interfaces book site:
http://www.designingsocialinterfaces.com/patterns/Main_Page

Interface Design Patterns (emphasis on infographics):
http://patternbrowser.org

Design4Mobile:
http://design4mobile.com

Endeca User Interface Design Pattern Library (emphasis on search):
http://patterns.endeca.com

Peter Morville's search and search-related patterns:
http://www.flickr.com/photos/morville/collections/72157603785835882/

Usability.gov provides a uniquely evidence-based library of interface design guidelines and recommendations. While not a pattern library as such, it is a valuable reference:
http://usability.gov/guidelines/index.html

The following websites are not pattern collections, but they do contain nice sets of general design examples. I use them when I needed examples or inspiration:

The GUIdebook Gallery:
http://www.guidebookgallery.org/

Pattern Tap (not the kinds of "patterns" described in this book):
http://patterntap.com/

Vandelay Design has many pages full of lovely web design examples, including e-commerce, nonprofits, churches, magazines, design portfolios, interesting navigation, and corporate websites. I refer you to only one of them here, and you can find the full list on this page:
http://vandelaydesign.com/blog/galleries/corporate-websites/

Books

If you're looking for more depth than this book can provide, the following list can offer you some good starting points. Obviously, there are far more excellent design books than can be listed here; these constitute a "best of" list that you can use to branch out and find more references. The list starts with general UI design books, and then lists some books on specific topics, such as graphic design, forms, information graphics, social media, and search:

Designing Web Interfaces: Principles and Patterns for Rich Interaction by Bill Scott and Theresa Neil (O'Reilly, 2009)

The Design of Sites: Patterns for Creating Winning Web Sites, Second Edition, by Douglas K. van Duyne, James A. Landay, and Jason I. Hong (Prentice Hall, 2006)

Designing for Interaction: Creating Innovative Applications and Devices, Second Edition, by Dan Saffer (New Riders Press, 2009)

Don't Make Me Think: A Common Sense Approach to Web Usability, Second Edition, by Steve Krug (New Riders Press, 2005)

About Face 3: The Essentials of Interaction Design by Alan Cooper, Robert Reimann, and David Cronin (Wiley, 2007)

The Design of Everyday Things by Donald Norman (Basic Books, 1998)

Information Architecture for the World Wide Web: Designing Large-Scale Web Sites by Peter Morville and Louis Rosenfeld (O'Reilly, 2006)

Universal Principles of Design: 125 Ways to Enhance Usability, Influence Perception, Increase Appeal, Make Better Design Decisions, and Teach through Design, Second Edition, by William Lidwell, Kritina Holden, and Jill Butler (Rockport Publishers, 2010)

The Non-Designer's Design Book, Third Edition, by Robin Williams (Peachpit Press, 2008)

Emotional Design: Why We Love (or Hate) Everyday Things by Donald Norman (Basic Books, 2005)

Web Form Design: Filling in the Blanks by Luke Wroblewski (Rosenfeld Media, 2008)

Forms that Work: Designing Web Forms for Usability by Caroline Jarrett (Morgan Kaufmann, 2008)

Defensive Design for the Web: How to improve error messages, help, forms, and other crisis points by Matthew Linderman and Jason Fried (New Riders Press, 2004)

The Visual Display of Quantitative Information, Second Edition, by Edward R. Tufte (Graphics Press, 2001)

Envisioning Information by Edward R. Tufte (Graphics Press, 1990)

Visual Explanations: Images and Quantities, Evidence and Narrative by Edward R. Tufte (Graphics Press, 1997)

Information Dashboard Design: The Effective Visual Communication of Data by Stephen Few (O'Reilly, 2006)

Now You See It: Simple Visualization Techniques for Quantitative Analysis by Stephen Few (Analytics Press, 2009)

Designing Social Interfaces: Principles, Patterns, and Practices for Improving the User Experience by Christian Crumlish and Erin Malone (O'Reilly and Yahoo! Press, 2009)

Designing for the Social Web by Joshua Porter (New Riders Press, 2008)

Search Patterns: Design for Discovery by Peter Morville and Jeffery Callender (O'Reilly, 2010)

And finally, here are the classic patterns books that started the whole concept:

The Timeless Way of Building by Christopher Alexander (Oxford University Press, 1979)

A Pattern Language by Christopher Alexander, Sara Ishikawa, Murray Silverstein, Max Jacobson, Ingrid Fiksdahl-King, and Shlomo Angel (Oxford University Press, 1977)

Design Patterns: Elements of Reusable Object-Oriented Software by Erich Gamma, Richard Helm, Ralph Johnson, and John M. Vlissides (Addison-Wesley Professional, 1994)

Index

About the Author

Jenifer Tidwell is a writer and consultant in interaction design, information architecture, and pre-design analysis. She has been designing and building complex applications and web interfaces for almost two decades. Her clients and past employers include Google, The MathWorks, nonprofits, and startups. She was one of the first designers to write patterns for user interface design, back in the late 1990s when the concept was first being applied to software. She lives near Boston, Massachusetts, with her husband, her son, and a small parrot.

Colophon

The animal on the cover of *Designing Interfaces* is a Mandarin duck (*Aix galericulata*), one of the most beautiful of the duck species. Originating in China, these colorful birds can be found in southeast Russia, northern China, Japan, southern England, and Siberia. The males have diverse and colorful plumage, characterized by an iridescent crown, chestnut-colored cheeks, and a white eye stripe that extends from their red bills to the back of their heads. Females are less flamboyant in appearance and tend to be gray, white, brown, and greenish-brown, with a white throat and foreneck.

These birds live in woodland areas near streams and lakes. Being omnivorous, they tend to have a seasonal diet, eating acorns and grains in autumn; insects, land snails, and aquatic plants in spring; and dew worms, grasshoppers, frogs, fish, and mollusks during the summer months.

The mating ritual of Mandarin ducks begins with an elaborate and complex courtship dance that involves shaking movements, mimed drinking gestures, and preening. Males fight each other to win a female, but it is ultimately the female who decides her mate. Mandarin ducklings instinctively follow their notoriously protective mothers, who will feign injury to distract predators such as otters, raccoon dogs, mink, polecats, eagle owls, and grass snakes.

Mandarin ducks are not an endangered species, but they are considered to be threatened. Loggers continuously encroach upon their habitats, and hunters and poachers prize the males for their plumage. Their meat is considered unpalatable by humans, and they are generally not hunted for food.

The cover image is from *Johnson's Natural History*. The cover font is Adobe ITC Garamond. The text font is Adobe Minion Pro, and the heading and note font is Adobe Myriad Pro Condensed.

Have it your way.